Scotland the Brave?

Scotland the Brave?

Twenty Years of Change and the Politics
of the Future

Edited by
GERRY HASSAN and SIMON BARROW

Luath Press Limited
EDINBURGH
www.luath.co.uk

In Memory of Kenneth Roy and Ian Bell

First published 2019

ISBN: 978-1-913025-02-1

The paper used in this book is recyclable. It is made from low chlorine pulps produced in a low energy, low emission manner from renewable forests.

Printed and bound by Bell & Bain Ltd., Glasgow

Typeset in 10.5 point Sabon by Lapiz

The authors' right to be identified as authors of this work under the Copyright, Designs and Patents Act 1988 has been asserted.

Contents

Acknowledgements

The purpose of this book is to understand the Scotland of the past twenty years, and to do so in a way which examines society, the economy and culture, and hence, politics and power in the widest sense. In so doing we have asked contributors to assess what has changed and what has not, and to make an evaluation of where we are and future challenges.

In such an all-encompassing project, there are numerous challenges. One is the breadth and balance of contributors, mixing the established with the emerging voices. Another is in style, combining different takes and tones – from the general overview to the specific, and from the conventional essay to the conversation between two and, on one occasion, three people.

Equally challenging has been where to draw the boundaries of such an ambitious project. Hence, we have included reflections on religion, art and football – the latter of which touches on wider issues about culture, place and identity in a world of globalising capitalism. We have planned this volume so that it makes a serious contribution to contemporary Scottish history.

A project like this is, by necessity, a collective effort. First and foremost, we would like to thank the stellar range of contributors who gave their time, insights and expertise for the following pages. We often asked the impossible in terms of briefs, and in each and every case were met with encouragement and positivity.

Sincere thanks are due to numerous people who gave advice in shaping this book. This includes Philip Schlesinger, Iain Macwhirter, Angela Haggerty, Peter Geoghegan, Willie Sullivan, Isabel Fraser, Madeleine Bunting, John Harris, Danny Dorling, Nigel Smith, Carol Craig, Katherine Trebeck, Joe Lafferty, Joyce McMillan, Michael Gecan, Kirsty Hughes, Mike Small, Jordan Tchilingirian, Sarah Beattie-Smith, Carla J Roth, Rosie Ilett and Vivienne Wilson. A big thanks to artist Ross Sinclair for working with us to come up with our striking cover, which succeeded in doing something different and eye-catching.

We would also like to acknowledge and thank Luath Press, Gavin MacDougall and all his staff. They have been passionate about this book and we would like to honour the wider contribution that Gavin and his team at Luath have made to the political and intellectual life of this country in recent years. They have made our public debates richer. We record our appreciation of this and our relationship with them.

Gerry Hassan
gerry@gerryhassan.com

Simon Barrow
simonbarrowuk@gmail.com

INTRODUCTION

Scotland the Brave?
Assessing the Past Twenty Years and Mapping the Future

Gerry Hassan and Simon Barrow

SCOTLAND HAS CHANGED dramatically over the past twenty years. Until 1999 Scotland was governed from Westminster and for 18 years (between 1979 to 1997) by the Conservatives, elected on a minority and diminishing vote. Domestically, politics was defined by single party domination of the system in which Labour were the beneficiary, and which the SNP and Liberal Democrats occasionally shook but did not seriously challenge. By the 1997 election, a sizeable majority of public opinion had given up on the old political order and coalesced around a home rule consensus that found expression in the 74 per cent vote for a Scottish Parliament in the 1997 referendum.

The establishment of Parliament aided a dramatic shift in the country's public affairs and ethos. Politics, voice and legitimacy that were once situated at Westminster became increasingly located at home over the next twenty years. Scotland changed in numerous other ways – from the economy, society, the public realm, place, culture to geopolitics. How Scotland has seen itself, and has been perceived by others, has shifted – aided by the movement of deep tectonic plates in each of these areas.

We are still in the midst of this change and the twentieth anniversary of the Scottish Parliament offers the opportunity to assess a Scotland beyond the narrow politics of devolution. In these pages we therefore address a wider canvas. This includes what has changed and what has not changed over this devolution era; understanding where, and how far, we have come, and what the contours and challenges of the future might look like. We review the consequences of this change, who and what have been the forces shaping it; who has gained and who has lost and assess the Scottish experience in the context of longer-term transformations here and across most of the developed world. This is a book about politics in the widest sense that touches each and every one of us in our everyday lives.

Scotland the International

The Global Picture

Scotland's transformation over the past two decades is part of a bigger global picture and involves homegrown change. It is important to understand the impact of the former. Across the West there has been a crisis of mainstream politics: the hollowing out of and discrediting of neo-liberalism – the idea that a corrupted version of markets and rigged capitalism should be the solution to most public policy choices – combined with the retreat of moderate forces of the centre-left and social democracy.

We have also witnessed the crisis of modernity – of left, right and nearly every other persuasion – and the related idea of progress, and with it the notion that the future was always going to be better than the present. In relation to this the time honoured twentieth century methods of agency – trade unions and collectivist institutions on the left and those of traditional authority and deference on the right – have retreated in the face of individualism, economic and social change and the onward march of the market (Arrighi, 2009).

In the place of this, new voices and movements have appeared. It is now close to *cliché* to talk about the rise of xenophobes and populists from UKIP to France's Front National (now National Rally), to the German AFD (*Alternative für Deutschland*), and the Trump phenomenon. But it is also true that other currents have emerged – Podemos in Spain, Syriza in Greece (before it had to face EU imposed austerity), the realignment of the German left and the left-wing upsurges in the British Labour Party and the US Democrats.

There has emerged the salience of identity and belonging – much of which relates to big questions and forces redefining society. Identity politics have come to be seen as critical and often fraught with battle lines on gender, sexuality, ethnicity, race and numerous other areas (Mouffe, 2018). They have become defined by charges and counter-charges with some using the assertion of their identity to find status and voice, while others have used it to claim this has all gone too far and is too atomising, precious and illiberal. What is often missed is that all politics has always, to some extent, been a form of identity politics.

These shifts have occurred against a backdrop of enormous changes in the world economy, the shaping of capitalism and how wealth and power is accumulated and exercised. Massive amounts of new wealth have become concentrated in very few hands. The Oxfam statistic reminds us that the 26 richest billionaires in the world own as much wealth as the 3.8 million people who comprise the poorer half of humanity. This is a scale of inequality that will never be redressed just by national governments, the philanthropy of the rich or 'trickle-down' economics (*The Guardian*, 21 January 2019).

At the same time, mainstream politics has struggled to address issues beyond the short-term: the electoral cycle, climate change, environmental damage, species extinction, the long-term demographics of the West and tensions around immigration and population movement. When there has never been more need for politics to involve leadership, honest conversations and taking difficult long-term decisions, it has never been so lacking. In this we have to ask: is Scotland really that different? Can we rise to the challenges of our times and can we be 'Scotland the Brave'? And, if we answer in the affirmative what does that entail and what would it look like?

Scotland's Journey Over the Past Twenty Years

The Scottish Parliament and devolution generated a new political environment, one which created numerous differences compared with the previous Westminster order. First, it brought democratic voice, debate and legitimacy to the heart of government – something that had been increasingly lacking.

Second, it injected accountability and scrutiny into aspects of public life that had previously been left unexamined. Sometimes formally via the Parliament, sometimes informally – through devolution acting as a catalyst in public life.

Third, it introduced a more pluralist politics, where all political parties, with the exception of the 2011 election, had to recognise and act in cognisance with the knowledge that they were popular minorities. Westminster politics and the distortions of the first past the post (FPTP) system had disguised this for decades.

Fourth, it reinforced Scottish politics as being characterised as social democratic and of the centre-left, even in the process moderating the voice of the Scottish Conservatives (at least in comparison to the direction of the British Conservatives).

Fifth, politics was further influenced by the fact that the main contestation in terms of parties and competing governments was, until the 2016 election, between Labour and the SNP. These two parties who placed themselves on the centre-left and often competed on the same terrain for the same voters.

Sixth, political debate, particularly in the first decade, became about public spending and its growth, allocation and winning extra remuneration. Even once retrenchment and austerity came, much of the political debate remained about spending and public services. This may eventually wither as the Parliament assumes more taxation powers, and more powers generally, but we have yet to see this effect.

Seventh, the establishment of a Scottish Parliament and Executive/Government led to these new institutions asserting themselves and accumulating more powers. Thus, local government faced growing constraints, while numerous public bodies underwent reorganisation that amounted to further centralisation and standardisation – a trend evident under Labour, the Liberal Democrats and the SNP.

Another dimension of devolution was that it contained within its own idea its own demise – with Scottish politics inexorably moving beyond its original parameters. The Scottish Parliament quickly became the main political institution in the country; the arrival of the Scottish Government produced an embryonic state and quasi-independence even before the momentum towards an independence referendum. At the same time, the constitutional framework of the UK struggled to adapt to and to accommodate a freshly assertive autonomy and voice north of the border.

Devolution and a New Public Space

The Scottish Parliament contributed to the creation of a new public space and stage, a new political system, and a different political culture. In this there were many continuities with the Westminster order as it manifested itself in Scotland, but it was also the birth of something new – with a dynamic and dynamism of its own.

In the course of twenty years, the Scottish Parliament and Executive/Government has established itself solidly, following a shaky start. There were the brief periods of the Donald Dewar and Henry McLeish administrations that never found their level – lacking both leadership and a sense of inner discipline, critics felt. The Jack McConnell administration stabilised the situation, but was widely viewed as uninspiring, characterised by the phrase 'do less, better' – hardly a clarion call to change the world.

Eventually, the new institutions found their feet, aided by the move of the Parliament from the General Assembly of the Church of Scotland in 2004 to the new Holyrood building designed by the late Enric Miralles, the Catalan architect and EMBT architects – its cost overrun was another blight in the Parliament's early years. A significant development was the decision of the SNP, upon winning the 2007 election, to rename the Executive as the Scottish Government – a symbolic move that spoke to the nationalists' ambition and aspirations for Scotland as a nation.

A defining characteristic of much of the SNP period in office – first under Alex Salmond and then Nicola Sturgeon – was a reputation for competence, widely acknowledged after the previous Labour-dominated era. Yet, as the years of SNP rule passed, this technocratic, managerialist approach began increasingly to be taken for granted and even discounted. Moreover, its growing limits became more apparent – particularly in light of the harsher climate of cumulative public spending constraints and Westminster imposed austerity.

Many observers started to ask: where was the radicalism, the ability to think longer-term and the willingness to ask difficult questions on a range of issues? Where was the boldness or desire for change on educational attainment, health service reform or local government taxation, for instance? Action on these and a host of other issues would create winners and losers, and hence political turbulence, which would require leadership and debate. Where in effect was the 'Scotland the Brave' that many people liked to think of?

The Strength of Scotland's Social Democratic Politics

Scotland over these past two decades has adopted a distinctive political path. It could be characterised as representing a communitarian and social democratic mindset – with an emphasis, where possible, upon universality and inclusivity over selectivity and targeting. There has been an explicit reference to a 'Scottish social contract' which connects all of us from cradle to grave and invokes a concept of citizenship which aspires to be enlightened and progressive (*The Times*, 7 November 2017).

In this, there was an element of self-congratulation and over-defensiveness in the face of criticism that characterised both the Labour and SNP eras. This has seen a lack of interest in detail and the distributional consequences of decisions – such as free care for the elderly, abolition of tuition fees and the Council Tax freeze – all of which assisted those on above average incomes and penalised the poor and disadvantaged.

This centre-left sentiment left several questions unexplored. Where, for example, were the guiding lights of Scotland's political prospectus? In terms of values these were, more often than not, beyond the official platitudes of the Government's strategy documents. The assumption was always that public services were informed by a set of progressive, humane and compassionate grounds. But this was often more implicit and rarely fully articulated so that it could be investigated along with the relationship between values, rhetoric and reality.

How otherwise could a social contract and a social democracy be a living, evolving one which renewed, adapted and improved in light of circumstances? The two main parties of the centre-left – the SNP and Labour – have both, over the devolution era, shown a conspicuous lack of interest in rigorous, intellectual ideas.

The SNP has suffered from a dearth of original thinkers, with the obvious exception of, on domestic concerns, the late Stephen Maxwell, with his case for left-wing independence and his critique of the Scottish middle-class settlement. There were also Neil MacCormick's ideas on post-sovereignty and the distinction between existential and utilitarian nationalisms (see Maxwell, 2012, 2013; MacCormick, 1999). Both men were part of the pre-Parliament generation, before the rise of the party's managerialist political class.

Similarly, Labour have produced no coherent political ideas over the period – for all the interventions of Gordon Brown and Douglas Alexander as well as Henry McLeish, former First Minister (see Brown and Alexander, 1999; 2007; McLeish, 2014; 2016). The last Labour thinker in Scotland with an impressive pedigree was JP Mackintosh, academic and Labour MP for Berwick and East Lothian, whose premature death at the age of 48 in 1978, illustrated the overall paucity of thought in the party (Drucker, 1982).

A larger point is the absence over the course of the past two decades of rigorously intellectual political work. There has been lots of politics beyond thinking about the Parliament – from commentators, activists, campaigners, NGOs, academics and policy experts. But something has been noticeably missing from the public sphere and what William Mackenzie called 'the community of the communicators' (Mackenzie, 1978).

This is not to say that there have not been ideas and initiatives to try to frame and understand society. But there has been a lack of deeper thinking and greater ambition, along with critical analysis, which has had an impact on the public sphere. The Parliament has instead reflected a sense of deep-seated pragmatism, drawing from the existing well of centre-left politics. Alongside this it has represented a sense of being – and an expression of identity and political community – not so much in terms of the detailed actions of the Parliament, but what it stands for and the very idea of it.

Moreover, the contested site of the public sphere has included an evolving politics and sense of place which has increasingly made Scotland feel like a different country from the rest of the UK. This complex, but fragile ecology has been underlined by its setting: a 'dualistic public sphere' alongside a London-centred public sphere – which continues to impact Scotland and has definitely dominated the airwaves post-Brexit vote (Hassan, 2014b; Schlesinger, 2019).

Elitist Scotland vs. Egalitarian Scotland

As Scotland has grown more autonomous and diverged from the UK/RUK, aided by the inexorable right-ward drift of British politics, it has made the need for more self-reflective debates about the state of the nation even more important. Hence, beneath an inclusive, Panglossian social democratic sentiment sits a set of characteristics which demand scrutiny and action. They raise the question of whether we are truly an egalitarian nation, or just a continuation of inherited elitist practices. These include the critical issues set out below.

First, Scotland's elite are unrepresentative and self-reproducing (as are elites in the rest of the UK) with 57 per cent of university principals and 45 per cent of senior judiciary being privately educated. This is compared with 55 per cent and 71 per cent across the UK. Our country emerged less elitist than the rest of the UK in parliamentarians: with 20 per cent of MSPs being privately educated (and 43 per cent going to one of Scotland's four ancient universities), compared to 33 per cent for Westminster's MPs (and 24 per cent going to Oxbridge). All figures are for 2015 (Social Mobility and Child Poverty Commission/David Hume Institute, 2015).

The aforementioned study concluded:

> the top of Scottish society is significantly unrepresentative of the Scottish population – though less so than the top of British society – with almost a quarter (23 per cent) of those in the professions we looked at educated privately at secondary education level compared to just over 5 per cent of the Scottish population as a whole and almost two thirds (63 per cent) having attended an elite UK university (Social Mobility and Child Poverty Commission, 2015).

Second, over the devolution era, Scottish measurements of inequality do not show any indication of progress in tackling this blight. Take the Gini coefficient – if it equals 0 it means everyone has the same income and if it equals 1 it means one person has all the income. One study gives an overall Scandinavian average rating of 0.25 and puts Scotland at 0.30 in 1996–97 and 0.34 in 2015–16 with it remaining in the 0.30–0.34 range for the whole two decades (Scottish Government, 2017; Pryce and Le Zhang, 2018). This makes Scotland only slightly less unequal than Great Britain over the period, a difference accounted for by the London-effect. Similarly, if we look at inequality by neighbourhood, proximity to crime, air pollution and housing quality, Scotland has not been making any real progress (Pryce, *op. cit.*).

Third, the seismic health inequalities which have disfigured Scotland for too long continue unabated. Many figures can be used to underline this, but one produced by Save the Children is stark: a child born in 2013 in Lenzie, a suburb of Glasgow, is predicted to live 28 years longer than a child born in Calton in the east end of the city in the same year. The harsh reality of this divide is that only 8.2 miles separate these two areas, working out at a 3.4-year life expectancy gap per mile (Save the Children Fund, 2013).

Fourth, Scotland has long been marred by a culture of violence – in which there has been improvement for the better recently. The country had a state approved practice of violence against children, only banning belting in schools in 1987 (with this happening due to pressure from the European Court of Human Rights). Today, despite this change and active proposals for a ban on smacking children, 22 per cent of children are still subjected to frequent physical punishment, mostly at the behest of their parents (Marryat and Frank, 2019).

Fifth, Scotland's record of political participation is not entirely positive in recent years. We can all be proud of the 84.6 per cent turnout in the 2014 independence referendum, but democracy is not a one-off. It is a continuous process. There has been widespread complacency among both Yes and No campaigners about the 'missing Scotland', and in particular the 'missing million' voters who had not voted in a generation having previously done so – and who turned out in the Indyref (Hassan, 2014a). Many seem to believe that this systematic exclusion has been permanently addressed by voting once in a referendum, oblivious to what has failed to come after 2014.

The reality is that Scotland's record of political participation, as measured by the minimum of turnout at successive Scottish Parliament elections, has never been as high as Westminster. Across five Scottish elections it has ranged from 58.2 per cent in 1999, 49.4 per cent in 2003, 51.7 per cent in 2007, 50.3 per cent in 2011 and 55.6 per cent in 2016. Westminster turnout over the period 1997–2017 has been 71.3 per cent, 58.1 per cent, 60.8 per cent, 63.8 per cent, 71.1 per cent and 66.4 per cent (Curtice, 2019). Thus, Scotland has become, Indyref apart, accustomed to the politics of a truncated electorate; those who vote are more affluent, middle-class and older than the electorate overall, and non-voters are poorer and younger. This has consequences for our political debate and the choices politicians feel they can make.

These and other salutary facts need to be placed centre-stage, both in assessing the impact of devolution, but also in critically informing discussions about the route-map for the future. The Scottish Parliament has accrued more powers through the Scotland Acts of 2012 and 2016, and more are coming its way. Beyond that, the way Scotland thinks, and talks, has gone through the democratic revolution of Indyref, which certainly contributed to a wider debate about the country's future. This should not be understood as an isolated event, with the normal service of top-down politics continuing as if nothing much had changed. But neither has it been transformational. There has been regression.

Different Scottish futures have been present in the past and have mobilised people to action. Such a vision was contained in the Labour story of Scotland in the 1950s and 1960s, with its focus on lifting up working-class people, widening opportunities and life chances. Similarly, the SNP prospectus offered in 2007 and 2011 was fundamentally future-focused. In 2007, informed by positive psychology, it emphasised the upside of a self-governing nation. Different visions of Scotland and the future were also evident in the 2014 referendum, galvanising a significant part of the Yes campaign. These mobilising stories are vital to the shape of the future which is being made in the here and now. It is to that future we now turn.

The Terrain of the Scotland of the Future

The Scotland of the future and of the next twenty years cannot, and will not, be a mere projection of today's country. At best, the linear optimism that is the inherent message of globalisation (ie that the only version of the future possible is an enlarged version of today in consumption, goods, and markets) has to be challenged (Hassan *et al*, 2005). It is a faux optimism that masks a profound pessimism – the future has already been decided by the rich and powerful and the rest of us have no choice but to buckle down and accept it.

The parameters of 'continuity Scotland', of devolution, business as usual and of institutional capture informed by the assurances of the managerial class will not be adequate in light of pressures coming down the line. How do we collectively find a set of directions which begin to sketch out the contours of what is to come?

Answers to this will not be found solely by looking at constitutional change, whether pro-union or pro-independence. The former needs to come to terms with the fundamental shortcomings of the UK as it is. How its economy, society and culture is increasingly focused on a winner-takes-all global class centred around London and the South East, and how all of this impacts Scotland and the northern regions of England.

The pro-independence movement cannot be based on the abstract principle of 'independence now – and let us worry about the detail later'. Apart from the fact that this offer is unlikely to bring over enough floating voters to win decisively, there is the warning from Brexit about winning a major constitutional referendum on a broad principle, but without any agreed offer. That will not happen in Scotland, but there is still political pressure to postpone all sorts of big discussions to the other side of a future referendum. This limits debate now and has a detrimental effect on the choices and style of the Scotland that will emerge in the future.

A more open-minded debate is needed. One which goes past the constitution and even politics. It should raise the question of who are the change-makers and what qualities do we need to nurture and nourish in the present to facilitate this? Where are the interpreters and makers of Scotland's future now? Some are already with us, doing the work and activities creating that change. They sit in numerous communities and organisations but are often found outside conventional settings. Instead, they are located in DIY organisations and the 'third Scotland' – of self-organising, self-determining activities – that emerged so powerfully in the Indyref campaign. This is more about an independence of mind, spirit and action – an autonomy of social practice – than constitutional change alone.

We see many examples of such action in the pages of this book. It can be found in the pioneering work of the Violence Reduction Unit (VRU) who contributed to challenging Glasgow's, and then Scotland's, culture of violence. Their initial strapline, 'violence is preventable, not inevitable', spoke to a refusal to accept the status quo and the fatalism that change was not possible. It then took on what were seen as immovable, taboo subjects like toxic masculinity, that sees men harm themselves, other men, women and children, as well as gang culture (Carnochan, 2015).

Such qualities can also be found in such initiatives as the Sistema Big Noise project. It set down roots in the Raploch estate in Stirling, using the power of music with young people to build confidence and social skills. It has proven so successful that it now exists in three of Scotland's other cities: Glasgow, Aberdeen and Dundee.

They can be found equally in the life-affirming work of Galgael in Govan, in the heart of Glasgow. This has, over the past twenty years, provided space and sanctuary by using the ancient Viking skills of shipbuilding to reach out to a troubled generation of men and women, aiding them through reskilling. But, even more than that, it contributed to people finding a new purpose and confidence in life, while remaking the idea of community.

Another example is the range of community buy-outs that came after the land reform legislation passed by the first Scottish Parliament. The experience of the island of Eigg pre-devolution has been followed by a number of other cases such as the island of Gigha and estates in North Harris, Glencanisp and Drumrunie, and South Uist: all of which have proven successful and sustainable. Yet, the impetus gained from the initial legislation slowly petered out – a product of over-complicated process, a failure of national leadership to champion local energies and, from 2007, the relative lack of interest from the SNP in continuing the momentum of change (Hunter, 2012). Still, the buy-outs so far have shown what could be achieved by small groups of people coming together, not giving up and not listening to naysayers and pessimists saying that nothing would ever change.

Some of the same virtues can be identified in the steadfast commitment of community projects such as the Govanhill Baths in Glasgow. They took on their local council after it closed the baths in 2001. The community stayed for the long term, dug in and won. They were handed back ownership of the baths in 2019 to develop an ambitious community-led, and owned, health and well-being centre. The neighbourhood is the focus of a chapter – looking at the mix of vibrancy and problems it contains – which, because it sits in First Minister Nicola Sturgeon's constituency, has attracted much right-wing media and commentary of a kind that is frequently not helpful and often not even bothered with accuracy.

If these currents of radical change are to be sustained, they need to find support, champions and resources. But its energy rapidly burns up and leaves one stranded, needing additional resources – an argument Fintan O'Toole explores at further length in his contribution to this book (O'Toole, 2014; see Walzer, 2015). They need a different kind of politics and a commitment to public services that can enter into genuine collaboration with places of innovation. This does not come easily and entails a fundamental rebalancing of how the state and public agencies act and relate to its citizens. It involves becoming a different kind of state. This was the implicit offer tantalising glimpsed in the latter stages of the 2014 independence referendum. But it is much harder to make real than the rhetoric suggests.

Maybe part of this promise in 2014 was a chimera that people wanted to believe. But it nonetheless captured the hopes and aspirations of a large part of Scotland who do not believe in old-fashioned state power no matter how benevolent it claims to be. Younger people in their twenties and thirties, in particular, feel let down and even abandoned by the state (which in most cases here means the British state) across the developed world. This requires a different approach to rebuilding trust and supporting people than simply hankering after the past.

There is a wide set of ideas and insights that can be drawn upon to chart our way to a different future. They point towards a path navigating away from the twin pillars of a supposedly enlightened, but often centralised and monolithic, state and of abandoning people to the mercy of an often-rigged market capitalism which lacks compassion or humanity in the harm it is inflicting – economically, socially and environmentally.

This path emphasises remaking relationships both in work and society. They are what gave rise to the Violence Reduction Unit. Such impact, the ideas of 'radical help', of self-organisation, remaking the state and the notion that the state has to have the courage and belief in people to let go in a manner which lifts people up, rather than abandoning them (Cottam, 2018; Goss, 2014). That, after all, was the vision inherent in books such as Lesley Riddoch's *Blossom*. *Blossom* found an audience in the Indyref, but it has not yet translated from an attitude into an actual practice (Riddoch, 2013). All of this enjoys a rich resonance with older Scottish radical traditions that predate the rise of Labour state-ism in the Independent Labour Party (ILP), and others emphasising self-government as an organising set of principles for society – not just relying on a Parliament in Edinburgh.

Such thinking showcases the limitations of inherited, dominant political perspectives – from conventional social democracy to the bankruptcy of the neo-liberal project. It also underlines that no matter how 'civic', progressive and outgoing our nationalism is in intent, it does not, on its own, offer a sufficiently imaginative guide for the future. In the words of Fintan O'Toole, civic nationalism is like 'a rocket fuel', it can take you far in the initial stages, aiding the setting up of a new nation state. But its energy rapidly burns up and leaves you stranded, needing additional resources (O'Toole, 2014; see Walzer, 2015). That future terrain is one centred on self-determination, which is localist, feminist, empowering and green.

The Problem with Britain Beyond Brexit

One important dimension that has to be taken into account in charting Scotland's future is the long-term direction of the British state, the crisis of that state and the exhaustion of the Tory and Labour versions of Britain, which have been exposed further, but not created, by Brexit (see Bogdanor, 2019).

The British state showed historic adaptability in legislating for a Scottish Parliament and a Welsh Assembly in 1997–98, preceded by affirmative referendums. It had the statecraft and intelligence to support the Northern Irish peace process leading to the path-breaking Good Friday Agreement (GFA) in 1998. This, of course, has been in danger of being undermined by Brexit and by the intransigence of hard-line Brexit advocates in the Tory Party.

But, long before Brexit, the UK had showed its long-term inability to reform and democratise. What we have seen in recent years has been the retrenchment of a unitary state nationalism, forgetting the inconvenient fact that the UK is not, in its character and make-up, a unitary state, but a union state made up of four nations.

In the years of devolution before Brexit, the UK saw Scotland, along with Wales and Northern Ireland, as boxes ticked, not as part of a larger story about an evolving, decentralising UK. There was no formalising of relationships between the devolved territories and the political centre. There was no codification or entrenchment of this supposed new settlement, and no remaking of Westminster and Whitehall. For all the talk over twenty years of the UK slowly moving to a federal or quasi-federal system, it has never amounted to anything substantive.

On the contrary, there has actually been retreat and denial. A remade UK had to ensure that its political core understood that it had to change and doing so – recognising that the way it did politics, and saw itself, was a problem. But, no real signs of this changing consciousness ever emerged under Labour, and certainly not under the Conservatives, with or without the Liberal Democrats. Instead, the United Kingdom has increasingly resembled a divided kingdom, with a unitary state mindset at the centre of what is, in fact, a union state. Then along came Brexit to add to these deep tensions.

Brexit is a product of a deeply rooted Euroscepticism in an English political imagination dominated by a reactionary form of nationalism. There are other Brexit sentiments, such as the historic Jeremy Corbyn-John McDonnell 'Left Exit' (Lexit) opposition to the EU. They have aligned themselves with this project and aided it, both in the 2016 referendum and afterwards. Brexit represents many failures, including that of pro-Europeans and progressives across the UK, but it is also a failure of alternative Englands to find voice and take on the forces of reaction and conservatism (Barnett, 2017). After all, there are numerous other English traditions and radicalisms which have at times found the strength and popular support to combine with Scottish, Welsh and Northern Irish sentiment to create majority coalitions for far-reaching change across these isles.

However, this alternative prospectus looks increasingly less likely in the future. This is not just because of the forces of backward English nationalism, which do not (for all their noise and disruption) speak for a majority in England and are probably still not even a majority in the Tories (although that may change). But because of the fragmentation and near-disappearance of any kind of homogeneous 'British politics' beyond Westminster. This makes it nigh impossible to conceive of a radical Labour Government coming to power under Corbyn, or a Corbynista successor, and implementing the kind of programme which it would like to do, and which deals with the structural inequities which disfigure the economy and society. It would either be blocked by establishment forces, fall through its own internal divisions, be scuppered by Brexit or otherwise dilute any radical plans, with the prospect of a reactionary backlash taking the UK further rightwards. All of this has implications for Scotland today and the future path it chooses to take.

Avoiding Scotland's Groundhog Days

In these tumultuous times it is understandable that some people want to cling to the idea that political change is easy. That all that is required is the 'will to power', a leadership with the right line and not compromising in the face of adversity. That, after all, has been part of the appeal of Brexit, Corbyn, Trump and even some independence claims pre- and post-2014.

Yet, it is also true that too many people in Scotland are trapped by events of the recent past, and this stretches out beyond 2014, and even the devolution era. They look to the landscape and transformation of the country over the last 40 years, particularly by Thatcherism and what came after. The Thatcher Government presided over hugely unpopular economic and social policies, from painful deindustrialisation, to public spending cuts and privatisation and the hugely divisive poll tax. It is difficult, 40 years after this political revolution, to begin to gauge how fierce this attack felt at the time to so many people in Scotland and elsewhere. It is heightened now by the Tory lack of a mandate and a widening democratic deficit between Scotland and Westminster.

The economic and social changes which the Thatcher Government encouraged and aided – from the decline of steel, iron, mining, shipbuilding and away from traditional male dominated industries, along with the rise of new, service sector employment, would have happened without Thatcher and her ideology. It would have occurred, as it did in many other countries, in a much more managed and humane way, while protecting profitable parts of manufacturing. People would have felt less that it had been imposed upon them with destructive force.

This is less an argument about Thatcherism than it is about how the past is remembered and interpreted, the role of collective memories and how these impact on the present and future choices (Torrance, 2009; Stewart, 2009). Hence, a powerful part of Scotland's political discourse after Thatcherism has been shaped by what has been called, in a very different context, the 'children of the echo' by Jarvis Cocker (Cocker, 2012). He was talking about the continued obsession with the 1960s and the mining of it with ever-diminishing returns. That decade was, he believes, a 'Big Bang' of imagination and creativity, which people have drawn from and referenced to, to the point that they have become plagiarists and copyists – Britpop being an obvious example of this, as Cocker concedes.

In Scotland, a large swathe of political debate on the centre-left and the left is seen through the prism of the 1980s and Thatcherism. It often adds the New Labour decade and Blairism onto the charge sheet, presenting them as an accommodation and even an extension of the dominance of the right. In this mindset, it is possible to frame most of the last 40 years of the UK in a carica-tured way, which takes away any nuance or attempts at change. Such a view was expressed by the likes of former Communist and UCS work-in leader Jimmy Reid – who was otherwise capable of highly genuinely creative thinking – when he stated: 'When New Labour came to power, we got a right-wing Conservative Government' (quoted in *Daily Telegraph*, 11 August 2010).

This is a Scottish equivalent of the 'children of the echo' that poses a sim-plistic, linear and bleak picture of the past. 1979 is presented as 'Year Zero', and everything that happened after seen as negative, a loss and imposed on us. This is contrasted with the Scotland of today, and more often than not with pro-independence views, to assume and assert the character of radical views in the present. Neal Ascherson was tempted to do this in the last stages of the 2014 debate, when he argued for independence on the grounds that the UK had degraded itself to a 'Serco state', defined by privatisation and outsourcing, while overlooking the presence of such activities under the watch of devolution (Ascherson, 2014). This is a classic case of over-stating differences, one which masks the difficult choices we face in Scotland about public services, opposing privatisation and developing new models.

Scotland After Devolution

A Politics of Self-Government

We have to come to terms with the complex shifts that have happened in our country and society over recent decades, both under devolution and beyond, and locate them in the context of longer-term trends. These include the weaken-ing of old collectivist norms, traditional forms of authority and power, and the rise of individualism – not all of the latter is reducible to right-wing reaction. For example, such a loosening up of society has aided Scotland to become more at ease with diversity, more multi-cultural, more pluralist and tolerant across a range of indicators – progress in LGBTQI+ rights being just one of the most striking. Connected to this is the decline of deference and hidebound forms of moral authority often associated with the Kirk, along with other types of social conservatism and the authoritarianism they often displayed. This has been an enormous gain for Scotland. Indeed, it has been such an all-encompassing change that it is often not even commented upon now. But it also raises serious dilemmas about what constitutes appropriate moral authority, and how we set agreed rules in a more diverse disputatious society.

Scotland has also experienced two 'Great Disruptions', seen in the indepen-dence referendum and then Brexit. The first a home-grown explosion of energy, and the second mostly imposed by English voters and motivations, with only a minority of voters in Scotland supporting it.

Some see the current climate of instability as one that calls for another Indyref as soon as possible. But this is a politics that puts process, the calling of a referendum and its timing centre-stage, rather than its substance. It chooses to ignore difficult questions. How it is possible to respect one majority while attempting to overturn it? How do we use referendums in a political culture which has not agreed a formal framework for them? That involves thinking about who calls them, how they are called, qualified and super majorities and how one mandate can supersede another. These concerns have all been fleshed out in public in the debate on a second EU referendum, or the 'People's Vote', but they are just as germane to any future independence vote. They are as much about how to hold people with different desires in some sort of commonly accepted democratic space, while dividing on a major change, as they are about the mechanics and calculation of the process.

The increasingly self-governing Scotland that is now evident, and which all of us have played our part in bringing into being, faces many difficult choices and debates. But, in this it cannot be reduced to a politics centred simply on the date of any future independence vote, or upon constitutional politics. Rather, it is about the sum total of our actions: how we act, interact and respect one another, how we build each other up and our capacity to be a different kind of society from the present.

That Scotland involves a politics that is about much more than Holyrood and its 129 elected politicians, or the Scottish Government and its formal powers. It is about a Scotland where the Parliament and its politics are a catalyst for, and reflective of, further and wider change; where it plays its part in encouraging and supporting people to take more decisions regarding their lives.

Twenty years ago, there were two competing visions of the Parliament and the devolution on offer. The first was of the Parliament as an intrinsic idea – an institution as an end in itself and as a political voice and expression. In this account, the Parliament speaks for Scotland, whereas previously there was no voice. The second perspective was of the Parliament as an instrumental idea – of a means to an end, to develop a Scotland where power was shared and diffused through the community of the realm and held by all of us to aid our betterment.

Of course, the two overlapped in a number of respects, but they also point to different ideas about political authority, voice and ultimately purpose. One is more essentialist and uncontested in the way it poses these ideas; the other more qualified, contested, fluid and open to constantly evolving. The former draws more from 19th century notions of sovereignty, whereas the latter sits in the tradition of pooled and shared sovereignty. Given Scotland has a deep-seated backstory of popular sovereignty (the 'claim of right') dating back 700 years, it is appropriate that we embrace it, renew it and apply it in our modern setting.

These two narratives illuminate the different paths Scotland has before it, one of which we have to choose. They have within them competing, contrasting futures: one where it is enough to have a self-governing Parliament and assertive Government; another where self-government amounts to the combined actions of millions of us as citizens, individuals and voters, practicing every day the democracy that Scotland could become and, in so doing, making us the kind of society where we make our collective future together. The first is about devolution and remaining within its paradigm or a very limited form of independence; the second is about transcending the constraints of devolution and involves a politics beyond the political classes. However, the constitutional question is shaped and handled, only one of these futures is worthy of the title 'Scotland the Brave'.

References

Arrighi, G. (2009), *The Long Twentieth Century: Money, Power and the Origins of Our Time*, London: Verso Books.

Ascherson, N. (2014), 'Scottish Independence: Why I'm Voting Yes', *Prospect*, September 2014, available online at: www.prospectmagazine. co.uk/politics/independence-referendum-why-im-voting-yes

Barnett, A. (2017), *The Lure of Greatness: England's Brexit and Trump's America*, London: Unbound Books.

Barrow, S. and Small, M. (2016), *Scotland 2021*, Edinburgh: Ekklesia and Bella Caledonia.

Bogdanor, B. (2019), *Beyond Brexit: Towards a British Constitution*, London: I.B. Tauris.

Brown, G. and Alexander, D. (1999), *New Scotland, New Britain*, London: Smith Institute.

Brown, G. and Alexander, D. (2007), *Stronger Together: The 21st Century Case for Britain and Europe*, London: Fabian Society.

Carnochan, J. (2015), *Conviction: Violence, Culture and a Shared Public Service Agenda*, Glendaruel: Argyll Publishing.

Cocker, J. (2012), 'The John Lennon Letters', *The Guardian*, 10 October 2012, available online at: www.theguardian.com/books/2012/oct/10/john-lennon-letters-hunter-davies-review

Cottam, H. (2018), *Radical Help: How We Can Remake the Relationships between Us and Revolutionise the Welfare State*, London: Virago Press.

Curtice, J. (2019), 'The Electorate and Elections', in Hassan, G. (ed.), *The Story of the Scottish Parliament: The First Two Decades Explained*, Edinburgh: Edinburgh University Press, forthcoming.

Drucker, H. (ed.) (1982), *John P. Mackintosh on Scotland*, London: Longman.

Goss, S. (2014), *Open Tribe*, London: Lawrence and Wishart.

Hassan, G. (2014a), *Caledonian Dreaming: The Quest for a Different Scotland*, Edinburgh: Luath Press.

Hassan, G. (2014b), *Independence of the Scottish Mind: Elite Narratives, Public Spaces and the Making of a Modern Nation*, London: Palgrave Macmillan.

Hassan, G., Gibb, E. and Howland, L. (eds.) (2005), *Scotland 2020: Hopeful Stories for a Northern Nation*, London: Demos.

Hunter, J. (2012), *From the Low Tide of the Sea to the Highest Mountain Tops*, Laxay: Islands Book Trust.

MacCormick, N. (1999), *Questioning Sovereignty: Law, State and Nation in the European Commonwealth*, Oxford: Oxford University Press.

Mackenzie, W.J.M. (1978), *Political Identity*, Harmondsworth: Penguin.

McLeish, H. (2014), *Rethinking Our Politics: The Political and Constitutional Future of Scotland and the UK*, Edinburgh: Luath Press.

McLeish, H. (2016), *Citizens United: Taking Back Control in Turbulent Times*, Edinburgh: Luath Press.

Marryat, L. and Frank, J. (2019), 'Factors associated with adverse childhood experiences in Scottish children: a prospective cohort study', *BMJ Paediatrics Open*, available online at: bmjpaedsopen.bmj.com/content/3/1/e000340

Maxwell, S. (2012), *Arguing for Independence: Evidence, Risk and the Wicked Issues*, Edinburgh: Luath Press.

Maxwell, S. (2013), *The Case for Left Wing Nationalism: Essays and Articles*, Edinburgh: Luath Press.

Mouffe, C. (2018), *For a Left Populism*, London: Verso Books.

O'Toole, F. (2014), 'It is not that Scotland might become a new state but that it might become a new kind of state', *Sunday Herald*, 7 September 2014, available online at: www.heraldscotland.com/opinion/13178696.it-is-not-that-scotland-might-become-a-new-state-but-that-it-might-become-a-new-kind-of-state/

Pryce, G. and Le Zhang, M. (2018), 'Inequality in Scotland: despite Nordic aspirations, things are not improving', *The Conversation*, 7

November 2018, available online at: theconversation.com/inequality
-in-scotland-despite-nordic-aspirations-things-are-not-improving-105307
Riddoch, L. (2013), *Blossom: What Scotland Needs to Flourish*, Edinburgh:
Luath Press.
Save the Children Fund (2013), *Child Poverty in Scotland: The Facts*,
Edinburgh: Save the Children Fund.
Schlesinger, P. (2019), 'What's happening to the public sphere?', paper to
Media, Communication and Cultural Studies Association Annual Confer-
ence, University of Stirling, 9 January 2019.
Scottish Government (2017), 'Poverty and Income Inequality in Scotland
2015–16', Edinburgh: Scottish Government, available online at: www.gov.
scot/publications/poverty-income-inequality-scotland-2015-16/pages/5/
Social Mobility and Child Poverty Commission/David Hume Institute (2015),
Elitist Scotland?, London/Edinburgh: Social Mobility and Child Poverty
Commission/David Hume Institute, available online at: assets.publishing.
service.gov.uk/government/uploads/system/uploads/attachment_data/
file/481851/Elitist_Scotland_Report.PDF
Stewart, D. (2009), *The Path to Devolution and Change: A Political History of
Scotland under Margaret Thatcher*, London: I.B. Tauris.
Torrance, D. (2009), *'We in Scotland': Thatcherism in a Cold Climate*, Edin-
burgh: Birlinn.
Walzer, M. (2015), *The Paradox of Liberation: Secular Revolutions and Reli-
gious Counterrevolutions*, New Haven & London: Yale University Press.

CHAPTER I

How Scotland Can Keep Breathing

Neal Ascherson

SOME PEOPLE HAVE a dream; I have a nightmare. It is to find myself locked in a dark, airless nursery cupboard, somewhere in the south of England, with Boris Johnson, Jacob Rees-Mogg, Theresa May and Paul Dacre, former editor of the *Daily Mail*. In the darkness, I hear their snuffling and sniggering as they crawl towards me.

I have a nightmare, because that is the future after Brexit. Britain – and not just England who voted for it – will become a place the young want to leave. The lights are being dimmed; the windows closed tight, the shutters firmly snibbed over them. Somewhere out there in the fresh air, people with many nationalities and languages will be coming and going as usual; lively, crazy, imaginative futures will be constructed in France or Italy or Poland. Often enough those futures will collapse and need new designers. But here in soundproofed Brexit Britain – a bit poorer than before, a lot duller – we'll scarcely hear the noises from outside.

Scottish culture will have to smash open airholes to keep breathing. But that's something we already know how to do. Remember how John Bellany and Sandy Moffat went to Berlin and brought back the fire of German Expressionism to Scotland. Or, how Ricky Demarco went to Kraków and returned with Tadeusz Kantor's theatre to inspire Scottish dramatists. Or how Lynda Myles went to France and Hungary and, aged 23, blew up the staid Edinburgh Film Festival with the *avant-garde* cinema culture she imported. Without European air, Scottish culture will begin to suffocate all over again.

Scotland still has a spare key to that locked cupboard in its pocket, a key tagged 'independence', if we dare to use it. But, Brexit itself is likely to happen now, whatever its form and political composition. We have had flirtation with the car crash of a 'No Deal Brexit' and the false hope of the supposedly less disastrous soft fudge Brexit. And yet, what these have shown is the hypocrisy in the soft options, and that the direction of travel is clear.

I used to think they'll spend four years trying to get out, and the next four years trying to get back in. Now I'm not so sure. To use Nigel Farage language, the English majority will feel that they have won back independence from foreigners, and with a few grumbles, they'll be content.

Europe, or more accurately the EU, is left in the lurch. George Soros is perfectly right about what needs to be done. Revive the idea of a two-speed Europe: a single currency integrated core, and a periphery of other nations preferring to stay with their own money.

Secondly, smash the German fogeyism of the European Central Bank – still in the lum-hat and stick-up collar age of banking. Show the bank how to help nations without forcing them to sit on the pavement and sell their frying pans and wedding dresses, like the Greeks.

This is easier said than done. So-called populism is the fault of European governments and EU policies, and the fanatical obstinacy of their neo-liberalism. To be dogmatic, the EU is coming apart basically because social democracy, or democratic socialism, betrayed its own people.

Two economic earthquakes – the collapse of Communist systems in 1989 and the banking disaster of 2007–08 – left winners but also more losers. People lost not only money and jobs but lost their feeling that their work mattered and was significant.

Socialists were expected to stand by those losers, their traditional constituency. But they had defected to collude with, and appease, the right. Blair veered to Thatcherism, the once great German Social Democrats destroyed themselves weakening the 'social model', Polish and Hungarian social democrats moved to forms of turbo-capitalism, and so on. So, they left a political vacuum. As a result, xenophobic, authoritarian and ultra-nationalist parties, but also welfare-ist, ones have rushed in to fill and colonise that vacuum.

Scotland's Dilemmas

Scotland pre-empted that. The SNP turned out to offer a benign variant of populism in which many people who felt like losers – the 30-year collapse of traditional industries, the sense that the nation was becoming a collective loser in the union – could take refuge. But what now in these turbulent times? I see this as a twice-dangerous moment. It is true that the Scots – unlike the English – still have that silver spare key to escape through Ukania's closed door. But will we use it?

The first danger is that Scots get increasingly put off EU membership. This is fatal. The truth is that an independent Scotland out with the EU would fall more rapidly into a 'Scotshire' dependency on London than the devolved Scotland we have now. The 'power grab' stushie with the Brexit Withdrawal Bill, which Scotland was never likely to win, shows how things will go. It is true there are reforms – heavy lifting jobs in Scotland needing state support and subsidy – which EU free competition rules would oppose. But much can be done in the interval between independence and admission.

By the way, pay no attention to vague threats of a veto, or to Brussels horror at the very notion of secession in one of its members. This is utter and transparent hypocrisy. No fewer than 20 out of the 27 EU's members post-Brexit will owe their existence to a secession opposed by a larger state or empire, starting with the Netherlands in the dim and distant 16th century. I have a list somewhere which I could go through, but I will spare you.

The second danger is better defined as a bewildering possibility. I mean the possibility of a real and permanent division in the self-government and independence forces and opinion. A point to emphasise is that the independence issue is here to stay. In 2014, it became a sturdy, plausible option for Scotland's future, it became part of the fabric, the furniture of who we are. Some wanted it, others did not. But it won't go away now, although it may take different forms and leaderships.

The SNP have governed Scotland for 12 years, and on the whole with a decency and humanity which has reflected the best of us and been an accurate portrayal of who we are. They have done this in spite of tendencies to over-centralise and to claim credit for things done by others. But they have not managed to deliver independence. They dominate political representation, speak for the nation at Westminster as the dominant voice and work for internal improvement. But the fires seem to have died down on the national question.

This is where the old Irish Home Rule party got stuck. At the end of the 19th century, it still held an overwhelming majority of Irish parliamentary seats. But, hardly noticed at first, a radical minority impatient for independence was building up behind them. And just a hundred years ago, in 1918, the dam burst. In the election that year, Sinn Féin won 73 of the Irish seats while the Home Rulers were reduced to a mere six.

Of course, Scotland is not Ireland. Behind that dam-burst lay centuries of colonial oppression, the tragedy of the 1916 Easter Rising, the Great War and London's insane decision in 1918 to impose conscription on Irish men. But independence movements do have similarities. Unfairly or not, impatience eventually breaks through.

'As If' Scotland

Being a Self-Governing Nation

Watching events in 2019 – the astonishing pro-independences marches across Scotland, apparently organised *ad hoc*, or the arguments over the Growth Commission report which has been contested both within the SNP and the wider Yes movement, I have to wonder: are we looking at the conception – not yet the birth – of a non-violent but implacably radical Scottish independence force in a way with some echoes to Sinn Féin one hundred years ago? So, it may be that a hard rain's a'gonna fall. How should Scotland dress for this change in the weather? Old Robert Monro, colonel of the Scottish regiment that fought in the Thirty Years' War, defended Stralsund against the imperialists and lost nearly 500 men in the siege. Afterwards, Sir Alexander Leslie was appointed the city's commander, and Monro wrote:

> having gotten a Scots Governour to protect them ... which was a good omen unto them, to get a Governour of the only Nation, that was never conquered...

I like that identity. Not lineage, landscape or wealth but simply unyielding guts under stress: 'the only Nation, that was never conquered'. Invaded, sometimes brutalised, yes – but not conquered. As another soldier, Marshal Pilsudski, used to say, 'To be beaten, but not to give in, is to be victorious'.

So, the kit for this weather is the brand called 'As If' Scotland – government, parliament and people – should act as if this country were already independent (as in many ways it is). The limits of devolution are a chain-link fence. Over there are reserved matters out with our competence etcetera, etcetera. But we should carry right on with our purposes until we bump into that fence, not slow down prudently well before we get to it. And, we should bring the big wire-cutters with us.

I admire the sentiment of the 2018 Common Weal book *How to Start A New Country* in that way. It just assumes – I think rightly – that the day will come when it's obvious that a majority will vote for Scotland's independence. So, you prepare. Even before the vote, you set up framework commissions to design the new institutions required. And you carry on with that detailed, sober construction over the three years probably separating a Yes vote from Independence Day.

That's walking right up to the wire, 'As If'... Or there's Clara Ponsati in St Andrews, Catalonia's education minister whom the Spanish Government wants to jail for sedition because she asked for independence. What happens if lawyers eventually deny her case, and the British Government advances to seize her for extradition? Do we let them take her, this honourable woman for whom Scotland feels both sympathy and responsibility? Or do we act 'As If', reaching for the wire-cutters and smuggling her into a chain of 'safe houses' across this country?

That would be illegal. But it would be like another crime, the 'theft' of the Stone of Destiny in 1950, which sent an unexpected flash of delight to millions. It was an authentic act, something not licensed by the Scottish Office, but something people in an independent country would have done. So, what happens now Westminster has overruled and vetoed all the Scottish Parliament's decisions on EU withdrawal or on ensuring the return of devolved powers to Holyrood? Or, when Scotland has finally been dragged out of the European Union against the expressed will of its people? Perhaps 21st century Scotland can do better than politely express 'deep disappointment'.

'As If' behaviour doesn't undermine the laborious arguments about currency or borders or debt sharing. On the contrary, it kicks them into higher gear. Colonel Monro got this right. He wrote in his journal, 'we are neither rich nor poore by what we possesse, but by what we desire'.

Section One – Scotland's Economy

CHAPTER 2

The Political Economy of Scotland
Twenty Years of Consequences

Craig Dalzell

POLITICS AND ECONOMICS are often spoken about as two separate agendas but in reality, politics permeates the entirety of our economy – and vice versa. Economic politics and the political economy are one. Scotland is a country of great ambition, and greater potential, but has been trammelled by economic choices made by us, and for us, over the past several decades.

It is the nature of politics that choices made decades ago can embed themselves into our political framework and limit the scope of our ambitions in subtle ways. The legacy of the neo-liberal programs of the 80s and 90s live on, not only in those who would adopt and succeed them, but also in those who fought and still fight against them. The legacy of the last two decades of rampant financial boom, devastating bust and then a decade of austerity is still in the process of creating the political paradigms that will, unless we take efforts to avoid it, control the political and economic debates for years to come.

The first decade of the 21st century was marked by the crescendo and death-scream of the legacy of the two decades before that. The marketisation of our housing sector and the liberalisation of our financial sector, in particular, have profoundly changed the way we interact with these sections of the economy and how they interact with us.

Housing is no longer about having a place to live in a community we love. For many, a house is an investment. It's a commodity. It's a replacement to the pension they once thought that they would receive. It's a 'step up the property ladder'. For a few, a house is a revenue stream – whether it is rented out to a tenant, or to an endless flow of tourists looking to 'live like a local' inside a block of flats populated almost entirely by endless flows of tourists.

For many still, a house is a dream. The idea of becoming a house owner is simply not feasible. The price their parents paid for the family home would not even cover the deposit required for a much smaller dwelling built today. Public rental housing is simply unavailable and to rent privately is to place one's self at the mercy of those who would treat you as a commodity. You will accept the rent increases as being as inevitable as the day you're evicted to make way for someone who can pay more – or for an endless flow of tourists.

Politicians will make promises of building more houses but either they get mired into committing to arbitrary targets – one more house than the other party built or are promising they will do – or they will build just enough to avoid 'distorting the market'. Private companies will, of course, never build enough houses to eat into their own profit margins. That would never do.

The liberalisation of the financial sector gave us the rise of 'quick' capital. Banks chased their profits off into the wild tangle of derivatives, credit swaps and other financial instruments too complex to be understood by even those who invented them.

These instruments, for a time, brought great wealth to those who wielded them not better than anyone else, but at least, faster or harder than those around them. A few would warn that the sector was lost and heading for disaster, but the lure of the now forestalled the vision of tomorrow.

For the great majority of us – those of us who did not dwell in those towers of glass, steel and money – the unfettered financial markets reached us in other ways. The retail banks no longer needed us as customers. Our meagre savings became an afterthought in their portfolios. Our needs mattered only insofar as how much they could turn our money into their money.

This has led to the gradual disappearance of our bank branches from our communities and the rise of internet and mobile banking. Finance as fast as you can click a button. No need to check to see if you can afford it. No need to check if your community needs it. There is no community. There is no society. Only individuals, their choices and their ability to spend the money that our app can lend you.

At the very worst of the pre-crash period, some of the banks realised that the buildings which hosted our businesses were increasing in value by more than the repayments on our mortgages. There have been cases of banks allegedly deliberately bankrupting their own customers so as to take possession of those buildings and other assets. This is the very opposite of a banking 'service'.

The 'casino capitalism' of the City of London, and elsewhere, has crowded out investment in our economy – especially in the small businesses that make up the heart of it. Why should a potential investor put money into a venture that may not return a profit for several years when they can just gamble it around the stock market for a few hours and make just as much money?

This is unsustainable. The economy of Scotland has slowly been hollowed out as our people have been caught in a financial vice. Our wages are stagnant or declining. Our housing and bills are growing more expensive. Our social protections stripped to the bone or withdrawn altogether. That 'fast finance' only keeps us able to spend until we hit our credit limits. And then what?

What happens to a consumer economy when it runs out of consumers?

We live in a country where the town high street is dying, independent shops are crowded out by multinational-owned superstores and then those superstores are edged out by even more nebulous internet-based companies. Our households are squeezed to the point that even these shops are seeing sales decline. An economy that watches pound-shops go bankrupt is one that is experiencing severe stress. We need to build something better than this. This is where politics has to take the reins of the free-market and gently direct the economy, rather than be directed by it.

Securing Finance

Managing and securing the financial sector in Scotland may come from publicly owning two key areas of it. The upcoming Scottish National Investment Bank (SNIB) has the potential of developing and strengthening the Scottish economy in ways simply not possible up till now.

The SNIB will amalgamate and sit alongside the existing schemes currently part of the Scottish investment landscape but will also be directed by missions set by the Scottish Government and according to a charter which specifies that its funding must be ethical and sustainable. Its key principle which will set it apart from the 'casino capitalism' of what we usually think of in the financial sector will be its adherence to 'patient finance'. This bank will specifically focus on those areas of the economy that require such a patient approach.

An investment bank with a mission: to actually support new businesses through that critical period before they become self-sustaining and then beyond as they look to build up their potential. It certainly has to work better than the previous examples of deliberate damaging behaviour.

But an investment bank can be so much more than just a business accelerator or SME growth instrument. The investment bank can support a new generation of public rental houses built not to maximise profit margins but to maximise the welfare for those who live in those houses. Disrupting the opportunistic 'housing market' in favour of a policy of providing warm, efficient and comfortable homes may sound jarring to some but isn't this just a symptom of the political trammelling that we've all been caught in due to the decisions of the past.

A key mission of the investment bank could be to support a network of publicly owned retail banks to replace the banks lost to the contraction of the commercial market and to change the face of banking in Scotland.

We need to challenge the idea that banking is too expensive to be a viable service for communities – especially those in remote and rural locations. Instead, we should consider it too expensive for these services to be withdrawn. The 'transactional banking' via the internet or mobile phone app that we've grown increasingly accustomed to might be fast and convenient, but you become less than a customer to these banks. Nothing more than a line in the spreadsheet which, as stated earlier, is almost irrelevant to the bank as it throws money after artificial derivatives in the search for profit.

We need to bring back 'relationship banking'. The idea that a bank hosts staff and a manager who are embedded in the community, who know you and your area as well as anyone else who makes their life there. These managers are far more able to decide if a certain type of investment is needed in the community or if a person is able to take on the responsibility of a loan. Far more able than a sophisticated black-box algorithm and far more able to justify their decisions should the need arise.

Examples are beginning to appear around the world of communities getting together to create their own local retail banks. There is no reason that Scotland could not do similar on a grander scale. The SNIB could support a network of nationally owned bank branches providing basic services without having to chase the insatiable demands of shareholders.

This is not just about maintaining a service for older people who are stereotyped as being unable to cope with internet banking, it's also about the businesses who rely on cash transactions and require ready access to cash deposit and withdrawal as well as other business services throughout the trading day. Towns without banks are towns without businesses. Without economies. Without life.

Future Foundations

With national level investment and community level management, Scotland has the opportunity to learn from the lessons of the past twenty years and to reject that model of economics. Instead of suffering a hangover from the 2008 crash for the next twenty years we could build something stronger, better and fairer.

There is the potential to build our communities around the rock-solid foundations of stable, patient finance; banks designed to support us rather than extract wealth from us. These banks would act as a financial oasis around which our businesses can sustain themselves. Patient finance will guide and develop a new generation of entrepreneurs and local shops which will help to recirculate money around the economy rather than pulling it away. As a local independent coffee shop is far less likely to move its profits through an offshore tax haven than a large chain brand, the national Government will benefit in terms of increased tax revenue and reduced vulnerability to being lobbied by those large chains that want to set up here.

A country with a stable, local economy is one with a very different political outlook to one that is reliant on fickle 'inward investment' or 'GDP growth' and always at the mercy of the next financial crash. Imagine the politics of a Scotland that spent twenty years building a sustainable, ethical economy that worked for everyone rather than just enriching the few who were already made wealthy by the previous twenty years. Imagine the politics that such a Scotland could pass on to the people who start to look twenty years beyond that.

CHAPTER 3

The Scottish Economy, Ownership and Control

Neil McInroy

SCOTLAND IS A wealthy country, with one of the highest GDPs in the world (Fraser of Allander Institute, 2016). However, nearly half of all wealth in Scotland is in the hands of the top ten per cent of the wealthiest people. Poverty, wage stagnation, underinvestment and low productivity are now entrenched features of the Scottish economy and its economies. Arguably, prevailing economic and economic development policies are failing to ensure that economic gains and wealth are delivering socially.

This essay believes that questions as to who has wealth, where it goes and who has influence over it are defining features of the Scottish economy. In this, we assert that there is a need to intentionally reorganize the Scottish economy. Where economic and social justice are viewed less as a mere 'after the fact' outcome of growth and wealth, and more hotwired into new forms of economic ownership and a distributed consideration of wealth.

Wealth in Scotland

Who Has It and Where Does It Go?

In the last decade, wealth in Scotland has grown much faster than incomes, with wealth now more than seven times the GDP. Furthermore, wealth distribution is hugely uneven, with the top 10 per cent owning 200 times more wealth than the bottom 10 per cent (a median wealth of £1.3 million compared to £6,000). Indeed, the wealthiest 10 per cent own 43 per cent of all wealth in Scotland, with the least wealthy 40 per cent only owning just 5 per cent (Bell and D'Arcy, 2018). Furthermore, in looking at wealthy individuals we see that some of the richest people in Scotland live elsewhere, including low tax countries such as Monaco or the Isle of Man (Brinded and Colson, 2017). This stands in contrast to 25 per cent of Scottish people who have less than £500 of net savings, and 7 per cent who have zero savings, or are in debt.

This inequality in wealth is in part driven by investment and capital flows. A key characteristic to this is how investment into Scotland is increasingly global. Investors have little or no attachment, connection or affinity to Scotland, its people, identity or its local places. Subsequently, investment returns are not readily recirculated into the local economy, through residency or affinity as they would be by local investors, but instead extracted out and away from Scotland.

While the action to capture international flows of private investment wealth, requires international cooperation and policy, this is not true for much publicly owned wealth. These identifiable stores of public wealth are, in the main, democratically overseen. However, these sources are not working hard enough for Scotland or being environmentally responsible. Public wealth is being extracted out of Scotland via offshore headquarters. For example, some PFI deals involving key public infrastructure is being delivered by offshore firms, and £543 billion of Scottish pension wealth is being extracted through being invested in foreign firms with shareholders registered in offshore tax havens (Whitfield, 2018). Furthermore, questions have been raised as regards links between Scottish pensions and investment in shale gas fracking, with claims that Scottish councils invest £972 million of pension fund money in overseas fracking companies (Friends of the Earth, 2018). Clearly there is a need and responsibility for pensions to accrue value for pension holders. However, Scottish pension wealth should be used responsibly, and be used to virtuously ripple through the Scottish economy, with multipliers as it does so.

How We Build a New Economic Ecosystem

In building a more economically and socially just Scotland, we must place more attention onto wealth. In a context of fast-moving capital, there are limits to any traditional central government 'after the fact' redistribution of wealth. By the time any wealth capture process is in place, the wealth may have already been extracted into the ether of the global economy, dividend payments to large shareholder driven corporations or simply offshored. In this the Scottish Government, local authorities and its people should embrace the rise of new social and economic movements around the world which seek to counteract these extractive forces, by advancing inclusion and reorganising the economy and wealth. This reorganisation is about ensuring that wealth is extracted less and is more broadly held, with more local roots.

Local wealth building is a practical systematic approach to economic development and is built on local roots and plurality of ownership (McInroy, 2018).

These ideas and actions around local wealth building counteract the idea of investment and trickle down. (Trickle down assumes that once investment capital had been enticed – often to our large metropolitan cores – wealth creation will flourish; the business supply chain will benefit and long lasting local jobs will be secured.) In local wealth building, social, and environmental gains are not an afterthought, but rather built in as a natural function of the economy. The aim here is to ensure a reliability of outcomes including jobs and meaningful work, equity, inclusion, economic stability and environmental sustainability.

There is a growing range of local agents, who are driving this local wealth building movement. This includes businesses, who are paying the Living Wage and growing their care and concern for employees, including the development of investment portfolios which reflect local need and place development (McInroy, 2017). It includes unions who, whilst somewhat fettered by often draconian national employment laws, are starting to support local activism and community organisation. In the social sector, we have many organisations developing co-operatives and economic alternatives that ensure wealth is more distributed and owned by the people who are producing the wealth. In the public sector, we are seeing a greater acknowledgement of the public pound (or democratised money), and how the commissioning and procuring of goods and services needs to be more local and flood through local supply chains (CLES, NEF and New Start, 2016). There is also a growing recognition of how land and property holdings and pensions funds should benefit local economies more. Above all and across all sectors we have a new movement of social innovation, which is seeking to build a better economy, with a growth in local currencies, local banks, community shares and community energy schemes. It is about unleashing activity around the foundational economy (Bentham *et al.*, 2013), co-operatives and post-capitalist entrepreneurship (Cohen, 2017).

At the heart of the local wealth building approach are four strategies for harnessing existing resources to enable local economies to grow and develop from within. A key part of this recalibration rests with anchor institutions as 'community wealth builders'. The term 'anchor institutions' is used to refer to organisations which have an important presence in a place, usually through a combination of being large-scale employers, the largest purchasers of goods and services in the locality, controlling large areas of land and having relatively fixed assets. Examples include local authorities, NHS trusts, universities, trade unions, large local businesses and housing associations.

Interest in the role of anchor institutions has arisen in recent years, through the work of CLES and across the world – notably the work of the Democracy Collaborative in the USA (Kelly and McKinley, 2015) – due to their potential to get involved in economic reordering, stimulate local economic growth and bring social improvements to the local community and environment. While the primary objective of anchors may not always be social justice, the scale of these institutions, their fixed assets and activities and their links to the local community mean that they are 'sticky capital' on which new local economic approaches and social improvements can be based.

There is a range of ways in which different public anchor institutions can leverage their assets and revenue to benefit the local area and local people. This includes:

Workforce of Anchors – often the biggest employers in a place, the approach anchors take to employment can have a defining effect on the employment prospects and incomes of local people. Recruitment from lower income areas, commitment to paying the Living Wage and building progression routes for workers are all examples of the actions anchors can take to stimulate the local economy and bring social improvements to local communities.

Anchor Purchasing – progressive procurement can develop a dense local supply chain of local enterprises, SMEs, employee-owned businesses, social enterprises, co-operatives and other forms of community ownership. This type of procurement is local enriching because these types of businesses are more likely to support local employment and have greater propensity to retain wealth and surplus locally. Of particular note, is the work by CLES in many locations across Europe and the UK – including work over ten years with Manchester City Council (Jackson, 2017) which has proven the significant benefit of a local authority anchor in bending what is locally purchased as regards goods and services and who provides them.

Critically, the process of purchasing goods and services (procurement) has historically been a challenge for municipalities and other institutions within our cities, especially when linking to wider local economic, social and environmental benefits. However, that perception and culture has changed. This is locally enriching because these types of enterprises are more likely to support local employment and have a greater propensity to retain wealth and surplus value locally.

Anchor Land, Property and Assets

Anchors are often major landholders and can support equitable land development (through establishment of Community Land Trusts) and development of under-utilised assets for community use. In terms of financial investments, directing pension funds to local investment priorities can bring transformative capital to locally rooted enterprises.

Ownership of the Economy

A desire for higher levels of social inclusion demand more self-generation of wealth, where social gains are wedded to the actual workings of the local economy. The long-term solution is therefore to redirect wealth and economic activity to employees and communities. This can be achieved through broader ownership models where more people have a stake in production and thus wealth is more readily harnessed for local good. Mutually owned businesses, SMES, municipally owned energy companies and local banks enable the wealth generated in a community to stay in that locality and play a vital role in counteracting the extraction of wealth.

This local wealth building work has proven outcomes, recent work in Preston, Lancashire has seen significant results and outcomes (CLES, 2018a) in local wealth capture, with work now being extended in numerous places across England, Wales and Europe (CLES, 2018b). Scotland has enduring issues, and these can be sourced back to question of wealth. In this, traditional taxation and forms of redistribution have a role to play. However, given the maturing of economic wealth extraction from nations and localities there is a need for much deeper policy intention, so that wealth is captured and more broadly held.

References

Bell, T. and D'Arcy, C. (2018), *The £1 Trillion Pie: How Wealth is Shared Across Scotland*, London: Resolution Foundation.

Bentham, J., *et al.* (2013), 'Manifesto for the foundational economy', Manchester: CRESC, available online at: http://hummedia.manchester.ac.uk/institutes/cresc/workingpapers/wp131.pdf, accessed 26 November 2018.

Brinded, L. and Colson, T. (2017), 'The 13th richest people in Scotland', *Business Insider*, 15 May 2017, http://uk.businessinsider.com/sunday-times-rich-list-2017-richest-people-in-scotland-2017-5/#13-lord-laidlaw-net-worth-795-million-scottish-born-laidlaw-who-now-lives-in-monaco-made-his-fortune-after-buying-a-us-small-publisher-in-1973-and-turning-it-into-the-institute-for-international-research-the-worlds-largest-conference-organiser-1, accessed 26 November 2018.

CLES (2018a), available online at: https://cles.org.uk/the-preston-model/, accessed 26 November 2018.

CLES (2018b), https://cles.org.uk/local-wealth-building/, accessed 26 November 2018.

CLES, NEF and New Start (2016), *Creating Good City Economies in the UK*, Friends Provident Foundation, available online at: https://cles.org.uk/publications/creating-good-city-economies-in-the-uk/ or dedicated website: https://goodlocaleconomies.cles.org.uk/, accessed 26 November 2018.

Cohen, B. (2017), *Post-Capitalist Entrepreneurship: Startups for the 99%*, Florida: CBC Press.

Fraser of Allander Institute (2016), *Economic Commentary*, Vol. 41 No. 1, University of Strathclyde.

Friends of the Earth (2018), *Divest Fracking: How UK Councils are Banking on Dirty Gas*, Friends of the Earth.

Jackson, M. (2017), 'Power of procurement 2: The policy and practice of Manchester City Council – 10 years on', CLES, available online at: https://cles.org.uk/wp-content/uploads/2017/02/The-Power-of-Procurement-II-the-policy-and-practice-of-Manchester-City-Council-10-years-on_web-version.pdf, accessed 26 November 2018.

Kelly, M. and McKinley S. (2015), *Cities Building Community Wealth*, available online at: https://democracycollaborative.org/content/cities-building-community-wealth-o, accessed 26 November 2018.

McInroy, N. (2018), 'Wealth for All: Building New Local Economies', *Local Economy*, Vol. 33 No. 6 pp. 678–687.

McInroy, N. (2017), 'We need a new social contract: A local one', in Leadbeater, C. *et al.*, *Flipping the Narrative: Essays on Transformation from the Sector's Boldest Voices*, New Philanthropy Capital, available online at: http://www.thinknpc.org/publications/flipping-the-narrative/, accessed 26 November 2018.

Whitfield, D. (2018), *Ownership and Offshoring of NPD and Hub Projects*, European Services Strategy Unit.

CHAPTER 4

Breaking with Business As Usual

Miriam Brett

Economics is the method; the object is to change the soul.

Margaret Thatcher

The Rise and Rise of the Free-Market

IT CAN BE difficult to pinpoint the precise moment that today's prevailing economic orthodoxy emerged. Not least because its guiding ideas are rooted in power structures that were shaped by and have survived waves of preceding concepts. However, the spread of the ideology we now know as neo-liberalism accelerated in the late 1970s, and Britain was right at the forefront of that process.

During this period, growth had begun to slow, and the demise of the Bretton Woods system initiated a radical reordering of the global financial landscape, while the collapse of the Soviet Union a decade later prompted widespread hostility to state-led economic models. The turmoil associated with these developments – coupled with a collapse of confidence in social democracy and centralised economic planning – paved the way for a new elite strategy.

Though the contemporary neo-liberal model is most closely associated with Western liberal democracies, its first testing ground was arguably Chile under the CIA-backed dictator General Augusto Pinochet. Alongside a series of gross human rights violations, Pinochet embarked on far-reaching economic reforms inspired by the free-market godfather Milton Friedman, and with a zealous group of Chilean economists known as the 'Chicago Boys'. Pinochet was characteristically ruthless in carrying out his reforms. He advocated deregulation, the privatisation of publicly-owned assets like pensions, and attacking workers' rights – policies that would go on to become painfully familiar responses to subsequent economic crises. Friedman hailed the economic reforms a success, describing them as a 'miracle'.

Chile became a laboratory of free-market reforms and, during the Thatcher-Reagan era, its example was adopted as a vehicle to propel the radical ideas forward. As with any theory, neo-liberalism can be elusive. It has been applied unevenly, developed and regressed in different places and times, and moulded all the while by its surroundings. But, at its core, it envisages an approach where markets are the primary means of organising, not only our economy, but also our society, expressed through its key pillars of deregulation and privatisation.

The role of the state, then, is primarily to nurture market forces, and in turn drastically and deliberately shrink the role of government, which is seen as a barrier to market growth at best, and an expression of communism at worst. The markets themselves are thought of as natural forces, and – unlike actual natural forces, which are regarded as fair game in the eyes of the markets – the so-called natural status of the markets means that they must be left entirely untouched. The infamous 'trickle-down' theory stipulates that a system benefiting the rich – characterised by tax cuts for corporations, high earners and asset owners – will eventually be of benefit to us all. In that sense, we just need to let 'nature' take its course.

In seeing the market as the primary means of organising society, the values of collectivism and universalism that were dominant during the post-war era have been corroded and replaced with market values like individualism and competition. Indeed, Thatcher herself famously said:

> They are casting their problems at society. And, you know, there's no such thing as society. There are individual men and women and there are families. And no government can do anything except through people, and people must look after themselves first (8 April 2013).

Attacking Society

The perceived hierarchy of human rights neatly illustrates the attack on society in the name of competitive individualism. Facilitated by a fear of collectivism associated with the Cold War, many market-based economies of the West stress the benefits of civil and political rights – which were seen to symbolize a lack of state interference – while social, economic and cultural rights, such as housing, are left to linger. There are obvious inconsistencies in this approach, not least that the court system, for instance, which is meant to guarantee our political and civil rights, requires significant state intervention in order to operate.

Nevertheless, in constructing a hierarchy of rights, supporters have been able to build a sleek and corrosive narrative that goes something like this: if individuals with political and civil rights work hard, they will earn enough to gain access to the luxuries of social, economic and cultural rights, like housing and education. Telling people that hard work alone creates wealth, that wealth equates to success and that ultimately human rights should be denied to people that are not wealthy might be wrong, but it suits the neo-liberal belief that the poor are responsible for their poverty. Stating that hard work alone creates wealth conveniently bypasses structural reasons for poverty and inequality, ignores evidence that some of the hardest jobs pay the least and overlooks the collective nature of wealth creation.

Author and activist George Monbiot summed up this conscious effort to shape culture when he wrote:

> so pervasive has neo-liberalism become that we seldom even recognise it as an ideology. We appear to accept the proposition that this utopian, millenarian faith describes a neutral force; a kind of biological law, like Darwin's theory of evolution. But the philosophy arose as a conscious attempt to reshape human life and shift the locus of power.

It was designed as an all-encompassing reimagining of culture and society, a model built to be so pervasive that it shields itself from criticism, deflecting blame to sections of society oppressed by the model itself. This logic has become more and more pronounced in the years following the 2008 global financial crisis.

The Financial Crisis

What We Failed to Do

The crisis should have been a wake-up call. Yet, in spite of significant protests and resistance from civil society, the collapse of the global economy was largely seized on as an opportunity to turbocharge financialization. Amid the panic, the right was more prepared than the left and floundering governments were told that 'there was no alternative' to spending cuts. Shock and awe programmes of austerity were implemented, aided by international financial institutions, some governments, ring-wing think tanks and corporate lobbyists. Again, the UK was at the forefront of this project.

One irony of the small state approach is that it often involves costly state interventions to rescue the economy – the financial sector, in particular. From September 2007 to December 2009, the Labour Government ploughed £137 billion of public money in loans and capital in a bid to stabilise the financial system. In 2010, the coalition Government embarked on a ruthless austerity programme to 'balance the books' on the backs of the poor by slashing expenditure to vital services while claiming that 'we're all in this together'. In a quick-fire sale, the coalition privatised public assets like the Post Office, removing our stake in maintaining an institution dating back hundreds of years. Since then, the Conservatives have quietly rolled back much of the little financial regulation introduced following the crisis, and requirements for trade union action have been tightened.

In so many ways, the shock doctrine policies shaping the UK's response to 2008 were a textbook example of what the 'Chicago Boys' had envisioned all those years ago in Chile.

Ten years on from the crisis and several years into an on-going austerity programme, many of the fiscal targets initially identified have been ditched and the economic recovery that was promised has not materialised. The UK is on track for the longest fall in living standards since records began, and the biggest increase in inequality since Thatcher. Last year, the Trussell Trust gave people in crisis a staggering 1,332,952 three-day emergency food supplies, up by over a million since austerity was first rolled out.

In an act of social violence, the welfare state has not just been slashed under austerity, but rather weaponised to target and harm the marginalised groups it was designed to protect. The Women's Budget Group stated that by 2020, households headed by women such as lone parents and single female pensioners will be about 20 per cent worse-off on average. Moreover, disabled people on social security have been hit with one million sanctions since austerity began. The situation is so dire that a UN inquiry in 2017 concluded that austerity policies amount to 'systematic violations' of the rights of people with disabilities.

Meanwhile, a decade on from the crisis, the UK financial sector is behaving as if nothing has happened. More than three-quarters of the EU's top-paid bankers and asset managers were UK-based, with 15 bankers and ten executives earning over €10 million. Staggeringly, research from the Sheffield Political Economy Research Institute (SPERI) found that a swollen City of London inflicted a cumulative £4.5 trillion hit on the British economy between 1995 and 2015. That is, two-and-a-half years' economic output. All the while, inequality between the richest 1 per cent and the rest of us continues to rise, as the Equality and Human Rights Commission predicts that without remedial action, the UK will become a 'two-speed society'.

Breaking With 'Business as Usual'

Scotland's place in all of this is complicated. On the one hand, our economic framework is, to a certain extent, predisposed by our place in the UK. In that sense, we reap the seeds sown in the Thatcher era, and our communities have undoubtedly been shaped by the market values that have dominated British politics for decades, hammered home with post-crash austerity. Yet the Scottish electorate were not won over by Thatcherism, and our voting record since has broadly reflected this. Moreover, devolution has changed the nature of our relationship with this model and, while some areas were accepted, there are clear examples of resistance.

Scotland's relationship with universalism hints at a lasting commitment to the post-War consensus. Premised on the notion that we as a collective society ensure that everyone can access basic services and rights, universalism is an enemy of the market society. In contrast to the neo-liberal hierarchy of rights – where the wealthy are afforded 'luxuries' as a reward for their perceived hard work – universalism protects and enhances the status of the poor by deconstructing inferiority tiers and relationships based on inequality.

When a person arrives at a pharmacy to collect a prescription, their class status is not enquired about, and the stigma attached to that enquiry and the differential treatment that follows is broken. Like the founding principles of the NHS, it is free at the point of use for all. Similarly, free tuition fees not only mean that class barriers are reduced by deconstructing a system where working-class students are shackled with tens of thousands of pounds of debt over a lifetime. Education is seen as something shared, not a commodity for individuals to purchase. The most recent example of universalism in practice has been the Scottish Government's baby box initiative, which was rolled out at a time when the UK Government was slashing universal child tax credits. Baby boxes provide each baby in Scotland – regardless of their family's income or wealth – with essential items for their new-born; an idea inspired by our Finnish neighbours.

Indeed, one of the most effective moves that Scotland could make is to not compare our journey with the UK as a benchmark of success. As with Finland's baby boxes, other countries are carving their own path and should act as our inspiration – many coastal communities globally thrive in balanced and diversified economies. The challenges faced by post-industrial cities are being faced by cities in similar predicaments abroad, and remote islands may be taking different approaches to sustainability that we could take inspiration from and vice versa.

This point is particularly true given that, even among our neighbours and allies, the UK is somewhat unusual. Alongside the dominance of finance in our economy, a 2002 Treasury encomium revealed that between 1980 and 1996, Britain accounted for an astounding 40 per cent of the total value of privatised assets in the OECD (Open Democracy, 2013). That is not to say that Britain is unique in its trajectory, but rather that it aggressively pushed the boat out. Take corporation tax. While the OECD average is 23.5 per cent (our neighbours in Germany and France sit at 30 and 33 per cent respectively) UK corporation tax sits at just 19 per cent, with potential further cuts lined up in the near future.

None of this happened in isolation. Our current dysfunctional economic model is the product of a concerted 40-year campaign by free-market ideologues, those that directly benefit from the steady accumulation of wealth and those paid to lobby on behalf of vested interests.

If Scotland is going to continue to shape its own path, it needs to be acutely aware of what it is up against. Fortunately, for all the money and power thrown at promoting free-market ideology, notions of collectivism and society have fought back. And that fact is a powerful reminder that the prevailing model does not represent the 'natural order of things', and that there is, in fact, an alternative. We just need to be ready to pursue it.

Section Two – A Social Justice Scotland for All?

CHAPTER 5

A Socially Just Scotland?

Kirstein Rummery

A Scottish Vision of Social Justice

SOCIAL JUSTICE IS an idea that has captured academic and political imagination. Building on the ideas of writers such as Sen and Nussbaum, it centres on the concept of the 'capabilities' that people need to be able to live meaningful lives, rather than focusing simply on income, poverty and inequality. The role of a responsible government under a social justice framework is to maximise the capabilities of citizens, and to address structural and individual issues that prevent them attaining the capabilities associated with citizenship. Whilst Sen refused to endorse a definitive list of capabilities, pointing out that functioning as a citizen is a highly contingent and context-specific (Sen, 1999), Nussbaum disagrees, and asserts that it is possible to agree on the central human capabilities of life, bodily health, bodily integrity, sense, emotions, reason, affiliation, self-respect and control over one's environment (Nussbaum, 2000). The state plays an important role in ensuring that citizens have the capabilities to access and protect these elements.

Social justice undoubtedly was an idea that underpinned the foundation of the Scottish Parliament. Donald Dewar proclaimed that:

> We are committed to promoting social justice and equality of opportunity for everyone in Scotland (Dewar, 1999).

His views were echoed in the case for independence made by Alex Salmond:

> an independent Scotland could be a beacon for progressive opinion... addressing policy challenges in ways which reflect the universal values of fairness (Salmond, 2012).

One of the first actions of the new Scottish Executive (later the Scottish Government) in 1999 was to publish a strategy paper outlining a vision of co-operative policy addressing social justice and poverty (Scottish Executive, 1999).

However, as evidenced by social policies, the Scottish Government and Parliament have at times struggled to articulate a coherent vision for social justice in Scotland. On the one hand, a commitment to universalism and supporting all Scots to be able to exercise the capabilities of self-determination (Sen, 1999) which are intrinsic to social justice has been apparent. There is a sense of social solidarity which underpins distinctively 'Scottish' social policies. A unifying Curriculum for Excellence, resistance to health policy reforms designed to increase competition and universal access to pre-school childcare have been some of the policies which reflect a desire to create a non-stigmatising, non-residual welfare state in which costs and benefits are shared. Not only does universalism in education and health reflect areas in which Scotland already had substantial policy levers with which to deviate from the rest of the UK prior to devolution; they also arguably disproportionately benefit middle-income citizens (and thus middle-class voters).

On the other hand, in 1999 Scotland had a reputation for being the 'sick man of Europe' in terms of health inequalities (McCartney et al., 2012) and income inequality was stark. There was clear pressure on the Scottish Parliament from day one to address this, and universal policies would likely make these inequalities wider. Targeted welfare in areas where there were significant inequalities has often been the preferred approach. This does undermine the claim to a 'fairer, more socially just' Scotland as the evidence suggests that means testing and targeting creates stigma, leading to a residual-ist, rather than a universal welfare state.

Social justice along gendered lines also featured in the political architecture of the Scottish Government. From the decision to abandon the Westminster electoral system of first past the post (which disadvantages women), the founding principles of equality of opportunity, the use of gender neutral language and the foundation of an Equal Opportunities (now the Equalities and Human Rights Committee), the machinery of governance was designed to allow policy to be developed which addressed women's access to social justice.

Social Justice Prior to the Independence Referendum

Despite most of the policy levers needed to address poverty and income inequality not being devolved, antipoverty policy has always been a significant driver in Scottish social policy. From 1999 until 2009 relative poverty fell from 30 per cent to 25 per cent, and child absolute poverty fell to 15 per cent over the same period (Scottish Government, 2018). The fall of unemployment over that period from 8 per cent to 4 per cent is probably largely responsible, as moving into work is the most reliable route out of poverty.

The first two terms of the Scottish Parliament saw Labour in charge and there was, therefore, not much policy deviation from the rest of the UK. The rise of the SNP from 2007 onwards saw some shifts in policy, although not significant at first probably due the lack of an overall majority in the Scottish Parliament. The 2008 banking crash also reduced funding, and therefore the policy levers available to address poverty in Scotland. A change in the focus of governance led to Single Outcome Agreements and the Scottish Government working in partnership with local authorities to achieve anti-poverty strategies. However, tensions between the Government and local authorities rose during a period of cutbacks in expenditure, not helped by a cap introduced to local taxation. This was a policy move that helped to cement the SNP's political popularity with centrist and middle-class voters, but which left local authorities struggling to meet statutory duties.

Issues such as free school meals – initially targeted at poorer children, but then extended to all Primary One to Three – and universal childcare – again initially targeted at low income families then extended – gradually moved policy from a targeted to a more universal approach. Other universal measures such as free prescriptions, free personal care and no tuition fees for home students at Scottish universities also extended universal provision. In terms of fairness, meaning equal access and solidarity, this was effective. But if fairness means income redistribution to tackle inequality then the Scottish Government has proved in policy terms to be less progressive. Free tuition has not resulted in more students from poorer backgrounds going to university, in contrast, educational inequalities in higher education in Scotland have grown in comparison to the rest of the UK (Riddell, 2009).

Moreover, the structural issues which underpinned women's relative lack of capabilities and inequality were not substantially addressed prior to 2014. An over-reliance on family care rather than investment in social care meant that 62 per cent of Scotland's unpaid carers in 2014 were women, with twice as many female as male carers relying on benefits. 95 per cent of lone parent households receiving income support were headed by women, and twice as many women as men relied on state benefits for their income. Horizontal and vertical occupational segregation meant that the pay gap for full-time working women was 13 per cent, rising to 34 per cent for those working part-time. 81 per cent of the austerity-mandated cuts to public spending following the 2008 banking crisis fell on women.

Claims to Social Justice in the Independence Referendum

The White Paper 'Scotland's Future' which set out a vision for an independent Scotland, which was essentially the SNP's vision that:

> With independence we can make Scotland the fairer and more successful country we know it can be... Independence will provide the opportunity to create a fairer, more equal society built around the needs of citizens... Social rights embedded in a constitution will put questions of social justice at the forefront of the work of Scotland's Parliament.

There was recognition that women were bearing the brunt of public sector budget cuts and of welfare reform:

> the Scottish Government's recent analysis concludes that women will also lose out because of how the universal credit system in particular is structured.

Women were key 'swing' votes in the 2014 referendum: whilst men are more likely to exhibit party and issue loyalty in voting behaviour, women are more likely to change party allegiance based on policies (Campbell and Childs, 2015). It became apparent that women may be a key 'undecided' group of voters and thus worth targeting in the vision of an independent Scotland.

The famous 'bairns not bombs' approach (the proposal to discard nuclear weapons and invest in childcare instead) was a tactic based on the uniting universalistic approach to fairness and social justice, recognising that 'independence... will... substantially bolster the financial case for a transformational change in childcare provision', creating 35,000 new jobs (primarily for women) and enabling more women to enter, or return to, the labour market. 27 per cent of the average income of Scottish working parents went on childcare, one of the highest in Europe and over twice the OECD average. The commitment was further framed as a social justice one: investment in childcare leads to better outcomes for children and working parents, creates jobs, creates wealth that is spent in the local economy, addresses child poverty and leads to improved educational attainment. However, the model of provision was predicated on the caring parent (usually the mother) working part-time or being able to supplement childcare costs out of wages – it did not provide fully wrap-around childcare. This meant that the proposal was most likely to benefit middle-class, middle income parents as poorer parents would either be unable to afford to work part-time or be unlikely to command enough in wages to make subsidising childcare affordable.

The White Paper also recognised that some welfare reforms were unpopular and considered to be unfair and against the principles of social justice. The rollout of Universal Credit, criticised for leaving families on benefits worse off and waiting too long for benefits to be paid, was to be halted. The Spare Room Subsidy, whereby low-income families were penalised for having a spare bedroom, was to be quashed. Benefits and tax credits for low income families were to be increased in line with inflation, changes to disability benefits were to be reviewed and the option to use a variable rate of taxation for higher earners was to be used. All of these were targeted benefits designed to ameliorate poverty, and to mitigate against the stigma of receiving welfare benefits.

Scotland at the time of the referendum was the location of significant social divisions. The income ratio between the top and bottom decile was 13.8 (as compared to 6.1 in Norway). Some progress had been made on health inequalities – the gap between mortality in the richest and poorest areas has fallen by 16 per cent since 2002, and the gap in infant low birth weight has narrowed by 31 per cent since its peak in 2004. However, in other areas, in such limiting long-term conditions, the gap has increased by 39 per cent since 2008, and in self-assessed health it has increased by 47 per cent over the same period.

Post-2014

New Powers, New Obligations

When independence was rejected in 2014, it was the task of the Smith Commission to reach a consensus on which further powers should be devolved to the Scottish Parliament. It took recommendations from over 14,000 organisations and individuals and worked with representation from the five main political parties in Scotland. The two pro-independence parties, the SNP and the Scottish Greens, were hopeful for the devolution of full taxation and welfare powers, to be able to control the economic and political levers for growth and the power to develop a fairer welfare system.

Most organisational submissions, particularly from the third sector working on social justice issues for specific groups, wanted further powers devolved. The Scottish Government had developed a much more co-operative and open style of governance since its inception. It left opportunities open to develop consensus around approaches to social justice that was problem focused rather than ideological (Cairney and Rummery, 2017).

The Smith Commission's proposal fell far short of full devolution, mainly in the face of opposition from the three main pro-Unionist parties. Instead, Scotland was granted the ability to vary income tax rates, control over disability and carers' benefits and the ability to vary the housing component of Universal

Credit. The majority of powers – pensions, child benefits, equalities and economic – remain reserved to Westminster.

Some policy deviation and experimentation has emerged from the post-2014 settlement. The Scottish Welfare Fund, begun in 2013, made nearly 300,000 payments totalling £164 million. Crucially, these are crisis grants not loans, and thus do not trap low income families in crisis in debt. The new social security system started by a wide-ranging consultation and the establishment of User Panels, as well as the establishment of a cross party ministerial committee which took evidence from experts. One of the first decisions was not to use the private sector to run welfare assessments. This was following research evidence that targets for reducing the costs of benefits had added significantly to the cost of running the system, and sanctions had taken claimants further away from being able to engage in paid work. It was also in response to concerns about the excess rate of deaths amongst the 'fit for work' group, implying that many were wrongly placed. Evidence suggests that the process of applying, and reapplying, for benefits is tremendously stressful and harms mental and physical health. The values of dignity, fairness and respect that are the foundations of the Social Security Scotland (and the decision to revert to the terminology of social security, rather than a neo-liberal welfare-to-work approach) sends a message of universalism, social rights and social justice.

It is clear that the post-2014 Scottish Parliament intends to continue with a mix of universal and targeted benefits to address social justice. However, its ability to take a radically different approach to social justice is constrained, partly by Westminster, but also by its own natural conservatism and path dependency. There was scope for considerable policy divergence prior to 2014 that was not enacted. Having control over social care and health funding did not lead to policy innovations to address the poverty responsible for much of the health inequalities facing Scotland; nor has it led to significant investment in preventative services. Scotland has an ageing population with higher rates of poor health than the rest of the UK. But no effort has been made to address local taxation or new ways of funding and providing social care (such as social care insurance) to address the crisis in social care.

The elephant in the room of Brexit is likely to inhibit policy innovation, for the simple reason of reduced policy capacity, forthcoming economic challenges and ongoing tensions between Holyrood and Westminster. The willingness to address social justice is undoubtedly there. But, the pragmatic political reality and resources to do so may be in short supply.

References

Campbell, R. and Childs, S. (2015), 'All Aboard the Pink Battle Bus? Women Voters, Women's Issues, Candidates and Party Leaders', *Parliamentary Affairs*, Vol. 68, Issue Supplement 1.

Dewar, D. (1999), A speech made at the opening of the new Scottish Parliament on 1 July 1999, available online at: www.ukpol.co.uk/donald-dewar-1999-speech-at-opening-of-the-scottish-parliament/, accessed 4 November 2018.

Nussbaum, M. (2000), *Women and Human Development: The Capabilities Approach*, Cambridge: Cambridge University Press.

McCartney G., Walsh D., Whyte B., *et al.* (2012). 'Has Scotland always been the 'sick man' of Europe? An observational study from 1855 to 2006', *European Journal of Public Health*, Vol. 22 pp. 756–60.

Riddell, S. (2009), 'Social justice, equality and inclusion in Scottish education', *Discourse: Studies in the Cultural Politics of Education*, Vol. 30 No.3 pp. 283–296.

Salmond, A. (2012), Hugo Young Lecture, available online at: www.theguardian.com/politics/2012/jan/25/alex-salmond-hugo-young-lecture, accessed 4 November 2018.

Scottish Executive (1999), 'Social Justice... a Scotland where EVERYONE matters: Milestone sources and definitions', available online at: www2.gov.scot/Publications/1999/11/SocialJustice, accessed 4 November 2018.

Scottish Government (2014), 'Scotland's Future', Edinburgh: Scottish Government.

Scottish Government (2018), 'Poverty in Scotland', available online at: https://news.gov.scot/news/poverty-in-scotland-2, accessed 4 November 2018.

Sen, A. (1999), *Development as Freedom*. New York: Knopf.

CHAPTER 6

Scottish Education Since Devolution

James McEnaney

SCOTTISH EDUCATION HAS always been independent from its equivalents in the rest of the UK. As far back as the 1707 Act of Union, and indeed even before that,

> its distinctiveness has been a mark of national identity to be defended against assimilation with England, and its supposed superiority has been a point of national pride. (Anderson, 2008)

Nevertheless, the restoration of a Scottish Parliament had a profound impact upon schooling in the nation, not least because those making the decisions, at the national level, about how children should be educated became far more accessible than had previously been the case. Pre-devolution, ministers and officials in the Scotland Office in London ultimately oversaw educational provision north of the border; as of 1999, when Holyrood assumed control of 'virtually everything' regarding education, power was brought significantly closer to the people of Scotland (Pickard, 2008).

Since then there have been nine Education Secretaries (although the title has varied) and it is worth noting that the position has only ever been held by either a Labour or SNP politician. In the years of the Labour-Lib Dem coalition Governments the education role, seen as one of the most important within an administration whose powers did not extend to areas such as foreign affairs, was always held by a Labour MSP due to the party's position as the senior partner.

Significant educational achievements in the early years of the Parliament included the abolition of 'Section 28' – a damaging and discriminatory legal bar on 'promoting' homosexuality in schools – in the year 2000, although the process of fully destroying the legacy it left is ongoing, having been spearheaded by the Time for Inclusive Education Campaign. In the same year, a spectacular failure to properly manage thousands of school students' qualifications became, understandably, a potent political issue, Scotland's new parliamentarians were able to pursue the matter

with an intensity and determination that would not have been possible in the Westminster Parliament.

Over time, 'investigations of educational issues as well as opportunities for legislation became hallmarks of Holyrood' while the relevant parliamentary committees

developed an expertise among MSPs that had never been possible for Scottish MPs in London (Pickard, 2008).

Further divergence between the Scottish and English school systems occurred when Scotland did not adopt the academies model introduced by the UK Labour Government in 2000. Schools would have been removed from local authority oversight and funded directly by central government. Instead, and in an attempt to 'develop the system within the Scottish tradition', a 'National Debate on Education' was instituted in 2003 (Pickard, 2008). Thousands took part in the consultation, with the responses shaping the next cycle in the development of Scottish education.

Curriculum for Excellence

In his foreword to a follow-up consultation on 'Assessment', 'Testing' and 'Reporting', then Education Secretary Peter Peacock said:

One of the most frequently raised issues in the National Debate in Education was assessment. The common view was that assessment for monitoring purposes often dominated the classroom at the expense of assessment for learning. Parents, pupils, teachers and head teachers all wanted that balance to be redressed: to put the focus back on assessment as part of learning and teaching to ensure that all children can reach their full potential, while maintaining the highest standards. Assessment of pupils' performance needs to be an enduring part of the system, but its focus in the classroom needs to be on supporting learning.

He also restated the commitment to

provide more time for learning by simplifying and reducing assessment, ending the current system of national tests for 5–14 year olds' (Scottish Executive, 2003).

In addition to the abolition of counter-productive standardised testing, these consultations ultimately led to the development of a new, three to 18 years approach to education known – some would argue unhelpfully – as the

Curriculum for Excellence (CFE). This would replace existing, but separate, structures and requirements for pre-school, primary and early secondary and senior phase pupils, offering instead a coherent and unified framework.

The idea was simple: to modernise Scotland's school curriculum and equip young people with 'the knowledge, skills and attributes needed for life in the 21st century' (Education Scotland, n.d.). This new curriculum would be 'less crowded and better connected and offer more choice and enjoyment' (Scottish Executive, 2004). It was supposed to be revolutionary and, at least at first, was built around a broad, cross-political and professional consensus that, today, seems almost unimaginable.

The problems with the development and implementation of CFE have been well documented but are nonetheless worth noting. The curriculum itself is overly, and needlessly, complicated, having eventually been constructed around an incoherent framework of 'Four Capacities' (the things we want young people to be), seven 'Principles of Curricular Design' (the ways in which we develop the overall structure of their learning) and more than a thousand 'Experiences and Outcomes' (the individual things that pupils would be able to do at different stages). Five 'Building the Curriculum' documents were also issued between 2006 and 2011, the latter of which was in five parts, with the whole series running to hundreds of pages.

Teachers also, with plenty of justification, complained about a lack of support from government agencies like Learning and Teaching Scotland (now known as Education Scotland following a controversial merger with the schools' inspectorate) and the Scottish Qualifications Authority. Local councils were also criticised – again, with plenty of justification – for insisting on obsessively bureaucratic tracking and monitoring systems (which perhaps is best exemplified in the demand to 'grade' students as 'Developing', 'Consolidating' or 'Secure' in relation to specific curricular levels, despite this act being counter to the very premise of the new curricular structure). Such approaches soaked up huge amounts of teachers' time and gave them little in return.

The end result of these – and other – failures was an audit-driven, tick-box culture which became increasingly focused on 'evidencing', rather than supporting, the work of teachers and pupils in Scotland's schools. The workload implications of this sort of approach were, unsurprisingly, entirely unmanageable, further undermining CFE and, ultimately, damaging the quality of Scottish education.

But, to properly understand the problems of the Curriculum for Excellence it is important to understand a larger factor: timing. The new curriculum made greater demands on educators than ever before. It emphasised teacher-led

development, moderation of everything from learning experiences to assessment materials and the goal of allowing schools to explore new approaches to
suit the communities they serve. At the same time, society was confronted with
the consequences of the worst financial crash since the Great Depression, which
were then exacerbated by the austerity agenda of the UK Government. This crisis, brought about as a result of political choices as opposed to economic necessity, inflicted massive social damage all across the country and, as ever, placed
the overwhelming majority of the burden on the poorest and most vulnerable.

As a result, additional barriers to education were constructed for many children and young people, while intolerable pressure was put on educators working within the schools' system. CFE was always enormously ambitious but, in
the face of such a profound socio-economic maelstrom, itself compounded by
a range of organisational failures, it became all but impossible for the original
vision behind the reforms to be realised.

2015 Onwards

The latest cycle in Scottish education arguably began on 18 August 2015 at the
Wester Hailes Education Centre. Under pressure as a result of data showing an
apparent decline in standards in Scotland's schools, First Minister Nicola Sturgeon sought to regain the initiative, delivering a speech in which she demanded
to be judged on her government's record of tackling, and eventually eliminating, the 'attainment gap' between pupils from affluent families and those from
deprived backgrounds. In attempting to tie educational improvements to electoral cycles, Sturgeon ensured that education would become more politicised
than ever before.

As part of the attempts to achieve her goal – regularly described since as
her Government's top priority – it was announced, amongst other things, that a
national system of standardised testing would return to Scotland's schools. Sturgeon confirmed that the data from these tests would be published and, although
the Government would not turn them into league tables, the First Minister
seemed unconcerned about the inevitably of others doing so (Sanderson, 2015).

Unsurprisingly, the policy became a lightning rod for criticism of Sturgeon
and her Government. Unions, parents' groups and academics immediately
expressed their opposition to the plans, with concerns around league tables and
'teaching to the tests' especially prominent. In November of the same year it
emerged that the Government had received no formal written advice as part of
the development of the policy, instead relying on four unsolicited emails and a
series of un-minuted meetings. The government was also forced to admit that

the formal consultation period on the framework itself did not begin until after the First Minister's announcement (Gray, 2015).

A few months later, having lost her parliamentary majority following the 2016 Holyrood election, Nicola Sturgeon replaced Angela Constance – who had struggled badly as Education Secretary – with John Swinney, her Deputy First Minister and most trusted ally. Swinney brought with him a reputation for unshakeable competence and his appointment was seen as a clear signal of intent. Despite this, SNP education policy has continued to be characterised by frantic mis-steps, controversy and mounting problems.

In August 2016, Swinney issued what he called 'definitive' guidance to tackle teachers' unmanageable workloads (Swinney, 2016). In reality it was little more than a paper – and PR – exercise. A few months later a new financial model, known as Pupil Equity Funding (PEF), was announced. This system would channel money directly to schools based on the number of pupils from deprived backgrounds but involved a simultaneous cut in funding to local councils. Concerns have been raised about the transparency of the model and schools' ability to make good use of the funding – in 2017–18, a 40 per cent underspend (amounting to nearly £50 million) was reported (Scottish Government, 2018).

In 2017, details of meetings with, and extensive lobbying by, Teach First – an expensive and highly controversial fast-track teacher training organisation from England – emerged, and it became clear that they had pushed the Government for policy changes that would allow them to expand into Scotland. A tender for a new route in the Scottish teaching profession was subsequently opened but Teach First ultimately withdrew from the bidding process, citing concerns over the timescales available and the funding models being proposed (McEnaney, 2017).

In an attempt to address the criticisms of CFE, a series of 'benchmarks' were published in the spring of 2017. These offered further information on what the 'Experiences and Outcomes' should actually look like in the classroom, but also tacitly accepted that the original documentation was not fit for purpose. Rather than simplifying curricular requirements however, many argue that these publications served only to further complicate them by burdening teachers, and therefore their pupils, with hundreds of pages of new material (Education Scotland, n.d.).

A much-heralded Education Bill – which had been promised in the 2016–17 Programme for Government as a means to secure changes to areas such as school governance – was also (embarrassingly) shelved in June 2018 when it became clear that the SNP would need Tory support to get it through parliament.

Throughout this tumultuous period, opposition to the imposition of standardised testing continued to grow, culminating, in September 2018, in a parliamentary defeat for the SNP minority Government. All other parties united to call for a halt to testing in Primary One, but John Swinney still refused to back down, stating only that he would consider the situation. Eventually, and after criticism that he had defied the will of the Scottish Parliament, he announced that the tests would continue while an independent review was carried out. The Parliament's Education and Skills Committee also began its own investigation.

These have been difficult years for Scottish schooling, with teachers, parents and, of course, pupils all affected; however, an opportunity for progress may now have presented itself, with the Government and councils finally coming to an eleventh-hour agreement with teachers for a new pay deal. As a result, the threat of the sort of nationwide teachers' strikes not seen in Scotland since the infamous industrial action of the 1980s has been averted. Having also committed to tackle other areas of concern for teachers, such as workload, career progression and Additional Support Needs provision, the SNP could attempt to build a new consensus around Scottish education, drawing support from across the professional and political spectrum. Whether or not they will do so is another matter.

It is impossible to predict the trajectory of Scottish education over the next twenty years, but two things are relatively clear. The first is that Scotland's 'attainment gap' will not be substantially closed by educational reforms that do nothing to address the socio-economic inequalities at the heart of the problem. The second is that, as things stand, being judged on their record on education is unlikely to help the SNP during the next election campaign.

References

Anderson, R. (2008), 'The History of Scottish Education, Pre-1980', in Bryce, T. and Humes, W. (eds.) (2008), *Scottish Education*, 3rd edition, Edinburgh: Edinburgh University Press.

Education Scotland (n.d.), *What is Curriculum for Excellence?*, available online at: https://education.gov.scot/scottish-education-system/policy-for-scottish-education/policy-drivers/cfe-(building-from-the-statement-appendix-incl-btc1-5)/What%20is%20Curriculum%20for%20Excellence?, accessed 27 November 2018.

Education Scotland (n.d.), *Curriculum for Excellence Benchmarks*, available online at: https://education.gov.scot/improvement/learning-resources/curriculum%20for%20excellence%20benchmarks, accessed 27 November 2018.

Gray, M. (2015), 'The four emails that led to @ScotGov's controversial standardised testing plan', *CommonSpace*, available online at: https://www.
commonspace.scot/articles/2925/exclusive-four-emails-led-scotgovs-con-
troversial-standardised-testing-plan, accessed 23 November 2018.

McEnaney, J. (2017), 'FOI victory reveals the full extent of Teach First's
Scottish lobbying', *Jmcemedia.wordpress.com*, available online at: https://
jmcemedia.wordpress.com/2017/12/13/foi-victory-reveals-the-full-extent-
of-teach-firsts-scottish-lobbying-blog/, accessed 16 November 2018.

Pickard, W. (2008), 'The History of Scottish Education, 1980 to the Present
Day', in: Bryce, T. and Humes, W. (eds.) (2008), *Scottish Education*, 3rd
edition, Edinburgh: Edinburgh University Press.

Sanderson, D. (2015), 'Sturgeon admits education reforms pave the way for
unofficial primary league tables', *The Herald*, available online at: www.
heraldscotland.com/news/13611159.sturgeon-admits-education-re-
forms-pave-the-way-for-unofficial-primary-league-tables/, accessed
22 November 2018.

Scottish Executive (2003), 'Assessment, Testing and Reporting 3–14: Consultation on Partnership Commitments', Edinburgh: Scottish Executive.

Scottish Executive (2004), 'A Curriculum for Excellence', Edinburgh: Scottish
Executive.

Scottish Government (2018), 'Pupil Equity Funding: school level spend
2017 to 2018', available online at: www.gov.scot/publications/
pupil-equity-funding-school-level-spend-2017-to-2018/.

Swinney, J. (2016), *Letter from Deputy First Minister*, Edinburgh: Scottish
Government.

CHAPTER 7

The Early Years
Are We Doing Our Best for Children from Birth to Eight?

Sue Palmer

DURING THE EARLY years of the Scottish Parliament, people noticed that all wasn't well with children's lives. For a start, they were growing fatter by the year – especially those growing up in poverty – which didn't bode well for their long-term health (Stakatis *et al.*, 2004). The discovery that around 50 per cent of children from disadvantaged homes also started school with a significant language delay had worrying implications for their educational future (I CAN, 2006). Then came a UNICEF league table for 'childhood well-being in the developed world', in which the UK was bottom – it looked as if there might be problems to come with mental health too (UNICEF, 2007).

Research about the huge significance of early childhood experiences in determining children's long-term prospects was pouring out from the USA. So, it was clear that – unless action was taken – there would be a high price to pay a decade or so down the line in bills for the NHS, social services and criminal justice. It was also clear that young children's lives had changed considerably over recent years. A combination of traffic-clogged streets, the breakdown of local communities and changes in parental working patterns meant young children were increasingly confined indoors and often engaged in sedentary screen-gazing. What's more, by 1998, the combination of sexual equality and a neo-liberal work ethic meant most mothers returned to work within a couple of years of their babies being born.

The Best Place in the World to Grow Up

The new Scottish Executive sprang into action. There was no way Scotland's existing state-run nursery schools could cope with the mushrooming demand for pre-school care so the new nurseries springing up all over the country were mostly privately owned. In 2002, the Executive set up a Care Commission, which henceforth would regulate and inspect all pre-school providers. It also commissioned a review of the school curriculum, resulting eventually in the Curriculum for Excellence. To bring all those pre-school providers into the educational fold, this began with an 'Early Level' covering education from three to six (Scottish Government, 2004).

A couple of years later, another project was commissioned, 'Getting It Right for Every Child' (GIRFEC). Over the next decade its principles for 'improving outcomes and supporting the well-being of children and young people' were introduced across all services, including health, social work, childcare, education and youth justice (Scottish Government, 2014). GIRFEC provided an eight-word definition of well-being – 'safe, healthy, achieving, nurtured, active, respected, responsible and included' – and workers across children's services learned to rattle off the mnemonic SHANARRI.

The early years (especially childcare, for which there was a growing and increasingly frantic demand) was now firmly on the political agenda. In 2007, Scotland's First Minister for Children and Early Years was appointed and in 2009, in partnership with COSLA (Convention of Scottish Local Authorities), the Scottish Executive began work on an Early Years Framework, a programme of national objectives for making Scotland 'the best place in the world to grow up' (Scottish Government, 2008). It was followed up by an Early Years Taskforce, which then spawned an Early Years Collaborative for invited practitioners from health, social work, education, childcare, etcetera. They were asked to set up local projects with a view to achieving transformational change.

Sadly, Scotland's early years sector has not been transformed. For the mainly female workforce (often under-qualified and poorly paid, always under-valued) there is still a daily struggle to provide appropriate care for young children in a cultural climate that grows less child-friendly with every passing year. It has not helped that they have been constantly bombarded with documents and bureaucratic demands from national and local bodies, nor that (with a planned expansion of funded childcare for 2020) there are problems with the 'mixed economy' model of provision (Scottish Government, 2016).

Scottish Culture and 'Early Childhood'

Scotland's Early Years Framework was based on the United Nations' definition of early childhood as

> the period from birth to eight years old... a time of remarkable growth, with brain development at its peak (UNESCO, 2010).

And perhaps the main reason that 'transformational change' hasn't yet happened is our nations deeply ingrained cultural assumptions about this age group; assumptions that amaze and horrify our northern European neighbours ('mad', 'crazy' and 'cruel' are some of the verdicts I have heard).

During the 20th century, Scots assumed most children would be cared for at home until they were four or five, when they'd go off to school. Scotland is unusual in this respect – 88 per cent of nations worldwide don't send children to school till they're six or seven. Only the UK and a handful of other – all bar one ex-British empire member – countries insist on such an early start (Palmer, 2016).

Once mothers expected (and were expected) to return to work as soon as possible, families were shocked at the cost of pre-school childcare and demanded state assistance. It was naturally assumed that the care traditionally provided by women should be free. It was also widely assumed that – as long as babies are healthy, and toddlers learn to walk and talk on schedule – childcare is just a matter of keeping the weans safe and supervised until they can start school.

Scots have great faith in the power of education. The Curriculum for Excellence claims that schooling will transform children into 'successful learners, confident individuals, responsible citizens and effective contributors' (Scottish Government, 2004). Our nation has – like much of the English-speaking world – failed to recognise the significance of traditional women's work in supporting children's early development and its huge contribution to successive generations' life-long well-being and success.

Not surprisingly, the public services inherited by Scotland's devolved parliament have developed to mirror these assumptions, and our approach to early childhood today is neatly divided between health, childcare and education, as follows.

For the first few years, children are catered for mostly through the NHS – midwives, health visitors, GPs and any other necessary specialist services. The emphasis is on keeping them alive and healthy.

From the age of three, the demand for pre-school childcare means successive governments have struggled to provide increasing numbers of state-funded hours within a mixed childcare economy. The job during this stage is generally seen as keeping children safe, healthy, achieving, nurtured etc, while mum and dad are at work.

Once children reach school age, the spotlight swivels to the three 'Rs'. Although the Curriculum for Excellence takes a light-touch approach to literacy and numeracy in the Early Level (three to six years) and talks about 'learning through play', the Scottish public, its politicians and much of the educational

establishment generally believe in cracking on with reading, writing and reckoning as soon as possible.

Political responsibility for the three stages of early childhood is also split
between health, childcare and education and is mostly, of course, concerned
with systems and funding. This tri-partite systemised approach is then reflected
back to the public by the media. At the time of writing, the main news items
relate to: Will the Baby Box burst into flames? Can the Government realise its
promise of 1,140 hours of funded childcare by 2020? Are tests of literacy and
numeracy vital in Primary One (as suggested by the Government) or potentially
damaging – as now argued by all the opposition parties?

What Children Need for Healthy Development

Scotland's cultural assumptions, the systems they have spawned and the media
coverage they attract do not sit comfortably alongside the biological realities of
child development. If Scotland really wants to be 'the best place in the world to
grow up', it'll take more than up-to-date medical services, SHANARRI-informed
childcare facilities and good, old-fashioned Scottish schooling. Once fundamental material needs are met, what children need most during early childhood
(pre-birth to eight years) is what lucky children have had through the millennia:
supportive, loving relationships with caring adults and plenty of opportunities
for self-directed, active, social play with their chums, as often as possible outdoors. Or, to put it briefly, love and play.

Human beings are, by our very nature, 'successful learners, confident individuals and effective contributors'. We are primed by evolution to develop a
vast range of skills and capacities during early childhood, including language
and communication skills, social know-how, problem-solving skills, resilience
and the ability to regulate our emotions and behaviour. So, we do not really
need a formal curriculum to become 'responsible citizens' either. But, now that
children's life-chances also depend on success in the education system, it's even
more important that they get plenty of love and play during their early years.

Close, loving relationships with adult carers help children develop the inner
sense of self-worth on which long-term human well-being depends (Oates,
2007). In the first two to three years, plenty of positive, playful interactions
with those adults lay the foundation of all social and communication skills. So
the best childcare during this early period is one-on-one, consistent, loving care
which – even with the best will in the world – isn't easy to provide in an institutional setting with a limited budget and, very often, under-qualified staff who
are so pre-occupied by myths surrounding health and safety that they don't even
dare cuddle the children.

As for play, neuroscience now confirms what early years specialists have long maintained: it's vital for children's physical, emotional, social and cognitive development (Pellegrini, 2009). In Western nations with a later school start and well-established kindergarten systems, opportunities for self-directed, active, social play (as often as possible outdoors where children can move freely and in natural surroundings which are good for their mental health) are considered an essential precursor of formal schooling.

But it is almost impossible for the under-eights to enjoy much of this sort of 'real play' in 21st century Scotland. Many nurseries have little in the way of outdoor facilities, especially for the youngest children. And even if a current government initiative to encourage more outdoor play in nurseries is a hundred per cent successful, it only extends till the year children turn five. Then they're packed off to school.

Scotland's early school start was less problematic in the past, when children could play out with their chums after school, at weekends and in the holidays. But most now suffer from extreme play-deprivation. Since 2013 we have a Play Strategy (Scottish Government, 2013) – a splendid document full of the noblest intentions – yet our children are still ranked among the least active in the world (BBC Scotland, 2016).

Mental Health, the Attainment Gap

What We Must Do to Stop Them Getting Worse

Scotland is currently in the grip of a child and adolescent mental health crisis, with frightening implications not only for the children concerned but for the nation as a whole. Yet, despite a great deal of lip-service to the fast-growing ACES movement (campaigning for action to prevent, or at least mitigate, Adverse Childhood Experiences), no politician has yet seen the need for root and branch reform of state provision for early years.

Scotland urgently needs coherent, well-funded policy-making (not just policy-writing) for this age range. We need a Minister for Early Years who will join up the dots between health, childcare and education throughout the age-range. We need a well-qualified, well-paid workforce, composed of people who love children and understand the significance of child development and play. And we need to learn from countries that have weathered the 21st century cultural storm better than Scotland. This means looking north, to the Nordic countries, for ideas about early childhood care and education.

Unaccountably, the SNP Government currently looks south to England in terms of much early years' policy. Take, for example, their response to the widening educational attainment gap between rich and poor. They introduced Scottish National Standardised Assessments in literacy and numeracy, starting in Primary One, when children are five (Upstart Scotland, 2018). All the international evidence points against such a policy which – as England has already demonstrated – narrows the curriculum, undermines relationship-based practice, marginalises self-directed play and puts unnecessary pressure on young children, not just in school but often at nursery too (British Educational Research Association, 2018). Given that children raised in poverty are likely to suffer more ACES than their wealthier counterparts, these national tests (if they remain) will increase the attainment gap in the long run rather than narrowing it.

There are three underpinning strands to Scotland's Curriculum for Excellence: 'Literacy', 'Numeracy' and 'Health & Wellbeing'. I recently came across a Primary One class that summed up Scotland's attitude to early childhood care and education. The teacher gave plenty of attention to 'Literacy' and 'Numeracy' but her nod to 'Health & Wellbeing' was 'We all sing the SHANARRI song!' The Scottish Government has been trilling a SHANARRI song for a decade. But, until it gets to grips with the 21st century realities of providing love and play for the under-eights, the long-term prospects for Scotland's children – and Scotland – are bleak.

References

BBC Scotland (2016), 'Scottish children "among least active"', 16 November 2016, available online at: www.bbc.co.uk/news/uk-scotland-37989247

British Educational Research Association (2018), *A Baseline Without Basis*, available online at: https://www.bera.ac.uk/researchers-resources/publications/a-baseline-without-basis

I CAN (2006), *The Cost to the Nation of Children's Poor Communication*, London: I CAN.

Oates, J. (ed.) (2007), 'Attachment Relationships: Quality of Care for Young Children' in *Early Childhood in Focus, 1*, Milton Keynes: The Open University.

Palmer, S. (2016), *Upstart: The Case for Raising the School Starting Age and Providing What the Under-Sevens Really Need*, Edinburgh: Floris Books.

Pellegrini, A.D. (2009), *The Role of Play in Human Development*, New York: Oxford University Press.

Scottish Government (2016), 'Discussion Paper – Early Learning and Childcare 1140. Hours Expansion', available online at: https://consult.gov.scot/digital-communications/childcare-expansion/

Scottish Government (2014), 'Getting It Right for Every Child', Edinburgh: Scottish Government

Scottish Government (2013), 'Play Strategy for Scotland: Our Vision', Edinburgh: Scottish Government

Scottish Government (2004), 'The Curriculum for Excellence: The Curriculum Review Group', Edinburgh: Scottish Government

Scottish Government (2011), 'The Early Years Framework', Edinburgh: Scottish Government

Stamatakis E., Primatesta P., Chinn S., *et al.* (2004), *Overweight and Obesity Trends from 1974 to 2003 in English Children: What is the Role of Socio-Economic Factors? British Medical Journal Archives of Disease in Childhood*, Vol. 90 No. 10.

UNESCO (2010), 'Early Childhood Care and Education', available online at: https://en.unesco.org/themes/early-childhood-care-and-education

UNICEF (2007), 'An Overview of Child Well-Being in Rich Countries: A Comprehensive Assessment of the Lives and Well-Being of Children and Adolescents in the Economically Advanced Nations', Florence: UNICEF Innocenti Research Centre.

Upstart Scotland (2018) *What Are the P1 Tests?*, available online at: https://www.upstart.scot/events/what-are-the-p1-tests/

CHAPTER 8

Higher Education and the Scottish Parliament New Players in an Old Landscape

Lucy Hunter Blackburn

Introduction

HOW SHOULD WE assess the effect of having a Scottish Parliament on the development of higher education in Scotland over the first two decades of this century? It cannot be simply by asking what has changed, because our universities would have done that, regardless of the wider political structure. That much is clear from observing the global picture: higher education worldwide looks different from the way it did twenty years ago. Should we look at all the ways Scottish higher education has developed differently from the rest of the UK? That supposes that administrative devolution alone would not have allowed an already distinctive system some further freedoms. What about limiting the impact of the Parliament to those things where there was a clear difference of political outlook north and south of the border? That would make most sense, but then the story risks being mainly, though not entirely, one about the impact of the SNP's decade in government, and that has been done elsewhere recently (Hunter Blackburn, 2017). To avoid repetition, this chapter does not attempt to provide a comprehensive account of where policy has diverged since 1999. It is instead a deliberately selective reflection on how the higher education sector has developed over the last twenty years, and where the establishment of the Parliament, and thus political devolution, fits in.

Higher Education in Scotland in 1999

When the Scottish Parliament opened, the Scottish higher education system was still adjusting to a number of major changes, principally the establishment of a separate Scottish Higher Education Funding Council and the creation of new universities out of the old central institutions, both of which took effect in 1992. As part of this general reconstruction, small specialist institutions for art and teacher training were being absorbed into existing larger bodies. Thus, as just two examples, Duncan of Jordanstone College of Art & Design was merged into Dundee University in 1994 and Moray House Institute of Education into the University of Edinburgh in 1998.

A significant new UK-wide institution had recently appeared in the form of the Quality Assurance Agency, established in 1997. Other longer standing bodies continued to play an important role, the Research Councils for research funding, UCAS for admissions, JISC for information technology.

As the Scottish sub-committee of the UK-wide Dearing Review noted, domestic student numbers had risen over the previous decade: between 1987–88 and 1995–96 the total 'age participation index' (API), which measured the proportion of young people entering some form of higher education, had more than doubled from 20.5 per cent to 44.2 per cent, and participation rates were higher than in other parts of the UK (Dearing, 1997). Some progress had been made since the previous decade in addressing the social class imbalance in university intakes. A substantial number, around 30 per cent, of undergraduates were undertaking shorter HE courses, mainly higher nationals, in local colleges.

Student funding and fee policy operated UK-wide, with only minor administrative differences. In 1998, a new system was adopted of means-tested fees, under which roughly one-third paid £1,000 upfront, one-third paid a proportion of that, and one-third paid nothing. At the same time, student grants had been abolished, and replaced by a new form of student loan, whose repayment was tied more closely to earnings. Both these moves were controversial across the UK, but it was fee policy which came quickly to be the dominant political issue, as the first Holyrood elections approached in 1999 (Hunter Blackburn 2016).

Trends From 1999

Picking up an inherited agenda, the new Scottish Government continued to oversee the merging of small institutions into larger ones. By 2018 only one free-standing college of art remained (in Glasgow) and no separate teacher-training colleges. Bell College was merged with the University of Paisley to create the University of the West of Scotland in 2007. New types of institution were developed. The University of the Highlands and Islands was a novel structure seeking to build on existing institutions to better serve a dispersed rural population, which gained full university status in 2011. In 2012, Scotland's Rural University College was formed by a merger of existing colleges and research institutes, creating another higher education institute which, like UHI and UWS, included a substantial amount of sub-degree teaching, spread across widely dispersed sites. All these developments might well still have happened, but for UHI in particular the advent of political devolution both gave the new Edinburgh government more freedom in how it took the project forward and increased its symbolic value as a new start.

The continuing rise in student numbers, at a similar rate to the rest of the UK (Bolton, 2018), built on existing trends, as did colleges' continuing substantial role in providing sub-degree courses. Widening participation was a political pre-occupation from 1999, but this was not distinctive to Scotland. Indeed, Scotland's performance relative to the rest of the UK was initially unremarkable. A different approach to fees may have fostered a certain amount of complacency. It was only with a change of First Minister and the establishment of a Commission on Widening Access (Scottish Government, 2015), and the First Minister's personal backing of new targets, that activity became more intense.

The electoral system for the Parliament meant that until 2011, and since 2016, governments were in coalition or minority, and so legislation has usually required the consent of at least two parties. In practice, unsurprisingly, primary legislation has been used relatively little to shape higher education policy. The earliest example, in the Parliament's very first years, took forward the outcome of coalition negotiations between the Labour Party and the Liberal Democrats, and the associated Cubie Inquiry (Cubie, 1999), creating a post-graduation payment ('the graduate endowment') in place of the previous brief regime of means-tested fees. The new SNP administration's act abolishing the endowment in 2007 required the support of the Liberal Democrats.

A 2005 act merging the Scottish Further and Higher Education Councils was largely technical and not contentious between the parties: as a piece of house-keeping, it might have happened without devolution. Although a parliamentary committee played an important part in its genesis, it would have been an attractive de-cluttering option to any government at some point.

Legislation reforming university governance took forward recommendations from a review (Scottish Government, 2012) and was more controversial. It drew on a cross-party alliance between the SNP and Labour, both regarding the universities as institutions in need of modernisation and greater accountability, with the changes strongly lobbied for by student and staff unions. The effects of these last reforms will only slowly become clear. Would they have happened without the Parliament? That seems unlikely: the legislation here was tied up with the continued government funding of fees, and the sense of entitlement to demand greater accountability associated with that, felt across political parties.

Alongside those clear cases where a distinctive approach to policy and legislation can be attributed to political devolution, the arrival of the Parliament has brought scope for greater scrutiny of universities and of government policy. It is less clear that this has had much impact on the development of the sector, although it is certainly the case that universities collectively and individually have put energy into courting parliamentarians. Pictures from receptions and show-case events in the Parliament's Garden Lobby are a regular feature in the timeline of anyone who follows Scottish higher education bodies on social media. The Parliament itself has struggled to impose much on government in this area. Early in its life, a parliamentary committee held an inquiry which prompted the Government to produce a life-long learning strategy (Scottish Executive, 2003). However, the conceptualisation of higher education as one part of an integrated life-long learning system did not endure. The inquiry's clearest legacy is the merger of the funding councils. There has not been a comparably influential move by a parliamentary committee in this area since. Nor, has the Government found the need to account to parliament much of a constraint on its policy-making.

Where the System is Heading?

Student funding is the most famously distinctive feature of Scottish policy-making, a distinction dating back to parliament's first years. It is unimaginable this divergence would have happened without political devolution. The different debate in England about student funding, the introduction of more private provision and regulation, all entangled, feels increasingly distant for those in Scotland. Scotland is often characterised as a system less driven by the market, this is open to question (Riddell 2016). It is certainly true, however, that the competitive environment in which Scottish universities operate is different from that in England, as far as it relates to local undergraduate recruitment. That seems unlikely to change soon.

Looking less at specific policies, the general relationship between universities and government deserves attention. This was always likely to be different in Scotland. A smaller sector, more able to caucus but also arguably less able to find room for dissenting voices, will have had a different relationship with any government than a much larger one. Once a separate funding council was established, moving the focus of discussion about the distribution of a large proportion of university funding north of the border, the scope for a distinctive university-government relationship in Scotland increased.

Political devolution has brought a further element to that dynamic. Universities have gained a new importance, to a new Scotland-based political class.

Often internationally visible, large enterprises in their own right, and more generally symbolic of long-time Scottish success, they are not like anything else the Scottish Government funds. The argument about tuition fees propelled universities into the centre of politics, but the utility of the universities to build the story of a new polity has kept them there. The universities were relatively quick to understand the opportunity. By the time of the White Paper in 2014, universities' central place in a distinctive new Scottish political narrative was well established.

Though the relationship has become more intense it is not necessarily easy. There has not been a repeat of the public war between ministers and universities over funding which occurred early in the devolved period. However, arguments over the legislation on governance exposed the vulnerabilities institutions feel in a system where government expects its control of funding to give it certain rights. By demonstrating the universities' ability still to mobilise a useful amount of support in the press and parliament, certain provisions were softened. Every so often, small signs of discord surface, for example over the cap on places, but almost always in a relatively low-key way.

The overall impact of this close, mutually dependent but sometimes edgy relationship has been that, for good or ill, Scotland has been outside many of the big debates in higher education taking place elsewhere in the UK. For twenty years there has not been a serious discussion about how big the system should be or the opportunity costs of continuing to invest so much cash in fee subsidies rather than anything else. For a long time, the rhetorical commitment to widening participation lacked any machinery to enforce it, and even now the gains made owe more to the fear of falling foul of a high-level political commitment than a systemic change to funding, for example.

Conclusion

Some of the changes observable in higher education in Scotland since 1999 would surely have occurred with or without the arrival of Holyrood: more students, institutional re-structuring, the widening of participation. Some however could only have happened with political devolution, most clearly the deviation from Westminster's fee and funding policies, bringing in turn a different approach to regulation and a different debate about the relationship between government and institutions. Beyond the specific technical differences, however, the Parliament has brought the physical presence of politicians making their careers on a clearly Scottish stage. For them the universities offer a particular sort of opportunity, and the same is true in reverse. We are still learning what the mutual dependence of a new political class and an older institutional power base means for higher education in Scotland.

References

Bolton, P. (2018), 'Higher Education Student Numbers Briefing Paper 7587', London: House of Commons Library.

Cubie, A. (1999), 'Report of The Independent *Committee* of Inquiry into Student Finance', Edinburgh: HMSO.

Dearing, R. (1997), 'National Committee of Inquiry into *Higher Education'*, *London: HMSO*.

Hunter Blackburn, L. (2017), 'Higher Education: The Story So Far', in Hassan, G. and Barrow, S. (eds.), *A Nation Changed? The SNP and Scotland Ten Years On, Edinburgh: Luath Press.*

Hunter Blackburn, L. (2016), 'Student Funding in the UK: Post-Devolution Scotland in a UK Context', in Riddell, S., Weedon E. and Minty, S. (eds.), *Higher Education in Scotland and the UK: Diverging* or *Converging Systems?*, Edinburgh: Edinburgh University Press.

Riddell, S. (2016), 'Scottish Higher Education and Devolution', in Riddell, S., Weedon E. and Minty, S. (eds.), *Higher Education in Scotland and the UK: Diverging* or *Converging Systems?*, Edinburgh: Edinburgh University Press.

Scottish Executive (2003), 'Life Through Learning, Learning Through Life', Edinburgh: HMSO.

Scottish Government (2015), 'A Blueprint for Fairness', Edinburgh: Scottish Government.

Scottish Government (2012), 'Report of the Review of Higher Education Governance in Scotland', Edinburgh: Scottish Government.

CHAPTER 9

Public Health Progress?

Gerry McCartney

Introduction

PUBLIC HEALTH IS a relative concept. Compared to the 1850s, and using life expectancy as a measure, the increase from around 47 years then, to around 79 years now, represents a remarkable improvement. Indeed, many of the previously endemic conditions such as cholera, typhoid and tuberculosis have been successfully reduced to levels that would have been unimaginable to our forbearers. All of this progress required the building of social housing, water and sewerage systems, the creation of the NHS and welfare state, the introduction of health and safety legislation, clean air acts and more. The health of a population is largely determined by the conditions of society: the economy, workplaces, housing, social security systems, culture and the environments in which we live.

Despite all of this progress, when the Scottish Parliament was reconvened in 1999, public health was a policy area that was rightly still the subject of substantial attention. Compared to other Western and Central European nations, Scottish life expectancy was (and remains) lower, and has improved more slowly (McCartney *et al.*, 2012). Since the early 1980s, mortality rates for young adult men and women hardly improved at all, largely due to increases in suicide, alcohol and drug related deaths. Furthermore, inequalities in health, defined as the systematic differences seen across the population ranked by socio-economic position, are wider that much of Europe and are, on many measures, increasing (Eikemo and Mackenbach, 2012; Scottish Government, 2017).

Excess Mortality

In the early days of the Parliament, work by the Scottish Council Foundation and the Public Health Institute for Scotland (PHIS) identified that the higher mortality rates in Scotland compared to the rest of Britain were not only due to greater poverty and deprivation. Some 5,000 additional deaths a year were initially 'unexplained' as 'excess mortality' and (unhelpfully) as the 'Scottish/ Glasgow Effect'. This led to a lot of silly reporting of the problem, perhaps best illustrated by an article in *The Economist* which suggested that it was 'as if a toxic vapour was arising from the Clyde'.

Subsequent research has since clarified that this excess mortality is best explained by a toxic combination of policies over the second half of the 20th century. The deliberate enticement of industry out of Glasgow (in particular), and the movement and break-up of whole communities through selective migration into new towns and peripheral housing schemes, left our populations much more vulnerable than in comparable cities elsewhere. When the shift to 'neo-liberal' policies was introduced in the 1980s this led to negative health trends across the UK, but more pronounced in Scotland because of these vulnerabilities (Walsh *et al.*, 2017). All of this, in combination with the well-recognised impact of socio-economic inequalities and poverty, was working through intermediate mechanisms including food, alcohol, drugs and tobacco. It has left Scotland with its comparably poor health statistics and wide health inequalities (Beeston *et al.*, 2013).

Public Health Policy Innovation

Of course, any description of a population's health should take a broad view to include mental health and well-being, as well as the ability of people to function within society. Scotland has led the world on the better measurement of population well-being, but the goal of improving and narrowing the inequalities in wellbeing remains challenging (Scottish Government, 2017).

The Scottish Parliament has proven itself to be a leader in many aspects of public health. It was one of the first countries to introduce a ban on smoking in enclosed public spaces, something which has been extensively evidenced to show substantial positive impacts on outcomes as diverse as heart attacks and asthma (Pell, 2008; Mackay, 2010). The recent introduction of a minimum unit price (MUP) for alcohol is a global first and, to the credit of the Parliament, has been introduced with the caveat that it is evaluated thoroughly. The approach of the Scottish Government to use a National Performance Framework (NPF) to identify the outcomes on which policy is intended to impact, and to link together the policies across areas which should make mutual contributions, is also a very welcome and innovative approach for government.

This has legitimised and supported the public health workforce to engage with policy-makers across government in recognition that the health of populations is more a function of the society in which we live, than just the health services that we have access to.

Public Health Challenges

Despite these positive developments, many population health trends are much less positive. These include mental health, obesity, drug related deaths and, more recently, overall mortality. Life expectancy in Scotland, in common with the rest of the UK, the USA and some other parts of continental Europe (Ho, 2018), started to decrease around 2012 for the first time since 1945 (Figure 1). Various suggested causes have been proposed, including austerity and the associated cuts to local government spending; recurrent waves of influenza; reduced value and increased conditionality in the social security system; and the rise in obesity.

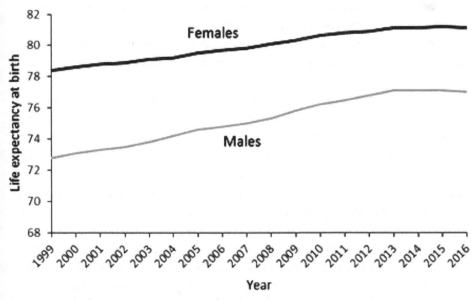

Figure 1 – Life Expectancy in Scotland, 2000–02 to 2015–17
(note shortened y-axis)
Source: National Records of Scotland.

Health Inequalities

Inequalities in health, the systematic differences in health outcomes across the population ranked by socio-economic position, are very large in Scotland.

Compared to rest of Europe, inequalities in mortality for women are the worst of all countries, and for men they are only better than countries in Eastern Europe. The premature mortality rate amongst those living in the most deprived 10 per cent of areas in Scotland is 825 per 100,000 per year, almost four times higher than the rate for those living in the least deprived 10 per cent of areas (Figure 2). The inequality does not only impact on the poorest communities, as there is a gradient across the entire population. Inequalities in health closely track trends in the fundamental causes of income, wealth and power inequality. As such, the inequalities that were high in the 1920s and 1930s, fell rapidly after the Second World War, during the period of welfare state building, to a low during the 1970s, before increasing rapidly during the 1980s and 1990s to the stark inequalities we see today (Beeston, 2013).

The most effective ways of reducing health inequalities is to reduce the inequalities in income, power and wealth in society. In general, policies that use regulation, taxation and legislation to make healthier products and activities easier or more affordable and unhealthier products and activities more difficult or expensive, are effective at reducing health inequalities. Good examples of such policies include legislation and pricing controls for alcohol and tobacco and subsidies for healthier foods and leisure activities (McCartney, 2013, Beeston, 2013).

Within Scotland, and in addition to the introduction of the ban on smoking in public places and the introduction of minimum unit pricing for alcohol, other policies have made a positive contribution. For example, the limited available powers to slightly reduce income inequality through the Scottish Income Tax powers. The Community Empowerment Act has also recognised the role that inequalities in power play in society and make a contribution to addressing some aspects of it. Perhaps the most important initiative to convene a ministerial group on health inequalities which recognized the importance of all policy domains in causing health inequalities and in reducing them. However, most policy which determines income, wealth and power distribution, such as most income tax and social security policy, is reserved to Westminster. This has created a tension where the Scottish Parliament is responsible for public health outcomes but many of the relevant powers are reserved. Indeed, the health consequences of changes to the social security system are now well recognised (Taulbut, 2018).

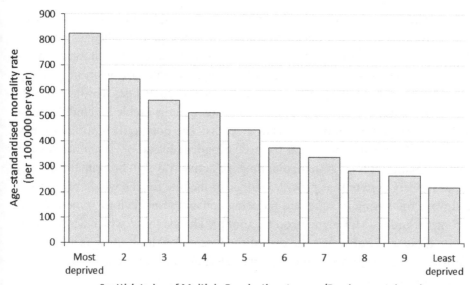

Figure 2 – Age-Standardised Mortality Rate (<75 years, Scotland 2016)
Source: Scottish Government.

Health Services

The NHS, and more broadly the health and social care system in Scotland, is the single largest spending area for the Scottish Parliament. Parliamentary scrutiny and interest in the NHS are very high as the system evolves to cope with rising demands and technological innovation. The Christie Commission recommendations and the move towards partnership arrangements for primary health-care and social care have marked a different direction for policy from much of the rest of the UK where privatization has been rapidly implemented. The full impact of the changes in Scotland have yet to be seen, but the intention is to reduce the potential for 'cost-shifting' between the NHS and local government and to promote genuinely more collaborative approaches which provide higher quality services with less institutional barriers. The extent to which funding has kept up with rising needs, the ability of the system to retain clear accountability and for resources to consistently be channelled into the most effective services has, however, meant that many health boards have struggled to consistently meet all of their financial and performance targets.

Future Population Health

Scotland compares well internationally on most outcomes. However, for most markers of health, and in particular for health inequalities, it compares very poorly. The Scottish Parliament has played a very important role in facilitating innovative and effective policies to change this, but many challenges lie ahead. As Scotland strives to become an environmentally sustainable nation, and to change its economy accordingly, it will require to make a transition that supports health and equality. There are many health challenges arising from the nature of society today which remain to be adequately tackled including obesity, health inequalities and drug related deaths. The potential solutions to these health challenges may be similar to those broader societal ones: a more sustainable and healthier food system; planning for active travel to become the norm; a social security system that provides sufficient income for the whole population; and ways of sharing income and reducing consumption such as some forms of carbon rationing (McCartney 2008a, 2008b). The extent to which Scotland can act on these is variable, but the rest of the world now look to us as a source of innovation and inspiration and it may be that our influence can go beyond our own shores.

References

Beeston C., McCartney G., Ford J., *et al.* (2013), 'Health Inequalities Policy Review for the Scottish Ministerial Task Force on Health Inequalities', Edinburgh: NHS Health Scotland.

Eikemo T.A. and Mackenbach J.P. (2012), 'EURO GBD SE: The Potential for Reduction of Health Inequalities in Europe. Final Report', Rotterdam: Erasmus University Medical Center.

Ho J.Y. and Hendi A.S. (2018), 'Recent trends in life expectancy across high income countries: retrospective observational study', *British Medical Journal*, Vol. 362 No. k2562.

McCartney, G. and Hanlon, P. (2008a), 'Climate change and rising energy costs: a threat but also an opportunity for a healthier future?', *Public Health*, Vol. 122 No. 7 pp. 653–658.

McCartney G., Hanlon P. and Romanes F. (2008b), 'Climate change and rising energy costs will change everything: a new mindset and action plan for 21st century public health', *Public Health*, Vol. 122 No. 7 pp. 658-63.

McCartney G., Walsh D., Whyte B. and Collins C. (2012), 'Has Scotland always been the 'sick man' of Europe? An observational study from 1855 to 2006', *European Journal of Public Health*, Vol. 22 No. 6 pp. 756–60.

McCartney G., Collins C. and Mackenzie M. (2013), 'What (or who) causes health inequalities: theories, evidence and implications?' *Health Policy*, Vol. 13 No. 3 pp. 221-27.

Mackay D., Haw S., Ayres J.G., *et al.* (2010), 'Smoke-free Legislation and Hospitalisations for Childhood Asthma', *New England Journal of Medicine*, Vol. 363 pp. 1139–1145.

Pell J.P., Haw S., Cobbe S., *et al.* (2008), 'Smoke-free legislation and hospitalisations for acute coronary syndrome', *New England Journal of Medicine*, Vol. 359 pp. 482–91.

Scottish Government (2017), 'Long-term Monitoring of Health Inequalities', Edinburgh, available online at: https://www.gov.scot/Publications/2017/12/4517.

Taulbut M., Agbato D. and McCartney G. (2018), 'Working and Hurting? Monitoring the Health and Health Inequalities Impacts of the Economic Downturn and Changes to the Social Security System', Glasgow: NHS Health Scotland.

Walsh D., McCartney G., Collins C., *et al.* (2017), 'History, politics and vulnerability: explaining excess mortality in Scotland and Glasgow', *Public Health*, Vol. 151 pp. 1-12.

CHAPTER 10

The Catalytic Converter
Twenty Years of Devolution Preserving NHS Scotland as a Nationalised Health Service

Anne Mullin

More equal societies bring major reductions in almost all the problems that become more common lower down the social ladder. A more equal society would enjoy better physical and mental health, higher standards of child well-being, less violence, fewer people in prison, less drug addiction and more equal opportunities for children. A more equal society is conducive to the psychosocial well-being of whole populations.

Wilkinson and Pickett (2018)

IT IS NOT possible to talk about Scotland's health service under devolution without acknowledging the divergence of the health systems of England, Wales and Northern Ireland with the Scotland that began under the Scottish Executive and is continued by the Scottish Government today (Doheny, 2015). The NHS is at a crossroads of devolved health systems with NHS Scotland progressing in a certain direction and the roads may never meet again. The direction of travel began to separate in 1996 when Scottish and select northern English authorities interpreted health legislation differently, choosing to resist any financial settlements thought to erode public services. In Scotland, Foundation Hospitals were largely rejected along with general practitioner fundholding. The National Health Service Reform (Scotland) Bill which was introduced by the Labour- Liberal Democrat Coalition of the Scottish Executive in 2003 further dismantled the internal market in the NHS in Scotland by abolishing NHS Trusts (Mooney and Poole, 2004). The Public Bodies (Joint Working) Bill in Scotland was passed into law in 2014 to further strengthen co-operation, collaboration and control as the central pillars of this system (Robson, 2014).

Scotland's successive governments had gradually removed market levers from the NHS and augmented bureaucratic levers to increase connectivity between specialist and community healthcare, ensure accountability and public engagement. Several eras of NHS restructuring have expanded holistic patient centred healthcare in the community by expanding the core primary care team with my own profession general practice as the hub. General practice has a unique gatekeeper function within the NHS. GPs refer patients to specialist services and provide continuous undifferentiated community healthcare via universal population coverage. GPs work at the messy end of healthcare with other clinicians in the core primary care team (eg district nurses, health visitors) and co-ordinate upstream preventative healthcare through serial encounters, practice organisation, collaboration with other general practices and with local communities. There has been significant progress across the UK in GP training and professional regulation (Gillies *et al.*, 2009), technology is changing how GPs interact with their patients and the feminisation of the workforce is now the normalisation of the workforce.

That said, the conditions that GPs work under in the devolved governments are very different. Scotland's NHS has no commissioning care groups and whilst GPs cannot cherry pick patients to streamline their workload (Brownleader *et al.*, 2018) a remaining challenge is to strengthen the gatekeeper role of GPs to reduce health inequalities, overconsumption of services and unmet need in Scotland's NHS (Leinster, 2014).

The founding principles of the NHS have been sustained over the course of devolution and there is no ambiguity about what 'nationalised' means for the NHS in Scotland (Doheny, 2015). Regulation of the health service is by several bodies, but ultimate accountability for standards of healthcare is to Scottish Ministers and the Scottish Parliament (Robson, 2016) and not the shareholders of an arm's length company.

In contrast, England's NHS Plan 2000 according to Kirkwood and Pollock (2016)

> set out a clear agenda for the privatisation of NHS services under the rubric of patient choice and in the absence of an evidence base.

Cutting and pasting policy from a system that relies on philanthropic organisations to provide healthcare to citizens who cannot access adequate healthcare (Long *et al.*, 2016) is not recommended.

Primary Care and General Practice

A Collectivist Political Tradition

Scotland has similar demographic challenges to elsewhere in the UK but there is no political motivation to prepare the NHS in Scotland to be market ready. Scotland's government uses many pathways to improve sustainable population health and well-being. De Maeseneer (2017) describes the multiple elements that complete this virtuous cycle of connected support 'better education, better working conditions and decreased unemployment, better housing conditions, access to safe food and water, will improve the structural determinants that influence the social stratification and address the 'causes of the causes'.

The history of a unified health service that was free at the point of need is a vital document to inform our shared memories of why the creation of a nation-alised health service was so ideologically appealing. It was a bold and radical step at a time of economic stress to write a social contract by integrating several distinct policy areas of National Insurance, Industrial Injury Insurance, Family Allowances, the NHS and National Assistance. It required a strong political lead-ership and a societal will to create the holistic welfare state that most have us have lived under. Griffiths (1948, foreword) argued that its aims went beyond the words and deeds of political actors:

> This scheme is, therefore, more than an Act of Parliament; it is an act of faith in the British people.

The establishment of the NHS in 1948 was devised to minimise UK differences in healthcare provision (Digby, 1999) but Scotland's NHS has roots that stretch over a hundred years. Universal healthcare had been provided for some time in Scotland by the Highlands and Islands Medical Service following the publi-cation of The Dewar Report (1912). The Cathcart Report (1936) went further and proposed a National Health Service for Scotland with coordinated general practice services extended to the whole population. The act which created the NHS enshrined many of Cathcart's recommendations and was passed in 1947 (NHS Scotland, n.d.).

General practice has always had its pioneers pushing at the boundaries of healthcare in the poorest communities from the earliest female GPs pre-NHS, who blazed a trail by providing healthcare for marginalised and non-profit-able patients who were mostly women and children, (Digby, 1999) to GPs who provided healthcare for families who were living in destitution and unable to afford their medical treatment (Glen, 2013). The early pioneers of general prac-tice wouldn't recognise today's paperless practice, the vast array of complex medical investigations and treatment choices. They would recognise the damaging effects of current UK welfare reform on health status and they would understand the language of destitution, food banks and premature mortality in chronically stressed patients.

I spent my GP training year in Possilpark in the north-west of Glasgow that was not the vibrant community where my grandparents had raised their family. That was a time when everyone walked into a job when they left school. The Possilpark that I worked in had its heart ripped out by deindustrialisation and after the decline of manufacturing it became one of the most deprived areas in Europe. It was blighted by a heroin epidemic with high mortality rates and morbidity in young people; an old person was anyone over 50, habitable housing stock was limited. For a young doctor in training it was very challenging work physically and mentally but the most important lesson in resilience was taught to me by the patients and senior GP trainers. The patients retained their community spirit and campaigned for better services, improved housing conditions and promoted the positive aspects of their community. My GP trainers extended this philosophy. They worked as holistic practitioners alongside their patients without national guidelines to inform them and promoted a joined up integrated health and social care model. They were ahead of their time and their profession, working at the margins of society but beyond the margins of their patient population in strengthening innovative community healthcare. There was no label attached to this way of working at that time although others were keen to label it. I recall being advised that working in this part of Glasgow required a 'particular type' of GP trainee and it was akin to 'medical missionary work'.

I will end my career in my third decade as a GP partner serving a 'Deep End' community in one of the one hundred most deprived GP practice populations in Scotland (GPs at the Deep End). The heroin epidemic has abated, new housing stock has improved many of the local streets, but employment remains precarious, austerity measures have impacted negatively on patient well-being and the inequality gap is widening (Oxfam, 2017). Over the years I have reviewed thousands of measurements of individual patient health indicators on a daily basis – blood pressure, smoking status, cholesterol. But, the real metric of my patient's health status are the small stories that I hear about the quality of their lives beyond the consultation tick box that reflect their lived-in experiences.

Look Back Before Looking Forward

The NHS has always had a complex bureaucracy that has required a large support structure to deliver healthcare. In Scotland the answer in my professional lifetime has been to reorder the delivery of healthcare provision that is focused on a local population and public health partnership, but not necessarily increase the headcount of whole-time equivalent GPs.

Local Healthcare Co-operatives (LHCCS) were introduced in 1999 that subsequently formed the basis of the structure the Community Healthcare Partnership (CHCP) that replaced the LHCCS as part of the NHS Reform (Scotland) Bill. These evolved structures were designed to give patients and staff a greater say in how their health services were delivered with an expanded community health provision including community nursing and pharmacy (Scottish Government, 2010).

There is a further reiteration of service delivery and new partnerships within NHS Scotland. Integration of health and social care is at the core of the new joint boards (IJBS) that have responsibilities to integrate adult social care services, adult primary care and community health services and some hospital services supported by the new 2014 legislation (Robson, 2016).

The central formula that includes the entire health spend and that determines GP numbers is complex with the bulk of the costs associated with hospital-based admission for acute services (ISD Scotland). But, in accounting and real terms, the data gathered about the community side does not seem to accurately reflect how much work, time and effort that is put into those community-based services. A relative shortage of GPs weakens the gatekeeper function for both elective and emergency work and time to care is not factored into the community budget (Mercer and Watt, 2007, Mercer et al., 2016). Moving beyond devolution the formula will require a bit of work. Future proofing the NHS across Scotland will require that it can predictively match provision with need, not necessarily with demand, ensure continuity of care for patients, improve the interface between the humans and technology at points of high risk for patients across the health and social care divide and support an on-going dialogue between service users and providers about intelligent use of a limited resource.

Tackling the Issues of Distribution

All Things Being Unequal

The UK has a nationalised health service that is not particularly generously funded by Western standards (as a per cent of GDP) and that does impact on the Scottish Government's ability to maintain ambitious standards of health provision that is aligned with other aspects of state support. Calculating real increase in health spend is complicated by reclassifying social care spend as health spend. The budgetary sleight of hand muddies the waters (Appleby and Gersklick,

2017) with reduced social care spend responsible for increasing the mortality rates in care home residents (Watkins *et al.*, 2017).

The end of health life expectancy 15 years earlier, higher rates of premature mortality and cancer incidence inequalities in Deep End communities will not shift in the right direction if the other elements of government policy cannot address the multiple ways that poverty and financial vulnerability mediate their adverse effects on health (Scotpho, 2018). The Scottish Government has progressed its protective policies to mitigate the worse of austerity and reverse the trend in increasing mortality rates across the UK and reduce poverty rates over the last ten years (JRF, 2017) but there comes a point where the straightjacket of Scotland's fiscal framework and deference to Westminster dictated policies stifle Scotland's potential to maximise its population, health and well-being. To create equality of opportunity with parity of outcome, the cultural transmission of other welfare provisions and a welfare system that is based on dignity and respect are necessary partners to maximise the potential of the health service in Scotland.

Conclusion

'The best anywhere becomes the standard everywhere,' noted Cochran and Kenney (2014). The essence of the NHS is inviolable because it is based on deeply moral behaviours – empathy, trust, and humanitarian support. Who would not want a health service that is patient-centred across the life course and is free at the point of access to it? Yet, the NHS has its critics, because like any big system the NHS is open to fault finding when things don't go well. This appears to be motivated by personal rewards for those who are increasingly ready to offload the responsibility of running the NHS to a myriad of disconnected for-profit organisations. This is surprisingly straight-forward if there is no political will to uphold the NHS founding ideology and over time it is possible to dismantle it in front of an unsuspecting public (Pollock and Roderick, 2018) sentence by sentence, clause by clause until legislation passed reduces the NHS to 'a public funding stream and a logo' (Pollock, 2017).

The Scottish Government has not pursued this agenda under devolution which should be celebrated because healthcare spend is money well spent and reflects our collective humanity. All lives matter to the NHS and it would be difficult to deny that the establishment of the NHS was Britain's greatest achievement in levelling the inequality gap. In Scotland our collective memory does not celebrate the history of the radical thinkers from over a hundred years ago who supported the principle of population-based healthcare. We should now look forward and consider today's debate about how much the health service contributes to health status. But is it academic if healthcare exists in a vacuum of welfare policies and the NHS is under threat from Brexit trade deals and changing rules of procurement? Scotland's NHS will not be immune (British Medical Association, 2018).

General practice currently is not given equal weighting to specialist services in health planning and developing care for complex health needs of their patients. This must change because providing time to care translates into time to think, plan and manage, and whilst undoubted there are remaining challenges to health provision in NHS Scotland, the aim is to make the Deep End shallow.

Scotland's NHS is at the heart of Scotland's progressive and humanitarian policies. It is incumbent on all of us to keep it beating and protect the principle of accessible and universal healthcare as a valuable contributor to Scotland's positive future.

References

Appleby, J. and Gershlick, B. (2017), 'Keeping up with the Johanssons: How does UK health spending compare internationally?', *British Medical Journal* Vol. 358.

BMA (2018), 'Beyond Brexit – International trade and health', available online at: www.bma.org.uk/collective-voice/influence/europe/brexit/bma-brexit-briefings/beyond-brexit-international-trade-and-health

Brownleader, S., Everington, S. and Applebee, J. (2018), 'GP at Hand is Destabilising General Practice', available online at: http://www.pulsetoday.co.uk/your-practice/practice-topics/pay/gp-at-hand-is-destabilising-general-practice/20036387.article

Cochran J. and Kenney C. (2014), *The Doctor Crisis. How Physicians Can, and Must, Lead the Way to Better Health Care*, New York: Public Affairs.

De Maeseneer, J. (ed.) (2017), *Family Medicine and Primary Care: At the Crossroads of Societal Change*, Leuven, Belgium: Lannoo Campus.

Digby, A. (1999), *The Evolution of British General Practice, 1850–1948*, Oxford: Clarendon Press.

Doheny, S. (2015), 'The organisation of the NHS in the UK: comparing structures in the four countries', available online at: http://www.academia.edu/12811258/New_Publication_The_organisation_of_the_NHS_in_the_UK

Gillies, J.C., Mercer, S.W., Lyon, A., *et al.* (2009), 'Distilling the essence of general practice: a learning journey in progress', *British Journal of General Practice*, Vol. 59 No. 562.

Glen, A. (2013), *In the Front Line: A Doctor in War and Peace*, Edinburgh: Birlinn.

Griffiths, J. (1948), *The Ministry of National Insurance. Family Guide to The National Insurance Scheme*, London: HMSO

Hart J.T. (1971), 'The inverse care law', *Lancet*, Vol. 1 pp.405–412.

ISD Scotland (n.d.) *Resource Allocation Formula*, available online at: www.isdscotland.org/Health-Topics/Finance/Resource-Allocation-Formula/resource-allocation-latest.asp, accessed 16 October 2018.

Joseph Rowntree Foundation (2017), 'Poverty levels and trends in England, Wales, Scotland and Northern Ireland', available online at: www.jrf.org.uk/data/poverty-levels-and-trends-england-wales-scotland-and-northern-ireland, accessed 16 October 2018.

Kirkwood, G. and Pollock, A.M. (2016), 'Patient choice and private provision decreased public provision and increased inequalities in Scotland: a case study of elective hip arthroplasty', *Journal of Public Health*, Vol. 39 No. 3 pp. 593–600.

Leinster, S. (2018), 'Training medical practitioners: which comes first, the generalist or the specialist?', *Journal of the Royal Society of Medicine*, Vol. 107 No. 3 pp. 99–102.

Long, S.K., Skopec, L., Shelto, A., *et al.* (2016), 'Massachusetts Health Reform at Ten Years: Great Progress, But Coverage Gaps Remain'. *Health Affairs*, Vol. 35 No.9 pp. 1633–1637.

Mercer, S.W. and Watt, G.C. (2007), 'The inverse care law: clinical primary care encounters in deprived and affluent areas of Scotland', *Annals of Family Medicine* Vol. 5 No. 6 pp. 503–510.

Mercer, S.W., Higgins, M., Bikker, A.M., *et al.* (2016), 'General Practitioners' Empathy and Health Outcomes: A Prospective Observational Study of Consultations in Areas of High and Low Deprivation'. *Annals of Family Medicine* Vol. 14 No. 2 pp. 117–124.

Mooney, G. and Poole, L. (2004), '"A land of milk and honey"?: Social policy in Scotland after devolution' *Critical Social Policy*, Vol. 24 No. 4 pp. 458–483.

NHS Scotland (n.d.), 'Explore the History of the NHS in Scotland', available at: www.ournhsscotland.com/history/timeline, accessed 18 October 2018.

Oxfam (2017), 'Building a More Equal Scotland: Designing Scotland's Poverty and Inequality Commission', available online at: https://policy-practice.oxfam.org.uk/publications/building-a-more-equal-scotland-designing-scotlands-poverty-and-inequality-commi-620264, accessed 14 October 2018.

Pollock, A. (2017), 'Tackling risks and harms', *British Medical Journal* Vol. 359 No. j4625.

Pollock, A. and Roderick, P. (2018), 'Why we should be concerned about accountable care organisations in England's NHS'. *British Medical Journal* Vol. 360 No. k343.

Robson, K. (2016), 'The National Health Service in Scotland', available online at:

www.parliament.scot/ResearchBriefingsAndFactsheets/S5/SB_16-100_The_ National_Health_Service_in_Scotland.pdf, accessed, 14 October 2018.

Scottish Government (2010), 'Study of Community Health Partnerships', available at: https://www.gov.scot/Publications/2010/05/06171600/4, accessed, 14 October 2018.

The Scottish Deep End Project (n.d.), *GPs at The Deep End*, available online at: https://www.gla.ac.uk/deepend, accessed 16 October 2018.

Watkins, J., Wulaningsih, W., Da Zhou, C., *et al.* (2017), 'Effects of health and social care spending constraints on mortality in England: a time trend analysis'. *British Medical Journal* Vol. 7 No. 11, available online at : http://bmjopen.bmj.com/content/7/11/e017722.abstract

Wilkinson, R.G. and Pickett, K. (2009), *The Spirit Level: Why More Equal Societies Almost Always Do Better*, London: Allen Lane.

CHAPTER 11

Housing Policy
Exposing the Limits of Devolution and Ambition

Douglas Robertson

Another World

HOUSING POLICY WAS considered a core power to be devolved. It was welcomed by those with an interest in such matters given the lack of legislative attention housing matters had received at Westminster. Scottish housing had always been considered somewhat different, given its historically poorer build standards and physical condition, plus the substantially higher rates of overcrowding – the result of the rapid construction of small, squalid tenement flats during Scotland's short yet rapid period of industrialisation (Checkland, 1981). The resulting 20th century response, the mass construction of public housing ensured a continuation of Scots peculiarism. Especially when compared to England, given that by the mid-1970s, 75 per cent of all its housing was owned either by a local authority, the Scottish Special Housing Association or a New Town Corporation. Housing policy was thus primarily seen as being about influencing practice within what is now unfortunately termed 'social' housing. Yet, by the time of devolution settlement, owner-occupation had already replaced public housing as the dominant tenure.

It was also the case that private housing differed from English norms, in that freehold was the norm, while leasehold, common throughout England and at that time ubiquitous within flats, remained a rarer tenure form. Further, property owners in Scotland were legally vassals, given the land ownership system was still feudal, one of the very last in Europe. There was thus always on any title, the feu superior, a feudal overlord to which you were legally required to defer certain property rights and obligations set down within the title. Although there were a few serious cases of feu superiors exercising such powers, most owners were ignorant of the potential implications, seeing feu superiors as an inconvenient oddity. Despite its legal standing, owner-occupation had grown fast, so that by 2005 it accounted for 62 per cent of the housing stock, almost doubling in the preceding thirty-years. Private renting, long a residual tenancy was still in decline, down to 9 per cent from 13 per cent three decades previous. That said, it had witnessed a slight fillip, the result of the reintroduction of a free-market in rents in 1988, the first time since the advent of rent restrictions way back in 1915 when most property was rented privately.

Long-term switching from private renting to owner-occupation, plus steady growth in private speculative house building, at a time when public spending on new council stock had all but ceased, partly helps explain such growth. However, it was the introduction of 'Right-to-Buy' legislation in 1980 which dramatically altered Scotland's housing profile, given half a million public sector properties were sold to tenants under these provisions.

Local authorities were allowed to reinvest sales receipts in the remaining stock. But, in terms of the effect on their Housing Revenue Account this was never a good deal, given the popular property which sold carried little outstanding debt, and housed a stable rent paying population. The property where the receipts were used to offset council borrowing were typically unpopular. There was a high turnover, they were costly to maintain, like the slum clearance stock, built in the late 1930s, or the system-build and high-rise developments of the 1960s, also constructed to address slum conditions. The housing sold was at deep discounts, 60 per cent maximum for a house, or 70 per cent for flatted property, depending on the length of tenancy. So, the resulting cash receipt was small, perhaps not always covering the outstanding debt. Such sales also cleared out a population of rent payers, leaving council house financing highly dependent on housing benefit.

Housing standards across the board were poor. Many millions of pounds had been expended on both housing associations and renovation grants to homeowners, to tackle residual slum housing, with the vast bulk of these monies being spent on Glasgow. Conditions within the council stock, which for over 50 years had not been particularly well managed, were also poor and deteriorating rapidly, given their markedly worsening financial situation. Again, nowhere was this more evident than in Glasgow, where Europe's largest landlord, the City Council, was having to spend 90 pence in every pound of rent money to pay debt charges. Hence, the entire stock was literally falling apart (Grieve *et al.*, 1986).

Table 1: Tenure Change in Scotland: 1975 to 2015.

	1975	1985	1995	2005	2015
Own occupation	33%	42%	58%	62%	58%
Private renting	13%	8%	7%	9%	15%
Social housing	54%	50%	35%	26%	23%

Source: Scottish Government, 2016.

Table 2: Tenure Change in Glasgow: 1975 to 2015.

	1975	1985	1995	2005	2015
Own occupation	25%	25%	34%	48%	45%
Private renting	5%	5%	5%	9%	18%
Social housing	68%	68%	65%	43%	34%

Source: GCC, 2017.

Radical Reforms

Donald Dewar, as First Minister, came forward with a very clear housing agenda. Although, the core element, the wholesale reform of Scots Property Law, was considered primarily a property law reform. This was accomplished through passing three acts: the Abolition of Feudal Title etc (Scotland) Act, 2000, the Titles Conditions (Scotland) Act, 2003, and finally the Tenement (Scotland) Act, 2004.

Dewar was also keen to address the serious concerns afflicting Glasgow's council housing, in part, because in representing Drumchapel, one of the city's four large peripheral housing estates, he was well acquainted with the issues. The Glasgow Housing Association, the country's largest ever stock transfer, involved 81,400 houses and a billion-pound public capital debt write-off, which ensured a privately funded investment package of four billion pounds (Audit Scotland, 2006). Other transfers occurred in Argyllshire, the Borders, Dumfries and Galloway, Inverclyde and the Western Isles, but other authorities promoting such a switch, namely, Dundee, Edinburgh, the Highlands, Stirling and Perth and Kinross and failed to secure the necessary tenant support.

Dewar's commitment to social inclusion also saw housing policy drive through a long argued blending of area renewal and community development into what was termed Social Inclusion Partnerships (SIPs). Unfortunately, although a lot of public money was thrown at these area-based initiatives, evidence gleaned from the Scottish Index of Multiple Deprivation, a data set setup established to monitor this initiative, failed to show any impact, given these places stubbornly remain the countries the most deprived (Robertson, 2016). Part of the issue here was that the entire program was so bureaucratically controlled from the centre, local participation proved hard to sustain.

The Labour-Lib Dem coalition also took the opportunity to get rid of the long despised Scottish Homes, the housing agency created by the Conservatives in 1988, given its predilection for privatisation. This was by and large through promoting stock transfers to housing associations, a policy this administration was now actively pursuing. Similarly, there was no real change in insisting that increasing levels of private investment were required to make up for the cuts in public subsidy. Communities Scotland, with its decentralised structure, yet more interventionist approach, was promoted as being socially conscious, given its role in delivering on the SIPs agenda.

The first administration was also lauded for working with a number of homeless experts, both practitioners and academics, to produce what has been described as one of the most progressive pieces of homeless legislation: The Housing (Scotland) Act, 2001. They achieved this by getting rid of the intentionally homelessness clause, ensuring local authorities had less ability to refuse housing.

Less lauded, but perhaps the most successful policy overall, was the introduction of the Scottish Housing Quality Standard (SHQS) in 2004, a basic housing standard expected of all social landlords. Communities Scotland were given responsibility to ensure the standards were meet by 2015, and currently, 90 per cent of all such stock does, with failures being mainly in older council stock. Within the Housing (Scotland) Act of 2006, a basic quality standard was also introduced for private rented stock, the Repairing Standard. Oddly, the quality measure for owner-occupation remained the tolerable standard. The measure designed in the 1960s to determine whether a property was a slum or not, and despite a few recent modifications still stands. Plans to unify all these tenure standards into a universal measure progresses, but at glacial pace.

The same legislation abolished the entire legal framework that had been in place for 30 years, which eradicated the countries remnant slum problem. The replacement 'Scheme of Assistance' allowed local authorities discretion in providing property owners with advice and guidance, practical help, or direct financial assistance, via grants or loans, when addressing serious disrepair. But crucially it is for local authorities to determine what assistance will be made available on the basis of local priorities and budgets. Area-based housing renewal, long a tenet of Scottish housing policy, was thus removed.

A 'Numbers Game' Plus Fragmentation

An SNP minority administration was then elected, to everyone's surprise, including their own. All incoming ministers were thus on a steep learning curve, and nowhere more so than in housing. The Firm Foundations housing policy paper reveals a lack of thought and essentially one ambition, a return to Macmillan's 1950s strategy of delivering more houses for less (Scottish Government, 2007). Local authorities were encouraged to return to the development fold, and along with housing associations and private builders to ensure 35,000 houses were built annually.

As with their predecessors, they immediately set about closing down a housing agency, this time Communities Scotland which, as no replacement was offered, brought to an end 70 years of having a dedicated housing agency to advise government. This action also, by default, finally separated funding powers from those of landlord regulation which had been long awaited.

Firm Foundation also tentatively suggested ending the 'Right-to-Buy', which was eventually announced six years later, which nonetheless was still highly symbolic given its totemic political status. A two-year notice period was included within the abolition provisions ushered in by the Housing (Scotland) Act, 2014, though incremental change in 2001 and 2010 had further tightened restrictions.

Perhaps the most interesting aspect of the Firm Foundations agenda, in terms of foresight, was its suggested reform of the private rented sector. Eventually, over a 12-year period, this came to fruition, with the most critical element, provision of an entirely new open-ended tenancy regime, being introduced by the Private Housing (Tenancies) (Scotland) Act, 2016. Now a tenancy can only be extinguished by the landlord under a set of statutorily prescribed grounds. Previously, the short-assured tenancy offered, but a six-month period, in an arrangement which neither the landlord nor tenant seemed fully conversant with. Enhanced security of tenure was also designed to help tenants access the range of additional rights, in relation to the Repairing Standard and other tenancy provisions, brought in by the Private Rented Sector (Scotland) Act, 2011, and further refined later in the Housing (Scotland) Act, 2014. The Scottish Government were certainly ahead of the curve:

following the global financial crisis of 2008, private renting rocketed and now accounts for almost 20 per cent of Scotland housing tenure. Or put, another way, the Scottish Government now has more tenancies than either local authorities or housing associations.

The crisis, brought about by woeful lending practices on low-value American real estate, not only played a critical role in destroying RBS, but it also transformed Scotland's housing system. During the immediate crisis, private developers were unable to sell property. There was also an immediate collapse in public funding. Chancellor Osborne's austerity package of 2010 presented an overall cut of 19 per cent to the Scottish Government. The housing budget however took a 35 per cent hit, although housing bodies showed this to be actually 53 per cent. Grant levels for housing development thus plummeted, ensuring only those with free reserves were able to bridge the widening funding gap.

This, in part, helped drive the rationalisation of housing associations, through mergers and takeovers, given many larger entities were keen to increase their portfolio, so they could borrow not from banks, but through issuing their own bonds. The Scottish Government, eager to protect its 'affordable' housing target, were more than happy to support this, even when this meant a loss of local control and accountability to larger development focused conglomerates, domiciled not just in Edinburgh and Glasgow, but also Manchester, Sunderland and Worcester.

With the 35,000 annual targets 'out of the window', the reworked Affordable Housing Supply Programme set a revised 30,000 'affordable homes' target for the 2011–12 to 2015–16 Parliamentary periods. Included here were 20,000 association 'starts', plus 5,000 council ones. They achieved 39,482 'completions', of which 22,523 were for association, 5,992 council, plus 3,473 for 'affordable' mid-market rent, and 7,494 'affordable' home-ownership, the latter two essentially being market products. Now in its third administration, there is a 50,000 target, over this parliamentary term, involving the same prevarication as to what exactly gets included within the 'affordable' badging.

Being obliged to adhere to certain UK polices, the Scottish Government is taking a 15 per cent stake in houses being purchased at up to £200,000. 'Help-to-Buy', projected to cost some £200 million, therefore, sits somewhat uneasily within a policy which seeks to address housing need. But for the small number of large private developers, it's been a lifeline, illustrating their considerable influence.

What is most surprising when reviewing devolved housing policy, is that so much of the housing legislative draws its antecedence from a single report: the Housing Improvement Task Force (HITF, 2003). This is surprising, because its ambition was to find ways to encourage owner responsibility for undertaking common repairs on multi-owned property. That said, its recommendations link directly to private landlord registration introduced in 2004; Houses in Multiple Ownership licensing, enacted in 2006; the aforementioned improvements in housing standards, the SHQS, in 2004, for social housing and the Repairing Standard for the PRS, in 2006; a linked complaints procedure, for private tenants, also in 2006; property factoring regulation, in 2011; letting agent regulation, in 2014; the introduction of the Home Report, in 2008; as well as the swathe of private rented sector reforms already mentioned.

Thus, it would appear there has long been something of a political consensus, in relation to slow incremental change, across this broad range of housing reforms. The HITF, established by the Labour-Lib Dem administration, set an agenda that was taken up and further developed by the three subsequent SNP administrations and, in doing so, relegated Firm Foundations to play mere second fiddle. With these recommendations, now largely worked through, perhaps there should be less of a surprise that the recent housing policy paper presents such a thin offering (Scottish Government, 2018).

Exposed Limits

Physically, the housing world that existed twenty years ago still looks similar, despite some new builds and extensive refurbishments. But underneath that physical *façade* the housing system has altered significantly. Long-standing totems of the housing scene have disappeared: there is no government housing agency, no 'Right-to-Buy', no Glasgow Housing Department, no area regeneration and now very few slums. Disrepair in private housing still persists, as does homelessness, even despite that progressive homelessness policy. Further, notwithstanding all the rhetoric around social justice and well-being, housing in policy terms, is still inextricably tied to construction jobs and the profits of 'spec builders'.

Yet, housing has always been about more than 'bricks and mortar'. We have long understood its role in defining someone's social status. But what has become more obvious, over the last decade, is just how housing assets tie into personal wealth, and from that a capacity to use that asset to earn an income, or to borrow or buy into additional housing assets. We have thus witnessed a return of rentier capitalism, so despised by Marx. This 'financialisaton' of housing helps explain the quite extraordinary accelerated growth of private renting, as well as short-let accommodation.

With 10,000 permanent Airbnb's in Edinburgh, and now over 20 per cent of its housing privately rented, should we be surprised that the city has the largest number of people residing in temporary accommodation, who also stay there for the longest periods. A housing policy that encourages new mid-market rental accommodation and celebrity homeless sleep-outs can never hope to address the real causes of that city's housing crisis.

Now added into the mix are the pernicious and cruel welfare changes, brought about by the austerity package, which made poverty a crime, while subjected those in greatest need to even less. The current roll out of Universal Credit holds the possibility of undermining social housing across the board, given the current reliance on Housing Benefit for 70 per cent of its rental income. So, to survive, these landlords find themselves becoming a contemporary poor house, which actively supports their tenants to secure an income, so they are able to pay the rent. While the 'bedroom tax' could be mitigated, the scale of these changes means they cannot.

This so succinctly exposes the limits of a devolved housing policy. While social housing and a significant element of private renting, is highly dependent on the Housing Benefit budget, which in Scotland currently stands at £1.7 billion, the entire Scottish Government's current capital housing budget is but 36 per cent of that. Out with that niche it is the market, and the lenders, who control everything else. That is the harsh reality of devolved housing policy; it is only influencing matters at the margins. Forty years back when more than half of housing was publicly owned there was real influence, but that is no longer the world we live in.

References

Audit Scotland (2006), *Council Housing Transfers*, Edinburgh: Audit Scotland.

Checkland, S. (1981), *The Upas Tree: Glasgow, 1875–1975... And After, 1975–1980*, Glasgow: University of Glasgow Press.

Glasgow City Council (2017), 'Glasgow's Housing Strategy 2017–2022', Glasgow: Glasgow City Council.

Grieve, R., Clark, L., Finniston, M. and Karn, V. (1986), 'Inquiry into Glasgow Housing' (The Grieve Inquiry), Glasgow: City of Glasgow District Council.

Housing Improvement Task Force (2003), 'Report of the Housing Improvement Task Force', Edinburgh: Scottish Executive.

Robertson, D. (2016), 'Groundhog Day, explaining 50 years of failed renewal', *Bella Caledonia*, 26 November 2016.

Scottish Government (2007), 'Firm Foundations: The Future of Housing in Scotland', Scottish Government: Edinburgh.

Scottish Government (2018), 'Housing Beyond 2021: Scottish Government Discussion Paper', Edinburgh: Scottish Government.

Scottish Government (2016), 'Housing Statistics for Scotland 2016: Key Trends Summary', Edinburgh: Scottish Government.

CHAPTER 12

Mark and Measure
Judging Scotland Through Punishment

Fergus McNeill

Introduction

IN ONE OF HIS LESS famous speeches, Churchill, perhaps plagiarising Dostoyevsky, once said this:

> *A calm and dispassionate recognition of the rights of the accused against the state, and even of convicted criminals against the state, a constant heart-searching by all charged with the duty of punishment, a desire and eagerness to rehabilitate in the world of industry all those who have paid their dues in the hard coinage of punishment, tireless efforts towards the discovery of curative and regenerating processes, and an unfaltering faith that there is a treasure, if you can only find it, in the heart of every man [sic]*, these are the symbols which in the treatment of crime and criminals mark and measure the stored-up strength of a nation, and are the sign and proof of the living virtue in it (*House of Commons, 20 July 1910*, emphasis added).

This seems an irresistibly apposite place to start. When and how do we punish? How much do we punish? Who do we punish? And why do we punish? The answers to these questions have much to tell us about who we have been, who we are and who we are becoming.

Let me start with my conclusion: when it comes to punishment, Scotland remains juvenile – perhaps even dangerously adolescent. We may have matured a bit in the last twenty years, but we have a very long way to go and, in this case, growing up is a matter of life and death.

Before We Were Born

Lesley McAra's (1999, 2005, 2008) pre-eminent work on Scottish penal policy-making before and after devolution, suggests that in the days of the Scottish

Office's Home and Health Department, civil servants and professional leaders conspired to protect Scotland from the chill winds of 'populist punitiveness' (Bottoms, 1995) that had started to drive change in the penal system of England and Wales. There, what Ian Loader (2005) termed the 'Platonic Guardians' in and around Whitehall, had been marginalised if not swept aside by the politicisation of 'law and order', crime and punishment, from the 1980s onwards.

Sociologists of punishment have been debating the causes and consequences of late-modern penal change for decades (see, for example, Garland, 2001; Wacquant, 2009). For present purposes, we can crudely summarise the story in this way: the major economic, social and political changes in the last quarter of the 20th century both provoked and reflected rising insecurity – not just about crime, but also about the precarity created by neo-liberalising societies with increasing levels of inequality. More existentially, confidence in shared belief systems (whether religious and political) waned. Collective or community provision of welfare gave way to individualism; we were told to insure ourselves against risks, to safeguard our own security and that of those we loved. There was, as Margaret Thatcher famously said, no such thing as 'society'.

In this wider climate, the resurgence of punitiveness was unsurprising; and the emerging 'penal state' or 'carceral state' capitalised upon it. On the one hand, it used punishment to control and manage the 'dangerous classes' from whom welfare had been withdrawn or for whom it had been made conditional and sanctionable. On the other, among the supposedly law-abiding, it used punishment to shore up its flagging legitimacy in the face of globalisation.

Baby Steps

As Loader and Sparks (2010) noted, this harsh climate posed huge challenges for the development of a 'better politics of crime and its regulation'. Indeed, Nicola Lacey (2008) went so far as to argue that, to insulate penal policy from the dynamics of populism, rates of imprisonment should be set by an independent commission, rather like the Bank of England's Monetary Policy Committee.

Scotland's baby Executive (and Parliament) didn't take long to start toddling towards penal populism. Criminal justice and, in particular youth justice, quickly became a site of political capacity building: Here was an area of real public concern through which the Executive could demonstrate its ability to govern (Simon, 2007). Particularly between 2003 and 2007, the Labour-Lib Dem Executive aped New Labour's Blairite approach; always tougher on crime than the causes of crime. The most visible or audible aspects of this retreat

from Scotland's vaunted penal welfarism was a puerile public discourse on
'ned crime' and the associated introduction of ASBOS and parenting orders.
Albeit that, in practice, these were very rarely used. More generally, McAra
(2008) describes this as a period of hyper-institutionalisation; new laws and
new quangos proliferated. Law and order, crime and punishment, had become
political and politicised in the new Scotland, and the effect was a paradoxical
'de-tartanisation'.

   In the background, despite falling crime rates, civil servants, practitioners and activists were becoming acutely worried by an accelerating rate
of growth in the prison population. Attracting less attention and provoking
less concern, the population under criminal justice social work supervision
also soared, drawing more and more Scots within the ambit of penal control
(Figure 1).

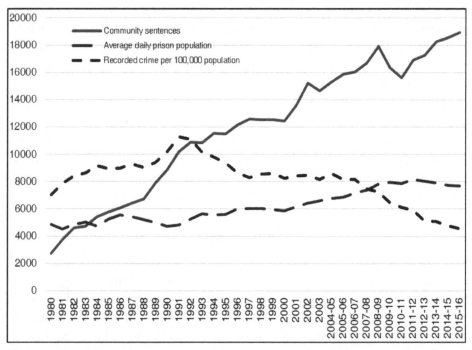

Figure 1: Number of Community Sentences, Average Daily Prison Population
and Recorded Crime Per 100,000 Population in Scotland, 1980–2016.
Source: McNeill, 2018.

   As Figure 1 indicates, Scotland's 'Platonic Guardians' (and/or the declining
crime rate) seemed to have restrained the growth in the prison population until
devolution, even if they had enabled a huge expansion of social work supervision. However, after devolution, in just eight years, the prison population
jumped from 6,000 to 8,000.

Adolescence

The election of a minority SNP Government in 2007 signalled a change in rhetoric and in approach. As I have argued elsewhere (McNeill, 2011), under Kenny MacAskill's leadership, the tone of penal policy changed, and the pace of penal change slowed. First aspiring for, and later (after their 2011 landslide) in anticipation of an independence referendum, the nationalists wanted to stress Scotland's potential not its problems, and to assuage rather than mobilise the population's insecurities and lack of confidence. Repeatedly, they stressed our cultural affinities to our more penal moderate neighbours like Norway or Ireland. More broadly, rather than re-legitimating the British state by evincing muscular responses to foreign or domestic threats, they aimed instead to legitimate constitutional change towards the project of an egalitarian, socially just, social democratic, independent Scotland.

Notably the first 'Scotland's Choice' report was about the direction of our penal system, not the question of independence (Scottish Prisons Commission, 2008). Its author, the Scottish Prisons Commission, was led by former First Minister, Henry McLeish, and was charged with exploring and addressing our over-use of imprisonment. In its report, recognising the social, human and fiscal costs of imprisonment, the Commission set a target to reduce the prison population from 8,000, to 5,000 (its 1980 level); an ambitious goal but a realistic one, they argued, in light of falling crime rates. Their 23 recommendations laid out how this goal might be achieved through the reform of prosecution, sentencing and release arrangements.

The Scottish Government accepted most of the Commission's recommendations (though it never endorsed the target) and embarked on various reforms: introducing a presumption against short prison sentences of less than three months and a new community sentence, the Community Payback Order, as well as establishing a Scottish Sentencing Council.

It remains difficult to judge the success of these efforts. The data in Figure 1 suggests a stabilisation of the prison population and then a slight drop. The average daily population has declined from a peak of 8,179 in 2011–12 to 7,552 in 2016–17 (Scottish Government Crime Statistics, 2018). Needless to say, this remains a long way short of McLeish's target, meaning that Scotland retains one of Europe's highest imprisonment rates.

But looking at this with a slightly longer historical lens, and taking into account Scotland's use of penal supervision, our current position is even more concerning. Between 1980 and 2015, our prison population rose from about 5,000 to 8,000 while the population under supervision climbed from less than 3,000 to about 22,000. As I have already noted, crime rates cannot account for the huge growth in our penal population. Indeed, in Scotland, there were ten times as many community sentences *per crime* in 2015 as there had been in 1980 (see McNeill, 2018).

Towards Maturity?

It seems therefore, that despite our best good intentions, Scotland continues to struggle for maturity in terms of penal politics. How should we respond? We could take Lacey's (2008) advice: admit that we can't trust ourselves with penal power and return it to our metaphorical 'mums and dads' – the civil servants and professional leaders who might act as Loader's 'Platonic Guardians' (2005). But, like Loader and Sparks (2010), and paraphrasing them, I fear that would merely leave us like Peter Pan and the Lost Boys, condemned to never grow up. The better – but also the harder – path is suggested in the conclusion of a recent Scottish study exploring how audiences respond to media reporting about punishment. Recognising the central importance of communicating censure in our appetite for punishment, Happer, *et al.* (2018) argue that:

> To encourage a more informed dialogue about the legitimacy or illegitimacy of different forms of punishment (whether imprisonment or community sanctions) may require us to move beyond the top-down approaches of 'better' penal reform campaigns or 'better' public relations strategies for probation. Rather, our findings suggest the need for a much deeper deliberative dialogue about punishment which has the potential to better exercise and develop our penal tastes; dialogue that allows us to recognise when satiating our appetites and indulging our tastes might in fact harm us and others (cf. Loader, 2009).

Of course, the question of what constitutes penal over-indulgence is a normative one that every polity must address. How we answer it depends ultimately upon (and, as Churchill said, reveals) what values we possess, prize and prioritise. To help us towards an answer, the late, great Norwegian criminologist, Nils Christie offered us some wise advice in his discussion of what constitutes a *suitable* amount of crime (and punishment) (Christie, 2004). He suggested firstly that if we believe in kindness, forgiveness and civility as values, then we ought to keep 'the institution of penal law' a small one; and secondly, that if we value living in cohesive, integrated societies, then we must restrain the growth of that institution.

On the evidence presented in this chapter, it seems obvious that, in Scotland, by allowing the rapid expansion of penal control – even when we have consistently aimed to shrink the penal system – so far, we have failed Christie's (1993) tests. As I have argued in a recent book about the pervasiveness of punishment in Scotland and elsewhere (McNeill, 2018), this expansion has tended to draw more of our people into the penal net, and the people caught up have been predominantly marginalized and excluded people living in the most deprived parts of our country. The greater the extent of their marginalization and exclusion, the more deeply they have been drawn into the penal net.

The dreadful human cost has been vividly illustrated in recent weeks in the case of 16-year-old William Lindsay who, two days after being remanded in custody to Her Majesty's Young Offenders Institution Polmont, took his own life (Reports in *The Scotsman*). One of *our* children, a product of *our* 'care', perhaps drunk and certainly distressed, walked into a police station and laid a knife on the counter, and rather than catching him in a safety net, *we* trapped him in a penal net from in which he hung himself. He will never get to grow up, but perhaps his story can help to teach us that, when it comes to criminal justice, we must.

References

Christie, N. (2004), *A Suitable Amount of Crime*, Abingdon: Routledge.

Garland, D. (2001), *The Culture of Control: Crime and Social Order in Contemporary Society*, Oxford: Oxford University Press.

Happer, C., McGuinness, P., McNeill, F. and Tiripelli, G. (2018), 'Punishment, legitimacy and taste: The role and limits of mainstream and social media in constructing attitudes towards community sanctions', *Crime Media Culture*, 7 May 2018.

Lacey, N. (2008), *The Prisoner's Dilemma: Political Economy and Punishment in Contemporary Democracies*, Cambridge: Cambridge University Press.

Loader, I. (2005), 'Fall of the "Platonic Guardians": Liberalism, Criminology and Political Responses to Crime in England and Wales', *British Journal of Criminology*, Vol. 46 No. 4 pp. 561–586.

Loader, I. (2009), 'Ice cream and incarceration: On appetites for security and punishment', *Punishment & Society* Vol. 11 No. 2 pp. 241–257.

Loader, I. and Sparks, R. (2010), *Public Criminology?*, London: Routledge.

McAra, L. (1999), 'The Politics of Penality: An Overview of the Development of Penal Policy in Scotland', in Duff, P. and Hutton, N. (eds.), *Criminal Justice in Scotland*, Aldershot: Ashgate/Dartmouth.

McAra, L. (2005) 'Modelling penal transformation', *Punishment & Society*, Vol. 7 pp. 277–302.

McAra, L. (2008), 'Crime, Criminology and Criminal Justice in Scotland', *European Journal of Criminology*, Vol. 5 No. 4 pp. 481–504.

McNeill, F. (2011), 'Determined to Punish? Scotland's Choice', in Hassan, G. and Ilett, R. (eds.), *Radical Scotland: Arguments for Self-Determination*, Edinburgh: Luath Press.

McNeill, F. (2018), *Pervasive Punishment: Making Sense of Mass Supervision*, Bingley: Emerald Publishing.

Scottish Government Crime Statistics, available online at: https://www2.gov.scot/Topics/Statistics/Browse/Crime-Justice/TrendPris, accessed 30 November 2018.

Scottish Prisons Commission (2008), 'Scotland's Choice', Edinburgh: Scottish Prisons Commission.

Simon, J. (2007), *Governing Through Crime: How the War on Crime Transformed American Democracy and Created a Culture of Fear (Studies in Crime and Public Policy)*, Oxford: Oxford University Press.

The Scotsman, available online at: https://www.scotsman.com/news/teenager-flagged-as-suicide-risk-takes-his-life-after-48-hours-in-prison-1-4827386, and https://www.scotsman.com/regions/glasgow-strathclyde/background-teenager-william-lindsay-died-in-custody-after-being-failed-by-system-1-4827410, accessed 30 November 2018.

Wacquant, L. (2009), *Punishing the Poor: The Neoliberal Governance of Insecurity*, Durham, NC: Duke University Press.

Section Three – Scotland's Public Realm

CHAPTER 13

Making Participation About People
An Exchange

Jim McCormick and Anna Fowlie

Dear Anna,

What is it to participate? In Scotland, there is a lot of emphasis on shared forms of participation – for example, community empowerment and renewing local democracy. Many consultations after devolution began like this. A policy-driven approach has often felt like a hard shift that hasn't yielded enough. Paying for public services by improving upon Council Tax? The hard choices have been ducked more than once. Participatory budgeting? A big idea but only allowed to influence spending decisions, so far, at the margins. Without any cynicism, I think it's fair to conclude that the promise runs way ahead of the practice.

If we look closer, there is another web of decisions that rely on our participation in everyday life, for example as workers, carers, parents and tenants. We draw upon a set of resources to participate – families, public service providers, our own endeavours, money, opportunities and luck. These are distributed very unevenly. And, for people who have few resources to count on, the capacity to take part and to shape the path life takes, can be especially restricted.

Our response to people living in hardship, facing adversities and struggling to cope is becoming gradually more enlightened. We know from people who have contributed to poverty truth commissions and fairness commissions that the process is painfully slow. Commonly people speak about the stigma of being in poverty. Interactions with public services are often disempowering and sometimes demeaning. Participation from this angle might involve being part of a grassroots movement to advocate for change, joining a union or a tenants committee. These steps make things better for many. But, in addition, we cannot overlook the powerful effects of participating in everyday decisions that affect your own life.

Scotland has a long track record of seeking to join up public services. Integration of health and care is the most visible example, building on a legacy of multi-disciplinary assessments and support found in health, education and social work locations. The idea of community hubs – or one-stop shops as they were called in some areas in the 1980s and 1990s – is familiar. If we can reduce the hassle people face in getting the help, they need quickly without being moved from pillar to post, the outcomes are usually better, and costs can be reduced. This vision of public services is fine as far as it goes. For many people much of the time, public services work well enough. I think the trouble is the models we have don't go far enough and have a conceptual flaw at the centre.

People who have complex lives, facing periods of adversity and vulnerability, tend to have poorer outcomes. In England, so called 'troubled families' were a policy focus of the coalition Government. Their troubles were framed in terms of the presenting issues – mental health problems, addictions, worklessness, struggles with parenting, youth offending – but rarely in terms of root causes, of which the biggest is persistent poverty. Much of the motive force seemed to be about the cost of reactive spending across multiple services. In Scotland, this framing wasn't used. The Christie principles of prevention seemed to offer a brighter outlook. But, here too, it is not uncommon to hear the frustration of officials due to high costs and poor outcomes. Some are identified as 'million-pound families'. But the problem here is also conceptual – how much of the public money spent trying to 'fix' complex and seemingly intractable issues has been shaped by the people who are supposed to benefit?

This is one of the themes in Hilary Cottam's recent book *Radical Help*. If public authorities are struggling to demonstrate how the large investment of money, professional skills and time is helping people to live better and more independent lives, shouldn't we pause and revisit our assumptions? What if the failures in the system are really about a deficit of trust, relationships and goal orientation? What if we inverted our approaches and started with the assumption that people have the innate capacity and desire to participate in order to improve their lives. What we sometimes lack is the support, connection or know-how.

Hilary Cottam's account of local experiments over a decade, co-designed with young people making their transition to independent adult lives, people stuck in the revolving door of seeking work and isolated older people, is hopeful and I think goes firmly with the grain of what Christie wanted to achieve. There are many dedicated organisations across public and community services with these insights in their DNA. Austerity has held them back, blowing them far off course from the local, light touch prevention that builds up capability and confidence as well as saving money. Getting back on course seems one of the biggest priorities of all if we are to live up to the promise of participation.

Best wishes,

Jim

Dear Jim,

I read your reflections on participation having just read the UN Raporteur's report on poverty in the UK. While less bleak, what you say chimes with that. Our citizens have been offered hope of a more participative, person-centred society, largely vested in public service reform. Yet most reform is tweaking round the edges, restructuring what already exists. The Christie Report is now ten years old. We all welcomed it and signed up for its aims, but have we delivered its aspirations?

In Scotland we have hopeful and inclusive political rhetoric and government policies. But that isn't enough. The aims still feel, and are even described as, radical. It seems to me that the inertia of bureaucracy and the lack of honest debate with the public, particularly voters, means that attempts to introduce new ways of doing things are undermined by having to simultaneously hold on to what we currently have.

Despite cross-party support for the National Performance Framework – the first attempt anywhere in the world to align national policy and delivery with the UN's Sustainable Development Goals – the debate in our Parliament remains focused on inputs and outputs rather than outcomes. That's not because people don't understand outcomes, it's because it's easier to bang on about numbers of police officers or teachers than it is to shift spend to prevention and well-being.

Yet if we were to shift our focus, that would involve genuine participation. We wouldn't have the divide we currently have between the private sector as the wealth generator, the public sector as the beleaguered cure for society's ills, and the third sector as an afterthought. Citizens and families come a faraway fourth. We can see this is in Norah Senior's recent report, Working Collaboratively for a Better Scotland, which seems to me to imply that the only collaboration needed is amongst the four big national public bodies with remits on enterprise and skills to support the private sector. Such a disappointment when the title promised so much more. If we want 'a better Scotland' the collaboration needs to go way beyond that and deeply into communities.

In the aftermath of the independence referendum in 2014, we were promised a Scotland that optimised new and astonishingly high level of participation in activism and political discourse by people who had been disenfranchised for decades. We haven't delivered on that. Yet we can only build a socially just Scotland with an inclusive economy if all of our citizens, all of our community and voluntary organisations are able to participate and are regarded as credible, equal voices alongside business and public authorities.

We hear a lot about the power of disruption and everyone these days is claiming to be a disruptor, yet the systems we have in place are all designed to resist that. Perhaps the most current example for me is the Independent Care Review, which is taking a genuinely disruptive approach. Young people who have been let down by every traditional construct, including family, are hugely emotionally invested in its success. They are participating in unprecedented numbers. We can't let them down.

Yours,

Anna

Dear Anna,

I agree with your sense of disappointment that we continue to fall short of the hopeful rhetoric we hear in Scottish public life. It is almost as if we are content to say the right things, especially if they put clear water between our priorities and those of Westminster, as long as we don't actually have to change very much. I say 'almost' because enough people are clearly not comfortable sitting in the gap between words and action.

The words from the Christie Report that resonate most with me are:

If we want a better Scotland, collaboration will have to go way beyond this, deeply into communities.

I think a number of questions flow from this.

First, what do we mean by collaboration – or its dictionary synonyms co-operation, participation, alliance or association? At its simplest, this involves people with their own distinct skills, interests and goals deciding to contribute to a shared endeavour. This can be for personal or wider benefit. More advanced forms lead to co-design and shared decision-making. To be effective, it should be based on an invitation to join forces. Partnerships which are really about going through the motions to achieve some form of minimum compliance rarely lead to positive change.

Second, what does it take to collaborate well? I think the fundamental point here is about power – who decides the purpose, who gets to shape the terms, who holds the purse strings and where does accountability sit? If decision makers are serious about achieving better outcomes and are searching for alternative ways to do this, they should be clear that no pathway will get them there without genuine collaboration – which in itself should change the definition of who the decision makers are. None of Scotland's big goals – well-being, inclusive growth, equity in school attainment, ending child poverty – is likely to succeed without galvanising public will at individual and collective levels. This needs to be resourced with time, money, care and a spirit of inquiry.

Third, going deeper into communities on the edge of the third decade of the 21st century could involve many new and creative approaches. Partly this is about harnessing technology. Partly it is about the diversity of Scottish communities, in culture as well as geography. And it is also about the power of stories aligned to the mapping of community assets. We can take what is on the surface a transactional approach – for example, the transfer of physical assets has been a positive disruptor in some remote and rural parts of Scotland. In reality, the relational elements of participation are almost always what make it stand or fall.

I've just been reading a tweet from John Carnochan who has learned more than most about this from his time in policing. He wrote, 'whatever the question, the answer is relationships'. Yes, there are caveats and complexities galore when it comes to shifting the place of participation in Scottish public life. But John's words are as a good a shorthand as I've seen.

How often have we framed collaboration narrowly between agency X and organisation Y, when experience tells us it is people with a clear stance or outlook and a will to flex rules and challenge norms who end up making change happen? These can be frontline staff and chief executives, young people with care experience (as you rightly draw attention to) and families living with addiction, mentors and whistle-blowers.

Participating to drive better outcomes is tougher at a time of prolonged austerity, when the struggle to serve people's basic needs gets in the way of longer-term participative work. But the need to do this – and to develop cultures of collaboration – is all the greater.

Yours,

Jim

Dear Jim,

Your reflections on what collaboration and participation actually mean resonate with me, as does John Carnochan's assertion that whatever the question, the answer is always relationships. As human beings, we are naturally relational. Organisations are made up of human beings, so why do they so often turn relationships into transactions? The terms 'collaboration' or 'collaborative approaches' tend in reality to be about co-operating. Things continue largely as they always have but the technology is more aligned or small pockets of funding are pooled. Or there are six-monthly joint management meetings.

However, I'm writing this just before Christmas and thinking I need to dial down my cynicism and turn up my natural optimism. More than ever, I think people do actually believe that relationships and how we do things are more important than what we do and preserving the system. It's just hard to do, especially when you've spent years working in the status quo, and it's hard to measure.

As you rightly identify, relationships are predicated on power and account- ability whether they are personal or organisational. I heard a group of young people aged between eight and 19 recently speaking about Brexit and saying what they needed most was stability, consistency and strong relationships, between people and between nations. How true is that! They said you need to keep focusing on our futures, not just the day-to-day problems.

As a Highlander, I reckon we could learn a lot from our rural and island communities. People living there know their communities only function if they all do lots of different things and maximise their expertise and resources (assets in today's language). The familiar demarcations of urban life don't apply, inter- generational interaction is normal. The health visitor talks to the social worker, the school knows what's going on in families. People get together to regener- ate their environment. They need support from public services to do that, not control or constraint. That might be money, but it's just as likely to be space or understanding.

I genuinely believe that if we focus on the outcomes in the National Per- formance Framework, believe in people and take away the barrier institutions put in the way of human relationships we can make Scotland the great place to live we know it can be. Where everyone has an equal chance and we use all our natural, financial and human resources for the good of our communities. To achieve that we really need to engage all of our citizens in what matters most; we don't do that by issuing lengthy written consultations about solu- tions we've already pre-cooked, we do it by honest and open dialogue. That's what I think participation is. It's about hearing people's views and experiences, respecting them and working together to make things better. We've got much better at articulating that and need to take the next step and do it.

There are good examples of where this is working. We know it's possible. While our public sector institutions are bickering about territory and money, are hidebound by risk averse practices, while our voluntary sector organisations are pushed into competitive short-termism and while the private sector is seen as focused on profit and reductionist employment practices, we won't build the cohesive society we need to address poverty, inclusion and equality.

We also need to stop thinking in terms of GDP, which measures financial success not wellbeing and doesn't take account of the environmental or human harm cause by wealth generation as a primary concern. An inclusive economy isn't about wealth for a few, it's about wellbeing and social justice for everyone.

So, in the twentieth year since we got back our own Scottish Parliament, let's be proud of what we've achieved and keep pushing forwards when the status quo tries to drag us back to how it's always been.

Best wishes,

Anna

CHAPTER 14

Banning the Box
Humanity and Leadership in Scotland's Public Services

Karyn McCluskey and Alan Sinclair

Karyn McCluskey worked in the police for 22 years in Sussex, Lancashire, West Mercia, Strathclyde and Police Scotland. In September 2016 she took up the post of Chief Executive for Community Justice Scotland. She was Director of the Scottish Violence Reduction Unit for the previous decade, which proposed a different way of addressing violence in Scotland. She has worked in a variety of areas within the NHS, East Africa and HM Prisons.

Alan Sinclair is an independent policy analyst who has written on early years development and is author of Right from the Start: Investing in Parents and Babies. He was previously Director of Skills and Learning at Scottish Enterprise and Chief Executive of the Wise Group.

*****

Karyn: A guy named Thomas Homer-Dixon wrote about the fact that complexity overwhelms us – and this idea that the experts don't really know what's going on and we feel paralysed by our ability to try and tackle some of these issues. He called it 'the Ingenuity Gap' – a gap between the problems that arise and our ability to solve them. ·

I think the 'Ingenuity Gap' is what really exercises me now and when I speak to other people about it, I can see them nod. They recognise that space as a place where innovation should be happening, where public services change and bring in people with lived experience, but we just don't do it.

Alan: It seems too many problems are too big. I've taken comfort from beginning to realise that many of the bigger problems in society are not actually different problems. They are the same problem expressed in a different way: poor attainment at school, violence, physical health, mental health. That problem is largely down to what happens to people in the first thousand days of their life, and what happens to a child in the womb, what happens to a child in the first days of life.

K: I agree.

A: A lot of these problems are the same problem. That's my first take. My second take is that the problem is another syndrome, which is 'Implementation Deficit Syndrome'. Policy-makers often don't know the sense of direction that they are going in, and instead are blown off course by short-term considerations, by the voting cycle or their position in the party.

K: I see the manifestations of hopelessness, that's what I deal with. Everybody's story starts, 'say when I was five', 'say when I was seven', 'say when I was three'. And so, nobody is hiding.

Whether you're talking about addiction, which drives so much of our offending, or the chaos that's in our prisons right now, hopelessness and alienation goes to the heart of it. Yet that ability for us to take that real step towards change hasn't really happened. I need to know what my direction of travel is.

I've been saying to people recently, 'Tell me what justice is for?' I've been met with deafening silence because nobody has really thought about what justice is for. Justice is technically for prevention. If you asked the public what they want the criminal justice system to be for, they want prevention as well. I think prevention is what my journey is about. My journey in Community Justice Scotland is about preventing more victims.

I did something bold and said I wasn't going to look at reoffending, I was going to look at prevention of offending. I believe that the foundations are there for us in Scotland to really make some radical changes. We've embraced lots of stuff around adverse childhood experiences, the impact of trauma, the benefits of building resilience. We can speak to each other, we have people in positions that can actually make the change and we don't change that often in senior positions, so we should actually be able to speak the uncomfortable truths amongst friends, and in a way identify the direction of travel, and yet we haven't.

A: I am a big advocate of prevention and that's why I am very heartened that the Victorians put in a water system and a sewage system which has seen us through to today. Prevention is just as important in health as it is justice. And the country that does really well in prevention, putting in Good Parenting Programmes, is Holland. They see it as a public health issue, not just a social issue.

K: Alas the Victorians also built prisons. They were so good at building them we still use them today.

A: The other thing is so much of public services are like a flashing light service, and that's because we respond when things go wrong and then everything kicks in. We have to try and get ourselves off flashing lights.

K: There's this marvellous piece by Adam Gopnik in *The New Yorker*. He argues there is no miracle cure in the history of medicine. Usually it was about building a standpipe, washing your hands and preventing the spread early enough – the same is true of crime. He said you'd have to look at the broken family, address poverty and a whole range of things before attempting to treat the symptoms. He said that's not really happened. What happened was a thousand small sanities (small acts of liberal virtue) where people chipped away at the edges and thought they had eventually gotten to the heart of the problem. Lots of people are waiting for the miracle cure. I don't think there is any big single solution.

A: I think there is not a single solution, but there is a coherent sense of direction if you choose to take it. Adam Gopnik wrote a book called *Through the Children's Gate*, and his sister Alison is a big writer on neuroscience and child development, and in fact they dubbed one of her books, *The Children's Brain*.

That sense of direction of change has to be simultaneously about what our public services do and what we do in our culture. What overlaps with both is the kind of mindset of what we are trying to achieve. I fear that too many public services have got this idea of providing a service and tackling a technical problem or tackling a cognitive problem – tackling a symptom. What we should be trying to do, is to help people to be more self-determining, to have more agency over themselves and their own lives.

*****

K: I think of one success we had in the Violence Reduction Unit (VRU) and in Community Justice Scotland. I've never been a 16-year-old boy who lived in Easterhouse that was brought up in domestic violence, I've never been in the criminal justice system, I've never been in care. So, I employ those with the expertise to navigate me through that. One example of this was when we were dealing with a policy written about expunging old convictions. One of my team here who has a very old conviction that still hangs over them to this day. It took them nine weeks to find out how to do it, how to get their conviction expunged. They then found out that when they were writing the policy, they hadn't bothered to think that people might need Legal Aid to do it because you need to apply to a Sheriff. They needed to do it all themselves, and it would have cost £3,500 to get their conviction expunged. Of the 147 people who have applied to have it done, only one has managed to do it. So, for the most disadvantaged people, we've written this wonderful piece of policy, and never worked out how it actually impacts them. A document not worth the paper it's written on.

A: Talking of memorable colleagues, I remember this one guy when I led the Wise Group for about twenty years. I was talking to one of our really good supervisors, Chris, about something we could do on a Thursday night and he said, 'I can't do Thursday, I go visit my pal on Thursday'. His pal was in jail for killing somebody. Chris had this blind loyalty to go and visit every Thursday, and he was one of our best supervisors because he was so diligent. He could speak to everybody, the site visitors, the boys who he was looking after, they all respected him.

One of our things in the Wise Group was getting the long-term unemployed into work. And we were good at it – getting six out of ten into work. One of the things that we decided early on was that people who had been unemployed would do a job of work for us, like insulating houses, then we would help them get a job, but getting the next job was their responsibility. But, when we were audited, they actually criticised us saying that we didn't help them get a job because they got it themselves.

K: I am in a building that is civil service now, and I have a very diverse, skilled group working around me. I realised how uncomfortable it is for lots of professionals to hear how poor we are at supporting people to make their own decisions and how unwilling we are to involve them. It still shocks me that here we are, so I banned the box in my civil service building. All I had to do was have a conversation with somebody from Head of Security.

A: What is the box?

K: It's the box that you need to tick to say that you've had previous convictions. 'I've got lots of people here', I said to the Head of Security. 'I'm going to employ lots of different people,' and he said, 'Convictions?' and followed up with, 'Well unspent or spent convictions?' I said, 'I don't know yet'. He sucked in his cheeks, and said, 'We don't really do that here'. 'All right', I said, 'I think you've mistaken this conversation. I'm not asking you for permission, I'm telling you what I'm going to do. And let me tell you this as the ex-Head of Intelligence, 10 per cent of the 3,000 people in this building have been less than perfect, so you deal with the unknown knowns.' And I just suddenly thought that the civil service is a massive organisation, yet we exclude the very people who we talk about in oak-bound rooms, around round tables. Who in their right minds would do that?

A: It is funny because anyone who's done any management knows you have to walk the job first, but then walking the job can be built into the job by having different people around you.

K: Our diversity strategy has always talked about age, sex, religion, gender and everything else. I always used to say, 'You're old and you're poor, or you're young and you're poor, you're black and you're poor, you're Muslim and poor, you're disabled and poor. Poverty is the thing. If you have money, it doesn't solve all of your problems, but it makes it better.'

A: My take on that, I'm slightly worried at times that we always overlook the poverty gap. I think poverty is so important but actually I think what is more telling is the poverty of behaviour of parents.

K: Fair point. In the VRU, we used to deliver 'David's Story' which was a story about a young person who commits an awful offence, I would say all the things that happened to them, and someone would always come up to me at the end and say, 'I know, but I had the same background as David'. And I would say, 'But who was behind your front door?' They will always tell me about someone who absolutely loved them, who mentored them and thought about them. Sometimes they mention a teacher. I used to go to prisons frequently, and I remember I used to be in Glenochil Prison, and my dad was the Head of Biology when I was in school. And these guys would always say to me, I was always slightly worried, 'Are you Mike McCluskey's daughter?' And I would think, 'Oh, they probably hated biology'. And they used to be like, 'Hey Mr McCluskey! He was the only person who took an interest in me, he remembered our names, he was a good man, he was a great family man'. Even though my dad is 80 now, I still go into town and people say, 'Mr McCluskey!', and I keep saying to him, 'That's the difference you make!'

A: There is a wonderful YouTube video on Ian Wright, the football player. And it's the same story. He is sitting in the stand doing an interview and his teacher from many years comes up. He hadn't seen him since school days, and Ian Wright could hardly talk, he was sobbing. He could hardly get his words together because he knew that he would have been down a very different course in life if it hadn't been for this teacher because nobody else was looking out for him.

K: John Carnochan always talks about bringing your whole self to work. I think because I've always sort of done that and tried to show discretion and put in the effort, whether I wanted to or not.

*****

A: A lot of people in their jobs are sick and tired, because they feel they've not been respected for whatever they're doing.

K: I don't have any challenges around touch or giving someone a hug or whatever else. And I don't think that makes me any less of a Chief Executive. What it does is make me human. I think if we regain and reclaim our humanity and set the tone for a better society, then maybe we will all start to make better decisions about what happens with public money. What happens to our kids, what the best decisions are, and maybe we will be bolder because I think we will make the bold decisions and we won't have that terror.

A: That's a perfect lead into what made the VRU tick and work, and to be as effective as it has been...

K: I work with lots of people who make themselves spikey because everybody has let them down. I work with men and women who have this shield up. They make themselves hard to love, and hard to like. I'm going to schools, which gives me huge joy, and I've always thought I wanted it to be better for kids. I think that the people who came to the VRU saw that. I think that even the people who surrounded me had that as well.

The VRU had a clear direction. I always say I could still shut my eyes and think about what success looks like – I know what a less violent society looks like. I can still imagine what it's like for a kid to grow up in, probably, not a lot of money, but certainly have the same life chances that my kid had.

I remember listening to a girl called Roza Salih, who was one of the Glasgow girls who helped prevent the deportation of one of her friends. I asked her, 'What motivated you?', she said, 'Anger and love'. And I thought, that's a wee bit of what motivated us – anger at the loss of life and a love for the people we met around us. So, the VRU were gatherers of people, whether that was in education or health, or wherever it was, and they had the same passion as Roza. The VRU supported these people we gathered, we found out what made them feel valued and just did that. That doesn't sound very skilful, does it really?

A: I used to find it strange because people would write things about the Wise Group saying, 'What a great idea! Training long term unemployed people to insulate houses and then get them a job, what a great idea and how you managed to combine all the funding, must've been a great idea that!'

I thought, well it's not really so much the idea, because the idea sort of came together, but I think what really did work was getting a very clear sense of purpose. We had a couple of objectives. One of them was to get these people jobs, and another was to insulate houses, so it was best to keep to that, don't go off onto too many other things. Keep to that focus.

K: I don't think we are very good at focussing on self-care. I think that when we deal with anxiety, stress and horror in many ways, that the horror that the people around us experienced was so much greater. We only had the one thing, we just wanted to reduce violence. Nobody really ever said no to us, because the question was always, 'Do you want to reduce violence?' And the answer was always, 'Yes'. Then all we had to do was argue how we got there.

Whether you were in early years, you were reducing violence. Whether you were in school, you were reducing violence. Whether you were in the police, you were reducing violence. It became everybody's agenda, and we worked really hard. It was an interesting thing in terms of partnership. I never really went into the emergency rooms and said, 'I want *you* to help *me* reduce gang violence'. I used to go into the emergency rooms and say, '*I'd* like to help *you* reduce your four-hour waiting target'.

So, it became a 'virtuous circle' because people shifted themselves. I didn't need to be in charge of it. I just wanted to give people the power to go and do something different. I think that's sometimes what organisations fail to do. They keep their staff and the people they work with so tight that we stifle innovation. We stifle discretionary effort. Sir William Rae, who was a Chief Constable, said that if your values are in the right place, if you put your values into practise and if you put the person at the heart of your decision-making, you'd usually do the right thing. He said, if you make a mistake but you tell me that your values are in place, and your integrity is there, then I'll support you. And I thought that was true leadership.

A: Politicians make mistakes, and they make them in a very public way. A couple of weeks ago I was at a crafts thing and saw these T-shirts. Instead of saying, 'People Make Glasgow', it said, 'People Make Mistakes'. We all make mistakes. I have made a catalogue of mistakes, I've done many right things, but I've made a catalogue of mistakes – but at some point, you just have to recognise them and move on.

K: I think authenticity helps because I think that you become that bit more reflective. I often get asked to do leadership talks, I don't know why really because I never really think very much about it. The only thing that I've learned from any leadership course is ensuring that I practise my values and I don't let them slip. I know that I do let them slip, particularly when I'm stressed, and I stress transmit.

I make sure I sit in my main office. I don't have an office, so people can say to me, 'No, that's not how we practise'. I was talking to some new prison officers yesterday and said to them, 'Tell me how you practise your values and how you make sure they are still in place, and how do you deal with stress?' And this young black woman said, 'I often just say, I'm going off the wing for five minutes,' and she sits and thinks about what makes her do the role that she does. And she puts her values back in place.

Then she goes back in, and I think how on earth did you develop at the age of 23? I didn't get it until the age of 40, and I actually think we need people to do that a bit more. It's going to require us to have a more robust set of values that we practise constantly. It's become that thing where people put those posters on the walls with the inspirational message. I've always thought your values were the hull of a ship – it's something that cuts through the water, that makes it strong and robust – and makes us able to sail in unchartered waters. For me that's always what it's been like.

A: The things that can make change more possible in Scotland have the same kind of features. That sense of purpose, the values and it's getting the people. There's got to be some systems underneath it all that starts giving people the discretion, the agency and recognition for what they're doing. Because often what we think of them is just changing systems.

K: When you look at Scotland now, our crime at a 42-year low, our murder levels are way down. We're spending less money on that, despite the horror around that. Each murder used to cost us around £1.7 million, it's probably somewhere around £2 million pounds now to investigate, so we are saving this money. In crimes we are down, but what is left is real challenging stuff, isn't it? Around people's mental health and trauma – that requires a whole different set of skills.

A: And people going missing.

K: People going missing. So that requires a whole different set of skills, and maybe we've embarked on a journey that we're not really fit to take on yet. We haven't got the framing.

A: Because the frame is, back into what I was talking about, that these are not different problems – these are the same problems.

K: I think that is what we do in public service, and I suppose in a way Campbell Christie's Commission was a way to try and overcome that. The problem is that often, when we are faced with these problems, we go in and do system change and public service change. We spend years in this complex process of change. And only see the very problem that we were dealing with, and not beyond it.

A: The other part of having a sense of direction is having it consistently. Too much of public life is a bit like a fashion show. It's pink, with white polka dots this year, and then next year it's green, and then black. That doesn't help because people get exhausted and cynical. In fact, we need more of this coherent narrative of what we are trying to do as a group of people and our culture and our society – there is not enough of it.

K: I do think right now is the time for it. I got to listen to Obama last year. He talked about the smallness of our politics, about the real complexity of society and what to do when somebody comes up with a big idea. What happens, however, is you get the interest groups and partisans who kick it around like a football until you lose the solution in the process.

A: Interest groups are a big part of this.

K: The other thing he said, and I thought, 'Oh grief! I sort of disagree with you right now', was about Martin Luther King Jr. and the quote that he had sewn into the carpet in the Oval Office. It wasn't MLK Jr. originally, he repeated it, and it was about 'the arc of the moral universe is long, but it bends towards justice', and I thought, no it doesn't. Awful things are happening right now. Things don't bend towards justice; you have to bend it.

There is the way we speak around our children in public policy areas. Even the age of criminal responsibility, which was a tragic eight years old in Scotland, and when we wanted to move it to 12 which, for the record was still too young, they should have pushed it to 16. There was a headline that said, 'Child Thugs Will Be Roaming the Streets'. Well, you're talking about nine-year-old kids!

A: We have to focus on the first thousand days, from preconception until two or three years old. At the moment, we like to talk about other things, away from that, but you have to ground this, and if we don't, I fear that we are going to keep treading water.

The other thing that I get slightly worried about is self-satisfaction. Like, 'Scotland's the best country in the world to bring up children'. The reality is we're about 16th best, and in some things, we are really poor, some things a bit better. We can too easily get self-congratulatory.

K: It's the same with violence, people talk about a reduction. It isn't enough, never has been. How much is acceptable? The truth is none. It's a relentless goal. And you always have to assess where you are, work out if it's changed. So, its utterly iterative, and sometimes in leadership, and I see it in public sector leadership frequently, people stay in a job for three years. I stayed in my job for 16 years, where it was both good and bad. That's really unusual now.

CHAPTER 15

Gender, Power and Women

Angela O'Hagan and Talat Yaqoob

SCOTLAND HAS BECOME an international reference point for gender equality policy and for progressive equality policy in the twenty years of devolution. This perception by external observers is accurate: there have been significant advances. Those of us living in Scotland and agitating for change have seen and sought to secure a more progressive approach to advancing equality in public policy decisions and eliminating discrimination from people's everyday lives.

We also know the limitations of what has been achieved and how much remains to be done. It is one thing to judge ourselves or be judged against the low benchmark that Westminster has become in terms of social justice since 2010 and to make political capital from that distinction. It is quite another to sustain political commitment to advancing equality of opportunity and achieving equality of outcome across economic and social policy, and in the experience of and participation in decision making on public policy and resources in Scotland.

The institutions of government created in 1999 have been held to the founding principles of openness, transparency, accountability, accessibility and equality of opportunity, creating a political environment suggestive of social justice and equality. The strength of political discourse around equality has been a distinctive feature of Scotland post-devolution. To put it another way, there is a lot of talk about equality. The very early days of the Scottish Parliament appeared to set a direction for the new institutions and what the 'new politics' might really mean.

By the end of 2000 there was an Equality Strategy in place, informed by conversations and consultations across Scotland, and the insidious 'Section 28' and its prohibition on the 'promotion of homosexuality' had been repealed by MSPs. That this was one of the first areas of action by the new institution suggested a political energy and appetite to legislate for and integrate social justice in the policies and practices of Scotland. The bitterness and bigotry that char-acterised the campaigns against the repeal of 'Section 28' revealed the extent of entrenched attitudes and prejudices that prevailed in Scotland at that time. The campaigns and debates around Brexit in 2016 exposed deeply rooted prej-udices around race, ethnic and national origin, and the pervasive racism that barely skulks under the surface in Scotland, as discussed by Claire Heuchan (Sister Outrider, 2016). These experiences are real and still raw and must serve to guard against complacency and falling into the trap of our own rhetoric.

In 2018, the Scottish Parliament passed the Domestic Abuse (Scotland) Act, creating a specific offence of domestic abuse which extends to the concept of 'coercive control'. This legislation, the culmination of years of campaigning by feminist organisations in Scotland, is another landmark for Scotland and for women in Scotland. It also exemplifies the very best of what is possible to do in an associative society, where the political process is open to engagement and challenge from outside the political parties, the institutions can be accessed by civil society organisations and dialogue is possible and can lead to change. Those characteristics, positive as they are, must also be continuously challenged and stretched so that the range of voices, perspectives and lived experiences that inform political decisions really are reflective of all of Scotland's diversity.

In this brief overview that follows we discuss some areas of politics and policy, reflecting on what action there has been to support the talk and what still remains to be done in relation to women's political representation and women's economic status and independence.

Women and Politics

In recent years Scotland has been considered a leader in progressive gender politics, in some ways it has been successful, with the world leading legislation on domestic abuse, a 50:50 cabinet and legislation for equal representation of women on public boards. However, a critical eye needs to be cast over how far rhetoric around gender equality has been met by action and whether the women who need radical policy and culture change the most, have genuinely benefited over the last twenty years.

Ahead of the creation of the Scottish Parliament, activists, led by trade union women, campaigned for 50 per cent women MSPs. In the first election in 1999, 48 women became (37.2 per cent) MSPs. Despite this being far from the 50 per cent target, it was considerably higher than expected and higher than any intake of a Westminster election (which in 2017 elected its highest proportion of women; 32 per cent). However, as with most fights to tackle institutionalised inequality, progress has not been linear. At the 2003 election, we gained a small increase to 39.5 per cent however, at the 2007 election, there was a considerable drop to 33.3 per cent. At the end of 2018, 35 per cent of the MSPs were women. This is despite a resurgence of the 50:50 campaign in 2014 and a commitment by four out of five parties to field 50 per cent women candidates at local and national elections.

It is particularly important to highlight the lack of diversity within the women elected since devolution. Despite a number of men of colour being elected in this time period, no woman of colour has been elected to the Scottish Parliament. Disabled women and carers are still grossly under-represented and working-class and non-university education women are barely present as high-level public decision makers in Scotland. In the current makeup of the Parliament, there is a higher proportion of graduates from the Universities of Edinburgh and Glasgow than there are women in total. The question remains then: can we have a progressive Scotland, with so much of the population failing to be represented in the highest office of the nation?

The independence referendum was a political turning point for many across Scotland, but its impact for women is of particular interest. Both sides of the debate targeted women voters but the No vote secured a higher proportion of votes from women compared to men (by 3 per cent). This is despite the Yes movement having a significantly more organised, local, women-led and women-focused campaign, (Women for Independence). There were ripple effects of this grassroots engagement of women: the SNP saw the highest number of women candidates in the 2016 Scottish Parliament elections and from those new faces elected, the majority were engaged in some way in the activities of Women for Independence.

Despite the grassroots activity and the diversity of campaigning including the No side's 'Many Cultures Better Together' or the spin off group 'Scots Asians for Yes', that diversity has failed to have an impact on the visibility of women of colour. None of the data currently available on voting records, turn out or political engagement in relation to the independence referendum can be analysed through an intersectional lens, meaning we cannot determine the impact the referendum has had on women of colour, other than the blunt instrument of counting candidates and elected officials. The sole victory in terms of representation was the election in 2015, of Tasmina Ahmed-Sheikh, the only woman of colour to have ever represented Scotland in Westminster. However, her seat was lost in the 2017 snap election.

While steps have been taken by parties to increase the diversity of candidates, the democratic system, the culture and parliament itself needs to change. Politics remains an exclusive environment, inaccessible for most people to participate. To be a candidate can require substantial sums of money and time, which few people have. Campaigning requires evening and weekends, for those with caring responsibilities this becomes near impossible and despite efforts, political activities often remain exclusionary for disabled candidates. For Scotland to be an equality world leader, political access and culture needs radical change. Without this, it is likely we have reached a plateau in Scotland's democratic progressiveness.

Beyond representation, women who are not white, educated, financially secure and who are not already engaged in political networks, have limited influence on policy-making. Too often the voices of working-class women, disabled women, women carers and women of colour are heard after the effects of a policy are felt, rather than them being around the table when the policy is being developed. This is most obviously apparent in the disproportionate impact of local council cuts on public services used by women and the impact of austerity measures and welfare reform on women's access to essential financial support.

Across civic Scotland and wider public life, whether in trade unions, in the media or the third sector, the same groups of women appear to be engaged and those described above continue to either be isolated from participation, or an unrepresentative small number of women from these communities are cornered into becoming spokespeople. In order for Scotland to become a leader on gender equality, an improved, accessible and intersectional approach is needed to open the doors of participation to women from all backgrounds. Whilst there is goodwill to increase access to Scotland's politics and policy-making, this is unlikely to have any meaningful impact until investment is made in real outreach within communities of women, moving away from an over-reliance on formal structures such as consultation responses and evidence to committees. Real lived experience needs to be reached out to, shared and heard. In 2016–17, the most recent data available, only 37 per cent of witnesses and experts giving evidence to committees were women. Only one committee heard from more women than men, the Equalities and Human Rights Committee. The committees with the lowest proportion of women experts were; Delegated Powers and Law Reform (28 per cent), Finance and Constitution (11 per cent), Local Government and Communities (27 per cent) and Rural Economy and Connectivity (14 per cent) (Scottish Parliament, 2018).

Women's Economic Status

Women make a significant contribution to Scotland's economy through paid work, with 58 per cent of women in full-time work (compared to 87 per cent of men), and through unpaid work providing unpaid care for children, family members and other relationships. Women also provide the bulk of care in the paid care economy, which is a key sector of Scotland's economy, but not formally recognised as such in the Scottish Government's Economic Strategy which has framed economic growth as the 'overarching purpose of government' since 2007.

In 2018 there were 2,642,000 people in employment in Scotland and 731,000 people described as economically inactive. Economically inactive is the terms used for

> any individual aged 16 to 64 who is not in employment, has not looked for work in the last four weeks, and is unable to start work within the next two weeks.

The options given as reasons for economic inactivity in the survey by the Office for National Statistics (ONS) are:

> being a student and not having or looking for a job
> looking after the family and/or home
> being sick (temporary and long-term)
> being retired
> being discouraged

These options are highly gendered given the distribution of care between women and men. They also ignore, and therefore further devalue, the economic contribution of carers, disabled and sick people who continue to pay taxes, consume goods and services, and are employers in their own right. This is a fundamental problem with how economic contribution is counted and valued. In Scotland, due in part to the work of the late Ailsa McKay, founder of the WISE Research Centre, and the wider activity of the Scottish Women's Budget Group, Close the Gap, EQUATE, Engender, and trade union activists, there has been an acknowledgement by the Scottish Government of the 'limitations of our economic models' (Scottish Government, 2012: 6). The number of current initiatives from the Scottish Government in the name of Fair Work, along with the expansion programme for publicly funded childcare are evidence of a changing discourse and policy activity around women and the labour market.

The Scottish labour market has experienced significant restructuring in the last decades as a consequence of recession, public service reform, reconfiguration of work and employment across different industrial processes and occupational groups. There has been a growth in part-time working for women and men, increasing by 12.4 per cent for women and 31.6 per cent in men working part-time since 2008. However, 75.2 per cent of part-time workers are women (Scottish Government 2016).

The intersectional dimensions of race, gender and class are more problematic to expose given the poor quality and availability of relevant data. According to Scottish Government data from 2016, and using their terminology:

Minority ethnic women experience substantially lower employment rates (45.0 per cent) than white ethnic women (70.5 per cent).

Employment rates for:

Minority ethnic males (71.6 per cent) were more similar to white ethnic males (77.1 per cent) (*ibid*).

These inequalities are a focus in the Scottish Government's Race Equality Action Plan 2017–21, which, according to the Equality and Human Rights Commission,

highlights the importance of employment in addressing racial inequality, and outlines actions which will aim to address the employment gap between people from white groups and people from ethnic minority groups (EHRC, 2018:34).

Women's pay and earnings continue to lag behind men's. The gender pay gap in 2018 is 15 per cent between men and women's average hourly rates and increases to 32 per cent when comparing part-time hourly rates. The gender pay gap has been constantly in focus by government in Scotland since 1999, with a range of policies and programmes introduced and organisations such as Close the Gap funded to work with employers and trade unions to tackle the causes of the gender pay gap.

A new Action Plan on the Gender Pay Gap by the Scottish Government is in process. Despite this focus on women's pay and earnings, unequal pay and specifically the disputes with local authorities have also endured throughout the period of devolution. With their origins in the local government reorganisation of 1997 and the introduction of the Single Status Agreement, local councils have been locked into discriminatory pay schemes affecting hundreds of thousands of women across Scotland, and into years of legal action as women have sought redress and compensation for unequal pay. Audit Scotland estimated that some £232 million has been paid to 50,000 workers through compromise agreements, reached after legal decisions confirming the discriminatory nature of pay agreements negotiated throughout the 2000's. The long-running dispute with Glasgow City Council has recently been resolved.

This protracted injustice against women is also a matter of public finance management and planning. In 2007, the Scottish Parliament Equal Opportunities Committee focused on the equal pay scandal in relation to resourcing through the Scottish budget process. Audit Scotland reported in 2017 on the

27,000 claims that were still live in the employment tribunal system then and estimated that since 2004 the cost of fighting and settling equal pay claims had been around £750 million (Audit Scotland, 2017).

Audit Scotland placed the responsibility for oversight with local authorities and elected members and through ensuring compliance with the Public Sector Equality Duty. Arguably the Scottish Government has ultimate oversight of public authorities and ensuring that Scotland's public finances are managed in such a way that women are not disadvantaged by receiving unequal pay and having pension contributions allocated and protected. The numbers of women affected over many years, and the huge sums of public money denied to these women in wages and pensions (and spent defending discriminatory pay systems) has scarred the lives of thousands of women as well as the equality credentials of successive administrations in government at local and national level in Scotland.

Looking ahead to public finance tests to come, the tax competences devolved to Scotland in the 2016 Scotland Act present significant opportunities for revenue raising, and a further set of gendered economic development challenges. Currently, of the 4.5 million adults in Scotland in 2018–19, only 2.5 million are income taxpayers. This means, two million adults, or 44 per cent of the total number of adults, will not pay income tax because their earnings are less that the personal allowance of £12,000. This incredibly tight tax base reveals the extent to which Scotland is a low wage or no wage economy. We have already set out the gendered dimensions of this problem in relation to women's earnings, unpaid work, and the gender pay gap. These factors all underscore the need for economic, skills and employment policies, to boost economic growth in Scotland to be based on robust gender analysis from the outset.

Key to integrating this gender analysis is the Scottish budget process. An international success story for its openness to scrutiny, developments around the budget process in Scotland has been further distinguished by the equalities analysis in the process and documentation. Scotland is the only country in the UK to produce an Equality Budget Statement as part of the budget process and documents. It is one of very few governments globally to do this. So far, so good. The Scottish Government's Equality and Budget Advisory Group is also a one-off in the UK and a rarity worldwide. What remains to do is to integrate gender analysis, within the wider equalities mainstreaming approach of the Scottish Government, into all stages of the budget process. The recommendations for expanded equalities scrutiny by the parliamentary committees made by the Budget Review Group in 2017 are an important driver to improve the openness, accountability and transparency of Scotland's public finances and policy decisions.

The final set of comments in our skim across gender, women and power in Scotland talk to the institutional support for advancing women's economic, political and social status. Women work hard in Scotland to press for feminist change in the public and private lives of women. There is a long and deservedly proud tradition of feminist activism in Scotland that pre-dates devolution and has continued since. Some organisations have come and gone, and others such as Engender, Scottish Women's Budget Group, EQUATE, STUC Women's Committee, Scottish Women's Aid, Close the Gap have endured, and new voices from different perspectives such as Women's Enterprise Scotland and Women for Independence (Independence for Women) have emerged and enriched the debate.

What has remained more constant in recent years are some of the limitations on these organisations and on the institutional 'machinery' for gender equality. Funding for women's organisations has been defended within the Scottish budget, and while gratefully retained it has not been increased in recent years.

The Equal Opportunities Commission was the statutory body for sex equality in 1999 and was replaced in 2007 by the Equality and Human Rights Commission under the Equality Act, 2006. The new body incorporated the existing commissions on sex, race and disability, into an expanded remit including human rights. For some this represented a dilution of focus on gender, conflating and equating 'equalities' issues and losing specificity. Concerns around the breadth of focus are also reflected in the maintenance of an 'equalities mainstreaming' approach by successive Scottish Governments, following the commitment of the first Scottish Executive to this approach as set out in the first – and only – Equality Strategy in 2000. The combination of funding constraints, including the consistently reducing budget and reach of the EHRC in Scotland and across Great Britain, and the formulation of a politics of equivalence in relation to equalities 'issues', means even greater pressure on feminist organisations to remain vigilant and maintain pressure on government to commit to and advance gender equality and women's economic, social and political status.

There is a preconception that Scotland has a more progressive and inclusive attitude. However, findings from social attitude surveys reveal only a modest difference between attitudes towards tax, education and inequality in Scotland from the rest of the UK (ScotCen, 2011). This idea of progressiveness can create complacency in the pursuit of radical equality. This is most notable when we review the lack of progress, and even simply the lack of available data to analyse policy impact, for women who experience multiple discriminations; sexism and racism, islamophobia, bigotry, classism or disabilism.

A stark illustration of how far we need to go on attitudes towards gender equality can be seen in the treatment of women activists and commentators, even with so-called 'progressive' spaces. Most recently journalist Vonny LeClerc and councillor Rhiannon Spear who have come under fire (largely from men) for highlighting the all-male line up of speakers at a pro-independence rally and the promotion of men in the Yes movement who have been accused of sexist behaviour towards women. Any movement campaigning for a more inclusive Scotland cannot have gender equality as a sidebar called upon when politically convenient, it must champion and embed gender equality at every turn.

Civil society organisations are only one part of the whole. Government, political parties, academia and research bodies, civil and criminal justice systems and our educational curriculum and institutions all have a role in maintaining the positive course set upon devolution and steering Scotland to become the more equal and socially just country we like to think we are.

References

Audit Scotland (2017), 'Equal pay in Scottish councils', available online at: http://www.audit-scotland.gov.uk/uploads/docs/report/2017/nr_170907_equal_pay.pdf, accessed 1 December 2018.

Equality and Human Rights Commission (2018), 'Is Scotland fairer? The state of equality and human rights 2018', available online at: https://www.equalityhumanrights.com/sites/default/files/is-britain-fairer-2018-is-scotland-fairer.pdf

Heuchan, C. (2016), 'Race, History, and Brexit: Black Scottish Identity', available online at: https://sisteroutrider.wordpress.com/2016/10/26/race-history-and-brexit-black-scottish-identity/, accessed 2 December 2018.

ScotCen (2011), 'Is Scotland more left-wing than England?', *British Attitudes Survey*, No. 42, 5 December 2011, available online at: www.scotcen.org.uk/media/176048/2011-is-scotland-more-left-wing-than-england.pdf, accessed 1 December 2018.

Scottish Government (2012), 'Equality statement: Scottish draft budget 2013–14', Edinburgh: Scottish Government.

Scottish Government (2016), 'Regional Employment Patterns in Scotland: Statistics from the Annual Population Survey 2016 Key findings for 2016', available online at: www.gov.scot/publications/

regional-employment-patterns-scotland-statistics-annual-population-sur-vey-2016-9781786529879/, accessed 1 December 2018.

Scottish Parliament (2018), 'Committee Witnesses – gender and repre-sentation' Research Briefings', available online at: https://digital-publications.parliament.scot/ResearchBriefings/Report/2018/2/27/Committee-witnesses--gender-and-representation#Appendix

Scottish Parliament Information Centre (2018), 'Labour Market Update: March 2018', available online at: https://sp-bpr-en-prod-cdnep.azureedge.net/published/2018/3/26/Labour-Market-Update--March-2018-1/SB%20 18-23.pdf

CHAPTER 16

Generational Gridlock Scotland?

Laura Jones

Generational thinking has always been reductive and condescending...
Here's your participation trophy: you old.

Adam Conover, *Millennials Don't Exist!, Deep Shift Conference (2016)*

FOR SOME REASON, I played a 1980s edition of Trivial Pursuit with my father when I was around ten years old. I don't know why we were playing for slices of plastic pie (or cheese, depending on your own upbringing) in a game I could never win. Maybe I found the packaging and neon pieces to be appealing, the quest for trivial knowledge irresistible. Maybe I was a young, budding masochist and loved a one-sided game, even not in my favour. Maybe my dad just enjoyed winning. I think about that game a lot and it was only through writing about generational gridlock that I connected some dots.

A cursory search of 'generational gridlock' on the Internet will only bring up a handful of results with international application, ranging from high unemployment rates across the Arab world in 2009 'creating a growing generational gridlock in the Middle East' (Queen Rania, 2009) to oppositional US analysis in 'Baby Boomers in Congress have given us gridlock: research shows Gen Xers will be more productive' (Rosen, 2016).

The first time I heard the term 'baby boomer' was during that game of Trivial Pursuit. I remember being sat on the living room floor in my hometown of Gardenstown in Aberdeenshire, picking up a musty, yellowing advert for the 'baby boomer' version of the game. I wondered if I would do better at that version than the 80s one, even though I had no idea what it meant. I worried that playing this particular game by these kinds of rules may never see me victorious.

Now, whenever I see a baby boomer vs. gen x/millennial headline, one that encourages a kind of generational opposition, that same feeling of hopelessness creeps over me. I feel hopeless that I, a millennial of 28 years, am expected to instinctively hate the baby boomers, as media often encourages. I didn't hate my father, a baby boomer, for winning at his game. I hated the game and its rules that just weren't made for me or my generation. In Scotland and the wider world, we're playing a losing game that is tipped in favour of the boomers, as voted for by the boomers to a large extent. That's the generational gridlock I've unfortunately come to learn and live by.

In Scotland, the main adopter of 'generational gridlock' is Gerry Hassan, who has said that within the Scottish political commentariat 'there has been little natural evolution or transition to a younger generation finding voice: this is in effect part of a generational gridlock'. (Hassan, 2014).

This may have been the case when this comment was made in 2014 but I would argue that in the four years since, though we still hear from the likes of Ruth Wishart, Joyce McMillan and Iain Macwhirter, we are now offered the younger voices from Vonny LeClerc in *The National*, digitally edited by millennial Stephen Paton; Sean Bell as a reporter for *CommonSpace*; and Robert J Somynne and Michael Gray within their new platform of *The Scotia* – to name a few. The shackles of said gridlock within Scottish political media are loosening so I'm more concerned about the millennial day-to-day life and within oppositional rhetoric as part of the gridlock.

Because generational brackets are inconsistent across official census and media internationally, I have to choose my own range for millennial definition (I roughly consider those born between the mid-1980s and mid-1990s to be the millennial generation and that the baby boomer generation is vaguely considered those born between the mid-1940s and mid-1960s). This indicates a dubious method with which to classify swathes of individuals. For convenience within this essay, I use these terms, but it is with reluctance.

Popular societal myth-debunker Adam Conover took generational bracketing and terminology to task in a keynote speech at the Deep Shift conference in 2016, revealing that Neil Howe and William Strauss coined the term 'millennial' in the US and launched LifeCourse Associates which interprets qualitative data of a generation's collective persona to allow marketers to target them efficiently. My reluctance to use the term 'millennial' stems from its identity not being created for any kind of representational accuracy; it was for the profit of two baby boomer gentlemen.

With that in mind, 'Generational thinking has always been reductive and condescending' (Conover, 2016). And, the media is only happy to portray millennials as lazy, narcissistic, and entitled, while baby boomers are rich, ignorant and selfish – which only further encourages us to repeatedly fall foul to vitriolic finger pointing between generations, an unhelpful side effect of generational gridlock. The younger millennials are first shackled by the decisions and voting powers of the generations before them, and *then* they are encouraged to blame and attack in what is simply generational opposition.

In a BBC article about the UK's 2016 vote to leave the EU, the headline panders to such opposition: 'Unequal Scotland: Baby boomers vs. millennials'. Independent adviser to the Scottish Government on poverty and inequality Naomi Eistenstadt is quoted in 2016 as saying:

> My generation is the last generation that is safe... I'm the last of the baby boomers, and I think it is absolutely appalling, the amount of free stuff I get at the cost of younger families, particularly families with children, and in fact working age adults with children (Fraser, 2016).

Eistenstadt makes an admission on behalf of her generation that many boomers in my life also acknowledge, but millennials cannot rely on the remorse of a generation. They must be engaged and aware as to the gridlock they've been gifted and seek ways to write new rules to a new game.

Glancing to Scotland and the 2014 independence referendum, millennials were arguably more vocal and visible than usual at the forefront of the Yes campaign, as seen in cultural movement National Collective. By campaigning through art in multiple mediums, gathering 4,000 members, and educating and inspiring young voters, National Collective was an admirable, albeit imperfect initiative by proactive, millennials. Indyref saw 96 per cent of 18 to 24-year-old voters opt for independence, 82 per cent for the 25 to 34 year olds (Burdz Eye View, 2014).

If that were not enough of a kick to the teeth to millennials, a no-deal Brexit, would cost every single millennial £108,000 between 2018 and 2050 (O'Carroll, 2018), looms ever nearer. Brexit is something that 72 per cent of voting millennials were against (Boult, 2016), that 62 per cent of Scotland was against (BBC News, 2016), and that two million new millennials are eligible to vote against since June 2016 (O'Carroll, 2018), should they wish. Sadly, with millennials being the lowest turnout for the Brexit vote (Parkinson, 2016), I can only assume a steady apathy across younger voters which may be remedied when they grow to the age at which to appreciate what kind of UK their parents and grandparents may have voted them into – a generational gridlock.

In future, millennials may be pushed out of apathy due to repeatedly oppositional headlines that populate our newsfeeds every day. The BBC couldn't resist the baby boomers vs. millennial slant as mentioned earlier, but the headlines get worse when we look to the US: 'Upset by political gridlock? Blame the baby boomers' (Montgomery, 2015) said the *Kansas City Star* in 2015. The AARP Foundation found some horrendous ones in 2014 including:

> Hey, kids, wake up!... Old people are doing everything possible to rob you of your money, your future, your dignity, and your freedom (Dunkel, 2014).

How about 'It's not revolting Brexiteer baby boomers that centrists should fear – it's the millennials' (Jacobs, 2018)? Give us strength. As a generation we are misrepresented and misunderstood across the board. We should not do the same to boomers, no matter how tempting it might be to rise to it, encouraged through today's goading online articles and social media. Living well is the best revenge and if any generation is best equipped to creatively play with the gridlocked hand that has been dealt by the boomers, it is the millennial generation.

By starting my publishing company, 404 Ink, with fellow millennial Heather McDaid in the wake of the Brexit vote in 2016, I wanted to take a stand against millennial misrepresentation and let the millennial voices I publish speak for me. By refusing to play the losing game of insecure employment that is the Scottish and UK publishing industry and beyond, by refusing to let No voters and Brexiteers determine my life in totality, I'm taking a personal and financial risk to escape the gridlock placed upon me by self-serving voters, whether boomer, Gen X or millennial. It's an undeniable struggle, and not possible for everyone, but the option to rip up the rulebook and start a new game is there, if you're able.

Sometimes the feeling of being locked in this lifestyle, one of constant insecurity while looking at a generation of considerable comfort, is exasperating. I currently barely afford to live in a rented flat in Edinburgh with my American partner, fearful for our future together in a post-Brexit, non-independent Scotland, while neither of us will ever catch a glimpse of the property ladder, let alone tread on a rung. I'm lucky to have undergraduate and postgraduate degrees but student debt follows me from one freelance job or zero-hour contract job to another. My publishing company is on the rise, but the idea of job security or a pension is laughable.

But, through my determination to resist apathy, oppositionalism, and to make my progressive, discursive, and confrontational publishing company a success by *my* rules, to safeguard my own and my children's futures, I hope to show millennials *can* prosper in a gridlocked existence, especially in a progressive Scotland. I voted Yes for Indyref, remain for Brexit, and always feel the same pang of loss I felt during that familial game of Trivial Pursuit, when a vote doesn't go my way.

'I would do better with the baby boomer edition,' I said to my dad, waving the old advert. 'Do you even know what 'baby boomer' means?' my father questioned. I was too embarrassed to say I did not. I thought that 'baby boomer' meant easy mode, a version for younger players that infants could win. Full of optimism, I did not realise that I would have failed at the baby boomer game just as much as I did with the 80s version.

Now, I choose not to fixate on the rules for prior generations. Now, it's my game, my rules.

References

Boult, A. (2016), 'Millennials 'fury' over baby boomers' vote for Brexit', *The Telegraph*, available online at: https://www.telegraph.co.uk/news/2016/06/24/millenials-fury-over-baby-boomers-vote-for-brexit/

Burdz Eye View (2014), 'Independence is definitely a generational thing', available online at https://burdzeyeview.wordpress.com/tag/millennials/

Conover, A. (2016), 'Millennials Don't Exist!', Deep Shift conference, available online at: https://www.youtube.com/watch?v=-HFwok9SlQQ

Fraser, D. (2016), 'Unequal Scotland: Baby boomers vs. millennials', BBC, available online at: https://www.bbc.co.uk/news/uk-scotland-38048492

Hassan, G. (2014), *Independence of the Scottish Mind: Elite Narratives, Public Spaces and the Making of a Modern Nation*, London: Palgrave.

O'Carroll, L. (2018), 'Millennials may lose up to £108k over 30 years with no-deal Brexit', *The Guardian*, available online at: https://www.theguardian.com/politics/2018/oct/25/millennials-may-lose-up-to-108k-over-30-years-with-no-deal-brexit

Queen Rania al Abdullah Media Centre (2009), 'Queen Rania urges the need to 'solve generational gridlock in the Middle East' during panel at the Clinton Global Initiative', available online at: https://www.queenrania.jo/en/media/articles/during-clinton-global-initiative-panel-human-capital

Rosen, D.L. (2016), 'How to Fix Washington: Elect Generation X', available online at: https://www.politico.com/magazine/story/2016/01/how-to-fix-washington-elect-generation-x-213566

BBC News (2016), 'EU referendum: Scotland backs Remain as UK votes Leave', available online at: https://www.bbc.co.uk/news/uk-scotland-scotland-politics-36599102

Parkinson, H.J. (2016), 'Young people are so bad at voting – I'm disappointed in my peers', *The Guardian*, available online at: https://www.theguardian.com/commentisfree/2016/jun/28/young-people-bad-voting-millennials-eu-vote-politics

Montgomery, R. (2015), 'Upset by political gridlock? Blame the baby boomers', *The Kansas City Star*, available online at: https://www.kansascity.com/news/politics-government/article17411765.html

Dunkel, T. (2014), 'A War Between the Old and the Young?', AARP Foundation, available online at: https://www.aarp.org/politics-society/advocacy/info-2014/the-generation-war.html

Jacobs, S. (2018), 'It's not revolting Brexiteer baby boomers that centrists should fear – it's the millennials', *The Telegraph*, available online at: https://www.telegraph.co.uk/politics/2018/09/11/not-revolting-brexiteer-baby-boomers-centrists-should-fear/

CHAPTER 17

Rainbow Nation
A Story of Progress?

Caitlin Logan

OVER THE PAST two decades, Scotland has experienced a sea-change in both legal equality and public attitudes towards LGBT people. Indeed, while politics has become sharply divided along constitutional lines, LGBT rights is a policy area on which each of the Scottish parties has come to largely agree.

Historically, Scotland was the country which dragged its feet on decriminalising sex between adult men for 13 years after England and Wales first lifted the ban in 1967. This was a decision thought to be driven by the views of religious bodies and the general public and supported somewhat by opinion polling taken in 1957 which indicated that 85 per cent of Scots opposed decriminalisation, compared with just 51 per cent in an English poll (MacNicol, 2017). It was, in large part, due to the hard-fought efforts of campaigners, including the Scottish Minorities Group, that the law in Scotland was equalised in 1980 after the European Court of Human Rights ruled in their favour.

Fast forward to the present day, and the leader of the Scottish Conservative Party is Ruth Davidson, an 'out' lesbian, who has recently given birth to her and her partner's first child. Nine other currently serving MSPs have spoken publicly about being lesbian, gay or bisexual, along with ten Scottish MPs. And after rafts of legislative reform in the Scottish Parliament, Scotland was ranked the best place in Europe for LGBTI equality for two years running in 2015–16, before falling to second place in 2017 and 2018 (ILGA-Europe, 2015–2018).

Like all progress, this transformation seemed to happen slowly, then all at once. LGBT activism developed as a strong force in Scotland throughout the 1980s and 90s with the formation of numerous campaigning and cultural organisations. When the Scottish Parliament opened its doors, the Equality Network had been set up to push for LGBT equality in Scotland two years earlier and the Stonewall Youth Project – which would become LGBT Youth Scotland in 2003 – had been in operation for almost a decade, while Stonewall Scotland, the younger sibling of Stonewall UK, was established in 2000, just in time to work with Scotland's newly elected members.

What Holyrood and the devolution settlement brought with it was a more direct line between these advocates and their representatives, and the scene was set for a strong partnership to be formed between civil society and the political class.

The Labour-Liberal Democrat Years

1999–2007

The Labour-Liberal Democrat coalition, elected in 1999, did not waste any time in demonstrating the devolved parliament's willingness and capacity to pass socially progressive legislation. Within its first year, the coalition announced its plans to scrap the now notorious 'Section 28', or 2a in Scotland, introduced by the Thatcher Government in the Local Government Act, 1986 to ban local authorities and schools from 'promoting' homosexuality.

Despite millions spent on advertising and public opinion polling by the Keep the Clause campaign, led by Stagecoach owner and major SNP donor Brian Souter, alongside a sustained campaign of negative media coverage, MSPs voted 99 to 17 to repeal the clause. Westminster would follow suit three years later.

Over the next seven years of the coalition's rule, successive legal reforms introduced by the UK Labour Government advanced the rights of LGBT people in Scotland. 2001 brought the equalisation of the age of consent; discrimination based on sexual orientation was prohibited in employment in 2003 and in the provision of goods and services in 2007; and 2004 saw the Scottish Executive grant consent for the introduction of Civil Partnerships for same sex couples, while the Gender Recognition Act, which allowed transgender people to change the gender on their birth certificates in line with an Equality and Human Rights Court ruling.

Meanwhile, the Scottish Executive took steps to cement its status as a champion of equality, from including LGBT people in its first Equality Strategy and providing funding in 2002 to engage LGBT people in policy-making, to equalising the rights of same-sex and mixed-sex cohabiting couples in 2006 and legalising joint adoption by same-sex couples the following year.

The SNP

The Early Years

The election of the first SNP minority Government in 2007 brought with it uncertainty: would the nationalist party, traditionally regarded as relying on support amongst some of Scotland's more socially conservative and religious voters, be bold enough to keep up the momentum on LGBT equality?

Despite the perception of an, at times, overly cautious approach, driven by a preoccupation with maintaining the goodwill of ideologically disparate communities (or in other words: pleasing all of the people all of the time), a continuing positive relationship with LGBT rights advocates has been borne out by the party's first 11 years in office.

In its first year of power, the SNP Government provided funding for the establishment of the Scottish Transgender Alliance – the first trans rights project to be funded by a national government in Europe – and it continues to do so in 2019. In 2009, a private member's bill introduced by Scottish Green MSP Patrick Harvie was passed unanimously to expand hate crime law to include offences aggravated by disability, sexual orientation and transgender identity. This made Scotland the first place in Europe to specifically protect against offences motivated by transphobia, one year before the UK-wide Equality Act, which put in place protections against discrimination based on 'gender reassignment' for the first time.

The SNP's first term also saw the introduction of new sexual offences legislation, which finally removed 'gross indecency' and 'sodomy' as criminal offences, both of which had historically been used to prosecute gay men.

Equal Marriage

Arguably the most contentious moment for the Scottish Parliament since the repeal of Section 2a came with the consultation on the legalisation of same-sex marriage, which began in 2011, three years after the launch of the Equal Marriage campaign.

Headed up by the Equality Network along with an alliance of other organisations, the campaign's eventual success was a testament to activists' commitment in the face of a drawn out political process and virulent opposition from a co-ordinated campaign by Scotland for Marriage and CARE for Scotland (Christian Action Research and Education) – both abundant with familiar faces from the 2000 Keep the Clause efforts, including the Catholic Church, the Free Church of Scotland and the England-based Christian Institute.

The question was initially raised in Scotland in the form of a petition put forward in 2009, but the Scottish Government argued it would be too logistically complex to achieve without legalisation in England and Wales. Thus, it was when Westminster launched its own consultation in 2011 – an important nod to the modern Conservative Party's new openness to socially progressive policy – that the wheels were set in motion in Scotland.

LGBT campaigners were kept on their toes for some time by the two-stage consultation, cabinet committee deliberations, and discussion with the UK Government in order to secure what were deemed as sufficient legal protections for religious opponents of same-sex marriage. But on 4 February 2014, equal marriage passed in the Scottish Parliament with 105 to 18 votes, and, while England and Wales ultimately saw their first same-sex marriages six months earlier, the law in Scotland has been commended for being more trans-inclusive, because it does not require people to gain the consent of their spouse before legally changing gender. Four years later, the Church of Scotland, which strongly opposed the legislation, has voted to draw up internal laws to allow ministers to choose to conduct same-sex marriages.

A Problem Solved?

With the pardoning of men who were convicted of historical 'homosexual offences' along with a public apology from First Minister Nicola Sturgeon in 2018, the fight for formal equality for lesbian, gay and bisexual people is in many ways a battle won. This legal progress is, on one hand, indicative of changing public opinion, and, on the other, a driving force in shaping social attitudes in itself.

By the time the equal marriage consultation began, a 2011 Scottish Social Attitudes Survey had shown that 61 per cent supported same-sex marriage; and by the time the first marriages were performed in 2014, this had climbed to 68 per cent. In 2000, when Clause 2a was scrapped, only 37 per cent of people agreed that same-sex relationships were 'rarely wrong' or 'not wrong at all'. By 2010, this had risen to 58 per cent, and by 2015 it stood at 69 per cent.

That being said, research suggests that discrimination and inequality is yet to be relegated to history. A 2018 report by LGBT Youth Scotland found that 92 per cent of LGBT young people had been bullied in education, and that one in five of those had left education as a result. That homophobic and transphobic bullying has not been sufficiently tackled is perhaps unsurprising, given that research by Stonewall Scotland in 2014 found that almost half of secondary teachers and 75 per cent of primary teachers were unsure of whether mentioning LGBT issues in schools was allowed. This demonstrates that legislation can only take equality so far: awareness raising, and education is integral to changing 'hearts and minds'.

Inclusive Education

Since activists Jordan Daly and Liam Stevenson launched the Time for Inclusive Education (TIE) campaign in the aftermath of the 2014 independence referendum, the question of how to make schools a more welcoming place for LGBTI young people – which had been high on the agenda of organisations like LGBT Youth Scotland for years – has gained new momentum.

The TIE campaign called for LGBT issues to be covered in initial teacher training, continuous professional development, and for the creation of new legislation to require schools to be proactive in tackling prejudice by including LGBTI identities in the curriculum (from history, to English, to sex and relationships education) and to record incidents of homophobic, biphobic and transphobic bullying.

Harnessing public and political support, including a majority of MSPs and Scottish MPs, the campaign catalysed the Scottish Government's decision to set up an LGBTI Inclusive Education working group in 2017. By the end of 2018, the recommendations of the working group, which consisted of education and equalities experts including Daly and Stevenson, were published, backing each of the aims put forward by the campaign – bar the introduction of new legislation *per se*.

Instead, it called on the Scottish Government to insert new outcomes into existing statutory guidance requiring LGBTI-related themes to be covered in the curriculum, to be monitored through school inspections, and for Education Scotland and the Scottish Qualifications Authority (SQA) to update their materials to reflect this.

The Scottish Government, in a landmark step, accepted the recommendations in full, to be implemented by 2021. Importantly, the working group included the Scottish Catholic Education Service, which signed off on the report, with no opt-out for any public school – another sign of just how far things have come since 'the Clause'.

Equal Recognition

Despite the leaps and bounds in other areas, trans rights continue to lag behind, as do public attitudes on the issue. The consultation on reforming the Gender Recognition Act to make legal gender change simpler, which began in Scotland in late 2017, closely followed by a similar consultation in England and Wales, has become the source of significant controversy.

The proposed reforms would remove the need for a psychiatric diagnosis before changing the 'sex' marker on a birth certificate, lower the age limit from 18 to 16, or 12 with parental consent, and introduce a third, non-binary option. Questions have been raised in the media over the impact on children's and women's safety and equality of allowing a self-declaration process, with considerable voice given to campaign groups set up to oppose the changes, such as For Women Scotland and Women and Girls Scotland and, south of the border, Fair Play for Women and Woman's Place UK.

However, as the reforms were backed by all five of the elected parties in Scotland in their 2016 manifestos in some form, and the country's leading feminist organisations have spoken out in support of the changes and emphasised their existing policy of trans inclusion based on self-declaration. With over 15,000 individuals and 100 organisations responding to the Scottish consultation, two-thirds of respondents backed all three of the main reforms.

This picture is the result of years of close partnership working between the LGBT and women's sectors, supported by the existence of a national trans specific project, and the fact that Scottish organisations have defined as 'LGBT' since the late 1990s; for example, while Stonewall UK only expanded to include trans people in 2015, Stonewall Scotland was an LGBT organisation since 2000.

Unfortunately this has not been enough to insulate Scotland from an increasingly hostile debate, with 15 members of the SNP, including three government ministers, four additional MSPs and four MPs signing a letter in April 2019 calling on the First Minister not to 'rush' the legislation, arguing that the reforms would amount to 'changing the definition of male and female'.

Meanwhile, others in the SNP have taken pains to reiterate their support of trans rights, with a large group of members and elected representatives being photographed with trans pride flags at the party's spring conference of 2019. Earlier in the year, SNP Councillor and TIE campaign chair Rhiannon Spear coordinated an open letter criticising negative and misleading media coverage around trans rights, signed by over 500 women in Scotland.

Polarisation around the topic led to the release of a statement by the Scottish Government Cabinet Secretary for Social Security and Older People, Shirley-Ann Somerville, in which she emphasised her own support for the rights of trans people and the Government's intention to address discrimination faced by trans people as well as working through the concerns which have been raised. This, and statements of support from the First Minister, are likely to give some reassurance to LGBT rights campaigners, but more than a year on from the consultation's closing date, a definitive response from the Scottish Government is awaited with nervous anticipation.

Looking Forward

Although the addition of the 'I' onto LGBTI has come into common usage, in many cases this is treated as a silent letter. Scottish campaigners, spearheaded by Equality Network, are seeking to change this by partnering with intersex people and organisations across the UK in order to learn more about their experiences.

While intersex people, who are born with variations of sex characteristics (including genitals, gonads and chromosome patterns), differ on whether they identify with the LGBTI community, it is considered that they share overlapping experiences. Established LGBT organisations in Scotland may be well-placed to replicate their successes to date with respect to intersex equality: indeed, in light of an increased push for such rights to be embedded into policy, the Scottish Government is due to launch a consultation on how to address the issues experienced by intersex people.

If Scotland were to introduce legislation which specifically protects against discrimination of intersex people, or against surgery or treatment of sex characteristics without informed consent, this would make it among one of the first in the world to meet UN recommendations by doing so (United Nations, 2016). This, along with gender recognition reforms, could well put Scotland back in the top spot for LGBTI rights.

In Scotland, LGBT equality has in many ways been 'mainstreamed', with even those on the right of the political spectrum speaking in its favour. None of this progress has happened in a vacuum, by accident or due to the simple goodwill of politicians: it has been the result of years of coordinated efforts on the part of activists who have been politically astute and, above all, resolute.

In many ways, Scotland's status as a small country has worked in campaigners' favour, allowing relationships to be formed and shared understandings developed. Now, as Scotland's LGBT organisations turn their attention to international injustices, it may well be that the world, too, can learn something valuable from the successes of a small nation.

References

ILGA Report (2015–18) 'Annual Review of the Human Rights Situation of Lesbian, Gay, Bisexual, Trans and Intersex People in Europe', available online at: https://www.ilga-europe.org/sites/default/files/Attachments/annual_review_final2018_web.pdf, accessed 29 October 2018.

MacNicol, D. (2017), 'Illegal to be gay – Scotland's history', BBC Scotland, 27 July 2017, available online at: https://www.bbc.co.uk/news/uk-scotland-40731733, accessed 29 October 2018.

Lough Dennell, B.L., Anderson, G. and McDonnell, D. (2018) 'Life in Scotland for LGBT Young People', LGBT Youth Scotland, available online at: www.lgbtyouth.org.uk/media/1354/life-in-scotland-for-lgbt-young-people.pdf, accessed 29 October 2018.

ScotCen Social Research (2014), 'Support for same-sex marriage in Scotland reaches all-time high', available online at: http://scotcen.org.uk/news-media/press-releases/2014/december/support-for-same-sex-marriage-in-scotland-reaches-all-time-high/, accessed 29 October 2018.

Scottish Government (2017) 'Sexual orientation in Scotland 2017: summary of evidence base, Scottish Government, 2017', available online at: www.gov.scot/publications/sexual-orientation-scotland-2017-summary-evidence-base/pages/7/, accessed 29 October 2018.

Stonewall Scotland (2014), 'The Teachers' Report', available online at: https://www.stonewall.org.uk/system/files/scot_teachers_report_2014_final_lo_res.pdf, accessed 29 October 2018.

United Nations Human Rights (2016), 'Fact Sheet: Intersex', available online at: https://docs.google.com/viewerng/viewer?url=http://interactadvocates.org/wp-content/uploads/2016/02/United-Nations_FactSheet_Intersex.pdf, accessed 29 October 2018.

CHAPTER 18

Race Equality and Nationhood

Nasar Meer

ANY ACCOUNT OF ethnic and racial minorities in Scotland since devolution needs to rest in a broader history of modern Scotland. What this chapter discusses are two specific issues that would be important for that history. The first details the present scale and experiences of racial inequality in Scotland, including what powers exist under the devolution settlement to address this. The second is the more nebulous but no less relevant question of national identity, and specifically how this cultivates a certain kind of political environment in which black and ethnic minorities negotiate post-devolution Scotland.

We might begin by recognising that Scotland has come some way since Martin MacEwen (1980) wondered if 'race-relations' in it were best characterised by 'ignorance or apathy' in Scotland. Yet even if the entirety of this complaint looks out of place, something of the charge remains. As recent studies have shown, about a third of black and minority ethnic (BAME) groups in Scotland continue to report experiences of racial discrimination, and a slightly higher number consider racial discrimination to be a widespread issue in Scotland (Meer, 2015 and Meer, 2017). Interestingly, the same research reports that 60per cent of respondents who had experienced discrimination in the last five y ears did not report it to any kind of authority. This was despite 82 per cent of the entire sample insisting they would encourage a friend or family to make a formal complaint if they thought they had experienced discrimination. What this implies is that significant degrees of both low-level and more obvious experiences of racial discrimination can go under-reported.

How should we understand this in a country where the prevailing political rhetoric leans against racial inequalities? One means is to refocus not on what politicians say but on everyday experiences, in which surviving racial discrimination is a normalised strategy. While limited, the lens of 'racial microaggressions' is useful here. These are the 'brief and common place daily verbal, behavioural, or environmental indignities, whether intentional or unintentional, that communicates hostile, derogatory or negative racial slights and insults' (Sue *et al.*, 2007). If we accept that the understanding of race and racism in Scotland cannot be reduced to a microaggressions alone, it might be adopted with caution to explain how BAME groups compartmentalise or bracket off racial experiences in their wider negotiation of social life. Of course, this is a complex social practice, but this reading is supported by studies that have undertaken precisely this type of work. Moreover, while we are talking here about subjectivity or people's perceptions, it equally tied to material and institutional inequalities, something quite easily demonstrated by pointing to structural racial inequalities in Scotland (Meer, 2018).

As the Scottish Parliament's Equal Opportunities Committee (2016) notes, despite equivalent education and skills BAME Scots are more likely to be unemployed or in low-paid work than their white counterparts. This was especially highlighted in the written submission from the Coalition of Racial Equality and Rights (CRER), which stated that:

> 17.7 per cent of BAME people interviewed for local authority jobs were appointed, compared to a figure of 31.9 per cent for white interviewees (2016).

It is a finding that sits in a broader employment gap between BAME and white people in Scotland, and which Scottish Government (2015a) data has shown to be significant (in 2013, 57.4 per cent BAME groups were in employment compared with 73.8 per cent of non-BAME groups). This discrepancy can be seen to permeate efforts to redress inequalities too, with the Modern Apprenticeships being the most prominent example, and where the proportion of people from BAME groups number 2.1 per cent against 5.2 per cent of those possibly qualified to be in receipt of one (Skills Development Scotland, 2016).

In some respect devolution has expanded Scotland's ability to pursue racial equality, even though matters of equality are formally reserved to Westminster in the Scotland Act (1998). Some of this is a reflection of contingency and some of this is a reflection of design, since a number of developments that can be traced to a distinctively Scottish, rather than UK, experience. First, while the primary legislation of public equality duties is set by UK statute, the secondary legislation that facilitates its operation across devolved areas is the responsibility of the Scottish Government. This means that, theoretically, the Scottish Government can go further than England and Wales (where the UK Parliament legislates *both* for primary legislation and secondary legislation). The question this raises asks whether Scottish Governments have diverged from the UK in these respects? Much depends on how this question is posed. For example, since devolution Scottish administrations have shown a commitment to mainstreaming race equality, in ways that go beyond the minimum required. An illustration of this is the Race Equality Framework (Scottish Government, 2016) that set out the Scottish Government's vision and strategy for race-equality over a 16-year period. The framework document itself reflects on the successes and limitations of prevailing race equality approaches in Scotland, and registers gaps in data and other kinds of practice-based knowledge that might hinder the delivery of effective race equality strategies. One civil servant central to its development characterises it as 'a point in the crossroads' (interview with author), something which reflects a feeling that it *may* (rather than *has*) facilitated divergence.

In this respect policy equally relies on the prevailing story about what contemporary Scotland is and wants to be, and here the discursive features of national identity are central. What is the evidence that appeals to nationhood that might be suited to address these challenges? When authors such as Hanif Kureshi and Salman Rushdie, and politicians including Diane Abbott and Bernie Grant, tackled Britishness in the 1980s they held a mirror up to white British society and asked, 'Who do you think you are?' Today it would be impossible to think of the identity of Britain without placing minorities at its core. Something similar is yet to happen to Scottish identity.

At the last census, 4 per cent of Scotland's 5.5. million population considered themselves 'minority ethnic' compared to 14 per cent in England (Scottish Government, 2018, Audickas, 2016, 4). Within this population, there are also different demographic dynamics. In Scotland, the largest 'visible' ethnic minority group were Scottish Asian populations at 2.7 per cent (compared to 8 per cent in England), whilst African, Caribbean and Black populations made up 0.8 per cent (compared to 3 per cent in England) (Scottish Government, 2018). The 2011 populations marked notable increases in both populations, Scottish Asian populations had doubled since 2001 (from 1.4 per cent), whilst African, Caribbean and Black populations quadrupled (from 0.2 per cent). In the coming decades, these dynamics are likely to continue and the ethnic minority population in Scotland is predicted to double what it was in 2001, approaching 10 per cent by the middle of the century.

The prevailing assumption of commentators and political actors is that Scotland has achieved a broadly inclusive 'big tent' national identity. In this view Scotland is comfortable with multicultural and multi-ethnic difference because it does not anchor itself in ideas of blood and soil. Of course, there is an instrumental logic to recruiting minorities into projects of nation-building. Politicians love to be photographed next to ethnic minorities in kilts or to attend events like the Scottish Asian Business Awards. As the sociologist of nationalism David McCrone (2001) put it some years ago:

> Better in terms of *realpolitik* to draw the boundary around as many as possible; better to have them inside the tent than out of it if one was trying to govern the kingdom.

While those seeking independence have a self-evident interest in nationhood, political actors of all hues are reaching for some ownership of nationalism. The unionist parties, after all, are named Scottish Labour, Scottish Conservatives and Scottish Liberal Democrats. And each – to misquote the political historian Tom Nairn (1975) – seeks to invite the masses into their version of Scottish history.

What is interesting is that there is also a strong and unambiguous trend not only among majorities, but among ethnic minorities, in identifying themselves with the nation (either as Scottish only, or Scottish-British, or Scottish plus something else). Scottish-Pakistanis, for example, are twice as likely to identify themselves as Scottish than their counterparts in England are likely to identify as English (who otherwise overwhelming identify as British).

Does this revise how Scottish identity is imagined by the majority too? Not necessarily, it would seem. In a survey of attitudes of Scottish majorities to claims made by minorities on nationhood in Scotland, McCrone and Bechhofer (2010), highlight a small but consistent 'ethnic penalty' that associates being 'Scottish' with 'being white'. They also note a weak relationship between residency and national identity and a strong relationship between markers such as accent and parentage. While higher rejection rates towards non-white in Scotland compared with England is concerning, Bechhofer and McCrone argue that it is important not to exceptionalise Scottish attitudes, for although they are slightly more exclusionary than English attitudes, they are not radically so. Interestingly, in their follow-up study, Bechhofer and McCrone (2012) found a closer pattern between England and Scotland when they looked to see whether national identity 'discriminates in terms of judging claims', something statistically affected by levels of education and/or age.

But this is more than purely instrumental and other nations have shown a marked inability to overcome ethnic barriers. In Spain's autonomous regions where a second official language is promoted, such as Catalonia, the Basque country and Galicia, immigration and ethnic minority diversity is deemed to present a particular challenge. Until recently the Basque Nationalist Party required four grandparents of Basque descent for membership of the party. In Canada, Quebec separatist leader and premier Pauline Marois and others have emphasised the importance of *Quebecois de souche* ('old stock').

Scotland's political nationalism therefore makes for a welcome contrast. All the same, its political pluralism is still more of an aspiration than a matter of fact. My research points to a number of ways in which political actors can be hesitant to remake Scottish nationhood. Take the issue of language. The national languages of Scotland include Scottish Gaelic, of which there are approximately 60,000 speakers. It has seen important advances in its recognition in recent years, such as the creation, in 2005, of *Bòrd na Gàidhlig*, a body charged with securing Gaelic as an official language that commands equal respect to English.

One rationale for setting it up was that Gaelic is an element of Scottishness because it's not spoken anywhere else. Yet other languages such as Scottish Urdu and Scottish Punjabi are more frequently spoken, and they appear to be taking on distinctive Scottish forms in terms of content and dialect. Nonetheless there is a consensus among political elites that they don't warrant status as one of Scotland's national languages. Religious pluralism is a more charged example. Irish Catholics secured various gains down the years as part of the Catholic emancipation in Scotland, most clearly symbolised by the restoration in 1878 of the hierarchy of the Catholic Church in Scotland. The typical response to bringing Muslims, Hindus and Sikhs into such settlements is that 'it would be extremely depressing,' one MSP told me:

> to think that in 50 or 60 years' time we'd repeated the mistakes in terms of other ethnic groups and other religions (interview with author).

There are some good reasons to be cautious about seeking to mirror one religious settlement in the present with something from the past, but thinking that recognising other religions in Scotland would be complicated by the country's sectarian issues is beside the point – how often does it occur to people that we are living in a country whose flag depicts a Christian cross?

It may be the case that, as the late Bashir Ahmed, Scotland's first ethnic minority MSP, put it:

> It isn't important where you come from, what matters is where we are going together as a nation (*Daily Telegraph*, 7 February 2009).

But this journey needs to occur within democratic and inclusive terms.

Scotland cannot rely on the view that in promoting itself as 'impeccably civic', it will secure a future in which ethnic and racial minorities are self-evidently included. Nation builders need to acknowledge ethnic hierarchies if they wish to pursue a genuinely pluralist project.

References

Audickas, L. (2016) 'Ethnic Minorities in Politics and Public Life', London: UK Parliament, available online at: obv.org.uk/sites/default/files/images/downloads/SN01156-Ethnic-Minorities-in-Politics-and-Public-Life.pdf, accessed, 4 June 2018.

Bechhofer, F. and McCrone, D. (2012), 'Changing Claims in Context, National Identity Revisited', *Ethnic and Racial Studies*, Vol. 37 No. 8 pp. 1350–1370.

Daily Telegraph (2009), 'Bashir Ahmad, Scotland's first Muslim MSP, has died', *The Telegraph*, 7 February 2009.

MacEwan, M. (1980), 'Race Relations in Scotland, ignorance or apathy?', *New Community*, Vol. 8 pp. 266–274

McCrone, D. (2001), *Understanding Scotland*, London: Routledge.

McCrone, D. and Bechhofer, F. (2010), 'Claiming national identity', *Ethnic and Racial Studies*, Vol. 33 No. 6 pp. 921-948.

McEwen, N., Swenden, W. and Bolleyer, N. (2012), 'Intergovernmental Relations in the UK: Continuity in a Time of Change?', *The British Journal of Politics and International Relations*, Vol. 14 No. 2 pp. 323–343.

Meer, N. (2015a), 'Looking up in Scotland? Multinationalism, multiculturalism and political elites', *Ethnic and Racial Studies*, Vol. 38 No. 9 pp. 1477–1496.

Meer, N. (2018), 'Race Equality after Enoch Powell', *Political Quarterly*, In Press.

Meer, N. (2015b), *Race Equality in Scotland, Challenges and Opportunities*, Glasgow: University of Strathclyde, available online at, strathprints.strath. ac.uk/53556/1/MeerN_IPPI_2015_Race_equality_in_Scotland_challanges_and_oppurtunities.pdf.

Meer, N. (2016), 'Self-reported discrimination in Scotland', in: Meer, N. (ed.), *Scotland and Race Equality, Directions in Policy and Identity*, London: Runnymede Trust.

Meer, N. (2017), 'Scottish BME Poll', available online at: http,//survation.com/wp-content/uploads/2017/08/Final-Scotland-BME-University-of-Edinburgh-Tables-5lop8-1.pdf

Nairn, T. (1975), 'The Modern Janus', *New Left Review*, I Vol. 94 November-December.

Scottish Government (2015), 'Analysis of Equality Results from the 2011 Census – Part 2', available online at: http,//www.gov.scot/Publications/2015/03/8716/0

Scottish Government (2018), 'Scotland's Census, Ethnic Group Demographics', Edinburgh: Scottish Government, available online at: gov.scot/Topics/People/Equality/Equalities/DataGrid/Ethnicity/EthPopMig, accessed 18 June 2018.

Scottish Parliament (2016), 'Removing barriers, race, ethnicity and employment' Edinburgh: Scottish Parliament, available online at: www.parliament.scot/parliamentarybusiness/CurrentCommittees/96080.aspx.

Sue, D.W. (2007), 'Racial Microaggression in Everyday Life', *American Psychological Association*, Vol. 62 No. 4 pp. 271-286.

CHAPTER 19

Managing Democracy

Katie Gallogy-Swan

THE SCOTTISH PARLIAMENT was founded on a promise of democratic renewal. Heeding the calls for popular sovereignty rippling across the UK, New Labour moved swiftly to deliver on this promise, though not without caveats. While limited powers ensured a specific remit of policy-making, reinstating the Scottish Parliament was also intended to manage the growing power of the Scottish National Party by ending the debate on whether home rule meant devolution or independence. As the Scottish Parliament has developed its own institutional culture in the years that have followed, the rhetoric of popular sovereignty has remained central to political discourse, particularly evident in the recent explosion of mechanisms to engage citizens in decision-making. However, the codes of such procedures in the Scottish Parliament have also inherited the managerial sheen of New Labour, begging the question of whether claims that successive Scottish Governments have delivered a more accessible parliament in fact simply hide how these processes carefully manage citizens' access to power. Ironically, twenty years on, the politicians and civil servants of the Scottish Parliament and Executive are faced with the same dilemma as New Labour in 1997: manage or transform Scottish democracy?

People living in Scotland engage with the Scottish Parliament through elections and public consultation. Elections enable citizens to directly select representatives based on manifesto commitments, while consultation lends legitimacy to policy delivery by using public engagement as a safety valve. How both are implemented and form part of the wider culture of the Scottish Parliament as an institution has significant influence on citizen trust in its democratic mandate. Getting to grips with, first, the way Parliament was founded; second, procedural norms and third, the political aims of Scottish Parties illuminates the common threads and priorities that have shaped the Scottish Parliament's impact on Scottish democracy.

Democratic Beginnings

The years following Thatcher saw a resurgence in interest in devolving power to regional representative bodies in the UK. In the aftermath of the failed 1979 referendum for Scottish Devolution, the Campaign for a Scottish Assembly (CSA), made up primarily of Labour Party members with some representation from others, quickly formed to campaign for devolution. Under Thatcher, their attempts got nowhere. In 1988 the CSA drafted the Claim of Rights signed by 58 of Scotland's 72 MPs, five of Scotland's eight MEPs, 59 out of 65 Scottish regional, district and island councils, and numerous political parties, churches, unions and other civic organisations; together, this formed the Scottish Constitutional Convention (SCC).

The Claim of Rights acknowledged the 'sovereign right of the Scottish people to determine the form of Government best suited to their needs'. This would be achieved by 'mobilis[ing] Scottish opinion and ensur[ing] the approval of the Scottish people for that scheme'. While problems abounded from the beginning over who exactly was defined as the 'Scottish people' considering the over-representation of self-appointed, older white men in the SCC, the political project for a Scottish Assembly was suffused with this rhetoric of civic inclusion, participation, and consultation. While the Claim of Rights has no formal legislative power, it continues to be invoked today to justify the Parliament, and more recently, the SNP's political priorities for independence.

Consensus Culture

The SCC came to be instrumental in pushing for the 1997 referendum. Key to its success was the joint efforts of Labour, the Liberal Democrats and civil society. This collaborative politics was to bear fruit in how the new Parliament would be formed: an electoral system designed to avoid majorities, and a chamber designed to lack an opposition. The Scottish Parliament has seen minority, coalition and, to much surprise, majority governments as a consequence. Most of the parties have worked together at some point – even Labour and the Conservatives, in opposition to Scottish Independence prior to the 2014 referendum. One of the consequences of this kind of politics is an elaboration of procedures of etiquette, for example the Guide to Collective Decision Making published in 2003 for the coalition Government of Labour and the Liberal Democrats. Policy documents which focus on the 'conduct of conduct' such as this have helped to enshrine an institutional culture that has been accused of bureaucracy, focusing more on administering and managing Scotland, rather than representing the people.

People and Party

The founding of the Parliament rested on a rhetoric of partnership between parties and civil society, but most importantly with the people. Indeed, the SCC undertook a consultative process to engage different communities on the question of devolution, further embedding public engagement as a hallmark of legitimacy in the Parliament's foundations. However, to evoke 'the people' necessarily raises the question of which people.

The notable absence of the SNP in the SCC marked the terrain of the different visions for home rule: for Labour, the aim was to build wider electoral support by successfully leading the regional assemblies, while the SNP believed the SCC was a distraction from campaigning for full independence. Capitalising on the same rhetoric of the 'Scottish people', it became easy for the SNP to undermine Labour's claims of representation in the years that followed the founding of the Parliament when it became evident that the political energy of the Labour Party was more invested in Westminster. Benefitting from the embedded belief in popular sovereignty for Scotland that had developed in campaigning for devolution, the SNP's messages for independence from Westminster gained salience, particularly in the aftermath of the financial crisis when the electorate delivered an unprecedented majority to the SNP at Holyrood.

Consumption Consultation

The focus on public participation was fundamental to democratic discourse in the Parliament's early years. Launching a series of consultations, guidelines on engagement, research into participatory methods and national standards for community engagement, public participation in decision making was crystallised as a technical exercise. When the SNP came to power in 2007, they upheld this status quo. In their community empowerment plan launched in 2009, the heavy emphasis on service delivery and local capacity building echoed the managerial-consumption style of New Labour's reframing of citizens as users and public bodies as service providers. This evidences a strain of neo-liberal thought which seeks to use the language of community agency to decrease state responsibility and incite local civil society to do things for themselves – the SNP's cornerstone policy on democratic engagement shared this influence with David Cameron's Big Society concept that was launched the very next year.

Democratic Deficits

While rhetoric of the people's participation and agency was deployed by all parties at the national level in Scotland for political ends, the centralisation of local democracy since the beginning of the Parliament tells a different story. Scotland has the least democratic local government in Europe. The average population size of a council is 163,200, compared to the EU average of 5,630. The average area covered by a council in Scotland is 2,461km, compared to a 601km average in the UK, and 49km in Europe. There is one councillor for every 4,270 people in Scotland, whereas in England, it is one to 2,860, and in Finland, one to 500 (Bort *et al.*, 2012). Turnout in council elections too, reveals the lack of trust and belief in Scotland's local democracy, and turnouts across elections in Scotland continues to be unacceptably low despite proportional voting systems. The democratic reality is that people don't have faith that democratic engagement will have an impact, despite the lofty claims of the Parliament's leaders.

Further, the focus on public engagement distracts from a constituency of interests which have benefitted from increased access to policy and decision-making since the Parliament's inception. The business community, who were largely against devolution, were flattered into 'partnership' with early Scottish Governments to neutralise their dissent and confirm that they shared the Government's economic interests in growth. Most recently, this was epitomised by the Sustainable Growth Commissions leadership under Andrew Wilson, a founding partner in corporate lobbying firm, Charlotte St Partners.

Indyref Democracy

Fifteen years on from the beginning of the Parliament, Scottish democracy got a shock injection with the independence referendum. The Parliament had failed to close the conversation on complete departure from the UK, and in fact had embedded the democratic rhetoric which enabled the SNP to win power. During Indyref, the decision between Yes and No caught the imagination and hopes of people across Scotland, and the number of local campaigners, debates, and creative projects focusing on the constitutional question fuelled a democratic blossoming.

In the aftermath of the No vote, the SNP initially continued to successfully position themselves as the party of the people, but it wasn't long before those mobilising during the referendum turned their attention to the democratic issues existing within Scotland. Notable policy outputs such as the Democracy Max project from the Electoral Reform Society in 2013, the Commission on Strengthening Local Democracy from the Convention of Scottish Local Authorities (COSLA) in 2014, and numerous papers from theorists and policy-makers on democracy all echoed the same need to decentralise power and build more meaningful engagement whilst also tackling the growing inequality which undermines equal access across Scotland's communities. To maintain credibility after such sustained and comprehensive democratic engagement during the referendum campaign, it was clear that the SNP needed to do more to satiate the public's appetite for voice and influence in the decisions which effected their lives.

The Deliberative Era

Keen to avoid the hypocrisy of democratic deficits at home while pushing for further powers to be released from Westminster, the SNP have revived the SCC-backed concept of subsidiarity, which in its purest form is centralising only those powers which cannot be delivered by a more local authority. To build credibility for the ambitious rhetoric of popular sovereignty and with the backing of a newly professionalised 'democratic sector', a range of new policies, tools, commissions and strategies have been launched by the Scottish Executive in the years since the referendum to innovate how the public can engage in decisions taken at Parliament. This has included the launching of What Works Scotland in 2014, the Community Empowerment Act in 2015; the relaunch of National Standards for Community Engagement, the Open Government Partnership and the Commission on Parliamentary Reform in 2016; and the Local Governance Review in 2018 in preparation for a new local democracy bill in 2019. These push the boundaries of former consultative processes at the Scottish Parliament: placing greater emphasis on power redistribution by increasing deliberation, inclusion and resources for public engagement. However, the history of technical guidelines to manage the parameters of engagement hangs heavy on these new pronouncements, and their release hasn't been without criticism.

Of particular importance is the criticism that the implementation of radical democratic tools such as participatory budgeting has focused on transactional rather than transformational approaches. Transactional approaches provide resources in response to direct requests, whereas transformational approaches have a bigger emphasis on power sharing between government representatives, local organisations and citizens. Achieving transformational outcomes from tools such as participatory budgeting requires resources to increase their deliberative quality and redistributive potential. And this demands a long-term commitment: developing the deep democracy such tools can engender requires patience as citizens and communities learn how to exercise and share power, co-creating a culture of participation – and making mistakes along the way.

Deliberation isn't necessarily emancipatory if it isn't connected to meaningful levers of decision-making and doesn't tackle uneven access to power. An alternative future to the radical potential of these tools is that parliamentary technocrats cultivate them as new sites of managing the hopes and ambitions

of communities. There is a risk that these tools will remain an extension of service delivery and grant-making, with no invested interest in strengthening trust
or engagement in Scottish democracy, meanwhile the lobby for big business
continues to define Scotland's economic trajectory. This will lead to the continuing degradation in meaning of buzzwords such as engagement, participation
and empowerment, and with a global democratic crisis engulfing political discourse, the stakes are too high for politicians in the Scottish Parliament to be
complacent.

These risks can be overcome with ambition, but such decisions are not easy
to take in times of austerity and fear in growing extremist movements. The Scottish Parliament's founding has developed a robust language of popular sovereignty and democratic renewal, but the outcomes have not matched the aspiration. Moving forward, the question facing this young institution is whether the
recent wave of democratic 'innovation' will be simply changing the parameters
of management, or indeed an opportunity to meaningfully release power not
simply with the aim to pursue independence, but to truly respect the sovereign
right of the Scottish people to determine their collective and individual futures.

CHAPTER 20

The View from Constitution Street

Jemma Neville

SITTING AT MY desk one day during the summer of independence in 2014, I noticed something unusual across the road. Sticky-taped to the panes of glass on a Constitution Street window were pieces of white A4 paper spelling out five words and a question mark in a child's deliberate but uneven handwriting: 'Do you want to play?' Five syllables (the first line of a haiku) and a direct, unambiguous question with a choice of two answers. I scrawled my response onto one sheet of printer paper, positioned it in my own window and waited for the reply. And so, began the first of many surprise conversations visible to all passers-by in the street, confusing Yes/No independence pollsters and reviving the Scottish ballad tradition of etching verse onto windows.

My neighbour Maddie is a true child of Constitution Street in Leith, Edinburgh. She has the scratched mirror that I salvaged from the old Port O' Leith ladies' toilets on her dressing table. Her parents met inside the bar and were married in South Leith Parish Church further along the street. Maddie's father, an Englishman, voted Yes to Scottish independence and is an active member of the local branch of the SNP. Her mother, a Scotswoman, voted No and is fervent in her disdain for Scottish nationalism. Such is how our lived experience and the people we meet shape our layered identities.

Constitution Street is about a mile's walk from the Scottish Parliament, the so-called 'People's Parliament'. For a school project on the Scottish Parliament, Maddie turned to her friend across the road for help. Her Primary Seven class had gone on a visit to Holyrood and it prompted us to talk about politics and about the Parliament building itself.

So, I think Westminster is like the main place where they decide what happens for the whole country and the Scottish Parliament is mainly for Scotland and I think, well, obviously the debating chambers are a lot different too.

Do you think we live in a fair country?

Yes, I think it's run fairly. Though I don't like how sometimes people with more money get treated differently to people with less money. And Brexit was not a good decision. Because, well mainly for my Mum's job. Like, she only gets paid if people buy things and people are kind of scared to now. So, she's not getting paid very well. And, also when you go to the airport, you're going to have to sign lots of papers and things to go to places like France.

Maddie and I continued our chat about the lay of the land. I explained that Scottish devolution came of age at the same time as our domestic human rights law. When I first studied law, some twenty years ago, the undergraduate course was called Civil Liberties. It is, by now, well understood that The Scotland Act, 1998, re-establishing a Scottish Parliament, embedded The European Convention on Human Rights (the Convention) into our constitutional and legal framework. If Scottish Ministers do not adhere to the Convention, legislation may be struck down by our courts or may result in a ruling from The European Court of Human Rights in Strasbourg. This applies to the functioning of all public bodies such as courts, schools, hospitals, prisons and local authorities.

The UK's Human Rights Act, 1998 is also over twenty years old and was introduced in Scotland ahead of the rest of the UK to coincide with The Scotland Act, 1998 and the re-establishment of the Parliament. In this way, human rights are often said to be in the DNA of Holyrood. The Human Rights Act was considered so important that it was protected from modification by the Scottish Parliament. It was also used to define the Parliament's powers to legislate.

In the last twenty years, there has been a succession of public interest legislation seeking to improve the lives of people: free personal care for the elderly, the abolition of tuition fees, social security and land reform. However, much less widely recognised is that paragraph seven of Schedule 5 of The Scotland Act devolves observing and implementing a range of international obligations. This includes those international human rights treaty obligations entered into by the UK but not fully incorporated into domestic law, most notably economic, social and cultural rights – such as the right to the highest attainable standard of housing and healthcare.

On my reading of current arrangements, there is nothing to stop the Scottish Government from enhancing existing human rights protections. A new Bill of Rights, or a written constitution, for Scotland could be a Human Rights Act 'plus'. This potential advancement of rights contrasts with the toxic climate surrounding human rights in other parts of the UK and the current UK Government's manifesto commitment to repeal The Human Rights Act.

I believe that now is the moment for a written constitution in Scotland. With human dignity at its core, the process of negotiating and agreeing the constitution, street by street, will give us back our sense of common place and purpose after a period of disorientating flux following the European Union and Scottish independence referendums. And, we need not start from scratch. The Universal Declaration of Human Rights (UDHR) provides a near-comprehensive legal framework to connect the global and the local. Drafted 70 years ago and widely referenced in other national constitutions and legal systems, the declaration has the status of customary international law.

> Where, after all, do universal human rights begin? In small places, close to home – so close and so small that they cannot be seen on any maps of the world. Yet they are the world of the individual person; the neighbourhood he lives in; the school or college he attends; the factory, farm, or office where he works.

So says Eleanor Roosevelt in her speech to the United Nations at the time. The small places close to home that Roosevelt spoke of are the places navigated amidst the ritual and routine of day-to-day life – the park, the bus stop, the pub, the kitchen table and the street itself. My street, Constitution Street, is economically and culturally diverse with a mix of old and new Scots living in the street's traditional tenement flats, high-rise tower block and sheltered housing. Maddie and I live in tenement flats. Tenement living locates perfect strangers, as we once were, in intimate proximity to one another. Our domestic lives are boxed and stacked, one on top of the other, in a precarious human tower. It is a form of social contract.

In her watercolour painting *Window in the West*, Glasgow artist, Avril Paton, depicts the external profile of a Glasgow tenement on a snowy winter's eve. Inside, the neighbours are continuing their intimate lives, seemingly oblivious to one another, and yet side-by-side and seen by the artist and us the viewer, they live in one single composition. A man sits at a computer, another draws open curtains to watch the falling snow, a cat sits in a window and Paton includes herself standing at the front door of the four-storey building. We see one another. And so, we see ourselves. The snowy scene could just as easily be Constitution Street or the street where you live or work.

I have lived on Constitution Street for the last decade and during 2017 and 2018, I set about interviewing over 50 of my neighbours, including Maddie, about our lives in common up and down the street. This personal research was set against the background of a period of immense uncertainty for the constitutional future of Scotland in the UK in the months preceding Brexit.

On 24 January 2017, the Supreme Court ruled that the UK Government could not remove the UK from the European Union without the legislative consent of Parliament. However, the same case also held that consent from the devolved legislatures, including the Scottish Parliament, was not required. The constitutional convention of the UK Government seeking the consent of the Scottish Government in matters concerning devolution had been proved to be just that, a convention and not a law.

The year and a half that followed, ahead of The European Union (Withdrawal) Act being given royal assent in June 2018, was a time of immense uncertainty for the constitutional future of Scotland within the UK. It was an interregnum of sorts while we waited for the balance of powers to settle. The collective mood was one of anxiety *en masse*. One thing we mostly agreed on was the need to improve people's lives, to hold onto our shared values and to try to navigate a way forward in the unchartered waters swelling in and around Brexit.

We needed both a compass and anchor that would protect our human rights beyond the party politics of the day. The idea of a written constitution drafted for, with and by the people of Scotland had been floated for some time by legal scholars. But, as the UK's constitutional arrangements became more and more choppy in the absence of a post-Brexit plan, the need for a rights framework became increasingly real to me.

Human rights law is guided by principles such as proportionality and minimum necessary restriction to balance individual freedoms with public interest. The overall duty of the state and its public bodies, to respect, protect and fulfil our human rights (such as the highest attainable standard of healthcare, housing and social security) is to ensure that we all can live out our lives with human dignity. In this way, the well-being and outlook of each of us individually can be seen as a living, breathing indicator of the collective health of the law and of the nation – our constitutional strength.

Semi-constitutional texts, including The European Communities Act of 1972, The Human Rights Act, 1998 and The Scotland Act, 1998, changed the relationship between people and state and placed limits on the absolute supremacy of UK parliamentary sovereignty. However, these were not permanent limitations, as seen with Brexit and the repeal of The European Communities Act. It did not offer the same long-term checks and balances that a written constitution might.

Significant environmental protections, aspects of employment law, privacy and data regulation and much anti-discrimination law will all be lost following Brexit. Considering this threat to our fundamental rights, the idea of a written constitution for the UK has been put forward by academics and civil society. But it is unlikely to gain any traction in the messy 'meanwhile' phase of the current political disorder and the strict doctrine of UK parliamentary sovereignty. However, the Scottish Government, either through current devolution arrangements, or in the event of a newly independent country, could seize momentum and legislate for a written Bill of Rights or a constitution framed by human rights.

Much like the interdependence of neighbours in a street, human rights are universal, indivisible and interdependent upon one another. Few human rights are absolute. They are subject to limitations and derogations, both legal and political in nature, and the most sensitive of balances embedded in human rights law is the relationship between the individual and the community.

A street is a particular type of community with clearly defined geographical boundaries. As neighbours, we are active participants in the negotiation and use of shared public space. In this way, the street is a type of commons and our feet do the work of the politics of encounter. When we pass one another to and from the small places side by side, we walk on common ground.

During my encounters on Constitution Street, I asked my neighbours questions, such as how do we want to live together? What are your hopes for the future? And, what do you want to leave behind? Rather than questions that resulted in the binary responses of Yes/No, Leave/Remain. Often, neighbours told me that no one had ever asked them these questions before. Unlike in the news coverage of the anxious, chaotic months preceding Brexit, my interviewees weren't politicians, lawyers or well-known commentators. They were people like you and me – shopkeepers, cleaners, carers, florists, musicians, architects, people of all faiths and none and school pupils. In opening up these conversations, I began to feel more grounded during a time of constitutional flux. The responses made real the application of human rights in practice. I was maintaining, or restoring, my own good health. I was setting out on a constitutional.

On Constitution Street, and streets up and down the land, Scotland has already changed beyond recognition since I was taught that human rights law was solely concerned with civil liberties or humanitarian crises in distant places. We now have an opportunity for Scotland to demonstrate international leadership with human rights. Regardless of whether or not Scotland remains devolved within the UK or becomes an independent country, we will always have an interdependency with our immediate UK neighbours and elsewhere in a globalised world. Neighbourhood, on any scale, is about mutuality and interdependence.

Scotland will continue to change at pace in the next two decades and beyond the Scottish Parliament. We will need many voices to tell our stories. By placing human dignity at the heart of public policy, a new constitution or Bill of Rights could be our window onto the wider world.

CHAPTER 21

Scotland's Environment Beyond the Fossil Trap
Imagining a Post-Oil Scotland

Mike Small

IN THE TWENTY years since devolution the ecological crisis has gone from critical to catastrophic and the emerging Scottish Government has strived to respond. It has had some limited successes in setting ambitious climate change targets. But, with energy, a retained power at Westminster, and without control over the North Sea, the Scottish Government has struggled to resolve and transcend environmental policy.

Successes include the closure of the Longannet power station in March 2016, which ended coal-fired power production in Scotland, and the overall growth of the renewable sector. The Scottish Government has set ambitious targets for renewable energy production. In 2005 the aim was for 18 per cent of Scotland's electricity production to be generated by renewable sources by 2010, rising to 40 per cent by 2020. In 2007 this was increased to 50 per cent of electricity from renewables by 2020, with an interim target of 31 per cent by 2011. The following year new targets to reduce overall greenhouse gas emissions by 80 per cent by 2050 were announced and then confirmed in the 2009 Climate Change Delivery Plan. Maf Smith, director of the Sustainable Development Commission in Scotland said:

> Governments across the world are shying away from taking the necessary action. The Scottish Government must be commended for its intention to lead the way.

A Mixed Blessing in Energy and Ecology

Scotland has significant quantities of fossil fuel deposits, including 62.4 per cent of the EU's proven reserves of oil, but also 85 per cent of the UK's hydroelectric energy resource, much of it developed by the north of Scotland Hydro-Electric Board in the 1950s. If energy is both our blessing and our curse this is not to say that some failures have not been entirely of their own making. The Scottish Government exists in a world unable or incapable of making the seismic changes required to respond to the climate crisis.

In 2018 *The Herald* reported:

> For the first time the scientists worked out Scotland's carbon budget under the international climate agreement made in Paris in 2015. They conclude that for Scotland to meet its global responsibilities it can only emit a total of 300 million tonnes more carbon dioxide – meaning it has to cut emissions by at least ten per cent every year starting now.

The report points out that if the world is to meet international climate targets 70 to 80 per cent of known fossil fuel reserves must stay in the ground. 'Scotland needs to begin an urgent and phased closure of its oil and gas sector', it says. Now this is going to cause some problems.

No-one really wants to do anything, even though the overwhelming evidence is that the world is teetering on the brink of catastrophic change. Real courageous leadership is conspicuous by its absence. No one wants to give up the lifestyle they've assumed is their right. At either end of the income scale in developed countries there's little appetite for change. Many of the wealthiest people have made their money from resource exploitation and can't see beyond it. Many people suffering in poverty don't see how this 'crisis' is to do with them or how they might have agency to change such a reality.

Many people who want to see an independent Scotland are still obsessed by the 'It's Scotland's Oil' trope of the 1970s. Many will no doubt claim that 'it will make no difference' and we should use every last drop. Of course, it's not Scotland's oil, its Shell's, Exxon's and BP's. And yes, we could tax them and yes, we could create an Oil Fund – but we would be doing so at least 30 years too late. Other emerging industries, and non-industries have far more potential and far less destructive impact. But our problem isn't just the obsession with oil, but climate polluters, and the exertion of corporate power.

Table 1: Scotland's Top 20 Climate Polluters

Plant	Tonnes of carbon dioxide emitted in 2016
Petroineos refinery, Grangemouth	1,650,000
Longannet power station, Fife (now closed)	1,640,000
ExxonMobile ethylene plant, Mossmorran	885,580

Combined heat and power plant, Grangemouth	614,863
SSE power station, Peterhead	602,641
Tarmac cement plant, Dunbar	537,029
Ineos Infrastructure, Grangemouth	495,214
Ineos Chemicals, Grangemouth	486,809
RWE biomass plant, Glenrothes	438,000
E.ON biomass plant, Lockerbie	370,965
Shell gas plant, Peterhead	356,334
Ineos Forties Pipeline System, Grangemouth	351,262
UPM-Kymmene paper mill, Irvine	279,483
Norboard chipboard factory, Cowie	268,160
Total gas plant, Shetland	235,234
Engie oil terminal, Shetland	211,741
Shell gas plant, Mossmorran	193,554
William Grant whisky distillers, Girvan	152,913
Repsol oil terminal, Orkney	144,206
O-I glass plant, Alloa	141,902

Source: Scottish Environment Protection Agency

Life Aquatic

As the light flashes on the very precise figures for Scotland to reach its climate change obligations – and the companies needing to be divested away from immediately – focus turns also to the disastrous state of our lochs, rivers and seas. The investigative project *The Ferret* have highlighted a full-length version of this video of lice infested salmon in a Scottish fish farm and been told that the Scottish Government confirmed officials would inspect it 'immanently'. A video shot underwater on 27 August 2018 inside a cage at Vacasay fish farm in Loch Roag showed hundreds of sea lice feeding on salmon with open wounds and damaged tails and fins

While the issues are being presented as an animal rights and cruelty issue (which it surely is) it also raises significant questions about, first, the 'Good Food Nation' and the constant cheerleading about salmon as the champion export of finest Scottish produce; and second, the rights of coastal communities to have their own marine habitats protected from these rapacious and damaging companies. If a company abused animals on land like this with a significant damaging impact on the wider countryside local communities would be rightly up in arms.

Who will win out? The natural environment and local communities who benefit little from these dire practices? Or, the handful of big companies leaching off the pretence that Scotland has high quality food standards? But as the UN announces it is taking its first significant steps towards legally protecting the high seas another new exploitation closer to home is emerging.

Marine Biopolymers has submitted a scoping report to Marine Scotland outlining plans to dredge for the kelp *Laminaria hyperborea* over a huge area of Scotland's West Coast. It is perhaps stating the obvious but:

> Kelps as primary producers and habitat providers play a key role in the maintenance of fish stocks and ecosystem structure, sustaining regional fisheries and the coastal communities they support.

As Ailsa McLellan stated:

> Marine Biopolymers want to tow a large-toothed dredge in strips through kelp beds ripping the entire plant up by the holdfast (killing it), then throw the holdfast over the side to 'facilitate survival' of invertebrates.

> Assuming any invertebrates survive this treatment, where are they meant to go when chucked back over the side? Their habitat is gone, the other invertebrates are not going to 'budge up' and make room for them, that's not how biology works.

> Kelp is long-lived a vital part of the habitat and much employment of coastal Scotland is reliant upon a healthy coastal ecosystem: fisheries and eco-tourism would all be jeopardised by the destruction of kelp beds.

> Moreover, climate change is happening. Its effects, such as increasing acidity and rougher seas are already being measured in our oceans. Kelp sequesters significant amounts of carbon, Kelp sequesters significant amounts of carbon, buffers acidity, and acts as a storm barrier for coasts.

She continued:

> Kelp dredging is currently not allowed in Scotland. Marine Biopolymers seek to change that and have submitted a scoping report to Marine Scotland with plans to dredge for kelp over a huge area of Scotland's West Coast. Kelp is one of the most biodiverse habitats on the planet, it protects coasts from erosion, absorbs carbon, buffers rising ocean acidity. We need it. Please call on MPs and MSPs to ensure that NO kelp dredging licenses are granted.

Precisely because the marine world is 'beneath' the, or out to, sea it is more vulnerable and needs our protection. It is inconceivable to continue to promote our land and coast as tourist destinations for their beauty and natural wonder and still allow this level of exploitation, or to conceive of us as a 'Good Food Nation' with lice-infested lochs.

The Heathrow Issue

The Scottish Government's attitude to aviation expansion is a prism on their environmental policy under devolution. How does anyone in Scotland benefit from a third runway at Heathrow? How is this in anyway in alignment with Scotland's (much vaunted) climate change emission targets? The Government's latest figures foresee aviation emissions rising by 7.3 million tonnes of CO_2 by 2030 if a third runway is developed at Heathrow airport – equivalent to the annual CO_2 emissions from Cyprus.

Heathrow expansion flies in the face of efforts to tackle climate change. As Friends of the Earth Scotland have said:

> The UK Government's proposal now needs to be approved by the Westminster Parliament. The Government has a minority of MPs and many Conservatives oppose this disastrous scheme. The votes of the 35 SNP MPs are likely to be crucial in the final decision.

Plastic Sea

In 2018 scientists on board the Greenpeace's boat MV Beluga II skirted round Scotland's coast collecting data on the concentration of plastic and micro plastics in the sea. Micro plastics are defined as pieces of plastic measuring less than 5mm in any dimension. All plastic waste tends to break down into micro plastics over time, and most of the plastic in our oceans is in the form of micro plastics. It is the first and possibly the only such research of its kind. Almost two-thirds of Scottish waters were found to contain micro-plastic pollution.

A total of 49 individual samples were analysed by Greenpeace's laboratory to determine the types of micro plastics found, and any chemicals or contaminants carried on individual micro plastic pieces. Despite the remoteness of Scottish coastal waters, and the low levels of coastal development of the areas surveyed, 31 of 49 samples tested contained micro plastics.

The survey raises profound questions about the state of our ecology and our responses to environmental problems. Greenpeace focused on the 'pristine' waters of Mull, Tire, Rum, Canna and the Western Isles precisely because these waters contain basking sharks, dolphins, whales and sea birds. Just as polar bears equal a climate change icon (people like bears), so sharks also play well in the public conscience.

At the launch of the report we had Tory Maurice Golden MSP and SNP Kate Forbes MSP talking about the Scottish Parliament's possible responses. Beach clean-ups were focused on and we were told to think of 'Ocean Optimism'. But if the West Coast is contaminated then that must mean the rivers are contaminated. We have created a product (plastic) that doesn't break down, is very cheap to produce and has multiple applications. Then we have created an economy based on mass consumption and a culture that thrives on throwing things away.

Kate Forbes has been leading the Final Straw campaign for an end to plastic straws and succeeded in the Parliament banning straws. Pupils from Glasgow's Sunnyside Primary School have persuaded Glasgow City Council to ditch plastic straws. The Scottish Government announced in September it will introduce a Deposit and Return Scheme for drinks packaging. Detailed proposals for a Scottish system are being worked up by Zero Waste Scotland at the instruction of Roseanna Cunningham MSP, the Cabinet Secretary for Environment, Climate Change and Land Reform, and a final design is expected to be published in the summer of 2019. Michael Gove has also suggested he would look at a similar scheme at a UK level.

Campaigners for the Scottish scheme have insisted their plans will go ahead regardless of whether it happens at a UK level, though obviously a UK-wide scheme would be preferable. Now both of these initiatives are to be welcomed and the deposit scheme has already been backed by more than ninety organisations, including businesses, local authorities, outdoor sports organisations and universities. A small fully refundable deposit on empty drinks containers has been proven elsewhere to reduce litter, boost recycling, and contribute to the circular economy and has widespread public support.

Post-Plastic Scotland?

What we need to be doing is thinking about the leap to a post-plastic society and departure from our throwaway consumable culture. If these measures are steps towards that goal, then that is good. If they are steps away from that goal by chaining us to ameliorative and negligible differences, then we need to be aware of that danger.

The idea of a Scottish food (and seafood) 'brand' being associated with being 'clean' and 'green' (itself highly problematic) is also potentially undermined by these findings and the reality of a 'Plastic Sea'. Environmental policies need to be allied to, and connected with, the wider aim of a rupture from consumer society and the reality that the production-consumption cycle is what fuels the climate crisis. Rather than a spurious 'Ocean Optimism' we should have a radical realism, face up to what is happening, and demand change at a level that has meaning.

The issues explored here are focused on the recent Scottish Government record on the environment. But successive devolved governments have failed to respond to the ecological crisis in a meaningful way. In part this is due to the limitations of devolved rule, but it is also in part due to a societal failing of all of us to 'give up' the lifestyle we have become accustomed to.

Ultimately it is due to the economic system we are tied into and a reliance on which has proven to be incompatible to the carrying capacity of the earth. To transcend this crisis will require not just constitutional change but massive political and economic rupture. That ultimately is about more than the Scottish Parliament and devolution, and even independence, but us as global citizens.

Section Four – Cultures of Imagination

CHAPTER 22

Twenty Years of the Press and Devolved Scotland

Douglas Fraser

Introduction

AMONG THE PLAYERS within civic Scotland who helped create the conditions for a Scottish Parliament, the nation's newspapers can take a (mostly) honourable place.

Over the preceding decades, they reflected back at their readers a growing sense of Scottish identity. They gave over their news pages to reporting the pressure for a Parliament, their opinion columns and letters pages to the national debate and they emphasised the distinctive facets of the nation's politics. Alongside the broadcasters in an era of few channels, they championed the nation's culture, both high and low, from sport to literature, drama and music.

For those who doubt that role, there are counter-facts to be found south of the border. With a much weaker print media and weaker broadcast offerings, the case for Welsh devolution was, at least until 1997, rooted in its language. Apart from broadcasters, there are few reporters to cover the Cardiff Bay Assembly, and few London papers covering Welsh affairs. In England, there was not the vibrant, confident, opinionated regional media with which to gain traction for proposals of devolution when the offer was made by Tony Blair's Government. There are critics of the Scottish print media, but this would be a different and culturally and politically poorer country without it.

One might have expected the dawn of a new Scottish democracy to give a boost to its newspapers. Cynics suggested that commercial interest was one compelling explanation for the editorial support for devolution given by titles such as *The Scotsman* and *The Herald*, and even more so by their younger, Sunday stablemates, *Scotland on Sunday* and the *Sunday Herald*.

The latter began publishing in February 1999. While a commercial proposition to retain readers from the weekday and Saturday editions of *The Herald*, it launched by making an explicit editorial appeal to be linked to the birth of a new dawn for a new Scotland. Yet such expectations were to be proved wrong. There were other forces at work on the newspaper industry – including the internet and changing reading habits.

Twenty years after the Parliament opened for business, and scrutiny by the fourth estate, Scotland's distinctive, indigenous news media is in a severely weakened state. The questions MSPs may well be asking over the next twenty years will be: whatever happened to the journalists, the coverage and scrutiny?; How do we combat fake news?; How do we communicate more effectively in the era that follows the mass media of the 20th century?

Here, however, is the place to reflect on the first twenty years – not only of commercial and circulation decline for the press – but of a rumbustious relationship with the new Parliament, of scandals, scalps and not a little silliness. It requires an understanding of what has happened to the marketplace in which the print media operates: relationships between journalists and politicians, and journalists with each other; how the SNP sought to neutralise the power of some powerful publishers and de-fang the venom from its critics in the media.

While there are parallels and contrasts with Scotland's news broadcasters over these two decades, that is for another chapter, addressed within these pages by Blair Jenkins. As a BBC Scotland journalist since 2008, I am too close and too contractually constrained to include it within this chapter.

First, though, some recollections. For nearly ten of those years, I was immersed in the coverage of the new Scottish Parliament as a print journalist. I wrote for *The Observer* and the *Irish Times* at the time of the 1999 election. The month after MSPs were first sworn in, I started as the political editor of the *Sunday Herald*, and I became the political editor of *The Herald* from 2004 until 2008.

The Coming of the Scottish Parliament

Having championed the Parliament going into the 1997 referendum, there was a sharp change of tack in press coverage in the year and eight months before it first sat. The narrative moved from an exciting new statement of national intent to the machinations in Westminster and Whitehall around the powers it would be allowed to take on, and internal battling – notably in Scottish Labour – about who would be allowed to stand for it (Fraser, 2004).

By the time we were reporting on their swearing in, the then dominant force in Scottish politics had already provided its observers in the press with a juicy range of stories of snubbed and resentful MPs. Denis Canavan, a Labour MP, was independently elected by an emphatic margin in Falkirk West having been told he was not good enough for Labour in the Scottish Parliament, serving as a rebuke to those who wished to exert control from party HQ.

Others nursed their grievance from the bars at Westminster and were quick to tell us of their unhappiness that MSPs were getting so much more media attention. They had someone else on their patch. In most cases, this was some-one from the same party, and in most cases, that was Labour. But there was the novelty of at least seven other list MSPs, mostly from rival parties, who could claim to represent their constituents in a national Parliament. It was striking that many MPs had failed to understand the likely consequences of the voting system in the Scotland Act 1998 which they had themselves voted through.

Only when Labour ceased to dominate constituency representation did this flow of stories abate. Those rivalries within Labour backbenches and at constituency levels had a parallel within Labour in office. The Blair Government contained several prominent Scottish MPs, most notably Gordon Brown. It appeared that the devolution of legislative power was to be balanced, in their minds at least, by a tightening of controls within the party.

Labour Pains

As Labour First Ministers, Donald Dewar, Henry McLeish and Jack McConnell expended much of their energy in battling with Whitehall to be given permission to diverge from the Blair Government's policies. Unnamed sources in those Westminster bars were happy to crow about Holyrood's losses. We were in an era when the Labour Government put the spinning of its message at the heart of operations.

Alastair Campbell, as Tony Blair's spokesman, took on legendary status as a master of the craft, and he inspired others – less able than him – to follow suit, both in London and Edinburgh. When Tom McCabe floated the proposal that the Scottish Executive should be renamed the Scottish Government, as that would be more understandable to the public, a telling and damaging reaction from Westminster was that

> they can call themselves a white heather club if they want, but they won't be a government (Hassan and Shaw, 2012).

The tensions provided a welcome flow of stories to those of us covering the new Parliament. In the first year, with Donald Dewar installed as First Minister, I recall an exhausting parade of mainly minor crises. He was surrounded by inexperienced ministers and special advisers, eager to try out the levers of power on the machinery of government. They generated sparks, which set off brush fires. After First Minister's Questions each Thursday in the temporary debating chamber on the Mound, an embattled spokesman would be put to work at slapping down and dampening the flames. That usually made for more copy, and the anonymous spinners would fan new outbreaks of heated embers.

The tensions and pressure on ministers were heightened by an extraordinary trial of strength between the print media and the then Scottish Executive over 'Section 28'. This was shorthand for a legal ban, introduced by the Thatcher Government, on the 'promotion' of homosexuality in schools. As Communities Minister in the first year, Labour's Wendy Alexander announced this would be repealed. For a socially conservative swathe of Scotland, she hit a raw nerve.

For nearly a year, which led the transition to Henry McLeish's leadership, the battle raged. Much of it took place in the pages of Scotland's newspapers. The *Daily Record* was then the dominant voice in the print media (though no longer the biggest seller) and vociferous for Labour, under the editorship of Martin Clarke. He had previously edited the *Scottish Daily Mail* and *The Scotsman* (and has gone on to build *MailOnline*) and brought a new intensity to those titles, as his journalists tore into Scotland's institutions. He had masterminded a ferocious monstering of the SNP's 1999 campaign, which left Alex Salmond and his team reeling, and vowing they would never again allow themselves to face such a relentless attack. The *Daily Record* was joined by other tabloids in attacking the ministerial team for having the audacity to liberalise a law which had never been used. Wendy Alexander and other ministers became household names.

The ammunition for this campaign was provided by Brian Souter, the businessman who funded a plebiscite, the Roman Catholic leader Cardinal Tom Winning and the tabloid editor-turned-PR man Jack Irvine. This was the use of media power in a blatant attempt to bully and intimidate a young, inexperienced ministerial team and Parliament itself. By June 2000, when the repeal votes finally took place, only Conservative MSPs opposed it, more out of deference to the Thatcher legacy than a belief that the clause was necessary. For the Scottish Parliament and for Scotland as a whole, the battle over 'Clause 28' can now be seen as a vital one (as then portrayed in the liberal *Sunday Herald*) both in terms of resolving the tensions between social conservatism and liberal social values, in favour of the latter, and also in facing down the bullying behaviour of an over-bearing tabloid media.

The fall of Henry McLeish, in 2001, demonstrated another strand of media coverage; the search for scandal and scalps. McLeish's slack management of his Glenrothes constituency office finances, sub-letting part of it and struggling to account for the financial gain, will be remembered by a humiliatingly weak defence that this was 'a muddle and not a fiddle'.

Small details of his arrangements kept dripping out and putting his court-room training to work. Conservative leader David McLetchie delivered the political blows which saw off the First Minister. McLetchie's leadership would suffer a similar fate, when a seemingly endless stream of revelations and questions about his taxi claims, ground him into resignation. In the Labour group, the rise of Wendy Alexander to the leadership for some years would itself be her undoing. She had funded her leadership campaign with opaque private donations. Unable to get out from under the pressure of questions, she also quit and soon left the Parliament for a more private career.

These were the early years of the Freedom of Information Act, passed by the Scottish Parliament, in parallel with one at Westminster. More public bodies were becoming more open. Journalists, notably Paul Hutcheon at the *Sunday Herald*, seized the opportunity to wield the new law against government and its agencies. The novelty of being able to pore over the minutiae of previously private documents was enough to justify publication. In the annual journalism awards, the resulting scalps were lauded and rewarded with trophies. Newspapers editors wanted more scalps.

The relationship between editor and political reporter was one which was different to that at Westminster. The big beasts of the lobby in the Commons had the clout within newspapers to tell their editors what the news line was; the lack of experience of many of those covering the Scottish Parliament, allied to the frenzy of coverage in those early years, meant that editors were dictating the terms of that relationship and the way in which MSPs, the Parliament and the Scottish Executive would be portrayed. At some distance, it was far from flattering. Yet the big scandals in those early years were small. David McLetchie failed to account for £11,500 of taxi receipts over five years. Likewise, for Wendy Alexander and Henry McLeish, they were not pocketing money, but failing to explain how fairly small sums had been handled. There was a repeated failure to get a sense of perspective.

The Holyrood building project helped change that. It was another dripping roast of a news story but involved a serious amount of public money being mishandled. There was a long period where no journalist was embarrassed by over-stating the developing scale of the fiasco, because every apparently wild claim of spiralling costs later turned out to be true. The news media covered it, again, in intense detail.

By the 2003 election, the incumbent First Minister Jack McConnell recognised that there was a burning fury across the country at the incompetence. This symbolic building was a symbol not of the new Scotland but of dysfunctional numptyism. The attacks were not on the Government or on opposition parties, but on the Parliament institution itself, and that was toxic.

One answer was a public inquiry, after the 2003 election. The other was, as Presiding Officer George Reid put it, to 'get in and get on'. It's worth recalling how quickly public anger was turned into a curiosity about this unique, signature building, and even pride in it. Press and public could then begin the process of separating 'Holyrood' from government and parties. The word Holyrood lost its toxicity and became the forum for heated debate rather than the focus of it. This was an important moment in the maturing of the Scottish public's understanding of the new institution.

For all the novelty, the media view of the Parliament was strongly influenced by the experience of Westminster. Not that many journalists had much experience from there. But there was a desire to make this feel like Westminster. One consequence was a failure by many to see that a coalition – and later, minority – government meant that small parties and small groups of MSPs could exert disproportionate influence. For eight-years, that meant the Liberal Democrats could exercise a veto on Labour. It brought new challenges for the politicians about how to manage those coalition relationships and how to ensure that one's partner party took the political pain for unpopular decisions or mishandled policy. It brought new opportunities for journalists. Some were slow to realise that the Lib Dems were not an affront to democracy, but a rich source of stories. Government, when run by two parties, was likely to be much more open. Disputes could and should be aired in public.

The understanding within the London media of the new Scottish Parliament and of devolution was in many ways woeful. Until Nicola Sturgeon and Ruth Davidson, there seemed to be more irritation than interest. The new technology of the print media, with multiple print plants, meant that Scottish editions could be printed with sometimes extensive Scottish coverage that never made it near the English editions. Although investing in Scottish journalism, London-based editors could be barely aware of what was going on at Holyrood, beyond a few headline stories that fitted into their narrative of devolution. The arrival of an SNP administration helped to change that. Alex Salmond had established himself as a significant figure at Westminster and was keen to deploy his media skills through the London media. Sometimes, oddly, this was to the exclusion of the media that reached his base and target audience north of the border. It also helped that Westminster's press lobby began to include a few journalists with at least some experience of Holyrood.

The SNP Years

The SNP's attainment of power in 2007 seemed to bring a sharp change. Even in a majority from 2011 to 2016, the party demonstrated an iron discipline about resolving differences. That discipline was partly under the dominance and intimidating eye of Alex Salmond as First Minister and was justified in the service of the party's aim of achieving independence. Whatever you make of the lack of open debate, or of acknowledgement of difficulty or problems, it has not been good news for journalists.

The focus on independence, and the deference to the cause and the leadership, has made for a much duller 12 years in the news pages. Alongside the discipline for this period, there were also important differences. Salmond liked to court elements of the press, set the agenda and make headlines. He considered himself a master of handling the media (and presumably still does) and helped as party leader and First Minister by those of a younger generation he had mentored. Kevin Pringle, though temperamentally unlike him, was Salmond's talented, key media adviser and spokesman, and was vital to developing and actioning media strategy. Nicola Sturgeon had also learned at the feet of the master, but as First Minister, she has not found it comes as naturally to play the media game. She has, instead, been more cautious (Geoghegan, 2017) – projecting an image primarily through broadcast. At the time of writing, 12 years into office, there are signs that this SNP self-discipline is coming under unprecedented strain. Supporters are straining against the caution of moves towards a second independence referendum, and the handling of allegations about Alex Salmond's behaviour while First Minister.

The rout of Labour in 2011 removed even more of the well-known figures who had featured in the soap opera narratives developed by newspapers in preceding years. The 'rainbow' Parliament of 2003–07, with its Greens and Scottish Socialists, had become SNP yellow yet largely grey through the tight discipline, while the flaring of firebrand rhetoric by and about Tommy Sheridan moved on to the law courts.

As this happened, print circulation was falling away. Between 1999 and 2019, circulation plummeted by at least two-thirds on many titles. *The Herald* now sells fewer than 30,000. *The Scotsman* has print circulation well below 20,000 and gives many of them away. It can claim to have far more readers online than it previously had, as content can be accessed for free. But its influence on public debate, as a forum for debate, has dwindled.

The *Press and Journal* in Aberdeen and *The Courier*, in Dundee, joined under the ownership of DC Thompson, stuck closer to their time-honoured formula of local, regional and heavily edition-ised coverage, and saw slower declines. Among red tops, the *Scottish Sun* had long since overhauled the *Daily Record*, just as its stablemate, *The Times*, now outsells both *The Herald* and *The Scotsman*. London titles could outspend Scottish-based ones, on coverage, breadth and in many ways on quality (Fraser, 2008).

The economics of printing allowed for more titles. In 2014, *The National* was launched, to tap into a pro-independence market. It hasn't reached far into the movement, but with meagre journalistic resourcing, it can tag along with its long-standing partner title, *The Herald*.

Advertising revenue was disappearing at least as fast as print sales, and without it, newspapers were stripped of resources. The business model was bust. While some – notably *The Times* – invested in the transition to a digital and print future, other newspaper managers simply slashed at costs, and shed journalists. *The Scotsman* stable was devastated by the pressure to bring down the vast debts built up by parent company Johnston Press. The head count at Holyrood has reduced. The reporters on the press corridor at Holyrood are now younger, less experienced and, thankfully, a bit less male and macho. For too many of the twenty years, there have been no women in the press corridor of the media tower. The Broadcasters and the Press Association, two floors above, have been more balanced. Either editors' reluctance to advance women journalists into political reporting, or the difficulty of persuading them to follow that path, is a continuing problem.

In the second decade of the Parliament, the newspapers' competitors have come to include blogs, vlogs, podcasts and campaigning websites. Facebook algorithms have become enormously influential in driving news traffic, more often to celebrity clickbait than to a discussion of Holyrood policy options. Twitter has become the main forum on which politicians and journalists engage with each other, with readers and voters. On phones in the palm of their hands, journalists and politicians are buffeted daily with insults, challenges and sometimes raw aggression. The clever politicians have deployed social media skills to reach their supporters directly, with less need for the conventional mass media. Nicola Sturgeon, as First Minister, is comfortable with the medium and set the standard for a natural, relaxed, direct engagement, without having to be ghost-written, as other, nervous political leaders are, by advisers and officials.

That new media was a powerful new weapon in the independence referendum campaign in 2014. The rise of the SNP, with a shaking up of party loyalties, led Labour – and Tory-loyal newspaper titles to tone down that stridency – and work out how to respond with the nationalist ascendancy. Their readerships were voting for several parties and could be found on both sides of the independence question – the deepening fault line in Scottish politics. Alex Salmond's determination, after the 1999 election campaign, that he would never again let the SNP and its cause face such a hostile press had been partially achieved by partly neutralising red tops. It had been partly achieved by the First Minister's assiduous courting of Rupert Murdoch, the global media tycoon behind *The Sun*, *The Times* and much else besides. This caused some embarrassment to Alex Salmond, when the phone-tapping scandal and the Leveson Inquiry rendered Murdoch politically toxic. It cast the SNP leader in a similar light to political figures at Westminster engaged in the undignified battle to win the support of the Murdoch empire and its newspaper titles.

The *Scottish Sun* swung behind independence, and the *Daily Record* cautiously calibrated its support for the Union to avoid alienating the other side. The view long held within the SNP, that it has been uniquely ill-served by a hostile newspaper industry is still commonly found on platforms such as Twitter. True, the print media cheerleading for independence is limited to *The National*, an echo chamber of propaganda, specialising in the imaginatively graphic variety on its front pages. But the four city papers – *The Herald*, *The Scotsman*, *The Courier* and *The P&J* – have usually sought to balance opinion because they serve a city and its region. They have known their readership covers many different views on many subjects, rather than playing to one market segment. For the tabloid tendency, where editors have sold the journalism of party loyalty, they have become significantly more nuanced on the independence issue, or at least become less hostile to that constitutional option.

Yet in a highly charged, partisan political environment during and after the 2014 vote, subtle shifts barely register with the most passionate and vocal supporters of their respective causes. Thus, in certain quarters, the result of the independence referendum is still – if not increasingly – seen as having been 'stolen' by the BBC and the *Daily Record*, with 'The Vow', signed by No-voting political leaders, in the final days of the campaign. For many, the debate is no longer a debate, but an echo chamber of reinforced opinion, and the hurling of abuse on social media instead of gaining an understanding of one's opponents. Neither Scotland nor the UK are alone in this.

Assertive, abrasive, unapologetic unionism can be found in the *Daily Mail* and the *Daily Telegraph*, but with falling circulation they are increasingly preaching to the choir. During the 2015 UK election campaign, The *Daily Telegraph* reported that SNP leader Nicola Sturgeon had told French diplomats that she preferred a Conservative victory to a Labour one. Hotly denied by Sturgeon and the embarrassed French consul-general, it didn't stand up too much scrutiny.

Such a story typifies one of the aspects of Holyrood reporting – in common with Westminster over the twenty years – that it has put far more effort and space into reporting the soap opera of individual ambitions and 'he-said-she-said' spats while putting less effort into exploring and understanding public policy choices. The latter can make for a duller read and requires a level of expertise that has been stripped out of newspapers, as specialist correspondents have gone, or been turned over rapidly. There is a price to be paid in democracy, in the public realm and in accountability. And, if it's a problem at Holyrood, it is more so at local government level, where part of the BBC licence fee is being used to fund press reporters, and where Dame Frances Cairncross has been commissioned by Downing Street to address the democratic deficit.

Twenty years on, Parliament and print media have evolved together: one a new kid on the Royal Mile; the other taking more than two centuries of history and adapting to new circumstances. Including editions of London papers, Scotland probably still has the widest range of national newspaper titles you will find in any media market of its size.

Few titles have disappeared, and some new ones have joined. Yet the newsstand presents a thin and pale imitation of the industry that threw its editorial weight around in the early days of the new democracy. That is far from being a bad thing, but parliament will continue to require a noisy, disputatious media and robust, well-resourced scrutiny. Despite the best efforts of those who work at Holyrood, it is not clear that is a job it can continue to do, adequately, for the next twenty years.

References

Fraser, D. (2008), *Nation Speaking Unto Nation: Does the Media Create Cultural Distance between England and Scotland?*, Newcastle: Institute for Public Policy Research North.

Fraser, D. (2004), 'New Labour, New Parliament', in Hassan, G. (ed.), *The Scottish Labour Party: History, Institutions, Ideas*, Edinburgh: Edinburgh University Press.

Geoghegan, P. (2017), 'The SNP and the Press', in Hassan, G. and Barrow, S. (eds.), *A Nation Changed? The SNP and Scotland Ten Years On*, Edinburgh: Luath Press.

Hassan, G. and Shaw, E. (2012), *The Strange Death of Labour Scotland*, Edinburgh: Edinburgh University Press.

CHAPTER 23

Broadcasting in Scotland

Blair Jenkins

IT COULD BE argued that not very much has changed in Scottish broadcasting in the twenty years since the restoration of the Scottish Parliament. 2019 might finally be the year when we do see the first real evidence of television catching up with devolution.

The launch of the new BBC Scotland channel, if not exactly revolutionary, is certainly both overdue and welcome. People in Scotland need a dedicated public space to explore and discuss the issues and opportunities facing the country and to see their own lives and culture reflected. The logic of having a distinctively Scottish television service has been clear for the last twenty years.

The new channel represents the most significant development in Scottish broadcasting since the launch of Radio Scotland in 1978. It will provide the biggest opportunity there has ever been for Scottish television content to be created and distributed for audiences in Scotland. It is also true to say that, with a slim budget of £32 million at launch, it already feels more like a starting point than any kind of final destination.

In 1999 spirits were very low in Scottish broadcasting. BBC Scotland had lost the long internal battle over its Scottish Six proposal (the plan for an integrated hour-long international, UK and Scottish news programme) while STV had moved firmly into its post-Gus Macdonald focus on cutting programmes and jobs.

The minority SNP Government elected in 2007 made broadcasting an early priority. The independent Scottish Broadcasting Commission (SBC), which I chaired, was set up to make recommendations for much-needed improvement. Its final report – including the key proposal for a new dedicated Scottish TV channel, the Scottish Digital Network – was endorsed unanimously in the Scottish Parliament.

Within the Commission, we thought it was important that there should be a secure and sustainable source of competition for the BBC in high-quality public service content produced for Scottish audiences. A distinctively Scottish channel had been a clear gap in UK broadcasting, a missing piece of the jigsaw.

A Changing Landscape

The SBC looked in depth at broadcasting in terms of its economic, cultural and democratic importance to Scotland. It was easiest to build wide support in the strong case for the UK public service networks to spend more money here. With the television licence fee remaining the only source of public funding for broadcasting, it was politically easier to move money within the BBC than to move it away from the BBC. Our demand for greatly increased network spending in Scotland resulted in additional tens of millions of pounds flowing annually into the Scottish creative economy, mainly from the BBC. The commissioning of this additional drama, comedy and factual programming brought a much-needed financial injection to the production sector, but also resulted in more Scottish content for audiences in Scotland.

However, the case and the support for the Scottish channel never went away, and in February 2019 BBC Scotland will launch a new service with some similarities to the SBC model. It's not the audacious and innovative start-up we had envisaged, but it does represent an important moment in Scottish media history all the same.

In the serial drama of Scottish broadcasting, there have always been two main elements to the plot: getting more UK production money spent in Scotland by the main television networks, and making good Scottish programmes aimed specifically at audiences in Scotland. Gaelic-language content has always constituted an interesting sub-plot.

Historically, there was a very similar dilemma for senior managements at both BBC Scotland and STV. It was important to sell UK-wide network programme ideas from Scotland to the BBC and ITV channel heads in London. But it was also important to opt out of those channels on a regular basis to make room for Scottish content. UK channel controllers tend to be less receptive to Scottish ideas when their own carefully-crafted schedules and pet programmes are being dropped or disrupted north of the border.

Tensions and conflict were almost inevitable. Some of the compromises were messy at best. We have now had 60 years of opt-out television services, with local schedulers always struggling on both BBC and STV to secure decent slots for Scottish programmes.

There was one important difference between the two broadcasters. STV always had more genuine corporate and editorial autonomy, but BBC Scotland always had more money to spend on programmes. Each eyed the other enviously. Both eyed London suspiciously.

Within the Scottish Broadcasting Commission, we thought that the commercial constraints on STV and the corporate constraints on BBC Scotland would always limit the scale and ambition of Scottish broadcasting. We proposed a new broadcaster, a dedicated Scottish Digital Network, as the most effective, proportionate and ambitious solution.

The remit for the digital network was outlined as including high-quality information and entertainment, news and current affairs programmes covering Scottish and international issues, and innovative and ambitious cultural content. I recall saying in interviews that it should be recognisably Scottish, but not relentlessly Scottish. Commenting on the BBC in Scotland, the Commission said there was

> a sense that the energy and vitality of modern Scottish life was not being adequately reflected (SBC, 2008).

The BBC now seem to have accepted our analysis and to have adopted much of this remit for their own proposal. I continue to think that it would have been much better if the new channel were coming from a new broadcaster with none of the baggage that the BBC brings, but that has not proved financially or politically possible.

Some people have argued that television channels are outdated concepts in the age of streaming services such as Netflix and Amazon. But traditional broadcasting is being supplemented, not superseded. There is certainly wider choice, more control is being exercised by audiences and convenience and personal preference are dictating viewing times more than channel schedules. This is particularly true for younger viewers. But broadcasting still has a power and impact that is almost impossible to replace.

This is very clearly the case in current affairs. It continues to strike me as a major failing of the Scottish broadcasters that there are no regularly-scheduled political discussion programmes with audience participation. In the 1990s these exercises in public engagement were important parts of the service on both main channels. It seems extraordinary at a time when there is such political energy and interest in Scotland – and so much to talk about – that there are no lively televised debates with ordinary members of the public actively involved. We need this kind of democratic forum to make sure that we see and hear the other person's point of view, not just our own.

Broadcasting is still a very important space for the exchange of ideas and opinions. Social media, for all its noise, seems incapable of fulfilling this role. Twitter is not somewhere you go to listen respectfully to other views – why bite your tongue when you can bite other people? We will benefit as a society from more open dialogue and more open minds. We need an accurate representation of our communities and our issues, which the BBC under its Royal Charter and under the Ofcom Broadcasting Code is required to provide.

It is certainly better that the BBC should create a new Scottish channel rather than one not existed at all. But we will need to see transparency in its operation and governance, and be vigilant in our scrutiny, if we are in effect to put almost all of our broadcasting eggs in this one basket.

Change at the BBC

The new BBC Scotland channel will be picking up a lot of tabs: compensating for the reduced spending and hours on BBC1 and 2; satisfying the SBC and public demand for a dedicated Scottish channel; providing the long-awaited integrated news service covering Scottish, UK and international news; and, last but not least, trying to appeal to the currently disappearing young audiences. All of this on a budget rather less than half of what the SBC thought would be necessary more than ten years ago. It is certainly a challenge.

That's one reason why the BBC will be pointing to the overall impact and distinctiveness of the new channel rather than just audience reach as the more valid measures of success. The shift away from linear broadcasting to viewing on demand makes this approach all the more necessary. The channel's content will almost certainly attract more viewing and comment online when it is shared on social media than when it is initially broadcast on the linear service.

With the new service launching, it means the end of separate programming for Scotland on BBC2 and we lose six hours a week on that channel in peak-time. There is no point in pretending that BBC Scotland can immediately make up for those audience losses for Scottish programmes. It can't. Ofcom thinks the share of total viewing achieved by the new channel in Scotland will be 'modest', with a working assumption of just over 2 per cent (Ofcom, 2018). Of course, it's not possible to estimate viewing levels precisely ahead of launch, but it's wise to be cautious.

The full details of the BBC Scotland schedule are not available at the time of writing. Those commissions which have been announced look generally crowd-pleasing and ratings-driven, which is perhaps understandable if you are launching a new channel with the difficult pre-existing obligation of an immovable hour-long news programme in the prime 9–10pm slot. We know the core content will be broadcast between 7pm and midnight, about half of it being original productions and the other half repeat transmissions.

The political context for the launch is problematic. That unanimous vote in the Parliament in 2008 was an unprecedented outbreak of political consensus in relation to broadcasting and not surprisingly it couldn't last. The SBC had said that 'broadcasting should not serve as a surrogate for the constitutional debate in Scotland' (SBC, 2008). This was ultimately a forlorn hope in a policy area which has become intensely politicised.

The BBC has put itself in the difficult position of being regarded with suspicion if not with outright hostility by large parts of the Yes movement for an independent Scotland. This is in part a legacy of its controversial and uncertain coverage of the Scottish referendum campaign. Whatever your view on that issue, it is undeniable that the BBC is not launching its new channel from a strong position in terms of the relationship with licence fee payers in Scotland. It was caught flat-footed by the referendum while new media (and indeed STV) did a better job of capturing the energetic and grassroots nature of the campaign.

Making an Impact

From the other side of the constitutional divide, the channel is seen as an unwelcome acknowledgement by the BBC of Scotland's distinctive culture and identity and indeed is assumed to be some kind of sop to nationalism. There will be many in both camps hoping for its failure. In these circumstances, audiences will be tough to attract and even tougher to hold.

On the positive side, this will be the best-funded media development we will see in Scotland in the foreseeable future. This is really it in terms of anything new with significant scale and resources. Importantly for all sceptics, the new channel is covered by robust impartiality obligations and a public service remit externally licensed and regulated by Ofcom.

We must insist on transparency and we must practise vigilance. Ofcom will formally review the performance of BBC Scotland against its stated promises and obligations, but the people of Scotland also need to take ownership and ensure that we get the service we need and deserve. Always remember, this is not an act of charity by the BBC. Our money is paying for it.

Most of all I believe, the new channel has to be talked about. Making an impact is more important than hitting a particular target for viewing figures. I hope to find things that are surprising and challenging, distinctive and innovative. It has to become part of the national conversation and quickly come to be regarded as indispensable. Whatever doubts I have about the BBC's ability to deliver such a service; I have to wish it good luck.

References

OFCOM (2018), 'BBC Scotland Competition Assessment: Final
    Determination'.
Scottish Broadcasting Commission (2008), 'Platform for Success', Edinburgh:
    Scottish Government.

CHAPTER 24

Arts in Hard Times

Ruth Wishart

IF YOU FEEL the urge to start a fight in an empty room, there are worse topics than funding the arts in Scotland. It has a history of many models; some discarded, some broken, others subject to periodic re-invention. A current example of the latter is something called Screen Scotland, an internal division of Creative Scotland, which was recently in receipt of a handsome and very welcome extra cash injection of ten million pounds.

When Creative Scotland was initially set up it consisted of a merger of the Scottish Arts Council and Scottish Screen, the film industries funding body. The latter always felt more subsumed than merged, and the screen community has never ceased to bemoan its lost autonomy. Given that the three newest members of the Creative Scotland board are all people with a screen hinterland, nobody is betting against a de-merger with a separate board.

But probably more significant than the lack of a dedicated, fully autonomous screen body has been the protracted effort to acquire a properly resourced studio; the subject of inter-agency wrangling these many years with various prospects gaining initial enthusiasm only to fail for a variety of logistical and planning reasons.

But then, just before Christmas 2018, Screen Scotland announced it was looking for tenders for the Forth Ports-owned Pelamis building in Leith, suggesting that Creative Scotland now sees long term leasing as the most promising solution to inward investment opportunities. The lengthy process was not helped by the fact that Creative Scotland and Scottish Enterprise (along with the Government) were jointly charged with the search. There has been long-standing tension between these organisations as to where the creative industries budgets and the overall responsibility should lie.

But in some senses, partially underwriting screen prospects is a comparatively simple process, given the dedicated and expanding pot and bidders all coming from the same sector. Funding all the other branches of arts and the creative industries has much more potential for internecine squabbling. The very phrase 'creative industries' has long stuck in the collective gullets of many arts practitioners who baulk at the thought of commercial operators getting their fingers in the funding cookie jar. It doesn't help that 'the arts, screen and creative industries' is an apparently immutable mantra which is emblazoned through all Creative Scotland's myriad strategic documents like seaside rock.

An Economic Contribution

Yet industries like gaming and animation have been growing in reputation and job creation with tens of thousands of employees and they make a handsome contribution to the national economy. Graduates and others who go into these industries are entitled to suppose their design skills are just as artistic as anyone else's. They also have a high preponderance of solo or small staff operations in need of seed corn support. What is arguably more contentious is using the funding round to give money to those agencies and organisations who support creative endeavour rather than solely to practitioners.

However, the more fundamental fault lines lie elsewhere. When the consultations for the latest Scottish Government cultural strategy took place in nine locations across Scotland, one of the recurring themes was what people in more rural areas felt was an enduring bias towards central Scotland projects. And there's a certain inevitability about that given the sheer weight of cultural organisations and enterprises that are located in the larger urban conurbations. But there's also a basic philosophical conundrum to unpick.

At one stage in Creative Scotland's early life it chose to try and refresh the parts of Scotland not currently housing cultural delights by a form of strategic commissioning. The motivation might have been admirable, but it profoundly altered the remit of the organisation from one which received and considered bids for funding, to one which was actively involved in determining the nature, and, most especially, the location of the successful bids. Unsurprisingly this caused unhappiness among applicants with excellent track records and credentials whose only real fault was operating in the 'wrong' part of Scotland. It was one of the factors in a widespread artists' revolt of 2012.

But there is an intrinsic problem within this which is genuinely hard to resolve. If there are two very good dance companies bidding for funds in the same area it's difficult to justify backing both, though arguably unfair to penalise either. Yet equally there is the perennially difficult, but essential task of nurturing innovative newcomers who, by definition, haven't built a following or a major reputation.

Balancing the Network

'Balancing The Network' is the name given to trying to square these circles, and it happens at Stage 4 of the funding application process when the senior leadership team and lead specialism officers discuss and debate the recommendations of the staff who have done all the initial assessments over the first three stages. (There is a persuasive argument that those organisations who have failed the criteria at earlier junctures, certainly those who fall off the wagon at stage one or two, should be advised of the outcome there and then rather than waiting for months to find out the worst.)

In essence Stage 4 is about examining the list of potentially successful bidders in the light of the perceived need for overall geographical spread, a decent range of art forms in various areas, and diversity of product and organisational size. It's arguably almost impossible at this stage to screen out all subjectivity, however aware the senior team are of the hazards of unconscious bias. The board approval is the final and fifth hurdle and, as the 2018–21 regular funding round indicated, is capable of throwing other spanners in the works.

There are other difficulties out with the control of the people taking the funding decisions. Using lottery money to underpin the financing of regular funding seemed a perfectly defensible notion when the lottery income went up inexorably year on year. Then the UK Government, wedded as ever to de-regulation, opened up the lottery market with the predictable result that the core organisation found money seeping away to a plethora of imitators, some more kosher than others.

It meant that when the 2018–21 regular funding round was being discussed in 2017, Creative Scotland was staring at a six million-pound black hole. Many scenarios were worked up internally on that basis, all of them horrible – one envisaged a 30 per cent cut in the government grant in aid. But all of them were guaranteed to decimate whole swathes of Scotland's cultural life. In the event the Scottish Government recognised nobody was crying wolf, and the budget settlement they gave not only made good the lottery shortfall but allowed the organisation itself a three-year deal rather than its annual settlement.

Bizarrely, just when a collective sigh of relief had gone up, it emerged that a handful of the most well-respected arts providers had nevertheless been taken out of regular funding. Such was the ensuing furore that most of them were re-instated at a subsequent emergency board meeting, but not before two board members – I was one of them – resigned. The Chief Executive and the then interim Head of Arts left the organisation within months. The interim chair's term expired one week after that meeting.

In fairness, that particular funding round was subject to some special circumstances – the application deadline had been in April, yet Creative Scotland, juggling various fiscal scenarios, only found what was in actually in the pot in mid-December following the Scottish budget. The helter-skelter process from that to a January board meeting on the 18th with a pre-arranged announcement to applicants scheduled for the 25th was not a recipe for considered judgement.

While the board felt it had neither the information nor the time to try to understand the rationale behind the high profile 'losers', the senior team felt it was being unfairly second guessed. The bottom line was that organisations which had sent in detailed applications by a spring deadline were still none the wiser as to the outcome nine months later. Being given funds to tide them over the gap site was welcome but, small compensation for the expanded uncertainty.

Future Burden

Undoubtedly there are ways in which the future burden can be eased for both staff and funding clients, some of which feature in the results of the external funding review swiftly undertaken by the new Creative Scotland chair. It's not easy in the village that is Scotland to employ external assessors with no obvious conflict of interest, but the recruitment of some more external expertise would ease the pressure on staff for whom almost every other aspect of their work has to be put on hold for months at a time while they plough through the bids. Brexit for the arty classes.

Externals are already used to assist the alternative funding stream, the Open Project fund, to which unsuccessful Request for Offer (RFO) candidates are often directed. Some of them would have been better aiming for that kitty in the first place, but it has always been seen as a poor relation to a three-year deal offering a degree of stability. And, like all arts kitties, Project Funds are always oversubscribed. The success rate runs at under a third.

The main RFO application process, whilst simplified from the early years, still relies on a one-size-fits-all approach which clearly disadvantages those small-scale applicants with slender human resources to gather and refine all the documentation demanded. And the forms themselves still need more attention from the anti-jargon police and their colleagues in the Campaign to Eradicate Unnecessary Duplication.

It might prove enlightened self-interest to be less prescriptive about the kind of business plan deemed acceptable, and to split the applications into different financial bands with the lower levels of ask subject to less protracted scrutiny as happens with the Arts Council England. (It is worth noting in passing that bureaucratic constipation is not helped by those arts organisations who somehow come to believe that appending dozens of pages of unsolicited appendices will help their cause. It won't. But it's a good way to cheese off the folks wading through it all.)

There are very specific criteria and guidelines deployed by all the in-house assessors, but it's not easy to ensure that these are interpreted in a uniform way, or that different specialism teams use interchangeable yardsticks for quality. How you screen out the human factor definitively is a conundrum few funding organisations can unravel. The recommendations are later re-examined by cross fertilised sector teams to add rigour to the process, but that can also throw up differences in the methodologies employed by individual departments. It is not an easy process, but I can attest to the efforts made to make it as fair minded as assembling such a complex national jigsaw can ever be.

Funding Pressures and More

The perennial complaint of cultural supplicants is that funding has become too process driven; that formulae and forms have been allowed to choke inspiration and ambition; that the application journey itself is liable to sap artistic energies to an unnecessary degree; that there are altogether too many boxes to be ticked; and there is a lack of transparency as to who makes the cut and why.

There is merit in some of these complaints even though Creative Scotland, following that major league stushie with its stakeholders, cut down its funding streams from 15 to three, and attempted to streamline the application process. But there is still a tendency, as noted, towards jargon infestation, occasioned perhaps because arts funding bodies are not immune from bureaucratisation. I never did share the outgoing CEO's attachment to having a ten-year plan against whose aims and ambitions all organisations were expected to test their bids. The concept always seemed more than a little Stalinist (though Uncle Joe only went for five-year strategies)! And the arts, of all places, need to be responsive and flexible to changing trends and demands.

The funding rounds and subsequent inevitable debates sometimes disguise the other work which Creative Scotland does in terms of sector and organisation development and brokering collaboration. During part of my spell on the board I chaired the inter-agency strategic group which produced a creative learning plan, among other things looking at the work of the creative learning networks in all 32 Scottish local authorities.

I remain an unapologetic enthusiast for the principles of the Curriculum for Excellence with its core aim of producing rounded citizens using their inherent creativity in ways which appeal to contemporary employers: lateral thought, team working, confident decision making. As the internationally renowned educator Sir Kenneth Robinson was wont to point out, creativity isn't a special quality bestowed on special people. 'If you're human it comes with the kit'. And that applies equally to teachers utilising creative ways of imparting knowledge across the curriculum.

So many other aspects of the operation are often obscured by questions over funding decisions, and staffers are often frustrated at being lambasted in public for these decisions without being able to respond in any detail given the need for commercial confidentiality. If you think there's potential for a bun fight when the 'winners and losers' are announced, imagine that amplified to the power of ten if everyone was privy to each other's bids.

Creativity and its Discontents

Creative Scotland began life with an executive duo appointed by an interim board. For a variety of reasons, which a well-developed antipathy to litigation discourages me from detailing, the inaugural team of Andrew Dixon and deputy Venu Dhupa ran into a major standoff with Scotland's cultural community. The successor CEO, Janet Archer, joined from the Arts Council England, one of many escapees from that body after a brutal round of cuts. She too 'lost the dressing room' and her deputy, the long serving Iain Munro, is now looking after the shop.

The same period has seen no fewer than three chairs. (Three and half if you count the six somewhat turbulent months Ben Thomson was interim chair following the untimely death of Richard Findlay.) Banker Sandy Crombie was the inaugural choice and served during the first firestorm surrounding the cultural community. Following Sandy, Richard and Ben, Jupiter Artland owner Robert Wilson now holds a chalice he will hope is less poisoned. His board will hope he is more consensual and less prescriptive than his immediate predecessor. Wilson's decision to instigate an independent root and branch review of the way regular funding is decided allowed many people inside and outside to vent their concerns; time will tell how many of the resulting recommendations are followed through.

The relationships between the chair and CEO of Creative Scotland and the Cabinet Secretary for Culture are clearly crucial. There is a balance to be struck between the Government respecting the supposed arm's length nature of their involvement with the agency, and the agency recognising that funding wheels need to be oiled by mutual co-operation. There have been occasions in recent years when the Government has leant on the organisation, perhaps because it lacked the necessary confidence in elements of its leadership. The letter of 'guidance' sometimes stretched the definition of that term. The departmental civil servants became overly prone to dispatching serial emails to senior staff demanding information.

It should also be noted, however, that when Creative Scotland has been most embattled it's been useful to have continuity at the Government end of the equation. After years of culture secretaries being changed with embarrassing regularity, the current incumbent has been around long enough to understand both the needs and the frustrations of the cultural community. It didn't hurt that she made it clear in one major speech that she didn't consider economic impact to be the overriding principle by which artistic endeavour should be measured.

What tends to achieve a fruitful relationship is having a chair who commands respect and knows the difference between pragmatic acquiescence and inappropriate subservience. And a CEO who appreciates and deploys his or her existing in-house expertise, and also gains the respect of his or her stakeholders. Funding chiefs will never win popularity contests, but they do need to speak human, and know how to delegate.

The Government leaves a footprint in other ways. It ring-fences funding for specific projects reducing the scope for flexibility within the agency. Nobody would argue against the merits of a Youth Music Initiative at a time when school music tuition is withering on the vine, but it means ten million pounds out of the core budget.

A Healthy Bedrock

The sorry state of music tuition in schools was flagged up by many when the Government agreed to fund Sistema projects in Scotland; first in the Raploch, Stirling, now in Torry, Aberdeen, Govanhill, Glasgow and Douglas, Dundee. Based on the Venezuelan model which led to the world-renowned Simon Bolivar Orchestra, it aims to give disadvantaged children new skills and confidence through learning and playing musical instruments. The results have been startling and heart-warming, but in an ideal world these would be projects building on a healthy bedrock of tuition throughout the state school system.

Having said which standalone initiatives, properly targeted, can give a country a significant bang for limited bucks, The Expo Fund gives indigenous companies and artists funding to appear at the Edinburgh International Festival and raise their international profile. Similarly, a touring fund for the five national performing arts companies – whose core support comes directly from government – has underwritten a number of important tours.

And there are other routes through which money for cultural enterprises can be levered. Cashback for Creativity – a subsection of the Cashback for Communities programme – uses the proceeds of crime to fund artistic endeavour sometimes in the most unlikely places. You can detect a delicious irony in the fact that it was the genesis of what became an arts strategy within Barlinnie Prison.

But all of these initiatives require to be carefully thought through. The late Sam Galbraith finding two million pounds down the back of his sofa having been lobbied directly by Scottish Opera, or Alex Salmond producing a cash rabbit from his hat for the Scottish Youth Theatre can only undermine the confidence of the sectors in the funding process being as neutral and rigorous as possible.

Dependence, Interdependence, Leadership

Arts funders are always keen on encouraging self-sufficiency and creative partnerships, and anxious that regular funding does not come to be regarded as investment in perpetuity. Yet here too there is the imperative of discouraging inappropriate dependency while recognising that some parts of the arts simply couldn't function properly without subsidy. Having listened to these debates up close and personal I can attest to the headaches they engender.

On the matter of leadership, the venerable Alasdair Gray once caused more than a flurry in the doocots when he suggested that Scotland had developed what he considered a self-harming habit of appointing people to top arts jobs from out with Scotland. That argument would only hold good if all the top jobs had gone to people of inferior quality.

When the inaugural board of the National Theatre of Scotland appointed Vicky Featherstone, it was regarded as a high-risk strategy. In the event, operating in tandem with John Clifford, she proved an inspired choice. Both she and Clifford have gone on to build international reputations. (On the other hand, the tenure of their immediate successor, also imported from England, is unlikely to feature in a resume of NTS' greatest hits.)

And you might easily argue that the Belfast born John Leighton, Director General of the National Galleries of Scotland, has been a greater champion of finding the means to respect and display its Scottish collection than a predecessor whose principal enthusiasm was the Italian school.

What is fair comment though, is the still visible reluctance in some quarters to believe home grown talent can possess the qualities of an apparently glitterier 'outsider'. 'I kent his faither syndrome' is no longer all-pervasive, but it is taking an unconscionable time to die off. And it's demonstrably true that while appointments from other countries can bring a welcome objectivity, they are also unlikely to be aware of either the history of or the nuances within the patch they inherit.

A final thought. Creative Scotland may be an imperfect vehicle to oversee and underwrite so much of Scotland's cultural activity. But to misquote Churchill on democracy: an arts funding agency is the worst way of disbursing essential funds – except for all the others.

CHAPTER 25

Beyond the Macho-Cultural Scottish Literature of the Last Twenty Years

Laura Waddell

'THE WHOLE WORLD needs creative women and seems to be unaware of its need' declared Willa Muir in 1925. Muir was a writer and translator, with a rare ability to size up Scotland's cultural concerns, writing with scorching wit on the national character. She critiqued petty parochialism and xenophobia, opposition to art and theatre and self-conscious, neighbourly hostility. Some of her words still ring true today.

Scotland is thought of as an exceptional nation by many; genuinely ground-breaking achievements of industry, innovation, and invention, and many can reel off men of letters whose works graced fast-flying printing presses. This can tint the national memory rosy, good for basking in, but clouding self-reflection.

Where are the women of Scotland in all this? We can count how many take a seat in our Parliament now as a barometer of cultural movement, but one wonders if so much has changed since Willa Muir was scathing of the

> Scotsman who thinks that 'intellectual argument' is the only kind of social intercourse, and who assumes tacitly that 'the women' are to be left out of it (Muir, 1936).

Lack of Parity

That great Scottish invention, the television, demonstrates a lack of women's parity with men a century after some women secured the vote as public voices on current affairs programming, while simultaneously reporting pay gaps and workplace sexual harassment. Muir was writing in a different context from the one we now live in, her achievements are all the more impressive for it, but in many ways, her words on equality burst from the page like a warning flare, signalling attitudes towards women writers that may be pervasive so many years on. Did the intellectual, creative woman, a woman like Willa Muir, get her due regard in the decades after?

I asked Adele Patrick, Lifelong Learning and Creative Development Manager at Glasgow Women's Library, what things looked like for women writers in the time period running up to Holyrood's creation:

> The cultural landscape that gave rise to Glasgow Women's Library was one where women's voices in all fields were hard to detect, muffled or silenced. There were some exciting developments in what would be the (ongoing) recovery of the lost canon of Scottish women writers from the mid-1980s and there was plenty of women active in writing groups but as far as publishing was concerned we lived mainly on a diet of North American and English fare with rare exceptions. In itself a mobilising force for the creation of the Library.

The universal or authentic experience has belonged to man with women writers offset. In 1991, Janice Galloway wrote:

> There is coping with that guilt of taking time off the concerns with national politics to get concerned about the sexual sort; that creeping fear it's somehow self-indulgent to be concerned for one's womaness instead of one's Scottishness, one's working-class heritage or whatever. Guilt here comes from the notion we're not backing up our menfolk and their 'real' concerns (Galloway, 1991).

Has anything changed in the years since? In the souvenir booklet of Glasgow being anointed City of Culture in 1990 you can see why Glasgow Women's Library emerged to put women on our shelves and minds; almost every cultural commentator included was a man. In it, Elaine C Smith wrote:

> I'm worried that instead of changing the image from the old macho-industrialised one we are simply changing it to the macho-Cultural one (Smith, 1990).

It's only one example, but it's difficult to imagine such skewed editing happening now, this book in the reader's hands as a contemporary contrast.

Women are more visible if not equally present in public life now to a backdrop of campaigns for parity on public boards and in parliament, while projects aiming to excavate women writers from a suffocating historical cloak continue.

Funding the Future?

In 2018, capping off a year of celebrating Muriel Spark, the Scottish Government announced funding of a complete set of Muriel Spark books for every library in Scotland.

> Muriel Spark is one of Scotland's greatest authors and it is fitting that we celebrate the centenary of her birth with this donation to libraries

said First Minister Nicola Sturgeon, noted champion of reading (Sturgeon, 2018). 2018 also saw a pathway in Edinburgh dedicated to Spark, the first physical thing to be named after her in the city of her birth, already host to an array of monuments to male writers. In 2016 Nan Shepherd became the first woman to appear on an RBS note. These initiatives, though positive, suggest those most celebrated in Scottish literature, and who in turn becomes canonical, is slow to evolve and include women writers.

Dr Stevie Marsden has examined gender in the Saltire Society literary awards, considered the premier book award in Scotland and a useful barometer for measuring esteem. In a 2019 essay she argues:

> Scottish women writers have been continually portrayed as playing lesser roles in the development of Scotland's literary and cultural development (Marsden, 2019).

Her research into the numbers shows:

> Despite critics arguing that there was a change in tide in the late 1980s and early 1990s regarding the balance in gender representation in Scottish literature… analysis suggests that Scotland's book award culture, and in turn, literary culture more widely, remains dominated by men (Marsden, 2019).

And that this trend continued into more recent decades:

> even though women writers comprised 32 per cent of all shortlisted entries for the Book of the Year Award between 1988 and 2014, they represented just 12 per cent of Book of the Year Award winners (Marsden, 2019).

This suggests writing by women has continued to struggle disproportionally in gaining national esteem. Christopher Whyte wrote scathingly in 1995:

> Much of contemporary Scottish writing has a narrow and drearily male focus… Scottishness is about drink and football, interspersed with brief episodes of violence in a home where cold, wounded and rejecting wives and mothers have little comfort to offer. What, one wonders, can the country described in these books offer women, children, and men with minds of their own? (Whyte, 1995).

For visitors leaving Scottish airports with a souvenir, the Scottish selection on offer seldom strays from books about gangs, murders, or politics in its most confessional capacity and rarely is it recently or attractively published. Nor does it reflect Scotland's impressive crime writing cachet which seems to punch above its weight. If what's on offer in these neglected retail spaces in 2019 has been selected by a buyer with an outdated 'no mean city' sentiment in the back of their minds, it's also noticeably macho. It's not reflective of the many excellent bookshops elsewhere; but it does give an insight into what is considered 'Scottish writing' in some outward-facing quarters.

The Publishing Scene

What is the Scottish publishing scene which underpins this, then and now? I asked Professor Claire Squires, Director of Publishing Studies at the University of Stirling, about the publishing of the last twenty years:

> Scottish publishing really started to see a renaissance in the late 1960s and 1970s, with the establishment of companies including Canongate, Floris, Mainstream and Polygon, and also the foundation of the Scottish Publishers Association. But the last two decades have also shown some key changes as well as continuities. Some established companies have closed or sold to companies outside of Scotland (eg Chambers and Mainstream). Other companies have come and gone (eg Cargo and Freight). Yet more have started, taking advantage of new technologies, platforms and alternative business models to establish themselves (eg 404 Ink).

Scotland's publishing scene has always been indie-heavy, akin to a flotilla of small boats, as reactive and innovative as they are vulnerable to difficulties of trading on a smaller scale. When Freight Books disappeared in 2017, after years of significant public funding, many debut Scottish writers on their list were put in a precarious position, some having to buy their own books at high rates to save them from being pulped. The suddenness of its departure could be described as an act of cultural vandalism; the duty of a publisher is not only to print books, but also to nurture writers. Fortunately, some of those writers have gone on to be picked up by other publishers such as Saraband and Polygon.

It is interesting to compare two small publishers bookending the run up to the Scottish Parliament and now; Rebel Inc. and 404 Ink. Publishing writers like Trocchi, Rebel Inc. injected a counter-culture vibe to the 90s lit scene. Founder Kevin Williamson said 25 years on:

> I was into literature, but I was immersed in the culture and philosophy of punk and DIY. And 'fuck the mainstream,' that was my philosophy and a dawning political philosophy too – of 'fuck London' (Williamson, 2017).

Undoubtedly they brought underground writers to the fore, making books relevant to a young creative community, but to a modern eye it's startling to look at the list of 52 titles and see how few women are among them, reminiscent of cult publishing in 60s and 70s US which reflected mainstream culture's gender bias. 404 Ink, on the other hand, launched in 2016 with the anthology *Nasty Women*, which was the bestselling book of Edinburgh International Book Festival that year and attracting compliments from Margaret Atwood, Shirley Manson and Nicola Sturgeon. Alongside talented working-class men of a millennial generation, they've published a queer anthology and books by women of colour, their rising prominence proving reader appetite. Although there are similarities, publishing outside the mainstream for a fresh, young audience looks quite different 25 years on, as non-masculine literary voices emerge. The same can be said of other emerging micropublishers and flourishing 'zine scene, where women creators are often a driving force.

Squires also comments on the business of publishing:

> Perhaps the biggest changes to publishing over the period have come in the wider context of book retail and digital technologies, with Amazon figuring large in both. These contexts have given publishers new opportunities but also represent significant challenge in building and sustaining commercial businesses in very tough trading conditions. But at the same time there's also been a strong and supportive ecosystem around literature and publishing, including via Publishing Scotland, Scottish Book Trust, and the growth of the literary festival, which has reached every part of the nation from the Borders to Shetland and developed incrementally in the last twenty years.

In the last couple of years there have been interesting developments supporting the infrastructure of that wider ecosystem. One of these is the Emerging Critics scheme by the Scottish Review of Books, aiming to hone the skills of next generation book critics, recognising the importance of specialised criticism when quality review spaces are declining, and reporting becomes more generalised. Beyond improving writing skills, the scheme also encourages participants to consider and influence critical platforms of the future. It affirms the practise of younger critics who can be estranged from print's in-house criticism. Like newspapers adapting to new models, arts criticism is still finding its feet digitally, and it's my belief we're only beginning to get a handle on the value of digital content and ownership of it. But as a tool for discoverability, and showcasing relevance to wider culture, healthy arts criticism is necessary for Scottish publishing.

As Gerard Carruthers commented in 2009:

> a healthy 'critical community' ought to comprise various and diverse critical voices. The future health of Scottish literary studies demands this, if it is to be in line with other areas of literary study and so as to be prevented from becoming merely a minor adjunct to the discipline of history (Carruthers, 2009).

Broadcasting is more difficult to engage, with BBC Scotland resistant to covering the Saltire Society literary awards, which in 2018 celebrated 30 years of a First Book Award recognising writers early in their careers such as Ali Smith, Louise Welsh, and Kathleen Jamie. The Irish Book Awards are televised; our less glitzy ceremony is better suited to documentary format, as suggested for many years. The popularity of Scotland's book festivals makes it surprising to see no hint of book coverage on the new Scottish channel. Dramatization is also a sticking point; the smaller scale of Scottish independent publishing is less likely to publish high volume hits favoured for the screen.

Publishing Scotland in 2018 established Scottish Books International. Irish literature has a very strong identity overseas; Scotland less so. Scottish literature has travelling and adventure in our traditional canon; this kind of investment in literary infrastructure is essential in supporting writers and their (often independent) publishers, in building cultural resonance and commercial potential. While Creative Scotland has funded these schemes and others, and the Scottish Government is a big backer of activities including Book Week Scotland, it stood out that there were zero publishers present at the criticised invite-only cultural strategy 'Culture Conversations' launch event in 2017.

Scotland and the UK

Scottish literature is somewhat estranged from a wider UK body of work. When asked for my views by an article by Houman Barekat on the novel and national identity (Barekat, 2017) I said:

> When a literary culture is positioned as external but in relation to a bigger and more centralized one – distinguished for all kinds of reasons, including local appeal sales, press and national funding bodies – it may give rise to work that is different in style from its bigger neighbour and conceives itself, in part, as 'different'. The indie publishing scene is thriving at the moment, and innovation often emerges in that context. Literary culture here is self-aware in national identity, and it is the other.

The argument that literature by Scottish women is doubly estranged still has been made before; I'd like to hope we are beginning to emerge from that. Continued dedication of institutions such as Glasgow Women's Library as well as the wider culture waking up to women is evident in the perspective of younger publishers who include women writers as default.

If masculinity has been a dominant theme of the past twenty years, drawing on long tradition of male writers is default on Scottish identity and history. I would like to see the Scotland which has slowly begun acknowledging women writers also recognise writers from other marginalised groups, particularly where national or cultural identities intersect. The campaign for a museum of slavery is beginning to take off; will we see more reckoning with Scotland's past beyond celebrating industrial achievement? I hope so.

Scotland's true enlightenment and a sober reckoning of its not altogether glorious history has some way to go as we examine hallowed rosters of success and those women intellects and writers whose contributions have been shunted from canonical ideas of national thinking. Willa Muir who wrote of 'formidable, outspoken Scotswomen' also wrote 'where women have no prestige of their own the community has no prestige' (Muir, 1936). Let us remember that as we consider the thinkers of Scotland, those whose legacies haven't always been graced the testimony of printed page, who as a result receive only a footnote in our cultural consciousness rather than their rightful place at the centre of a whole and healthy national body of literature.

References

Barekat, H. (2017), 'Innovation and the Decline of the English Novel', *Times Literary Supplement*, 20 April 2017.

Carruthers, G. (2009), *Scottish Literature*, Edinburgh: Edinburgh University Press.

Galloway, J. (1991), *Meantime: Looking Forward to the Millennium*, Edinburgh: Polygon.

Marsden, S. (2019), 'Why Women Don't Win Literary Awards: the Saltire Society Literary Awards and Implicit Stereotyping', *Women: A Cultural Review* Vol. 30 No. pp. 44–65.

Muir, W. (1936), *Mrs Grundy in Scotland*, London: George Routledge.

Muir, W. (1925), *Women, an Enquiry*, London: The Hogarth Press.

Smith, E.C. (1990), *Glasgow 1990: The Book*, London: HarperCollins.

Sturgeon, N. (2018), *Muriel Spark Books for Every Library*, 21 November 2018, available online at: https://www.gov.scot/news/muriel-spark-books-for-every-library/

Williamson, K. (2017), 'A Cultural Call to Arms: Rebel Inc. 25 Years on', *The Skinny*, September 2017.

Whyte, C. (1995), 'Introduction', in *Gendering the Nation: Studies in Modern Scottish Literature*, Edinburgh: Edinburgh University Press.

CHAPTER 26

The Carrying Stream
Twenty Years of Traditional Music in Scotland

Mairi McFadyen

MY AIM HERE is to offer a brief overview of the past twenty years of traditional music in Scotland. Since devolution from the UK in 1999, through the early years of the new millennium and later the independence campaign in the years leading up to 2014, Scotland has witnessed a blossoming of cultural confidence and consciousness. Music has played a vital role in this process. This era has also seen huge changes in terms of policy and practice; the pace of globalisation and the digitisation of contemporary culture has necessarily transformed the contexts of performances as well as the choice and style of music.

With unprecedented numbers of professional performers, an ecology of community music organisations offering tuition for children and adults, a vibrant culture of community-based sessions happening at the grassroots and highly successful international festivals, traditional music is flourishing in contemporary Scotland. This is a far cry from certain versions of 'traditional' culture in the 20th century given shape through the likes of Harry Lauder, Brigadoon and the White Heather Club.

A Modern Traditional Story

The modern story of Scottish traditional music has its beginnings in the 1950s. An oft-cited moment was the 'discovery' of Traveller singer Jeannie Robertson, brought down from Aberdeen by folklorist Hamish Henderson to perform at the first People's Festival Ceilidh in Edinburgh in 1951. For the first time, those living in the urban centres were introduced to the music and song of the Scottish Travellers and to the Gaelic song and piping traditions of the Hebrides with Flora MacNeil and Calum Johnston. The Folk Revival movement which was to follow was a powerful time of musical exploration and political activism with far reaching international connections – particularly with the USA. At home in Scotland, an infrastructure of performance platforms such as clubs, festivals, record labels and publications began to coalesce. The instrumental revival and exploration of the 1970s was the decade in which commercialisation began to take root and when professional touring bands became a reality. Glasgow-based group The Clutha popularised the idea of a 'Celtic band,' which consisted of fiddle or pipes leading the melody.

The accordion also gained in popularity due to the renown of Phil Cunningham, whose distinctive style was an integral part of the band Silly Wizard. By the end of the 1970s, lyrics in the Gaelic language were appearing in songs by *Na h-Òganaich*, and with Runrig's album *Play Gaelic* being the first major success for Gaelic-language music in 1978. By the 1980s, globalisation gave rise to a new commercial genre of 'world music'. Names like Dougie MacLean, Runrig and Capercaillie took music to a new level commercially, reaching international audiences. By this time too, it was becoming more common to hear folk and traditional music in mainstream media. A critical mass of recorded material, thanks to new labels such as Greentrax (1986), allowed for weekly radio programmes such as BBC Radio Scotland's *Travelling Folk*.

As a reaction to political disenfranchisement in the era of Thatcher's Government, this decade saw something of a cultural renaissance and a celebration of cultural forms rooted in the vernacular experience. Perhaps the most famous example here would be the Proclaimers brothers from Leith. In the Highlands at this time, the Gaelic language was in serious decline. McGrath's play *The Cheviot, The Stag and the Black, Black Oil* (1973), featuring traditional music and song, had made a huge impression across village halls. Music has the power bring people together in conviviality, creating a space to rehearse and perform alternative realities. Runrig's Calum MacDonald later wrote, 'this was a generation angry but inspired and desperate to reclaim a heritage' (Martin, 2006). Such motivations fuelled the beginnings of the Gaelic *fèisean* movement in the Highlands and Islands, which provided access to traditional music along with instrumental tuition rooted in Gaelic culture and began the process of re-connecting people to their language, culture and their music.

The decade of the 90s welcomed a wave of new bands and artists such as Shooglenifty and Wolfstone who embraced new influences from other genres such as rock, pop and jazz, composing new material and pushing the boundaries of tradition. This experimentation was aided by new technologies, a freedom that inspired composers such as Martyn Bennett who worked creatively with samples of archive recordings and explored urban dance and electronic music. Another pioneer of innovation was the late piper and prolific composer Gordon Duncan, whose infamous bagpipes setting of AC/DC's heavy rock anthem 'Thunderstruck' was unleashed during Edinburgh International Festival's 1999 Piping Series.

Celtic Connections

Glasgow's Celtic Connections festival burst on to the scene in 1994, representing a critical mass of enough world class musicians for a very large festival: this was Scottish traditional music in its new international context of 'world music' arriving as part of mainstream popular culture. With the inclusion of country music stars on the bill, this development divided opinion, although arguably this is a musical style which emerges from the same well-spring. Today, the festival features over 300 concerts, ceilidhs, talks, free events, late night sessions and workshops as well as an extensive educational programme.

In the run up to the opening of the Scottish Parliament there were a number of key developments that demonstrated the emergence of Scottish traditional music into national cultural and political life. For the first time, there was major state support for the arts in cultural policy: the then SAC's *Charter for the Arts* (1993) stated that:

> Scotland's cultural heritage in all its forms should be preserved, augmented and made accessible to the public.

From seeds planted in the Isle of Barra in 1981, the community-led education model of the Gaelic *Fèis* soon spread across the Highlands; in the Lowlands the Scots Music Group, emerging out of the Adult Learning Project's (ALP) radical agenda implementing Freirian adult education and community development, began in Edinburgh in 1991, closely followed by the Glasgow Fiddle Workshop in 1992 and Scottish Culture and Traditions in the North East in 1997. The 'Traditional Music in Scotland Report' (Francis, 1999) was published just months before the opening of the Scottish Parliament. Of course, one of the decisive moments in Scottish political and cultural life was the performance of Robert Burns' song 'A Man's A Man For A' That' by singer Sheena Wellington at the Parliament's opening. This song – celebrating liberty, equality and universal human rights – was a bold statement of intent, placing the radical and ideological heritage of the Scots tradition at the forefront of future national ambitions.

Growth and Development

Since the opening of the Parliament, the growth and development of the traditional music and the policy and frameworks that support it have been unprecedented. In terms of education, the early years of the millennium saw developments and pathways in formal education opportunities, with *Sgoil Chiùil na Gaidhealtachd*/National Centre for Excellence in Traditional Music in Plockton (2000) and the introduction of new degree-level courses in traditional music performance at the Royal Conservatoire of Scotland (Formerly RSAMD) and Lews Castle College in Benbecula, alongside the more traditional degree courses in culture and heritage elsewhere.

Another significant development since 1999 has been the introduction of new awards schemes such as the BBC Young Traditional Musician of the Year in 2001 and the Hands Up for Trad's Scots Traditional Music Awards/*Na Trads* in 2003. These were created to celebrate Scotland's traditional music in all its forms and to create a high-profile opportunity to bring the music and music industry into the spotlight of media and public attention, while at the same time recognising community projects, venues, publishers and others who make up the ecology of the traditional arts scene. During the early years of the awards, bands like Back of the Moon, Blazin' Fiddles, Daimh, artists like Karine Polwart and Gaelic singers Kathleen MacInnes and Julie Fowlis were new on the scene and were recognised as part of this early project. Era-defining bands included Session A9, the Scots Song group Malinky, hybrid musical collaborations such as Salsa Celtica and the highly experimental band LAU, who transformed traditional dance forms like jigs and reels into exciting new musical structures.

Representations of traditional music in the media have certainly increased on radio and television through broadcasting from BBC Alba (2008) and elsewhere. Developments in internet technology and social media platforms have brought with it a new world of opportunities for sharing and connecting and an emerging visual and video culture. This advancement has revolutionised broadcasting, with smaller micro level programmes and podcasts available on digital radio.

Both globally and locally, the discourse of the 'creative and cultural industries' are altering traditional forms of creation and dissemination. This particular moment in cultural policy-making also reflects a broader ideological shift in the technologies of cultural governance, symbolised by things like audits and the trend towards evidence-based policy in the context of this 'era of public management'. In the UK, this development had a clear beginning in New Labour's UK 'Creative Industries Taskforce' of 1997 – the link between the cultural sector and economic growth has formed the basis of almost every policy document written on the creative industries since.

This approach is twofold: the state takes on the role of 'cultural impresario' using trade and industry methods to 'sell' culture; at the same time, culture is used to promote or 'sell' the nation. The SNP Government in Scotland has embraced this approach wholeheartedly since they came to power in 2007. Since 2010, traditional music activity has been supported in the mainstream by the funding body Creative Scotland; as a consequence, much of the support and policy for traditional music is delivered within a highly professional and commercial context. The name-making, logo-driven culture of neo-liberalism demands of artists to be a brand, a business, an export. This is mirrored in the development of cultural tourism and increased 'festivalisation,' where traditional music is packaged and offered up for global consumption on the Homecoming stage. Traditional music and musicians may benefit from this situation in financial terms, but many sit precariously and uncomfortably within such an ideology.

'Traditional music is, at its heart, a community phenomenon' (TMF). Many musicians involved in this scene speak of the sense of community that folk and traditional music engenders. Underpinning traditional music is the ethos of hospitality: sharing what we have as people gather together, welcoming the stranger. This is perhaps embodied in the idea of the *cèilidh*, which means 'to visit'. In Scots it means a gathering. Out with the professional festivals and touring scene, Scotland has a vibrant culture of community-based sessions happening at the grassroots alongside a network of community music organisations offering tuition for children and adults as well as access to local resources. Within the current policy paradigm, however, the radical agenda of the 1990s community work has taken a back seat. This is not to undermine the important work that these organisations do both locally and nationally, but rather to recognise the strong neo-liberalising tendencies that dominate policy and cultural production and today.

Different Models

Counter to the prevalence and enthusiasm for the creative industries worldwide, UNESCO's report on the Creative Economy (2013) recognises that there are different kinds of economic models – from co-operatives and non-profits or sharing systems – and that these may offer more appropriate models for cultural activities which represent other sources of value for people beyond the economic. UNESCO's 'Convention for the Safeguarding of the Intangible Heritage' (2003) encourages state support for the living performance of cultural traditions in the communities in which they are practised, emphasising the intrinsic value and national importance of traditional music and its value to local and community life.

In the context of the creative industries, this throws up a conundrum: framing traditional music as both an export brand and as a cultural practice in need of safeguarding due to the threat of globalised economisation. In the current constitutional set-up, Scotland has no direct pathway to official UNESCO recognition: the convention recognises only state parties and the UK has not signed up (it is unlikely that the UK will take part any time soon; they have a long-standing resistance to certain UNESCO initiatives, dating back to the early 1980s). This said, freedom from official bureaucracy has provided an opportunity to interpret policy differently. Drawing on the civic national model of citizenship laid out by the Scottish Government, cultural heritage policy – unlike elsewhere in Europe – embraces and recognises the diversity of cultures found in Scotland, which includes the indigenous languages of Scots and Gaelic as well as that of immigrant communities. Recent work by TRACS (Traditional Arts and Culture Scotland) and BEMIS has highlighted the creative potential of our diverse cultural heritages in local communities across Scotland (and their global connections). With sympathetic implementation, such policy could raise awareness and support the sustainability of those cultural practices that define the groups, communities, regions and the plural national identity of the contemporary nation.

The constitutional question came to a head in the independence referendum of 2014. This was a seminal moment in Scottish culture in which music and song played a vital role. Far from recreating exclusionary nationalisms of the European past, traditional music was largely mobilised here within the discourse of an inclusive civic nationalism, (McFadyen, 2018) as a 'Welcome Table' for 'New Scots' (Mackenzie, 2014). By 2014, almost all public political statements from traditional musicians advocated an independent Scotland, a trend which reflected the wider arts community as a whole. Whether or not the very public alignment of the traditional music community with support for independence in cultural and political discourse gives a skewed view of the opinions of the whole scene, it is certainly true that not since the 1960s had this community been so politically active.

Independence of Spirit

Many commentators consider the referendum process to have been a hugely creative and formative period in Scottish politics. The movement had its critics; notable here is the particularly prominent voice of composer Sir James Mac-Millan. For many, the campaign was the beginning of a personal cultural discovery, a catalyst to search out the cultural heritage of traditional music, song and folk culture. This growing awareness, recognition and interest has left a legacy of growing cultural confidence, hugely important to an emerging sense of both cultural possibility and national identity. Since the events described, Scotland has seen more and more 'folk culture' and traditional music made visible in mainstream culture, for example through the film *Hamish the Movie*

(2016), a biopic of Hamish Henderson, Adrian Moffat's *Where You're Meant to Be* (2016) about Traveller singer Sheila Stewart, and the staggering success of Celtic Connections hitting the one million pound mark in ticket sales.

Another significant cultural moment in recent years was the live orchestral staging of Martyn Bennet's GRIT on the stage of the Edinburgh International Festival (EIF) in August 2016, with new director Fergus Linehan at the helm. The original studio album (2003), incorporating archive recordings, was a tribute to the voices of Scotland's cultural past, from both Scots and Gaelic traditions. The EIF has historically been the realm of 'high culture' and the world's elite art, holding to the 20th century ideals of cultural democracy from which it emerged: the idea that the masses could be civilised by giving them access to culture that was not their own. It was certainly not the cultural space for the Traveller voices of the early People's Festival Ceilidh nor the electronic breakbeats of 90s rave culture. In this sense, staging GRIT was an act of defiance. A bold step on the journey to an exciting future – a future where traditional culture is not a shackle tying us to the parochial past but a potent source of creative cultural possibility.

Other significant moments include 'A Night for Angus' at Celtic Connections in 2017, a tribute to the life and work of Shooglenifty's fiddle Angus Grant; and Runrig's farewell concert to an audience of tens of thousands celebrating 45 years and leaving a legacy celebrating Gaelic, Highland and Scottish music. Other notable developments include Karine Polwart's expansive multi-genre theatre piece 'Wind Resistance' in partnership with Pippa Murphy, which stands out as something vital. Taking as her inspiration the miraculous teamwork of migrating geese, she has built a cycle of song and spoken word that explores how we all depend on each other. In terms of global connections, Jamaican artist Brina has been working with local artists revisiting the songs of Robert Burns as part of a Scottish-reggae fusion and collaborating with artists such as Gaelic hip-hop artist Griogair Labhruidh, breaking musical boundaries between traditional and urban genres. Here, 'the national finds its expression in the local expression of the universal' (McKerrell and West, 2018)

Cultural investment in and support for traditional music over the past twenty years has paid off when we see a new generation of distinct creative voices now performing, teaching and contributing to the culture. The generation of musicians who were wee in the 1990s – many of whom grew up and learned their craft in the context of community education organisations described above – include, for example, fiddler Lauren MacColl, recently commissioned by *Fèis Rois* to compose new music inspired by the life and prophecies of renowned highland prophet The Brahan Seer; Piper Ross Ainslie, a student of the late Gordon Duncan, pushing the boundaries of piping yet further still; harpist and singer Rachel Newton, leading a national conversation on gender issues in traditional music; Lori Watson, celebrating the local traditions of the Scottish Borders; singer Siobhan Miller, as at home with a traditional ballad as a modern pop song; and composer Mike Vass, whose recent commission 'The Four Pillars' (2018) celebrates the major tune types of the Scottish fiddle tradition – the slow air, the march, the strathspey and the reel.

Bands such as Breabach from the Highlands and Fara from Orkney give voice to distinct local traditions and bands such as Niteworks, Treacherous Orchestra and the Kinnaris Quintet push the music in exciting new directions. There is a generation even younger still, with singers such Robyn Stapleton, Iona Fyfe and Hannah Rarity in the Scots tradition; Mischa MacPherson, Ellen MacDonald and Josie Duncan in the Gaelic, and a wave of young bands such as Talisk, Eabhal, Inyal, Heisk and Assynt. This is a generation that takes devolution absolutely for granted. They have no cultural cringe and are eager to celebrate and share in a sense of identity and belonging through participating in traditional music. This cultural transformation has been something of a revolution in front of the eyes of the generation who have witnessed it.

This paints a vibrant and flourishing picture, although we should be conscious of criticisms of the whiteness of musicians, audiences, educators and entrepreneurs involved. This is a music of its place: grounded yet outward looking. Tradition here is understood not as fixed in history, but as a carrying stream, connected to a global ocean of cultures, moving forward through time in a way that is inclusive of all those who live in Scotland. The performance of South African soprano Pumiza Matshikiza's rendition of Henderson's 'Freedom Come All Ye' at the opening of the Commonwealth Games in 2014 embodied this aspiration. It is my hope, whatever political future lies ahead, that the collective voice of Scotland is a confident and inclusive one and that those who perform and craft identities in and through Scottish traditional music remain committed to an open and plural notion of what that might mean.

References

Martin, K. (2006), Fèis, The First Twenty-five Years of the Fèis Movement, Portree: Fèisean nan Gàidheal.

McKerrell, S. and West, G. (eds.) (2018), Understanding Scotland Musically: Folk, Tradition, Policy, Abingdon: Routledge.

McFadyen, M. (2018), 'Referendum Reflections: traditional music and the per-
    formance of politics in the campaign for Scottish independence', in Simon
    McKerrell, S. and West, G. (eds.), *Understanding Scotland Musically: Folk,
    Tradition, Policy*, Abingdon: Routledge.
MacKenzie, E. (2014). 'Eilidh MacKenzie: Scotland – the Welcome
    Table', available online at: http://nationalcollective.com/2014/06/05/
    eilidh-mackenzie-scotland-the-welcome-table/
Traditional Music Forum, available online at: www.traditionalmusicforum.org

CHAPTER 27

Architecture and Design

Jude Barber and Andy Summers

The Parliament sits in the land. Scotland is a land... it is not a series of cities. The Parliament should be able to reflect the land in which it sits.

Text from competition-winning entry by Enric Miralles/Benedetta Tagliabue (EMBT Architects, 1998)

IT IS CHALLENGING to recall exactly what we were both doing when the devolution referendum was announced on 11 September 1997. One of us was studying architecture at Edinburgh College of Art and had just voted for the first time in any national election. The other was working as an architectural assistant in practice within Edinburgh's Old Town after completing a Master's in Architecture at the University of Strathclyde. In 1998 the architect Enric Miralles' studio won the international competition to design the new Scottish Parliament building and there was much discussion and debate around its design, location and cost.

After a turbulent and fractious construction process Donald Dewar, Scotland's first-ever First Minister, finally stood in the newly completed Scottish Parliament building on 1 July 1999 declaring that

today there is a new voice in the land, the voice of a democratic Parliament. A voice to shape Scotland, a voice for the future.

Although we would not meet until 16 years later, both our lives and work were filled with boundless energy, healthy critique and youthful optimism echoed in Dewar's statement.

Shortly after this, the Lighthouse Scotland's Centre for Architecture and Design – was opened as part of Glasgow's wider 1999 UK City of Architecture and Design celebrations within the former offices of *The Herald*, designed in 1845 by Charles Rennie Mackintosh. The building and associated programme via the newly formed Architecture Design Scotland, promised a genuine commitment to the exploration of ideas, design ambition and educational activities.

Twenty years after devolution is a timely moment to reflect on the creation of the Scottish Parliament, its policy, its action and its influence on architecture, design and the public realm. And, what the next twenty years might hold.

Design and Civic Life

Our everyday lives are rooted in design and spatial politics. In his 2012 book *Why We Build*, the author and critic Rowan Moore states:

> Architecture is about power. The question is how that power is delivered; to whom, by whom and for whom.

Consequently, our built environment shapes social identity and reflects our civic priorities. Despite the efforts of many, the majority of development is driven by aggressive market forces and associated, reactionary development planning. In 1961 the late Jane Jacobs stated that, 'This is not the re-building of cities. This is the sacking of cities', which still rings true for many people today – particularly the most vulnerable.

Over the last ten years the Scottish Government, NHS Scotland and partner agencies have sought to address inequalities and enhance civic engagement via their co-created 'Place Principle'. This positive initiative encourages public organisations to work collaboratively to not only improve public health, but also the places where we live, work and meet. This work was led from the front by the former Chief Medical Officer Sir Harry Burns on his appointment in 2005 – via the publication of *Equally Well* in 2008 – which clearly communicated, evidenced and connected public health inequalities and the built environment.

Also, in 2015, the Scottish Government approved the Community Empowerment Act and established Community Planning Partnerships, which seek to positively encourage civic participation and influence over the built environment. Communities are invited to take a lead in the planning and delivery of local land, buildings and services. Some positive examples can be seen around Scotland in both rural and urban areas. They include initiatives from the Tayport Community Trust in Fife and the community buy-out of the coastal village of Findhorn in Morayshire.

So, with the clear connection established between good design, participation and civic life, who might be the champions of architecture and design within Scotland's public sphere? Surprisingly, there is no Minister at Holyrood with architecture specifically in their portfolio. Instead, architecture and the public realm sits across a number of ministerial posts including Local Government and Housing, Culture, Tourism and External Affairs. Fortunately, there are some key political champions fighting for the public realm. Andy Wightman MSP has championed key policy changes in land reform, planning and community empowerment since coming into office. Aileen Campbell MSP, as Cabinet Secretary for Communities and Local Government, has also taken an active and positive lead around the 'Place Principle' and tackling health inequality.

Architecture and Design Scotland is the executive non-departmental public body that seeks 'to promote the value good architecture and sustainable design adds to everyone's lives'. After optimistic – and well-funded – beginnings in 2005 it now leads some important, yet modest, education and design conversations. Whilst this work is central to the national conversation, it unfortunately lacks sufficient legislative influence and authority.

Over the past decade The Royal Incorporation of Architects in Scotland (RIAS) has suffered from direct influence and control. Despite chairing the Scottish Parliament Cross Party Working Group since 2016, it has not effectively influenced key quality issues such as procurement, policy, sustainability and the production of the built environment. It ran a well-funded and highly promoted Festival of Architecture in 2016. However, this did little to communicate the complexity and contradictions involved in the making and shaping the built environment. During 2017–18, a group called A New Chapter (of which both authors played a role) campaigned to reform and re-energise the RIAS. The RIAS has since gone through significant changes and now promises to be a more effective and influential voice in civic society.

Scotland must continue to build a strong alliance of agencies working in tandem to effectively address the key issues affecting health inequalities, the environment and the public realm. This must include landscape architects, ecologists, engineers, hydrologists, health professionals, educators and sociologists. Health professionals are currently leading the agenda and conversation and the 'Place Principle' – with its multi-agency thinking – offers a strong platform going forward.

Devolution and a Policy on Architecture

The establishment of the Scottish Parliament and the transfer of legislative power was an opportunity for specific focus to be placed on architecture and design in tandem with the enhanced remit on housing and planning previously under the remit of the Scottish Office. The excitement and potential for new possibilities primarily coalesced around the new 'Policy on Architecture for Scotland' published by the Scottish Executive on 5 October 2001. The publication of the policy really felt like a watershed moment, where well-designed buildings and places would become the norm, with quality and the common good embedded within our civic life and public realm. Devolution created a time of such energy and optimism – a moment of decisive change and momentum for Scotland. Or so it felt.

The ambition of the original version of the 'Policy on Architecture' was plain to see, with 40 published points of action to meet the five primary objectives. Importantly an international perspective was included, reflecting the aspirations for architecture and design in Scotland to look outwards in order to make new connections and join wider conversations. The policy was revised in 2007, where a more holistic emphasis on the wider built environment began to emerge, aligning more closely with planning. The word 'place' also began to be used, as a point of coalescence where architecture, design and planning came together in real time. In 2013 the policy was revised again to the current in-use version – and we will come back to the term 'in-use in a moment.

Upon reflection of the 2001, 2007 and 2013 versions of the policy a subtle but perhaps critical change in language is evident, beyond the proliferation of the word 'place'. In 2001 the word 'investment' could perhaps be read as the central aim of the policy: investment in architecture, investment in quality, investment in the people of Scotland. Over time however 'investment' has faded, and the word 'value' emerges as pre-eminent. This change is important. 'Investment' suggests a transfer, an undertaking, where the onus is on the benefactor (here the Scottish Government and its various agencies) to lead, inspire, fund and act to engender worthwhile results. 'Value' shifts emphasis, a shift where the onus and associated expectations rest more on the beneficiaries to prove their worth in the reflection of a more passive benefactor. This shift could be attributed to the change in public finances from 2008 onwards in tandem with a noticeable – and fully consequential – depreciation of momentum and activity from the centre. For example, the funded National Programme of projects, exhibitions and publications on architecture and design – produced by Architecture Design Scotland, via the Lighthouse – essentially evaporates around this time.

Picking up on the term 'in-use' helps us to reflect on the current relevance and effectiveness of the policy on architecture, perceived or otherwise, in the day-to-day creation of our buildings and places. In summary, the policy feels entirely forgotten about, with very little debate or scrutiny about its content or stated deliverables respectively. Beyond the (limited) use of the Place Standard Toolkit, used to holistically assess existing neighbourhoods or places for pending (re)development, the Policy on Architecture appears to be devoid of active momentum, appreciation and value. Looking back at the original policy from 2001 one can't help feeling that we, collectively, are wasting this opportunity.

Policies on architecture, in a worldwide context, are rare. In any industry or profession commitment from central and local government is critical to the overall effectiveness of the policy itself. However, in Scotland, if we wish any policy on architecture to be a conduit for progressive change, raising standards and bettering design which results in an internationally recognised culture of architecture, then we as architects and designers need to make sure we have a policy on architecture which is fit for purpose. This requires the Scottish Government to better communicate and enforce policy 'on the ground' at local authority level and for a reformed RIAS to take a lead with its membership and affiliations. It is up to us to propose, draft, agitate for and demand a better, more effective policy if we are to have any policy on architecture at all which is worth publishing and pursuing.

Fairy Tales and Horror Stories

The publication of the 2001 'Policy on Architecture' was an achievement and promised so much. Its intentions are noble, with admirable examples of good practice from around the country. Notwithstanding this, for those working at the coalface in architecture and design, it has become a fairy tale of sorts. Modelled on a Scandinavian approach to design it contains key references from the inspirational Danish architect and urban designer Jan Gehl, such as 'First life, then spaces, then buildings: The other way around never works'.

While this is entirely admirable in principle, it is challenging for most clients and design teams to consistently deliver in practice while working within a landscape of funding cuts, 'stuck' 1980's local authority thinking, ridiculously low design fees (in both the public and private sector) and the lack of on-the-ground, inter-agency working.

In parallel with this, the Scottish Government has implemented ambitious national projects such as 1999 'Homes for the Future' in Glasgow Green and the 2010 'Highland Housing Fair' near Inverness. Both aimed to raise the bar for everyday design and delivery of architecture and the public realm. They encouraged architects, engineers and landscape architects to explore ideas, realise their ambitions and showcase good design to the general public. To a large extent these projects perfectly captured the optimism of devolution and should be applauded. Young practices were offered new opportunities, clients and the wider public could visit great architecture and politicians could laud them as a success.

The positive traction generated around devolution during the early 2000s was evident in the work of many housing associations and cultural organisations who produced some excellent architecture including Dance Base in Edinburgh, the Dundee Centre for Contemporary Art, Castlemilk Stables and Gorbals Regeneration projects in Glasgow. Several rural practices, led by Dualchas in Skye, delivered elegant and thoughtful residential and community buildings rooted in their context.

More recently, the Scottish Borders Education team are delivering ambitious new schools and the Gorbals Housing Association continues to develop new housing and amenities at Laurieston in Glasgow with architects such as Stallan Brand, Page/Park and Elder & Cannon Architects. Scottish Canals has also developed an innovative client and developer relationship, facilitating and delivering positive and nuanced regeneration work. Several projects have recently won UK-wide recognition such as the Big Lottery funded Barmulloch Residents Centre in North Glasgow by Collective Architecture and the Nuclear Decommissioning Centre in Wick by Reiach and Hall Architects. Such exemplar buildings and spaces are, and will be, consistently profiled in policy documents. However, they unfortunately are the exception, not the rule.

The backstory to the positive design examples, policy and political endorsements is that the majority of buildings that most people interact with – and places they visit – are poorly designed and adversely affect their health. In some instances, new buildings are literally harmful and tragic. Horror stories such as Grenfell and the Edinburgh PFI school scandal spark the most obvious attention and rage. Which begs the question 'Why were these disasters allowed to occur at all?' Author Darren McGarvey succinctly answers this question in his 2017 book *Poverty Safari*:

> This inferno [Grenfell] was a preventable disaster; a confluence of human error and industrial-scale negligence.

'Race to the bottom' procurement models, aggressive 'value engineering' processes and a lack of control over design and quality enables such negligence. These behaviours are at the centre of current public led procurement models – and this has to change.

Another, less dramatic horror story is the slow, nauseating effect of the housebuilder-led suburban model and the damage this is causing to public health, the environment and civic society. This forceful and thriving model is characterised by the individualistic dominance of the car, low density development, cookie-cutter design, limited provision of shared, local amenities, a propensity towards gated communities and the lack of any contextual design response – which flies in the face of good policy, sustainable practice and current public health agendas.

In parallel with this, the exclusion and alienation that many poor communities experience in relation to the design and development of their neighbourhoods, along with growing levels of homelessness, is a national disgrace. Jimmy Reid's famous speech delivered on his inauguration as Rector of the University of Glasgow in 1972 described such alienation as:

> The feeling of despair and hopelessness that pervades people who feel with justification that they have no real say in shaping or determining their own destinies'

Good architecture and high-quality design should not be considered the 'icing on the cake' to development or a 'nice to have' for those who can afford it. The value and benefits that quality design can bring must be embedded into both practice and procurement. There must also be better opportunity for innovative young designers and smaller studios to work creatively to deliver buildings and places within both the public and private sector.

Tin 2018, Scotland's acclaimed contribution to the 16th international architecture exhibition the Venice Biennale – entitled 'Happenstance' – brought together artists and architects to work with Scottish young people 'to discover what 'Freespace' means to them and their communities'. The abundance of optimism and colour within the project and its presentation was infectious but did seem to lack rigorous and critical debate regarding the harsh reality faced by most people at the margins in Scottish society – and how this plays out within the character, form and ecology of their built environment. A key action for architects, political leaders, and organisations working to promote good design in Scotland is to urgently turn the bi-annual Venetian fairy tales into concrete reality for all – particularly for those who do not currently have control over what happens within their own neighbourhoods. Architects, landscape architects, engineers and creative thinkers must be central to this.

Diversity and Plurality

Collaboration and Grassroots Activism

The apparent stagnation of and engagement with the current policy on architecture is perhaps diametrically opposite to the reality of the contemporary architecture and design scenes in Scotland. Current activity at grassroots and areas of emergent practice is vibrant, engaged and resourceful. Commonly self-initiating and often self-organised there is an increasing diversification and deepening plurality of individuals, groups, companies, organisations and platforms across multiple disciplines which are creating new work of high quality, forging new connections beyond their respective areas and acknowledging with intent the contemporary cultural, political, social and economic contexts of which they are part.

This mosaic of activity thrives on cross-programming between artforms, embraces collaboration and enables work, which is distinctive, well-produced and of an international standard. In architecture, the Architecture Fringe is disrupting the previous staid formality of architectural culture in Scotland. Inspired by the Scottish Government's then-upcoming Year of Innovation, Architecture & Design, the Architecture Fringe was founded in 2015 with the intent of developing a new, critical community of voices to challenge each other, support new work, encourage a wider conversation about architecture and design in Scotland and to engage internationally with other people and organisations. Over just three years the Architecture Fringe has initiated, inspired and invigorated a broad spectrum of activity in architecture, art, activism, dance, music, photography and live performance – all exploring, questioning and challenging current practice within our built environment.

Other and mutually-supportive initiatives have also emerged in the same period, from the Voices of Experience living archive, rediscovering forgotten women who have shaped our towns and cities, to the Test Unit summer school prototyping new approaches to urban development and to *Crumble Magazine*, a self-initiated in-print journal by students at the University of Edinburgh– award-winning and stocked around the world from London to Hong Kong. Other critical organisations and platforms which have emerged include Local Heroes, a curatorial and commissioning agency which presents and promotes products, design and the design industry in Scotland to an international audience and Graphic Design Festival Scotland, founded in 2014, which promotes Scotland as a hub for creativity and design and is a key industry event with their annual open international poster competition now attracting almost 7,000 entries from 102 countries.

Along with organisations and initiatives such as Custom Lane, Missing In Architecture, The Stove Network, SEDA, *Fearann Land*, Atlas Arts, Make Works, Creative Dundee, Dundee Design Festival, Creative Edinburgh and the Edinburgh and Glasgow Tool Libraries activity, lateral thinking and a commitment to hard work in architecture, design and making; activism is in abundance in Scotland. This flourishing in plurality across diverse geographies is an important but complementary counter-balance to government-only top-down activity. Since the re-establishment of the Scottish Parliament a new generation and new era in contemporary, creative civic society has emerged. The interconnected, pan-regional collaborative nature inherent within this generation is greatly aided by social media. To make connections and be aware, very easily, of what other people are doing at the other end of the country in real time is a critical aspect of contemporary Scotland.

Conclusion

You never change things by fighting the existing reality. To change something, build a new model that makes the existing model obsolete.

R Buckminster Fuller

When we consider the future of Scotland's buildings, places, land and society for the next twenty years, where might architects and designers best focus their attention and energy going forward? At the recent 24th Conference of the Parties to the UN Framework Convention on Climate Change (COP24) the head of the International Union of Architects (UIA) Thomas Vonier stated that:

Current practices in the built environment are unsustainable. The built environment is a major consumer of energy and natural resources and a massive producer of waste. Furthermore, how we build can exacerbate inequalities and affect health. The built environment is part of the problem, but through the potential of planning, architecture and design, it is also a crucial part of the solution.

The urgent need to address and mitigate climate change – and how this might reduce inequalities – has to be a key priority going forward for architecture and design in Scotland. Holistic sustainability within all aspects of our contemporary activity – in design, planning, production, construction, health and in our environment – requires commitment, action and enforcement in policy throughout our multi-agency, collaborative approach.

The Saltire Society's 1944 publication *Building Scotland* by Alan Riach and Robert Hurd contains a powerful and poetic foreword, written by the then Secretary of State for Scotland Thomas Johnston:

And in this beautiful land of ours, the free people who inhabit it, and who have paid such a high price for their freedom, will, in the better days that are to be, surely insist that the architecture of their buildings, public and private, shall be worthy of them.

CHAPTER 28

Scottish Football in the World of Global Money

Jim Spence and David Goldblatt

Dear Jim,

Viewed in a global, certainly from a European, perspective, Scottish foot-ball has been hit harder by globalisation, and fallen further, than counties of comparable size and sporting pedigree – Croatia, Portugal and Belgium, for example. I think that the legal changes in football's labour market – the Bos-man decision – is just one, albeit important, facet of a wider series of economic, technological and cultural changes that have contributed to the relative decline of Scottish football.

One could argue that Scotland's decline begins some time before this. In 1967, close to the peak of Scottish industrial output and employment, Celtic won the European Cup, Rangers lost the final of the Cup Winners Cup, and the national team beat England, the then holders of the World Cup, and the Scot-tish press declared them 'World Champions'. In the early 1990s, despite a quar-ter of a century of brutal deindustrialisation, that ripped the heart of Scottish football's core constituencies, you could still imagine that there might be some kind of parity with the English neighbours. You had, after all, qualified for five consecutive World Cups (1974–1990) to England's three. While the latter's clubs had been banned from European competition, after the Heysel tragedy in 1985, Scotland's club had attracted amongst the best of England's stars – Terry Butcher and Mark Hately for example. And, as late as 1995 Paul Gascoigne's destination of choice, after his Italian misadventures at Lazio, was Rangers.

However, after nearly a quarter of a century of change, there is now no comparison economically between the two top leagues, precious few linkages left between Scottish and English football and absolutely nothing can be done about this. Thus, in the 2000s Scotland continued to supply a steady stream of players to the Premier League, not to mention up to a quarter of its managers. But those numbers have dwindled as Scots must compete against the entire world for English clubs' attentions. Yes, there was late flash of European success, but it was a pale shadow of the past. It is hard to imagine that any Scottish club will be contesting in the final of a European tournament any time soon.

In what are now a global market for fans, sponsors and players, and a European market for tournament prize money, small country teams, even those as hegemonic as Celtic and Rangers, are going to find it impossible to compete. The Old Firm have explored all the exit options, cornered as much of the Scottish market as is possible without entirely vaporising everyone else, and still nothing doing. Add to that the long-term secular dissipation of Scottish football's iconic and urban industrial core and this is a recipe for serious decline.

But, the achievements of clubs at the apex of the game, even of the men's national team, might not be the be-all-and-end-all of what constitutes football success. Certainly, while Rangers were undertaking their purgatorial journey through the lower leagues, and though Celtic monopolised the league ever more firmly there was some space for another kind of Scottish football to appear.

Since 2012 the Scottish Cup been has won by Hearts, Hibs for the first time in 104 years, and by Inverness Caledonian Thistle and St Johnstone for the first time ever. In this Scotland, nation and football have appeared less Glasgow-centric and less Central Belt-centric than they have before. A particular plus is that Hearts, since Romanov's departure, have been transformed under the part ownership and zero-bullshit managerial leadership of Ann Budge – the most powerful and important women in Scottish football to date. The introduction of normal and responsible business and accounting practices has been a revolution by itself. But Budge, who is selling her share to the supporters' trust, and Hearts are pioneers of a new wave of social ownership in Scottish football.

The economic and demographic dynamism of the Highlands has also been represented by the arrival in top-level football of not just Inverness Caledonian Thistle – from the fastest growing city in the country – but its rural highland cousin, Ross County from the tiny market town of Dingwall. Scotland can still claim to have the highest number of professional football clubs, per capita head in the world, and a level per capita attendance exceeded only by Cyprus, and there is whole hinterland of amateur, junior and women's football that doesn't seem to be a part of anyone's equation. The women's game has been especially inspiring for many of late.

So, how can there be more of all of this? Certainly, part of the answer is what to do about the Old Firm? The danger of drifting back into some kind of dull lopsided Glasgow-centric duopoly awaits – but it would be good to think more widely than just this.

David

Dear David,

The short answer to your question about how can there more of all of this is that there can't and won't be, in my view. The hegemony of the big two in Glasgow is so great and so historically pronounced that it has traditionally been, and will continue to be, impossible to challenge on any serious and regular basis. Their reach throughout Scotland is vast and shows no sign of decreasing. In Dundee, a friend of mine who runs one of the city's Celtic supporters' clubs, estimates that there are between six and eight thousand 'Celtic minded' folk. Only a very small proportion of these will attend games at Celtic Park, but the key thing is they definitely don't attend matches at Dens Park or Tannadice, where the base home support is around five thousand at each club.

Even if Rangers never again become the force that operated previously from Ibrox Park, the numbers are still stacked against the rest of the Scottish clubs. Unless Celtic take their eye off the well-rounded marketing ball which they've so assiduously created, it's difficult to see how any other club can get close to challenging them on a regular and sustainable basis.

Aberdeen, currently the fifth best supported club in the country are averaging around a third of Rangers home crowds and a quarter of Celtic's, so they too even if the new stadium sees an uplift at the turnstiles, fall well short of being able to match the Glasgow pair in terms of depth of quality they can attract, since the wage differentials are so substantial.

The truly depressing thing about this, if you are not a fan of either of the big two, is that the rest of the Scottish game has been complicit in its meek acceptance of the situation. Elements such as gate sharing, which at one time created a slightly more even playing field, have long since been voted away; such was the acquiescence of the other clubs in their own guaranteed subservience. Any possibility of an American type set up where revenue is much more evenly distributed, is frowned upon not only by fans of Celtic and Rangers, but other clubs also. Tribalism wins out over a level sporting playing field every time.

Celtic and Rangers have been on the horns of a dilemma for a long time. Both are potentially huge businesses stymied in an environment where their growth is by nature limited because of the size of population, TV revenue etc. However, the gap between them and the rest is too big to bridge on anything approaching a regular basis.

Jim

Dear Jim,

Scottish football feels like a rather grim lesson in the contemporary realities of capital accumulation, in which increasing inequalities create a tiny, and increasingly impregnable, elite. This applies both within Scotland, and then as you say, to its few leading clubs once they step outside of Scotland, though in the latter case, they are the marginals.

If you are right that this situation is, for the foreseeable future, impossible to alter, then Scottish men's professional football offers a rather gloomy prospect, with such a narrow range of storylines and narratives, locking the game and the version of Scotland it constructs into stasis – and one linked to the nation's imperial geography and sectarian divisions. Not that these are not a vital part of Scottish history and identity, but Scotland is so much more and so much more complex than this. Presumably, this state of affairs will lock the men's national team into the similar state of permanent marginality, telling the same story of unrealised national potential, over and over again. Is that how you see the future? Is that a future anyone in Scotland feels good about? If not, what other futures are available?

Rather than concentrating then, on 'what to do about the Old Firm'? Or, even 'what to do about the men's national team? Maybe we, and the Scottish football authorities, should just stop talking about them all together and be thinking about all the other ways of playing, following and enjoying football. What would such a programme look like?

It would certainly prioritise more people having more fun playing more football as its starting point, and not just kids, but every age group. There's a lot of bang for your health buck from getting old folk's playing walking football. Given the impossibility of reform, perhaps even of progress for the moment in the men's game, maybe it should prioritise the women's national teams. Let's see what a reversal of the current expenses of the two teams, for say five years, does.

Either way, some version of Iceland's extraordinary community football programme, should be the template for investment in facilities and coaching, and the mobilisation of an enormous reservoir of voluntary energy and talent.

And maybe there is something to be said for Uruguay's approach to its men's national team, which has over performed in the most amazing way over the last decade or so. Knowing that they will lose their best players at a young age to the global labour market, an intensive effort is put into nurturing the national youth teams, not merely technically – though there is lot to be learnt from Uruguay in this department – but socially, educationally and emotionally. There is something, I think very Scottish about that. Football was introduced to

Uruguay by William Poole, a Scottish teacher, and for all the ravages of the last 40 years, the Scottish educational system retains real autonomy and difference from the catastrophe that has befallen England.

Of course, questions of money, power and politics remain unaddressed, but let's just dream a little. That's one of the things football is for.

David

Dear David,

The current situation appears on the whole to be accepted by the bulk of fans, who I think are so inured to and accepting of it that change seems completely improbable. Ultimately, I suspect it comes down to what football represents for most fans. If it is about community, camaraderie and a few drinks before and after the game, then many if not the majority of fans will accept a continuation of things.

The occasional good cup run, and a re-establishment of place in the natural order of things for the big city clubs, should ensure that revolutionary talk is confined to the margins. In many ways our football mirrors our politics. We often talk the talk, but seldom walk the walk, when it comes to radical change. Scottish football, like Scottish politics, is essentially conservative and technocratic.

By and large my experience is that the folk who run football clubs, chairmen and boards, are 'movers and shakers' in other walks of business life and tend not to take kindly to supporters telling them how to spend their money or take decisions. We could bring in more equal redistributive methods tomorrow, if the clubs would vote for it. Wage caps, shared gates and merchandise could revolutionise competition. However, the chances of it happening are slim to none.

The tendency to view fans as anything other than tribal may be somewhat cynical, but it's also true in my experience. Supporters see the game through a prism of irrationality and clan type belonging. Take a simple example. Fans of say Dundee United and Dundee will blithely castigate glory hunting Celtic fans from the Lochee and traditionally Irish area of the city but see no irony in the Angus Arabs travelling from Arbroath and Montrose to see United, or the Capital Dark Blues from Edinburgh to watch Dundee FC.

Looking for general agreement and equitable views among football fans on most subjects in the game is like looking for the yeti in a white out. That divide and rule tactic serves the status quo well, and ensures that only marginal changes, masquerading as creative thinking, passes for radicalism in the game here.

I was in Iceland over ten years ago to see them play Germany. It was only a few days, but I jaloused that they are a very different people and society from us in Scotland. I'm not sure that we have either the energy, inventiveness or the desire to be as egalitarian as they seem to be in organising their football. We I feel, are much more hierarchical and amenable to a doff the cap system.

The job of a journalist is to be sceptical not cynical. I am sceptical of serious change being enabled in Scottish football, and that means in my view that the current orthodoxy will prevail, and that any changes or advances in women's football, the club game, or schools' football and greater rates of participation, will be minimal.

Jim

Dear Jim,

I admire your clear-eyed assessment of the emotional texture of Scottish football, its deep conservatism and its real structures of power. So, how is a manifestly unjust and dysfunctional social order justified and maintained?

Fans, like consumers and voters are depicted as irrational, tribal, distracted and divided. The lassitude of mainstream football culture in Scotland, the acceptance of an obviously broken and rigged system in return for a small space of camaraderie, *craic* and ritual, is not I feel confined to football. Indeed, it sometimes appears to be the *modus operandi* of our lives. Our leaders in football, business and politics, the movers and shakers as you call them, often seem self-interested, contemptuous of the views of the public, and all too ready to take power and status achieved in one realm and imperially transfer it to another.

Finally, you argue that Scotland remains short on the kind of social solidarity and entrepreneurial social energies that drove Iceland's footballing miracle, too wedded, these days, to pre-existing hierarchies. Talking the talk but not walking the walk. Certainly, any social order rests on apathy and disengagement as much as consent, our own included.

But whatever we say and think, there will be change. Today's quiescent fans will soon be dead. Will the next generation, already demographically smaller, replace them or will FIFA 2027 and Football Manager be their games of choice? How long will the memories and images of mid-century industrial Scotland, like England still sustained and reproduced in football, serve as a sufficient liturgy? Is there only inertia, nostalgia, quiet decline and decay ahead? Maybe you are right. In which case my question is, how shall we live with that?

David

Dear David,

Despite myself and my attempts to remain positive I'm afraid I see little light at the end of a dark tunnel. I have so far excluded mention of the SFA, Scottish Government, and central government. The reason is simple. The first represents the clubs. But in reality, the clubs, as their own power brokers, are also their own closed shop to use the old industrial terminology. That closed shop is impervious to most change never mind radical change, and there is little organised opposition to challenge them, with the exception of a few honourable folk in the game.

Those who might and do challenge are few in number; many will fall by the wayside fighting the good fight in a doomed rear-guard action as small guerrilla units, and others may succumb to temptation to embrace the mantra that it's better to be inside the tent pissing out, than outside the tent pissing in. That approach of course usually ends like it did for the frog carried across the river by the scorpion.

As far as national and local government is concerned, I discern a watery interest only. The game, whether it be sectarian behaviour, the alcohol ban, or the level of investment required for effectively assisting private companies, isn't worth the candle to them. They have many more important things to tackle, and their possible involvement meets with negativity and cynicism from many fans.

The culture of the game is undoubtedly changing and just as very few folk play the lute anymore, fewer and fewer of the younger demographic appear to be as involved as perhaps our generation were, and are, in supporting the game. It is much more international in flavour and the ability exists to be a knowledgeable football fan supporting Barcelona, or Juventus, or Liverpool from afar, without the messy requirement to pay 22 quid to see your local top league side, or 14 quid to see a team a couple of divisions lower.

On Saturday past, without a senior game to cover, I went along to a junior match in the Kirkton housing scheme where I was brought up. Lochee Harp were playing there while their new stadium is being built, in part of a deal with a large car outfit. Many years ago, Harp could attract crowds in the high hundreds and often the low thousands for cup games, yet I estimate there were around 30 or 40 attending on Saturday.

At all levels the game is having to fight for its stake in the community. Strangely, I have a notion (no more than that) that junior football with local lads playing could, if marketed differently, be restored to some of its former glory. At professional level the link between the community and players at bigger clubs strikes me as more tenuous than ever. Players come and go on a succession of short deals, no real roots are put down, and I wonder what the relationship is now supposed to be between 'Your Club' and players from here, there and everywhere who know little and care less for the history and traditions of the place they are playing in.

For every determined supporter who desires to tackle those who exercise power in Scottish football, there are ten, who have neither the energy nor the interest. I think the game will simply roll onward, with the occasional highs and lows, maintaining its central place in the hearts of fans, but each passing year, the numbers will get fewer to paraphrase the old song. My fear is that someday no one will watch here at all.

Jim

Dear Jim,

Tell me it ain't so, but I feel like I am reading an obituary, or at least one in the making. You conclude by writing that 'the game will simply roll onward', but your final thought is an altogether more morbid one: 'my fear is that some-day no one will watch at all'. Are you saying that Scottish football, trapped in the same institutions, tribalism and narrow visions that currently sustain it, will become increasingly culturally marginal, and but for its very highest echelons, abandoned?

I think you are, and you have made a very good job of arguing why there isn't much that can be done to stop this. It is hard to find fault with your analysis of the game's institutional inertia: the self-serving and defensive nature of the SFA, the power and allure of patronage, the thousand ways that conservative institutions sap the soul and make change impossible. Nor, from what you say, is it clear quite what can be done about the sharp decline in the playing of football or the equally sharp rise in fan's global tastes, not to mention the ante-diluvian menu of hot drinks available.

So, maybe this is a moment for changing what we can change – and that includes how we look at the problem in hand. Raymond Williams argued, 'That to be radical is to make hope possible rather than despair convincing'. I am not, for example, as despondent as you about the possibilities of a state funded, grassroots revival along the lines of Iceland, though with a Scottish twist that embraces existing strengths like the junior leagues. I know too, that the old men that run the game and set its tone will die and pass, and that the generations that have lived through the turmoil of recent years will not just turn into replicas of their hapless elders. I want to believe that both young and old will eventually tire of their smart phones, and their neck ache and re-engage with the real world of play.

David

Dear David,

It's not like me to be this gloomy, I admit that after having reported on the senior game for over 30 years and seen the inside of a topflight club for a short consultancy spell, I do have serious concerns for the future.

It depends I suppose on what we want from our football, and for me ultimately, domestically it has to be a range of possible top league winners. I simply see no possibility of that happening, unless we embrace a much more egalitarian and socialist type distribution of income.

Such an approach is unlikely to happen. We have I think a great capacity to fool ourselves in Scotland into believing that we are a potentially socially just and a left of centre nirvana. The rather harsher truth is that the tribalism inherent in our game means there is little pause for thought as opponents are tossed into the financial wilderness of the lower leagues to stagnate and fossilise, losing the next generation of fans into the bargain.

I see little reason to think that a future generation should necessarily be any more radical than their current conservatively minded parents and grandparents in relation to changing the game. It is one thing for such a generation to embrace modern communication techniques and write opinion pieces on statistical analysis and soccer ball economics. It is another to challenge those holding the levers of power and recalibrate in a way which actually might challenge your own club's status and power. That though is at top level. If we are concerned for the notion of true community and prepared to accept that football is, at heart, a participatory sport for community involvement, then I'm more positive.

There are also plenty of junior and amateur clubs where enjoyment and fulfilment can be had. Increasingly I wonder if some might start to turn their backs on the professional game and embrace instead a more localised form of football at amateur and junior level. It has a long and honourable tradition, perhaps we may be about to see the wheel reinvented as folk return to a simpler form of enjoyment, free from the dictates of the real business of professional football, which at heart, is really all about money and power and privilege.

Onwards and upwards!

Jim

References

Barrow, S. and Goodwin, P. (2016), *Transforming Scottish Football: The Fans' Manifesto*, Glasgow: Scottish Football Supporters Association.

McLeish, H. (2018), *Scottish Football: Requiem or Renaissance?* Edinburgh: Luath Press.

CHAPTER 29

Religion and (Beyond) Belief in Scotland

Simon Barrow with Richard Holloway and Lesley Orr

RELIGION AND BELIEF – the latter term now denoting a range of life-stances and philosophies, both religious and non-religious – has been foundational to the story of both ancient and modern Scotland, for both good and ill. Yet, as part of what might be termed as 'the national conversation' they feature very little outside the guild of specialists dedicated to such matters, or to the shrinking but increasingly diverse group of people who are active adherents. Throughout this book, for example, there are fewer than a dozen explicit references to religion in public life, most in passing. Yet globally, the use and misuse of religion, broadly defined as cultural systems of behaviours, beliefs, practices, ethics, texts, sanctified places and organisations (Holloway, 2016), has direct relevance for billions of people – the great majority of the world's population.

This can be hard to recognise and understand for people reared in those parts of Europe, including Scotland, most impacted by secularization – the historical processes in which religion loses social and cultural significance (see Davie, 2015; Brown, 2009, and Bruce, 2002). It is perhaps most difficult for the increasing number of younger people whose upbringing includes little or no contact with organised religion, a significant percentage of whom have been entering the worlds of commentary (Barrow, 2012) and scholarship over the past couple of decades.

Religious Decline and Diversification

So, one of the important developments we recognised in our conversations is that the proportion of people in Scotland who describe themselves as having no religion at all has reached its highest ever level over the past few years, according to ScotCen's latest Scottish Social Attitudes survey (ScotCen, 2017). These research findings indicate that nearly six in ten (58 per cent) now say that they have no religion, up 18 percentage points on 1999, when the figure stood at four in ten (40 per cent). There has been a fall in religious identity across all age groups, although it has been slowest among those over 65 years. Even so, there has been an 11 per cent increase in the proportion of over-65s who said they had no religion between 1999 and 2016 (from 23 per cent to 34 per cent). The increase among those aged 50 to 64 has been 24 percentage points (from 33 per cent to 57 per cent). Young people are, perhaps unsurprisingly, the least likely to be religious. Three-quarters of young people (74 per cent of 18 to 34) now say they have no religion, compared with 34 per cent of those over 65. There is no sign that these trends are abating.

At the same time, Scotland over the last twenty years has seen a parallel shift among those for whom religious affiliation or association is important. This is one away from Christianity and towards other religious and philosophical traditions. Christianity remains the largest faith in Scotland. In the Scottish section of the last official UK census (GROS/ONS, 2011), 53.8 per cent of the population identified as Christian (declining from 65.1 per cent in 2001). The largest religious grouping in Scotland, engaged with 32.4 per cent of the population, is the Church of Scotland (Presbyterian), which remains the recognised national church, though not an established one. The Catholic Church accounts for 15.9 per cent of the population and is especially important in west Central Scotland and parts of the Highlands.

In recent years other religions have established themselves solidly in Scotland, both through migration and differential birth rates. Those with most adherents in the 2011 census were Islam (1.4 per cent), Hinduism (0.3 per cent), Buddhism (0.2 per cent) and Sikhism (0.2 per cent). Other minority traditions include the Bahá'í Faith and various Neopagan groups. Organisations actively promoting Humanism and non-religious secularism, included within the 36.7 per cent who indicated no religion in the 2011 census, have been growing notably. Since 2016, Humanists have conducted more weddings in Scotland each year than either the Church of Scotland, the Catholic Church or any other religion (HSS, 2016).

Changing Stories

The story of my lifetime has been accompanied by the decline of religion in the secular sociological paradigm, observes Richard (Holloway, 2013).

This was set out starkly by Callum Brown in *The Death of Christian Britain* (Brown, 2nd edition, 2009). But then the strange thing was that the 70s onwards saw the bucking of that trend.

He refers here to the growth of evangelical and fundamentalist beliefs, the link between religion and some of the major global news stories of the last decade and more (from 9/11 to abuse scandals) and to the mutation of faith in institutional religion towards more amorphous, eclectic and syncretic forms of belief – part of a much wider Western trend (Smith and Barrow, 2001).

Nevertheless, the combined and sometimes competing influences of the Scottish Enlightenment, the Kirk, and the change connected to immigration continue to exert themselves. Healthy scepticism, moral rigour and growing diversity are weaved in and out of the recent story of Scotland in some important ways. In terms of diversity, for example, Islam has long been a prominent part of society in Glasgow. Scotland's first mosque was opened there in Oxford Street in 1944 and Sandymount Cemetery became the first burial site for Muslims during the same era. Since then, some 70,000 Muslims with roots or connections in Pakistan, the Middle East and elsewhere have called Scotland home. They have struggled with prejudice and misunderstanding, experienced welcome and undergone significant social upheavals (*Sunday Herald*, 2018).

Society Beyond Church

One of the trends we all recognised early in our conversations was the demise of the Kirk as a major force in public discourse. Both Richard Holloway and Lesley Orr see the emergence of the Scottish Parliament as perhaps a decisive moment here. The General Assembly Hall of the Church of Scotland hosted the Parliament until the completion of its permanent home at Holyrood (Seiwert-Fauti, 1999). Suddenly it was Scotland's restored national assembly, bestowed with devolved powers, which became the centre of attention and national conversation. 'Reporting of Kirk statements and activities in the media declined at that time,' observes Richard. 'There was a recognisably secularising trend in reporting and commentary'.

Other attitudes changed over time, too. Lesley identifies hostility to religion as more noticeable over the past twenty years, but also notes that

faith plays an important role or background influence in the lives of many women I know active on gender, justice and peace issues.

She is a member of the Iona Community, the radical, communally oriented, peace-and-justice outgrowth of the Church of Scotland, which has since diversified significantly – but also aged and failed to attract younger people.

> Religion is just not part of the routine thinking or culture of many people nowadays.

The anger and disillusion brought about by abuse crises in the Christian churches (though far from restricted to them) has added to the 'bad taste' that religion can leave for a growing number of people, both Lesley and Richard acknowledge.

> But many thousands of people are still inspired by the likes of Dorothy Day, Martin Luther King and Desmond Tutu,

Orr adds:

> Faith has been vibrating way outside the churches and hierarchies, and indeed has been shaking them. Prophetic faith can still be a major force for transformation (see Orr *et al.*, 2020).

The sheer scale of the crisis of affiliation, recognition, confidence and resources that faces the institutional churches in Scotland is, however, something that they still fail fully to comprehend, all three of us feel. The culture and language of a body like the Kirk is increasingly impenetrable to those outside its confines, despite some efforts to modernise and widen its appeal. At the same time, those inbred cultural and ideological features can act as a barrier to a deeper understanding of what is happening in the surrounding and suffusing cultures across the regions of Scotland, urban and rural. All this ought to, perhaps, have been expected to produce a more substantial ecumenism (collaboration and coming together) among the churches, more active co-operation across faiths, and more exchange between religious and non-religious people on ethics, value and life-stances. Yet the institutional structures for Christian ecumenism, in particular, have been receding. One response to decline or the threat posed by loss of perceived and actual centrality in national life is a retreat into zones of safety, some of which (like 'messy church' for kids and families) may be far less accessible to a wider public than they like to think.

Another shadow side linked to religion is the persistence of sectarian attitudes and behaviours in Scotland – seen in marches and football matches, but not simply attributable or blameable on one set of social institutions or manifestations. The extent to which communal tribalism wears religious language or clothing significantly is a hotly debated issue. Anti-Catholic prejudice is strongly felt by those it impacts, alongside Islamophobia and anti-Semitism. Many within Scotland's committed faith communities recognise the potency and danger of religiously aggravated intolerance, discrimination, hatred and violence, and seek deep resources within their own traditions which can address and combat these positively.

Even so, the religious bodies remain deeply divided on issues where prejudice and bigotry play a notable role – most especially on issues of sexuality and the inclusion or exclusion of LGBTQI+ people within their societies and in the wider culture. There is deep conservatism and fear within Christian and other circles on such questions, but also a surge of acceptance and change. The speed with which same-sex partnerships and marriage have emerged and been widely accepted over the past twenty years is breath-taking, given the centuries of rejection preceding this. Religious voices have been strong in movements for liberation and reform, but they have also been a major obstacle, as churches run to catch up with an ethical tide that challenges their claim on moral precedence. Sharp debates exist on the place and role (or otherwise) of religion in public education, too. Painfully but unavoidably, we need to be able to recognise church as a conducive context for abuse, and link action in the future to address this more directly to the long history of ecclesiastical patriarchy and misogyny.

A key challenge in describing Scotland today and tomorrow in its continuing relationship with religion and belief (that 'and' being used by equalities bodies to denote the non- and a-religious character of belief) is one of language. All three of us favour a secular Scotland, by which we mean a plural culture where beliefs coexist and contend without privilege in the public sphere, and where the state neither prescribes nor proscribes religion *per se*. But that word 'secularism' can also be used to advocate a strictly eliminative approach. More dialogue is needed here.

What we are looking at in Scotland is a 'mixed belief society', rather than one that can simply be labelled secular or religious. The era of Christendom (where a certain kind of religion conveyed blessing on rulers in exchange for protection and privilege) has come to an end. What will take its place is still up for grabs. None of us wish to see a return to any kind of imperial religion, in Scotland or elsewhere – though we note disturbing signs of this in the US right now. But we also recognise that spirituality is important in grounding life in human (and for many, transcendent) values and practices. We recognise that the loss of religious institutions can also mean the loss of centres of gravity or specific taxonomy for some kinds of conversation – on ethical concerns, for instance – as well as the loss of actual local communities of engagement. How to construct diverse, rooted moral communities for sustaining the good life is one question that these brief reflections on religion and (beyond) belief in Scotland, and the wider world, leaves tantalisingly hanging.

*****

These reflections on the current religious and secular situation of Scotland arise from two separate recorded conversations involving the three of us – a think-tank director with a background in ecumenical relations and theological education (the principal author), a former church leader engaging in an open and critical way with the societal impact of belief, and a feminist scholar and activist engaged with religion. We sought to be conscious in our exchanges of both the scope and limits of our experience, research and understanding.

References

Barrow, S. (2012), 'Religion and New Media: Changing the Story', in Mitchell, J. and Gower, O. (eds.), *Religion and the News*, Farnham, Surrey: Ashgate.

BBC (1999), 'Kirk's home hosts moment of history', 1 July 1999, available online at: http://news.bbc.co.uk/1/hi/special_report/1999/06/99/scottish_parliament_opening/378263.stm

Brown, C.G. (2009), *The Death of Christian Britain: Understanding Secularisation, 1800–2000*, Abingdon: Routledge.

Bruce, S. (2002), *God is Dead: Secularization in the West*, Oxford: Wiley-Blackwell.

Davie, G. (2015), *Religion in Britain: A Persistent Paradox*, Oxford: Wiley-Blackwell.

General Register Office for Scotland (2011), 'The Office of National Statistics – 2011 Census in Scotland', Edinburgh: GROS (now National Records of Scotland).

Holloway, R. (2016), *A Little History of Religion*, New Haven, CT: Yale University Press.

Holloway, R. (2013), *Leaving Alexandria: A Memoir of Faith and Doubt*, Edinburgh: Canongate Books.

Humanist Society Scotland (2016), 'More than 4,200 Humanist weddings took place in Scotland last year', Edinburgh: HSS.

Mitchell, J., Orr, L., Percy, M. and Po, F. (2020), *Wiley Blackwell Companion to Religion and Peace*, Oxford: Wiley-Blackwell, forthcoming.

ScotCen Social Research (2017), 'Scottish Social Attitudes Survey', Edinburgh: ScotCen.

Seiwert-Fauti, U. (2019), 'How the Scottish Parliament has changed the nation's identity', *The National*, 11 February 2019.

Smith, G. and Barrow, S. (2001), *Christian Mission in Western Society*, London: CTBI.

Sunday Herald (2018), 'Just how welcome are Muslims in Scotland?', 26 August 2018, available online at: www.heraldscotland.com/news/16599716.just-how-welcome-are-muslims-in-scotland/

Section Five – Place and Geographies

CHAPTER 30

The Land Question

Andy Wightman

Introduction

LAND REFORM IS the process of changing the relationship between land and society. This relationship is one of power. It is about legal power (reform of land tenure), economic power (fiscal reform), and political power (law-making and land use decision making).

Across the world, land reform has been the means by which power has been redistributed from elites. Whether in Latin America, Africa or Europe, most countries have had their land reform moments when – as a result of decolonisation or revolution – the deep structural rules that monopolised land were overthrown and land was redistributed, tenure strengthened for marginalised populations, an' women's rights improved.

The United Kingdom never had such a moment, but its history is littered with all the ingredients that led to reforms in countries across Europe. The reasons for this are rooted in the un-reconstructed power of elites in the UK; in particular, the stranglehold of landed power in the UK Parliament's House of Lords until very recently. It is important to note that in large measure the laws that govern land relations across Britain were framed by male landowners.

It was the legal certainty of landownership that enabled British landowners to raise capital secured against their land to finance the industrial revolution. It was primogeniture and the ownership of land by men that embedded patriarchy and inequality. Today, in the UK, growing inequality of wealth is in substantial part explained by whether you own property or not.

Scotland has a distinctive history regarding land. Feudal tenure was not abolished until 2004. Primogeniture was only abolished in 1964. The ownership of private land is among the most concentrated of any country in the world. Home ownership only rose above 50 per cent after 1990. Unlike many other European countries, Scotland has not developed a property-owning democracy.

Instead it has been, for much of the 20th century in the grip of aristocratic feudal landlords in rural and urban Scotland and a local state in which public housing has been responsible for housing people in proportions seldom seen outside the former socialist states of eastern Europe.

The Significance of the Scottish Parliament

Central to this condition has been the lack of agency by the people of Scotland in debating and determining their own affairs. The campaign for a Scottish Parliament was designed to correct this anomaly whereby Scotland's laws were made by MPs who overwhelmingly did not represent the voters of Scotland. In relation to land laws, not only did the House of Lords act as a barrier to reform but the Secretary of State for Scotland secured only very few legislative slots in a parliamentary programme dominated by the needs of England. The consequence of this legislative neglect was a failure to modernise the Scots law of property even where proposals were non-contentious.

The ownership of land in Scotland has long been a totemic issue for radicals and a good example of the kind of topic that self-determination could tackle. Throughout the 1990s, a succession of campaigns by rural communities on the Isle of Eigg, the Knoydart peninsula and on the crofting lands of Assynt had emerged in response to decades of neglect, absentee landlordism and frustration.

By the mid-1990s, it was simply a matter of time before a Labour Government was elected on a commitment to establish a legislature in Edinburgh. The United Kingdom comprises three jurisdictions and the UK Parliament never provided adequate time for the passage of Scottish legislation. These reforms such as the abolition of feudal tenure that was first proposed in the 1950s never became reality until the establishment of a Scottish Parliament with direct accountability to the voters of Scotland and with no hereditary House of Lords to block such proposals.

Within months of the 1997 election, Donald Dewar had established a high-powered committee of civil servants under the chairmanship of Lord Sewel, the Land Reform Policy Group. In a fast-paced period of work, the group prepared two consultation papers before publishing a final report in January 1999. Intended as an agenda for the new Parliament to be established later in the year, it contained a wide range of recommendations including new legislation on public access, the establishment of national parks, reform of tenement law, abolition of feudal tenure and strengthened rights for tenant farmers.

With the establishment of the Parliament, a legislature elected by the people of Scotland now had the ability to change the law governing the ownership and use of the land of Scotland. Not everyone welcomed the change. Landed interests, long used to exerting influence through the House of Lords and unelected Scottish Office Ministers such as Lord Lindsay, Lord Sanderson, Lord Mansfield, suddenly had to answer questions in front of committees of MSPs.

Land Reform in the Democratic Era

The first session of the Scottish Parliament was dominated by legislation designed to modernise and reform Scots land law:

> Abolition of Feudal tenure etc (Scotland) Act
> Agricultural Holdings (Scotland) Act
> Housing (Scotland) Act
> Land Reform (Scotland) Act
> Leasehold Casualties (Scotland) Act
> National Parks (Scotland) Act
> Title Conditions (Scotland) Act

On a more practical level, the most significant legislative achievement was the complex and long overdue abolition of feudal tenure. The ability of feudal superiors to dictate what their feudal vassals could do with their property had given rise to numerous conflicts with homeowners, for example, prevented from carrying out modest alterations to their property.

Despite these reforms, however, land reform continued to be framed and approached over the next decade as a topic that concerned rural communities and their relationship with landed estates. Discussions of land reform were almost always conflated with support or opposition to community land ownership. Wider questions about fiscal policy, succession law, wealth inequality, housing policy and land governance remained absent from debate.

From 2003 until 2011, attention to land reform faded from view. The incoming SNP Government in 2007 instructed civil servants that 'enough has been done on land reform' and wound up the Land Reform Branch within the Scottish Government. It was clear that for now, the job had been done and the central questions of power, accountability and equity in access to land remained undeveloped, unanswered and ignored. Part of the reason for this was a failure by civil society, academia and others to pick up where the Land Reform Policy Group had left off and to maintain the momentum that had been established from 1999 to 2003.

To reform Scotland's land laws, the assumptions they generated and the power structures they perpetuated requires determination, focus and political will across many election cycles. For too many politicians, land reform was about treating symptoms of structural inequality rather than a long-term programme for eliminating it. Other European countries had their revolutionary moments. The UK and Scotland did not. In the face of human rights law and embedded legal conventions, securing outcomes that reflect modern European norms is a substantial political project.

Frustration with the failure of the minority SNP administration of 2007–2011 to advance the cause of land reform led to growing calls for a more determined approach by Holyrood. Ongoing conflicts between land-lords and tenants, wishful thinking about ending the influence of the Crown Estate Commissioners, a realisation that the housing crisis facing your people is, in substantial part, a crisis in the land market, all contributed to land being pushed up the political agenda. In a stark admission of the lack of thinking that had taken place since 1999, the SNP promised in its 2011 manifesto to establish a Land Reform Review Group to revisit the agenda and inform new legislation.

By time the Interim Report was published in May 2013, the two mem-bers of the group had resigned leaving only the Chair in place. The insipid and poorly-informed report was widely criticised, and the Government moved to strengthen the group and appoint an adviser with knowledge and experience in the topic.

The Final Report was published in May 2014. In contrast to earlier criti-cisms, the report was widely welcomed. It admitted, candidly, that

> at present, the Scottish Government has no integrated approach to land reform and Scotland has not had a land reform programme for ten years.

It argued that

> significant changes are required to make Scotland's system of land ownership a more efficient and effective system for delivering the public interest.

The report was wide-ranging, analytical and ambitious and its recommenda-tions reflected a broad sweep of land reform from urban to rural and marine issues. They included longer and more secure tenancies for private housing tenants, new powers of compulsory purchase, the establishment of a Housing Land Corporation to acquire land, new arrangements for common good land, the devolution of the Crown Estate, removing exemptions from business rates enjoyed by owners of rural land, giving children the right to inherit land, pro-hibiting companies in tax havens from registering title, protecting common land from land grabbing, reviewing hunting rights, limiting the amount of land any one beneficial owner can own and introducing a wide range of new powers for communities to take more control of the land around them in towns, cities and the countryside.

Of the 62 recommendations, 58 were within the full-devolved competence of the Scottish Parliament. The Group defined land reform as

> measures that modify or change the arrangements governing the possession and use of land in Scotland in the public interest.

At long last, here was a definition that was comprehensive and inclusive.

The work of the Review Group led to the Land Reform (Scotland) Act, 2016 but many recommendations remained unfulfilled despite further work by civil servants. The challenge of ensuring ongoing political commitment to the hard work of structural reform of well-established power structures remained.

The final recommendation was designed to overcome this political inertia – the establishment of a Scottish Land and Property Commission to provide research, advice and support for future land reform measures. Established in 2017, the Scottish Land Commission is now actively undertaking research and publishing policy papers on a wide range of topics such as compulsory sale orders, land value capture and, importantly, human rights. Conventionally regarded as a limiting factor in land reform as a result of the provisions of the European Convention on Human Rights, the debate surrounding the passage of the 2016 act emphasised that land policy should equally enhance and uphold human rights (to housing for example).

Future Challenges

Scotland is now better placed to deal with the breadth and depth of issues arising from the way in which land is owned and used. Although huge amounts of work lie ahead, there is now a more sophisticated and nuanced appreciation that land relations are central to a range of policy areas including housing, planning, climate change, equalities and wellbeing.

A range of analyses published during 2018 highlighted ongoing wealth inequalities (which are running at twice income inequality) in Scotland arising as a consequence of how land is governed and how housing wealth in particular is distributed and taxed (or not). Three times as many households are living in the private rented sector compared to 1999. With parental wealth being as important a factor as incomes in determining the prospects of home ownership, the politics of land is now part of a debate on intergenerational inequality. All political parties will have to respond to the strain caused by housing costs consistently outstripping incomes.

Attempts to tackle housing shortages remain conditioned by a reluctance to challenge the privileges of the home owning class and the inequities of rising housing costs. This is most starkly illustrated by the persistent failure to abolish the regressive Council Tax, which remains based on property values established in April 1991.

Land reform is about changing the legal, administrative and fiscal relationship between society and land in order to deliver public policy in areas such as housing, development, the environment, agriculture and forestry. The potential gains are immense and a radical programme of reform over the next decade and beyond could fundamentally alter the nature and distribution of power in Scotland.

CHAPTER 31

The Place of Gaelic in Today's Scotland

Malcolm Maclean

GAELIC DEVELOPMENT IS not just about language learning but aiming to educate Scots about their cultural DNA. To paraphrase James Baldwin:

> What Scots do not know about Gaelic reveals, precisely and inexorably, what they do not know about themselves.

Gaelic was invisible in Scottish public life until the closing decade of the 20th century. It had no place in politics, commerce or education and if you spoke Gaelic in a court of law you were 'deemed to stay silent'. This has changed dramatically as Gaelic television, arts events, education and signage have made the language far more visible in the 21st century. The Parliament's Gaelic Act of 2005 was a historic milestone on this journey.

After centuries of political repression, the act was a major step towards Gaelic normalisation and an important gesture of reconciliation and political goodwill. Addressing this ancient fracture in Scottish culture was a healthy step for Scotland and did much to raise confidence and expectations in the Gaelic community. The Official Status that came with the 2005 act has led onto significant legislation on Gaelic medium education, Gaelic language plans for public services and vital progress in creating a Gaelic learners culture.

Unfortunately, this welcome progress has been undermined by failure on other fronts. National progress on Gaelic language learning has been accompanied by a sense of marginalisation in the communities where Gaelic is still spoken by the majority and survives against long odds as a living language in daily use. The biggest disappointment in terms of official policy towards Gaelic has been the Creative Scotland (CS) failure to sustain strategic support for Gaelic arts and cultural development. This is the new paradox of 21st century Gaeldom.

Good News for Gaelic and Scotland

Gaelic is probably the oldest language in non-Mediterranean Europe. It is a couple of thousand years older than English and 500 years ago it was spoken by 50 per cent of Scots.

The 2011 Census found 57,600 Gaelic speakers and 87,100 people in Scotland with Gaelic language skills (1.7 per cent of the population)

The highest proportion of people with Gaelic language skills (61 per cent) was in *Eilean Siar*/Outer Hebrides with 74 per cent of them using Gaelic at home. Gaelic speakers in the Highlands and Argyll and Bute number 7 per cent and 6 per cent respectively with a further 10,000 Gaelic speakers in greater Glasgow and almost 6,000 in the Edinburgh area.

Gaelic medium primary school education (GME) has grown from 14 pupils in 1985 to 3,278 in 2018. There is now a total of 5,607 involved in GME from early learning (nursery) to secondary level and GME pupils match or outperform monolingual pupils in all subjects, including English.

Gaelic language plans mean that Local Authorities have committed to more GME and Gaelic learner education and other public bodies have expanded their provision of Gaelic services.

Learngaelic.scot provides resources for adult Gaelic learners and Skye's Gaelic college, *Sabhal Mòr Ostaig*, delivers full-time study, short courses and distance-learning for beginners.

Economic impact research carried out by Highlands and Islands Enterprise and *Bòrd Na Gàidhlig* (BNG) shows the economic value of Gaelic to the Scottish economy to be between £82 million and £149 million.

The BBC ALBA TV channel is one of the major Gaelic successes of recent years. BBC Alba contributes to Scottish culture, identity and economy and creates internationally-recognised programmes that are watched by more than 10 per cent of the population every week. MG ALBA has created 290 FTE jobs, and GVA of £12.5 million. Of this, around a hundred jobs are based in the Outer Hebrides and Skye, with wages above average for the area.

BBC Radio *nan Gàidheal* provides a national daily radio service that reaches more of the people it is aimed at than Radio 1. It connects Gaelic communities across Scotland and the world and offers a kind of cultural bloodstream for the Gaelic community.

Gaelic arts, music and culture are recognised throughout the world and add to Scotland's reputation as a country with a rich and diverse heritage. The Gaelic creative industries contribute to Scotland's cultural and economic growth through literature, publishing, film, digital media, visual arts and music recording.

The *Fèis* movement's 47 tuition-based festivals bring Gaelic arts learning opportunities to 6,000 young people annually. *Fèis* events reach an audience of 70,000 annually and that figure rises to 450,000 when TV appearances and YouTube hits are taken into account.

Gaelic television is responsible for 95 per cent of the Scottish traditional music on UK TV. This exposure and the impact of the *Fèis* movement have been driving forces behind the resurgence of Scottish traditional music since the 1990s.

VisitScotland's regular Visitor Survey confirms that finding out more about Gaelic was of interest to a third of the visitors to Scotland.

Public attitude surveys confirm that the majority of Scottish people now show substantial good will towards Gaelic. 81 per cent of believe that Scotland should not lose its Gaelic traditions, 70 per cent believe there should be more opportunities to learn Gaelic, 65 per cent believe more should be done to promote Gaelic and 53 per cent want to see Gaelic used more in everyday life. Younger people are even more positive.

Downsides to Success

The first downside to this progress has been centralisation of authority and financial control in BNG, the public body established by Parliament to take responsibility for Gaelic development. Gaelic history and geography have given the Gaels good cause to be deeply resistant to centralisation making it an unfortunate model for BNG to follow. This 21th century centralisation is also a rewinding of history in that the key characteristic of the Gaelic breakthrough period in the 1980s and 1990s was *de-centralisation*.

Following the 1886 Crofting Act the old Highland Land League had morphed into the Gaelic membership organisation *An Comunn Gàidhealach* (ACG) who became the spokespeople for the Gaelic community throughout the 20th century. By the 1980s, however, the world was becoming too complex for any one organisation and the challenges facing Gaelic culture were intensifying. State support for Gaelic was non-existent so Gaelic communities began to vote with their feet and new and independent Gaelic initiatives began to emerge.

They represented different interest groups from a playgroup's movement, a new parents organisation, a new learners organisation, local history societies, new arts initiatives such as the *Fèis* movement and *An Lanntair* and the Gaelic college *Sabhal Mòr Ostaig*. ACG's leadership role was displaced by a new organisation, *Comunn Na Gàidhlig* (CNAG) in 1984 who were state-funded to take an economic development approach. CNAG's strategic development role included advocacy for the emerging Gaelic sector and their classic campaign for a Gaelic television service that secured eight million pounds a year from the 1991 Broadcasting Act. Most of the big policy initiatives on Gaelic were underway prior to devolution. Gaelic medium education was supported by both government and local authorities in the 1980s and 1990s and continued by the Scottish Parliament. The same was true of the Gaelic arts and the Scottish Arts Council (SAC). Despite CNAG's lead body role in these developments the defining characteristics of the late 20th century Gaelic resurgence were organisational diversity – mostly social enterprises – and geographical dispersal.

The centre of gravity of 21th century Gaelic development is now in the BNG base in Inverness with support from their satellite office in Glasgow. Inverness was a controversial base location from the outset and was seen as neither fish nor fowl. A Hebridean base would have brought BNG closer to the largest Gaelic speaking community and the Gaelic jobs and career opportunities would have been especially welcome in a region struggling with depopulation. Alternatively, a BNG base in Edinburgh would have brought the new national agency closer to the decision makers in the Scottish Parliament than neutral Inverness.

BNG's Inverness base has contributed to a growing distance and tension between the agency and the language's traditional heartlands in the Hebridean communities. The failure to base full-time staff on the islands or even open a BNG island office, has compounded a sense of disempowerment. This mainland centralisation crystallises and symbolises a wider disconnect between Gaelic speaking island communities facing massive socio-economic change and the completely sluggish response from government and its agencies. This potential disconnect between the carriers of the language and the professionalised language and media sector is a class and a geographical issue to a degree – rural speakers vs. urban professionals – and it should not be ignored.

Unfortunately, it has been. An as yet unpublished 2017 research study into islanders' attitudes towards BNG found mounting levels of open disappointment, criticism and alienation. The consultation I attended in my owncommunity was unanimous in its concern. Majority Gaelic speaking island communities feel abandoned by BNG as they struggle with the economic and cultural challenges of depopulation, demographic shift and language maintenance.

A key reason for this lack of BNG presence in the islands is the numerical targets they have been set by government. The agency's success or failure is to be measured in the numbers of new Gaelic speakers recorded in future census figures and these targets are most achievable in large population centres. This has led to an urban bias as BNG focusses its limited financial and human resources on cities in pursuit of the necessary numbers.

The positive development here has been the creation of a Scottish Gaelic learners' culture. The absence of a strong learner's culture in the past was a key strategic weakness so this is a very welcome development. The vast majority of Irish and Welsh speakers identify as learners which is why their numbers are so much greater. Gaelic is the first language of the vast majority of Scotland's 57,000 Gaelic speakers and there are probably more first language Gaelic speakers in Scotland than among Ireland's 500,000.

The Irish accord a high status to their first language Gaelic speakers that has not yet been nurtured in Scotland. Ireland's Gaelic communities play a vital strategic role in Irish language learning through a network of Gaelic immersion summer schools that have hosted generations of learners from the cities. In turning away from the islands, the Scottish model seems to be going in the opposite direction.

Gaelic is spoken throughout the Scottish diaspora, but it is in Scotland's Hebridean communities that it has survived into the 21st century. As a Glasgow Gael I welcome BNG's work in the cities, but the islands are where Gaelic is still spoken by the majority of the population. The creation of an urban learners' community should not be at the expense of the traditional Gaelic communities in the islands. Both communities are essential to Gaelic language survival and this should not be an either/or equation. The riches of Hebridean language, heritage, history and identity are among Scotland's greatest cultural, social and economic resources and should be a cornerstone of any Gaelic language learning strategy. There are no examples of a language diaspora surviving without a homeland community where their language is spoken by the majority of inhabitants. Scotland's islands, however, seem marginal to the current BNG agenda.

A second downside to the 21st century Gaelic story has been the damage done by CS to the momentum Gaelic arts and cultural development. One of the first and most culturally significant acts of CS was to torpedo 25 years of highly productive Gaelic arts development work by their predecessor the SAC. The 2012 decision by CS to withdraw hard-earned funding status from the Gaelic arts development agency, *Pròiseact Nan Ealan* (PNE), was an ill-advised, unexpected and an unexplained body-blow. The CS torpedo hit PNE below the waterline and, following three years of struggle, it finally sank in 2015. CS decisions had rendered it unworkable and forced the closure of the only Gaelic arts production company.

This ended a highly successful, multi award winning, SAC development strategy that created an embryonic Gaelic arts infrastructure and a whole new sector of the Scottish arts. This success at local, national and international levels was reportedly seen by CS as too independent and too ambitious for an organisation based in the sticks of the Outer Hebrides. The toxic combination of arrogance and ignorance that characterised the early days of CS eventually became a national controversy that forced the resignation of the CEO and his deputy. The regime change that followed brought a degree of stability to the infant CS, but this came too late for PNE and the Gaelic arts. CS had no idea of how to remedy the damage they had done and have continued to flounder ever since.

Organisations will always come and go as they outlive their usefulness, but the key issue here is the abject failure of both CS and BNG to produce any kind of alternative strategy. A highly critical 2015 editorial in the West Highland Free Press challenged CS to state their strategy for Gaelic arts development – if they had one. They have never responded. Several years later this sustained CS avoidance of any coherent Gaelic arts development strategy has moved the issue beyond ignorance, arrogance and the law of unintended consequences. It now constitutes a hostile act.

The absence of such a strategy is not a marginal arts matter. Ensuring the survival of Gaelic into the future is one of the most critical cultural issues facing Scottish society. It is not a responsibility the key arts agency delegated by government to dispense millions of pounds of public funding can ignore. It is an abuse of the arms-length principle for CS to pay lip service to government policy and the declared will of the Scottish Parliament while failing to take meaningful strategic action. The key word here is *autochthonous,* which means a language and culture that no other government has responsibility to support. Gaelic is a uniquely Scottish responsibility which has been jeopardised by CS failure to plan strategically, failure to invest and failure to understand.

BNG share responsibility here. Their inertia on this issue suggests a lack of vision and ambition and a disturbing degree of weakness but the CS/BNG relationship is not one of equals and CS must take the primary responsibility.

Why Does This Matter?

The arts are the arena in which languages and cultures will survive or die in the 21st century. They are therefore especially significant in the Gaelic context and language planning without an arts strategy is to enter the arena with your hands tied behind your back. Motivation is a primary factor in language usage and the arts capacity to engage hearts and minds makes them a powerful motivational tool.

Internationally renowned linguist, Professor David Crystal, sees the arts and artists as our best hope of addressing language death. A language becomes extinct every two weeks and 90 per cent of the 6,000 languages spoken today will have disappeared by the end of this century. Gaelic is in the top 20 per cent of languages in terms of the number of speakers.

The 'Linguarts' research study by the Interarts agency in Barcelona surveyed the relationship between language and cultural policies across Europe and found none. They concluded that there was a completely illogical separation of these two policy areas that worked against the best interests of both arts and language and was 'ultimately unsustainable as it represents poor value for public expenditure'.

Both BNG and CS have invested in Gaelic language plans but neither have a Gaelic arts strategy. Ten years ago, CS, BNG and HIE requested a national Gaelic arts strategy that was later commended to Parliament by culture minister, Mike Russell MSP. Its most radical proposal was for public agencies to work together to agree jointly-funded strategic initiatives that required critical investment to get off the ground but would benefit them all. This was a direct challenge to the funding fiefdoms managing multiple small grants in CS/BNG and offered a way to think bigger and get better value for the public pound. It was promptly shelved and buried without trace.

The Scottish arts are not a level playing field and 25 years of modest SAC investment, no matter how productive, has not reversed 500 years of institutional hostility and neglect. The Gaelic arts and cultural infrastructure remain seriously underdeveloped and the current CS/BNG policy of small grants to multiple small projects – no matter how successful they may be – does not constitute a development strategy. A vibrant music scene, for example, can mask a hole in the middle of the picture which is the Gaelic language itself. A strategy to develop flagship productions and creativity in the language in song, drama and the written and spoken word is urgently required. Denying strategic development investment will condemn the Gaelic arts to permanent cottage industry status.

What Can Be Done?

In the 1980s a generation of very bright Gaels identified key strategic challenges and set out to overcome them. The negative of wall-to-wall English language television was turned into the positive of a Gaelic television service. A language seen as economically irrelevant has become an economic driver and a valuable job qualification. The absence of endorsement by any one political party was transformed into cross-party political support. What was widely regarded as a localised language issue to do with the remote north-west is now recognised as a national cultural asset with learners throughout the country. I had the privilege of a ring-side seat at some of these developments and see the issues I have highlighted here as the problems of success. They are serious problems, nonetheless.

Despite the progress of recent years Gaelic remains on very thin ice. The effectiveness of the 2005 act has to be judged against hard outcomes, as well as good intentions and the Parliament must, after twenty years, consider how its undoubted goodwill can be translated into more effective outcomes. This commentary suggests four actions.

A Gaelic community's strategy. BNG's centralising impetus means vital and energetic island communities are becoming passive observers of – rather than active participants in – a national Gaelic development process.

A national Gaelic arts strategy. CS has demoted the Gaelic arts sector and are pursuing a cut-price, one-size-fits-all approach lacking vision, ambition and investment. This is a sector that had grown and flourished in the immediate pre-devolution era and any assessment of Holyrood's record on Gaelic over the past twenty years, should ensure it is a policy area which is critically reviewed.

A review of GME secondary school provision. This remains disappointingly inconsistent and many children who go through GME primary schooling fall off a cliff as they approach secondary.

Reinforcement of BNG's Gaelic language plans. These have been a central plank of BNG strategy but can create a tick-the-box mentality in public agencies who then fail to fulfil their Gaelic commitments. The challenge here is to ensure that the implementation of plans is rigorously monitored and sufficiently resourced to deliver the spirit as well as the letter of their Gaelic responsibilities. As the Parliament enters its third decade it should mark this coming of age by appointing a Gaelic Commissioner to oversee the delivery of Gaelic plans and monitor future language and cultural progress.

References

Bòrd Na Gàidhlig (2018), *Gaelic Today and Tomorrow,* Inverness: Bòrd Na Gàidhlig.

Crystal, D. (2000), *Language Death,* Cambridge: Cambridge University Press.

Delgado, E. (1999), *Linguarts. Language and Cultural Policies In Europe,* Barcelona: Interarts Observatory.

MacPoilin, A. (2018), *Our Tangled Speech,* Belfast: Ultach Trust.

Olsberg (2016), *Impact of MG Alba's Production Investments,* Stornoway: MG Alba, HIE.

CHAPTER 32

Edinburgh Calling

George Kerevan

SCOTLAND'S CAPITAL CITY is a chameleon whose economic and political fortunes have gyrated wildly over the centuries. Begun as a military encampment high on a fortuitous volcanic plug, Edinburgh came to life in the Middle Ages as a strategic garrison town. The Port of Leith forged Scotland's golden link in the chain of great Baltic trading centres of the Hanseatic League. A rising urban bourgeoisie, stiffened by intellectual and political ties to revolutionary Protestant Europe, ensured Edinburgh became the pivot for Scotland's capitalist transformation – ideologically, financially and socially.

The city lost some of its political clout with the Union of 1707, but this loss can be exaggerated. By its nature, the Union settlement bequeathed Scotland's domestic affairs – legal, religious and educational – into the hands of a smug, conservative and oft-times ruthless Edinburgh petty bourgeoisie. This middle-class elite has dominated the city – and Scotland – ever since. True, 19th century industrialisation and the slave trade saw a temporary shift of wealth and influence towards the dark Satanic mills of Clydeside. By mid-20th century, Edinburgh's Old Town was an under-populated slum and its immigrant Irish proletariat dispatched to damp new housing estates on the city's fringes.

The Backstory of Edinburgh's Recent Renaissance

In the nick of time, Edinburgh managed to recover its economic and social dynamism. Partly this was aided by Glasgow's deindustrialisation and urban planning suicide. As a result, Edinburgh's petty bourgeois elite of lawyers, accountants, bankers and academics finally escaped the hegemony of Glasgow's fast-eroding industrial class. Edinburgh's renaissance was also due to the accident of the International Festival and its ever-inventive Fringe, which refurbished the city's cultural and internationalist credentials – even if the snooty Edinburgh hoi polloi preferred classical concerts to the *avant garde* Traverse Theatre.

In the decade and a half before the return of a Scottish Parliament in 1997, Edinburgh's revival took a distinctly social democratic turn, spearheaded by a youthful and radical city administration. This was the first majority Labour council in the capital's history. Its progressive values – consciously influenced by Ken Livingstone's maverick GLC – stood in sharp contrast to Scottish Labour's unsavoury tradition of clientelism and civic inertia. The new council declared itself a nuclear free zone, set up a women's committee (initiator of the famous 'zero tolerance' campaign against domestic violence), and gave out free needles to halt the spread of AIDS.

But, the city administration also pursued a radical interventionist policy in the local economy through its own public-sector development company, Edinburgh Development and Investment. The result was a complete refurbishment of the capital's infrastructure with a new conference centre, concert hall, business park, technology incubators and central banking district. At one point, Edinburgh's capital investment programme was bigger than the rest of municipal Scotland put together – the result of artful financing by a civic team that consisted of former Trotskyists (including myself).

Many of these changes were achieved through a curious alliance between the council and key members of the Edinburgh elite, the banks and big assurance companies. The political horizons of Edinburgh's financial bourgeoisie – buttressed by private schooling and membership of the all-male New Club – were conservative (and Conservative and Unionist). But just occasionally some in this elite had an inkling of something different. Angus Grossart and Iain Noble used the advent of North Sea oil to create *ab initio* the first Scottish merchant bank. For Noble it was a quick step to imagining an independent Scotland free from the domination of his rivals in the City of London. By century's end, Edinburgh's financial class had recovered a certain entrepreneurial spirit and (in a rare burst of civic engagement) actively collaborated with the city council to modernise the capital's infrastructure.

Edinburgh's New Place in 21st Century Scotland

With the return of the Scottish Parliament in 1997, Edinburgh seemed destined to recover its historic role as a political capital, while eclipsing Glasgow as Scotland's premier financial and intellectual hub. As Glasgow's population continued to decline with the flight of the middle-class to the suburbs, Edinburgh enjoyed a demographic boom. The Old Town slums of the 1960s became, in turn, student flats then expat investment vehicles selling for London prices. Some dared anticipate Edinburgh as the capital of an independent Scotland.

However, the next two incendiary decades proved to be a strange lacuna in the capital's history. One in which the city as a *polis* failed to stamp its mark on events. Paradoxically so given the momentous tide of change: the destruction of Labour's smothering political hegemony in Scotland, the rise and fall of Edinburgh-based RBS as the world's biggest bank, an independence referendum barely lost, followed by a Brexit that threatened to cut the city off from its traditional European hinterland. Blame for the city's failure to influence events or create a bigger profile lay with a series of soggy coalitions on the local council and an increasingly complacent Edinburgh middle-class more bent on making money than exerting a positive political influence.

Of course, the Edinburgh of the past two decades was an outward success. Population rose continuously from just under 450,000 to *circa* 513,000 – a 14 per cent jump driven largely by inward migration and reflecting the capital's economic boom conditions. Add in the exploding Edinburgh dormitories of West, Mid and East Lothian, and the conurbation has the most dynamic demography in Scotland. By the 2030s, Edinburgh's population will likely have breasted 600,000, an historic climacteric that will put it ahead of Glasgow.

Yet despite this explosive growth, the capital's development strategy has proven a catastrophic disappointment in key respects. Construction of a new tram line – an unnecessary prestige project – turned into a financial and planning catastrophe, rightly depriving the city's incompetent Liberal Democratic administration of its majority at the 2012 municipal election. Massive cost over-runs and construction delays resulted in plans for a comprehensive tram network being sharply curtailed. When the truncated service finally limped into operation in 2014 it had become an international by-word for municipal incompetence.

The tram fiasco was far from being Edinburgh's worst planning failure. With the city's population exploding, it was an easy call to let developers make a fast buck by churning out endless, identikit estates, eating deep into Edinburgh's green belt; or throw up anonymous apartment buildings shoehorned into nooks and crannies in the town centre. The new SNP Government at Holyrood added to the debacle by ordering local authorities to deliver arbitrary quotas of land for house building. The intention was to over-ride nimbyism and stimulate construction to boost economic growth after the 2008 recession. But the consequence was a Stalinist centralisation of planning that gave builders the chance to cover prime farmland in concrete.

Other European capitals had a less parochial vision, sensing (correctly) that a truly successful global city is one that pioneers and takes risks. Instead, Edinburgh retreated into its traditional petty bourgeois risk aversion. Early plans to make the city a laboratory for green and sustainable housing technology – on a par with Stockholm's Hammarby Sjöstad – quickly disappeared. An innovative proposal by Edinburgh architect Malcolm Fraser to return housing to Princes Street, and reanimate the city centre, remained a paper project. True, there is Richard Murphy's wonderful homage to Vienna's classic *Werkbund* social housing, in the shape of his 2013 Wharton Square development. But Murphy's effervescent project is marooned deep inside the new Quartermile district, a crowded facsimile of the worst of the over-priced, plate glass high-rise developments that pollute London's contemporary East End. Murphy's Wharton Square is a searing indictment of the utter failure of recent Edinburgh councils to take social housing seriously.

The lacklustre, derivative architecture that fronted Edinburgh's demographic and economic expansion of the past two decades is a metaphor for the city's conservative, philistine petty bourgeoisie. Even at the height of the banking boom, there were no flamboyant skyscrapers: traditional petty bourgeois understatement remains in vogue. Nor was there (American-style) conspicuous private sponsorship of major new art venues. Apart from a revamp of the city's main museum complex in 2008, and a modest upgrade of the Scottish National Portrait Gallery in 2011, wealthy Edinburgh has done nothing much to improve its cultural endowment since the 1990s. Culturally, the capital has been in retreat. The once influential newspaper, *The Scotsman*, has become a pale shadow of its former self, with circulation crashing from a daily 120,000 at the start of the century to barely 10,000 over-the-counter sales in 2018.

Edinburgh as a Finance Centre

The period saw one major new bank development – RBS headquarters at Gogarburn. Symbolically, this is hidden on the outskirts of the city, in a hundred-acre wood near Edinburgh airport. It cost a ludicrous £350 million to build in the campus style beloved of US high tech firms. Opened in 2005, it stands as a monument to the hubris of Fred 'the Shred' Goodwin, the bank's CEO. Goodwin used borrowed cash to fund international acquisitions, temporarily making RBS the biggest bank on the planet. When financial markets froze in 2008, RBS teetered on the verge of bankruptcy and had to be nationalised by the then Chancellor of the Exchequer, Edinburgh MP Alistair Darling. The collapse of the capital's two main banking houses – RBS and HBOS – should have proved catastrophic to the city's business reputation. It didn't. Edinburgh bankers stick together, even if the older generation were scandalised by Fred Goodwin's brashness. After 2008 they simply vowed to keep a lower profile.

It wasn't long before Edinburgh began hosting a new wave of financial groups and fintech companies, facilitated by the city council's liberal (or neo-liberal) attitude to speculative office building. Edinburgh benefits from the agglomeration of scale that comes from being the UK's second biggest financial centre, with circa 50,000 workers employed – 15 per cent of the UK total. The city's financial bourgeoisie proved adept at cashing in on the global bull market in equities and bonds triggered by central bank quantitative easing. Its fund managers now have anything up to a trillion dollars of foreign assets under local direction. Baillie Gifford, a secretive private partnership located discretely in the lee of Calton Hill, is one of the largest global investors in Amazon and Tesla electric cars.

Baillie Gifford's success is a metaphor for the Edinburgh of the last two decades. Forget the SNP's moderate version of interventionist social democracy. The reality of contemporary Edinburgh is its embracing of the neo-liberalism paradigm in all its glory: the domination of a global finance capital, a debt-financed and ultimately unsustainable property boom that gives the illusion of prosperity and a consumer economy based increasingly on entertainment – restaurants, pubs, shops, taxis and hotels. Flash rather than substance.

– Like some sleazy Latin American metropolis, Edinburgh is a city of social extremes. The city ranks in the top quartile for incomes in Scotland but is in the bottom quartile for indicators of poverty. In the most deprived parts of the city, the proportion of households living below the poverty threshold jumps to a third. The work force is split between a highly educated professional elite and a precariat whose real incomes have been static for over a decade.

Edinburgh's increasing social divide is nowhere clearer than in the colonisation of the city centre by a burgeoning student population with its ghetto of new-build, undergrad housing complexes. Modern Edinburgh could be rechristened Student City. By 2016, the student population (including further education colleges) had risen to over 80,000. A staggering 55 per cent of Edinburgh employees have a university degree, more than in London (52 per cent), Bristol (48 per cent), or Manchester (43 per cent).

It is this complacent middle-class Edinburgh that voted overwhelmingly against Scottish independence in 2014, by 61 per cent to 39 per cent. A more even vote in the capital would have narrowed the outcome by a considerable margin. Yet this same middle-class city voted 74 per cent for Remain in the 2016 Brexit referendum and felt chagrined by the UK result. A lesson, perhaps, that Edinburgh's petty bourgeois insularity has consequences.

Where does petty bourgeois Edinburgh go in the next twenty years? Perhaps Brexit will drive the city's middle-class to one of its rare bursts of political energy, to embrace the path of Scottish independence glimpsed by the late Iain Noble? Perhaps the long-overdue global revolt against neo-liberalism – on the right as well as the left – will finally and fatally undermine the shaky economic foundations of the Edinburgh financial class? Perhaps there will be a progressive political revolution in the municipal City Chambers and Scotland's capital will become a global laboratory for post-capitalist living? One way or the other, and almost counterintuitively, Edinburgh could be the pivot on which Scotland's future turns.

CHAPTER 33

Glasgow
A Knowledge City for the Knowledge Age

Brian Mark Evans

CITIES AND CITY regions are increasingly the drivers of economic growth (EU 2012). Glasgow is Scotland's largest city and the centre of its only true metropolitan economy with a population of between 1.2 and 1.7 million depending on how it is measured. According to the Scottish Government our cities are 'centres of knowledge, innovation and culture' and can build on these strengths to 'develop internationally investible propositions based on skills in science, technology, innovation and creativity' (Scottish Government, 2016). Today, Glasgow is growing again with a 2.5 per cent increase in population and a 1.5 per cent increase in workforce since 2008 (National Records of Scotland, 2017).

A Short History of Glasgow

There are aspects of context and history embedded in the city's DNA. Glasgow originated as an ecclesiastical centre located on high ground above the lowest fording point of the River Clyde. The city's name, emblems and earliest traditions date from these early medieval times. The literal translation of the Gaelic *Glaschu* has become the *Dear Green Place* of the city's ecclesiastical founder St Mungo with myths of birds, trees, bells and fish still represented on the city's escutcheon. Early Glasgow had little strategic significance in Scotland, rebellion and war largely passed it by, however, it's location on the West Coast with a safe harbour, fertile agricultural valleys and a plentiful supply of coal – the raw materials of the industrial revolution – presented Glasgow with a very significant opportunity for industrialisation, immigration and export.

In this way, a small medieval burgh experienced exponential growth in the 19th century to become an industrial and manufacturing behemoth. For two centuries Glasgow outgrew successive suits of architectural clothes leaving them threadbare and soiled. When this expansion and enterprise came to a sudden halt in the years after World War Two, the city's economy slumped with the fabric of the city damaged and worn out and the people tired and unhealthy. Glasgow's narrative over the last 50 years, however, has been one of determined transition through levels of social upheaval and economic challenge only experienced by other cities in times of war. If Glasgow escaped these privations in early history, the citizens paid their dues several fold in the second half of the 20th century. Since the 1970s, Glasgow has been changed through processes of land remediation, renewal of city fabric and built heritage, landscape enhancement, economic regeneration and the renaissance of communities.

Regeneration gathered pace in the 1980s when major events helped reposition the city's reputation by hosting the most successful of the UK's Garden Festivals in 1988, winning European City of Culture in 1990 (beating out Athens, Florence, Amsterdam, Berlin and Paris no less) followed by the UK City of Architecture and Design in 1999. The 20th Commonwealth Games in 2014 is the most recent in a line of successful *pacing devices* that have become the talisman of a city transforming itself. Brand marketing has played a role helping to dispel negative stereotypes that were a barrier to inward investment. Campaigns that began with 'Glasgow's Miles Better' in 1983 and most recently 'People Make Glasgow' in 2013 have worked because they have managed to find authenticity and resonance with citizens and visitors alike and they have kept pace with the city's transition.

Glasgow's Fortunes from the 1980s

The turnaround in the Glasgow economy is due in part to action that flowed from a McKinsey report of the late 1980s that was used as a blueprint for a new phase of economic activity based on services (particularly financial), software and tourism (McKinsey, 1985; OECD, 2002). McKinsey commissioned the late Gordon Cullen, one of the UK's foremost city thinkers and visualisers, to produce an aesthetic vision of the city centre looking back from the future. The work captured the collective imagination and was underpinned by an economic strategy to back it up. *Glasgow Action*, a short-burst public private partnership instigated a programme that has led on to the creation of the city's International Financial Services District which has attracted blue-chip companies including Tesco Bank, Shell and JP Morgan Stanley (IFSDG, 2019). From a modest start, several companies now have global IT, software and other specialist functions – notably JP Morgan's global software centre.

Business services now make up 35 per cent of the city's economy and Glasgow headquarters a number of major international companies such as engineers, The Weir Group, and power specialist Aggreko alongside internationally-owned players such as Scottish Power and the Clydesdale Bank and smaller high-growth companies like Castle Precision Engineering and luxury hi-fi specialist Linn Products. These businesses link Glasgow to international markets, develop Glasgow's skills and graduate base and attract international talent to the city. Today the Blythswood New Town is home to one of Scotland's major concentrations of Knowledge Intensive Business Services (KIBS), proof positive that inward investment into the city is migrating talent from these large companies into a small high-end home-grown knowledge bureaux of engineers, lawyers, designers, marketeers and accountants who supply design, information and knowledge products and services into the larger companies (Evans, Lord and Robertson, 2018).

Led by the two powerhouse universities, Glasgow has become important in life sciences (especially medicine and medical technologies) and engineering and Scotland's pre-eminent centre for the creative industries, particularly print, broadcasting and film-making with the recent announcement of the Channel 4 Creative Hub alongside the BBC, STV and others on the River Clyde Pacific Quay campus.

In parallel with economic development, the 1990s and 2000s have seen attention focused on neighbourhood regeneration using the creative and cultural industries to support regeneration, redress planning decisions undertaken in the 1960s and 1970s and implement programmes to tackle worklessness and exclusion to accelerate the transformation of run-down, post-industrial areas into work-life areas inhabited by artists and creative professionals that help stimulate a growth in popularity and land value (Florida 2002; 2018). While there remain challenges (the percentage of working age adults remains persistently low) the Glasgow economy is greatly improved from twenty years ago and completely transformed from the twenty before that. The city can now speak to a large, strong and deepening financial and business services sector alongside ongoing strengths in innovation, technology, engineering, life sciences, tourism and events. The Glasgow economy is rebalancing and arguably returning to its economic roots as a global trading city – trading on its skills and talent, innovation, technologies and business acumen (Evans, *et al.*, 2015).

The River Clyde, for so long a backwater flowing between extensive areas of vacant land, the residue of shipbuilding, has seen considerable renewal along its banks with the International Financial Services District, the Digital Media campus, the new Riverside Museum (by architect Zahah Hadid), strengthening the Scottish Exhibition and Conference Centre with eye-catching buildings by Foster and Partners – the 'Armadillo' conference venue and the SSE Hydro Arena, a 13,000-seater auditorium, all revitalising the riverfront while retaining references to the city's past with the retention of industrial artifacts including the Finnieston Crane and the Tall Ship Glenlee at the Riverside museum. All welcome and working towards a rejuvenated river through the city. But even with new residential neighbourhoods like Glasgow Harbour and, upstream, the Athletes Village from the 20th Commonwealth Games, regeneration of the River Clyde is a major undertaking and remains a work in progress.

Glasgow provides an interesting case study as a city that has combined a variety of approaches and initiatives using its creative and cultural sectors to aid regeneration including investment in cultural assets and the emergence of creative industries, artists' workspaces and studio complexes. The central message of the City Economy Conference in 2018 was that Glasgow has moved past the first wave of regeneration foreseen in the McKinsey report to a new and second wave that builds on the previous advances while refocusing on the city-region's historic role as Scotland's engineering and technological heartland.

Sustained effort and real progress in the city's East End are now re-directed to North Glasgow continuing a radical programme of social housing investment and delivery at a rate and a pace unseen elsewhere in Scotland or the UK. This strategic spatial direction of effort into structured regeneration of place is of vital importance and should not be understated. History and geography have combined to create the need for, and a capability to deliver, regional planning in the west of Scotland with a long-standing history of working at the metropolitan scale extending back to the Clyde Valley Regional Plan of 1946 prepared by Sir Patrick Abercrombie and Robert Matthew that sought to balance urban land use and greenfield land release and advocated Green Belts and Regional Parks which remain strong components of current strategic planning. The establishment of the Strathclyde Regional Council in 1975 until it's disbandment in 1996 saw a number of Structure Plans prepared and updated biennially to remain current.

In 2009, the Structure Plan process was replaced by Strategic Development Plans for the metropolitan area as concise and visionary documents with a focus on development, infrastructure and green-space issues and co-ordination of cross (local authority) boundary initiatives and projects. The latest was adopted in July 2017. This system of strategic planning has served Glasgow and the Clyde Valley and estuary well. Strategic planning is under threat from current Scottish Government reform and, with the increased importance of the new city-region deal in Glasgow and the west of Scotland, (and Scotland generally), the demise of strategic planning seems a premature, and possibly retrograde, step.

A 21st Century City

At the turn of the 21st century, Frank Arneil Walker wrote that designing for place demands an ability to reconcile the *genius loci* (the spirit of place) with the *zeitgeist* (the spirit of the times) – a simple, elegant concept to grasp, if a deal harder to describe, teach and practice (Walker, 2011). There is a continuous and passionate discussion about the *genius loci* in Glasgow but, significantly, there is also an established consensus that the spirit of place is somehow environmental, cultural, spiritual and expressed in cultural inheritance, the built heritage and the natural environment – the *Dear Green Place*. The *zeitgeist*, however, is an altogether more complex challenge in the febrile environment that presently exists where Brexit runs the risk of creating a stasis throughout the UK. This must not come about, for beyond Brexit and Scotland's own constitutional question, lurks a basket of international forces that may combine to be toxic or benign to society and community.

Recent research for UN Habitat identified a number of revealing conclusions about trends affecting cities of the developed north from Vancouver to Vladivostok and, by extension, for Scotland and Glasgow (Evans, *et al.*, 2017). Glasgow is not alone in reflecting on the first two decades of this century – UN Habitat takes a duodecennial view since the first global conference on the human habitat in 1976. Today, six global trends are driving the *zeitgeist* in cities at the start of the 21st century: ageing, low fertility, migration, climate change (of itself polyvalent), automation and artificial intelligence (AI) – in essence demographics, climate change and technology. Ageing Western societies have insufficient children to sustain them and require immigration to reduce the average working age of the population, while automation and AI replace lower skilled but valuable jobs like driver, and extreme weather and flooding make living and working more problematic, especially for the elderly and the vulnerable. These international forces of globalisation interact with one another and can, without intervention, become toxic. They are manifest in cities in a number of ways.

Urban Concentration: The combination of the *jet age* and the *net age* has compounded urban concentration. The predicted *death of distance,* whereby the entrepreneurial class takes off to the islands to telework over fibre broadband, has proved to be a myth (Cairncross, 1997). Certainly, there are those who desire remoteness, but they are comprehensively outnumbered by those who seek the face-to-face buzz of the city. Recent research has shown that the centripetal effect of urban concentration is present in Scotland's cities as it is in cities across the global north (Evans, Lord and Robertson, 2018).

A Change in the Urban Paradigm: Over the last two decades, there has been a paradigm shift from the *industrial city* to the *knowledge city* where knowledge is the principal means of production that requires no spatial requirement beyond proximity.

City-Regions are Important: nearly 60 per cent of the KIBS (Knowledge Intensive Business Services) jobs in Scotland are located in Edinburgh, Glasgow and Aberdeen. Add to these the three city regions and the figure rises to over 80 per cent. Our knowledge future is urban and regional.

Governance and Leadership: Management of these trends in the *zeitgeist* is necessary as is recognition of the consequences, but this is not sufficient. Effective leadership is required with vision, clarity, skill, transparency and a degree of political courage to face down the hypocrisy and dissimulation pedalled by many commentators. To combine the effects of these forces in a benign manner requires vision, leadership and a designed response. Scotland's national objectives, performance frameworks and indicators together with national outcomes are all very important. It is important to measure things, but it will take consensus-building to bring about change.

The Scottish Government is to be complemented in its early adoption of the UN's 17 Strategic Development Goals (SDGs) formulated after the Paris Agreement of 2015. The recent drive to community activation and engagement is welcome – essential in fact. But the gulf between community activity and national planning is too great, even for a small country like Scotland, especially one with an extensive and diverse geography. There needs to be a regional mechanism of spatial mediation in the provision and delivery of infrastructure between community and nation and this is vital in a true metropolitan region like Glasgow and the Clyde Valley. In this respect, the city-region deals are an imaginative and welcome step in regional delivery, but without strategic spatial plans, they run the risk of becoming scattered where projects and infrastructure are delivered without the benefit of a spatial rationale. Regional (strategic) planning therefore remains necessary in the mediation between the *zeitgeist* and the *genius loci*.

Glasgow's local authority is alert to these interactions and the formation of a city-region cabinet involving all eight local authorities is most welcome to design responses appropriate at the metropolitan level where an explicit consensus is required to bring about coordinated and considered action in the safeguarding and enhancement of the *genius loci*. Glasgow is making great progress but the fragilities that remain are particularly sensitive to these changes. Working with government and business, Glasgow – and all cities – must manage these international trends carefully and design intelligent responses or we will face attrition of what we hold dear.

Recent research now makes clear that the transition from industrial to post-industrial is only half of the story for cities like Glasgow transitioning in the contemporary era. The factors identified above are the drivers of city economies today:

> it is now proximity to knowledge rather than proximity to resources that is the primary driver of city growth (Swinney and Thomas, 2015).

A *Century of Cities* classifies British cities as either *'replicators'* or *'reinventors'* where the top performers have reinvented themselves as knowledge-based economies based on global businesses, skilled workers, strong links with universities and research establishments and other factors. Most of the top performers have a relatively low dependency on manufacturing, mining and the other staple industries of the late 19th and early 20th centuries. By contrast, the *'replicators'* (mostly in the North of England and Midlands) have tended to be highly dependent on traditional industries that have contracted sharply or disappeared entirely finding themselves in a cycle of decline, replacing employment in declining industries with a new generation of routine, low-skill, low-wage jobs in call centres and logistics (Swinney and Thomas, 2015).

Can cities cross paths from being replicator to reinventor? This is a key question for, and finding from, Glasgow's transition. Reviewing the differences between the decades discussed earlier, the answer for Glasgow is clearly yes, even if, by comparison with pre-eminent European and North American examples, there is still some way to go. Glasgow should move past considering itself as a *post-industrial* city and start to think and act as a *proto-knowledge* city – and arguably the city does so albeit implicitly. Glasgow's new knowledge geography is remarkable: over 120,000 students study in an arc of knowledge that extends from the University of Glasgow (in the UK top 20), through The Glasgow School of Art (in the global top 20) and the Royal Conservatoire of Scotland (in the global top 5), Glasgow Caledonian University, the University of Strathclyde (in the UK top 40), interspersed with a number of highly rated colleges of further education. Within this arc sit the clusters of international business and KIBS jobs highlighted above. This is one of the most intensive knowledge clusters in the UK and it extends out into the metropolitan region with the University of the West of Scotland and other further education colleges.

In spite of the effort, expertise and commitment described above, challenges of urban poverty and social polarisation persist in large metropolitan areas across the UK where an ageing demographic structure and cultural diversity still feeds suburbanisation, sprawl and, in some cases, shrinking of cities. This remains a risk for the Glasgow city-region. The European model of the city aspires towards a dispersed polycentric network of medium-sized, human-scale and compact settlements that are culturally diverse, socially inclusive, environmentally friendly, economically vital and peacefully and democratically governed, while providing high-quality public spaces, public services and carbon-free mobility solutions. The fundamental principle underlying this model is a concern to take account of all aspects of sustainable development in an integrated manner, often described as the *compact city* model (OECD, 2012) and it is a fundamental precept of Glasgow's current City Development Plan (Glasgow City Council, 2017).

There is a very substantial literature about Glasgow's culture, character and form, about the nature and determination of its people and its ability to confront and overcome adversity. These attributes led to recognition for Glasgow as a member of the global Resilient Cities Network by the Rockefeller Foundation. Compact, resilient and competitive were recently described as the three key characteristics necessary for cities in the knowledge age (Evans, *et al.* 2018).

Historical, structural and geographical factors exert a powerful influence on the fortunes of cities, but this does not mean that their fate is predetermined. The winding up of the regional councils in 1996 gave the former district councils considerably more authority, capability and powers and Glasgow City has since continued to build institutional capacity in capability, expertise and delivery as well as explicitly working with partners to demonstrate thinking and action strategically, and in pursuit of knowledge capability. The last two decades have been a period of lightning-quick change characterised by that emblem of the times, the mobile phone that has gone from a 'brick' to the 'city in your pocket' (Kopomaa, 2000). The coincidence of timing between the 21-year span of the City Economy conference, the lifetime of the Scottish Parliament and the interval between the UN Habitats is striking. It is hard to avoid the conclusion that, in the developed north at least, there is a coincidence of forces influencing cities between the scores of years bracketed by 1960s–70s, the 1980s–90s and the first two decades of this century. It is hard also to avoid the conclusion that there was a definite *fin de siècle* blossoming of arts and culture and economic optimism in many cities extending from the late 90s through the noughties that has morphed into something considerably less appealing after a decade of credit crash, austerity, populism, Trump, Brexit and the resurgence of the right wing.

Glasgow has fared well over the last twenty years. It has come to terms with itself and its road to reinvention. In the Scottish Government there are centralising forces at play and ironically the metropolitan nature of Glasgow may be better understood in the wider international area where membership of the UK's Core Cities group provides more pertinent peer group of cities beyond a perennial and zero-sum comparison with Edinburgh. Scotland does not yet totally comprehend, or is apprehensive of, a Glasgow for what it is – a metropolitan city with a population of 1.7 million, 35 per cent of the Scottish population, 12,000 students, 30 per cent of the country's top universities and 40 per cent of the further education provision. There is a faint air of institutional bias against this precept that seems to favour the significant, but ultimately impractical, growth of Edinburgh and an east coast axis over embracing the emphatic role that a strong metropolitan Glasgow can play in Scotland, the UK and Europe.

Once a source of great pride, the epithets of 'Second City of Empire' and the 'workshop of the world' have come to be seen for the shibboleths that they are with a widening realisation that the wealth of empire was founded on colonialism, exploitation of peoples, countries, resources and slavery as well as extracting a great price from Glasgow in terms of the state of its environment and the health of its people. In common with other cities of the UK and the USA, there is greater humility and contrition in such claims today.

Glasgow has moved on without denying its glory days and its dark decades. If not yet self-confident, there is at least growing awareness and belief that continuing the effort and energy may bring the city and its region to a tipping point over the next two decades. There remains a great deal to be done. The health inequities from *The Glasgow Effect* remain and will take decades to eradicate, but today this is a health challenge, not a health problem, and the city has simultaneously developed centres of excellence in life sciences along the way.

Fragility remains, and the trends described in this piece that underlie Brexit – the demographics of ageing, fertility and immigration, the employment consequences of automation and AI coupled with climate change – are such that Glasgow bears a greater fragility from Brexit and the loss of freedom of movement. The city is alive to these threats.

Reflecting on change over the decades rather than years makes differences more pronounced and trends easier to perceive. There can be no doubting the significant and substantive change in Glasgow's fortunes from the 1960s through to the first two decades of the 21st century.

With these in mind and with the spectre of Brexit, we might nevertheless posit that 2020 might well be the year when Glasgow can truly claim that it is no longer a post-industrial city but is now truly a proto-knowledge city – a city that is compact, competitive and resilient, that earns its living through knowledge and is managing the challenges of demographics, climate change and AI.

References

Banfield, E.C. (1970), *The Unheavenly City*, New York: Little, Brown and Company.

Breen, A. and Rigby, R. (1996), *The New Waterfront: A Worldwide Success Story*, London: Thames & Hudson.

Cairncross, F. (1997), *The Death of Distance: How the Communications Revolution Is Changing Our Lives*, Cambridge, MA: Harvard Business School Press.

Clark, G. (2016), *Cities, Global Cities and Glasgow – Some Reflections*, University of Strathclyde, International Public Policy Institute, Occasional Paper.

Clydeplan (2017), 'Strategic Development Plan – Delivering Growth in the Glasgow City Region, Glasgow and the Clyde Valley Strategic Development Planning Authority', July 2017, available online at: https://www.clydeplan-sdpa.gov.uk/images/ApprovedPlanHighRes.pdf

European Union (2012), 'Territorial Dynamics in Europe: Regions and cities in the global economy', Espon Programme, available online at: https://www.espon.eu/topics-policy/publications/territorial-observations/territorial-dynamics-europe-regions-and-cities

Evans, B., Badynia, A., Elisei, P., *et al.* (2017), 'Housing and Urban Development in the Economic Commission for Europe Region – Towards a City-Focused People-Centred and Integrated Approach to the New Urban Agenda, Habitat III Regional Report', United Nations, available online at: https://www.unece.org/fr/housing-and-land-management/projects/habitat-iii-regional-report.html

Evans, B., Lord, J. and Robertson, M. (2018), *Scotland's Urban Age: Aberdeen, Glasgow and Edinburgh in the Century of the City*, Edinburgh: Burness Paull, available online at: http://campaigns.burnesspaull.com/urban-age/static/pdfs/Urban_Age_Full_Report.pdf

Evans, B., Tait, S., Kane, K., *et al.* (2015), 'Glasgow – A City of Continuing Traditions', in Glowinska, J. (ed.), *Poszukiwanie modelu inteligentnego miasta. Przykład Gdanska i Glasgow (Searching for a Smart City Model: Gdańsk and Glasgow)*, Warsaw: Wolters Kluwer SA.

Florida, R. (2018), *The New Urban Crisis*, London: One World Publications.

Florida, R. (2002), *The Rise of the Creative Class*, New York: Basic Books.

IFSDG (2019), *International Financial Services District Glasgow*, available at: http://www.ifsdglasgow.co.uk/why-ifsd

McArther, A. and Kingsley-Long, H. (1978), *No Mean City*, 4th edition, London: Corgi/Random House.

McKinsey and Company (1985), *The Potential of Glasgow City Centre*, Glasgow: Scottish Development Agency.

Myerscough, J. (1988), *Economic Importance of the Arts in Glasgow*, London: Policy Studies Institute.

National Records of Scotland (2017), 'Projected Population of Scotland (2016-based): National population projections by sex and age, with UK comparisons', available online at: www.nrscotland.gov.uk/files//statistics/population-projections/2016-based-scot/pop-proj-2016-scot-nat-pop-pro-pub.pdf

OECD (2012), *Compact City Policies: A Comparative Assessment*, Green Growth Studies, Paris: OECD.

OECD (2002), *Urban Renaissance Glasgow: Lessons for Innovation and Implementation*, Paris: OECD.

Scottish Government (2016), 'Scotland's Agenda for Cities', Edinburgh: Scottish Government.

Skills Development Scotland (2018), 'Regional Skills Assessment: Glasgow City Region, Summary Report 2018', available online at: www.skillsdevelopmentscotland.co.uk/media/44074/glasgow-city-la.pdf

Swinney, P. and Thomas, E. (2015), *A Century of Cities: Urban Economic Change Since 1911*, London: Centre for Cities.

Understanding Glasgow, the Glasgow Indicators Project, available online at www.understandingglasgow.com, accessed 3 January 2019.

Walker, F.A. (2011), 'Grasping the Thistle', in *Urban Identity: Leaning from Place II*, Evans, B.M. Macdonald, F. and Rudlin, D. (eds), London: Routledge.

CHAPTER 34

Conversations About Our Changing Dundee

Gillian Easson and Michael Marra

The Year of Dundee

SO, 2018 WAS a high-profile year for the city of Dundee and her citizens, and 2019 looks set to continue that. Both authors were born and raised in the city; have left and returned; and have been active in the city's policy environment as Dundee has garnered headlines around the world. 'National Geographic Cool List', one of world's most 'design-savvy' cities (CNN), 'thriving, creative' and one of the best places to visit in Europe (Lonely Planet), 'buzzing' (Vogue), a 'hot destination' (Wall Street Journal), 'Britain's coolest little city' (GQ) and on and on. It is all a bit of a departure.

The vast increase in media attention on the city has been driven by the opening of the V&A Dundee, the first branch of the venerable London institution of design outside of London. The £80 million modernist masterpiece by the Japanese architect Kengo Kuma opened to great fanfare on 15 September 2018 after well over a decade of agitation, planning, fund-raising, cost increases and delays. The critical reaction has been overwhelmingly positive, and the reputational impact has met, even exceeded, the aspirations of those who conceived of the project.

The V&A project nested within a broader waterfront redevelopment is actually a marker stone in a cyclical process of reinvention for the city. Once Scotland's second largest urban settlement when the eastern seaboard hosted the principal trading routes, Dundee has spun through cycles of growth and decline since the industrial revolution and the rapid growth driven by shipbuilding and textiles. The city of the late 20th century became known for industrial departures through Caledon, Timex and NCR. That trend continues with the November 2018 announcement of the closure of the Michelin tyre factory which had been manufacturing in the city for over 40 years.

The opening of Dundee Contemporary Arts in the same year as the Scottish Parliament reflected a shift in the city's economic policy focus from industry to culture and the benefits of a knowledge economy. Inclusivity was at the time, and remains, a concern.

A Dundee Conversation

Michael: Were you home when the DCA opened in '99?

Gillian: No. I was coming back, just coming back from art school and didn't plan to stay long back in Dundee.

M: That was the start of the city embracing this pretty woolly idea of culture-led-regeneration.

G: It took me a long time to step foot in the DCA at that time, and understand it was actually for folk like me, even with having an arts education.

M: Those barriers of perceived exclusion are certainly still around. But this investment in culture as economy is a really old thing. In Dundee it goes back at least as far as to when the McManus Galleries was established as the Albert Institute in the mid-19th century.

G: In 1867 – It was the 150th anniversary last year.

M: You're good at the dates. It was part of the same process really. Decline of whaling, an investment in culture and particularly in learning, education and self-improvement. So, it differs in the lack of focus on the tourists and more of a focus on the population.

G: For citizens, yes, there's always been a focus on and investment in culture for people who live here as well as those who visit. The V&A is part of the city's bigger design ethos, Dundee was designated as the UK's only UNESCO City of Design in 2014 – another marker in our journey. That wasn't about a single museum. It's about everything happening here, from engineering, innovation, drugs and pharmaceutical design, to fashion and video games.

M: All areas where the design element comes through as part of the lineage of the city. It's more of a constant than an industry which waxes and wanes.

G: That's what I find interesting when other global cities visit us, is that they are generally focused on business and economic growth of their design sectors, we don't have that cluster of design businesses of scale here. For us, it's about working across the city's public, private and third sectors to increase understanding of the potential of design in improving the quality of our lives. During a recent visit here by other UNESCO Cities of Design, other cities couldn't get over how connected everyone was, particularly how the private sector embraced partnerships with our design community. It's definitely about the scale of our place. It's talked about a lot. But there is a truth there.

M: There is a 'small is beautiful' aspect to that (Schumacher, 1973). But I really wonder in political economy terms if familiarity can be the enemy of progress. That inertia can only be broken if there is an appetite for change, an ambition, that is widely shared. And I do think we have that now in the city.

G: On the lineage: how much do you believe in the whole idea that the video games sector started because everyone had stolen ZX Spectrums from Timex?

M: I do think the spill over effects of investing in knowledge and technology is real. Lots of literature would say that is the case. So, building familiarity with technologies will help a population to apply them. But the idea that Dundee made *Lemmings* and *Grand Theft Auto* because you could get three computers for a fiver in the Nine Maidens pub? Maybe. There is a definite clustering effect through the 90s with the city making big hits in a hits-based industry and others thinking it was a possible and reasonable thing to do for a living.

G: We recently heard from one of the *Lemmings*' lead developers, who actually credits the Kingsway tech college's Thursday night club, where all the gamers hung out and nobody really followed what they were up to. Sometimes things are serendipitous rather than overly constructed. Even if the lineage of investing in culture and learning is a long one the proposition of the V&A coming to Dundee was still met with considerable scepticism in the city and further afield. The development of the project began in the mid-2000s in the University of Dundee's Duncan of Jordanstone College of Art & Design and was dreamt up by then Dean, Professor Georgina Follett.

M: The biggest barrier to the University developing through recruitment of students and staff in the early to mid-2000s was the external perception of the city. The post-industrial malaise images. What did it physically look like and feel like and the general reputation? The job was to try and help the city change that reputation. Georgina thought of creating this relationship with the V&A and making design the thing.

G: Well that seems to have worked hasn't it? The media and external perceptions of the city have definitely changed. Even now, the city still feels very real and not too polished – There's something about Dundee that isn't really replicated anywhere else. It would appear that if the success of culture led-regeneration is to be measured by tourism and image then the policy shifts of the last twenty years in the city are a conspicuous success.

M: If the image is actually changing then the Universities have a responsibility to capitalise now. They started this and won over the council, the UK and the Scottish Governments to back it. I persuaded Jack McConnell to back the project in 2007 and you do feel part of the responsibility for where this has got to. Of course, the building and the funding of it was obviously the hard bit. And that has not been without pain. The choice to spend money on this museum is money not spent elsewhere.

G: I don't believe that Dundee would have accessed this kind of capital without a major national flagship project. The money that came for V&A would not have been available for other things.

M: But the logic behind the critique is entirely reasonable, isn't it? We can talk about PR and reputation but we have one in four kids living in poverty; massive underemployment; the council targets an unemployment figure that is completely meaningless because we have the highest proportion of citizens disengaged from the labour market of any city in Britain, and those figures have not improved in decades. They are getting worse not better.

G: There are so many people doing incredible work across the city's communities, yet there are still big issues and needs – basic Maslow's hierarchy of needs to be met. The fact we are still speaking about this even now is pretty crazy. In the years since the advent of the Scottish Parliament the political make-up of the city of Dundee has changed markedly, even if the social challenges have not. In 2003 Labour lost a parliamentary seat for the first time since the 1974. By 2015 the SNP held every parliamentary seat, Westminster and Holyrood, in the city and were in power on the city council for the first time. The 2007 election was a political turning point across Scotland and the rising SNP targeted the city to become their first urban powerbase.

M: For a short period of time there was actually political competition in the city. Between 1999 and 2007 Labour and the SNP were fighting on reasonably even footing, though the trend was increasingly towards the nationalists. It was possible at that point to extract opportunities and concessions from both parties. We won a significant boost for life science funding by putting McConnell and Salmond on the same stage days after the other in 2007. And then Jack backed a feasibility study for the V&A which pushed Labour Councillors to back the project against the wishes of council officers and the SNP fell into line as a consequence. They all wanted to look like they shared the ambition and vision.

I do think that devolution has made that kind of transactional politics possible in a way that it rarely was with Westminster. Dundee's voice has been heard as a result.

G: I'm much further away from local politics than you, however activities like the cross-party group that you set up for the UK City of Culture bid brought regular people like me into the mix. I remember being in Parliament and feeling very proud of Dundee and its ability to have everyone behind us with a shared goal. More of that please.

M: The kind of political competition we have had has really been about exploiting those small differences in a fairly homogenous politics. A more plural conversation would be more difficult to exploit. But it might feel a bit more fundamental. The big questions of poverty and whether the kind of economy we have works at all really, those are missed in the conversation of marginal differences.

The Future

M: So, what does the future hold? Do you think it's possible to marry up the culture-led regeneration story with the real social problems? Is the culture side of things not vulnerable and fragile?

G: We co-designed Dundee's first Creative Industries Strategy and found that people still find it difficult to make a living from their practice here. 87 per cent of Scotland's creative businesses have less than five employees. We have a real challenge of retaining our emerging leaders.

M: I heard you talking about this at the University's Festival of the Future. The panel seemed to be saying that to work in a creative or technology sector in the city you basically have to create the industry yourself and assume leadership. That's great. But the next stage seems to be the problem. How do you move on or up when there are few other companies? The culture needs to be communal and supportive rather than ultra-competitive.

G: Absolutely. Collaboration across sectors is something we're always trying to encourage. Competition doesn't really work in a small city like ours. Within the Creative Industries Strategy there's a contributor's quote I reflect on a lot, which says:

> Although we can't predict the jobs of the future, we can create the conditions to ensure they emerge.

We need everyone on board to figure out what's next.

M: I also worry about what happens when the hype dies. Once you've been cool how do you cope with not being cool? That's not something I've ever had to worry about myself. But it feels like the kickback for Dundee is going to come.

G: I don't think we've ever sought these PR accolades though. It's not in our nature to be seeking personal praise or glory as a city. We've always been realistic about it and we don't dismiss the city's problems. Let's take the good coverage while it's going. We'll be OK if and when it's gone. There are longer-term benefits through the changes which can be very real and have the potential to catalyse our next steps. We're hosting a panel session tonight exploring how video games can address young people's mental health problems, with health practitioners and games developers. We also have to use the UNESCO status to hook into more opportunities around the world and persuade people to invest and create jobs here, to go with all the good sentiments.

M: And we can't stop at investing in the waterfront. We need to keep investing in the physical side of the city. Better housing all over and lots more zero-carbon living in the city centre, bringing people closer together. A new concert hall, a new central library like the one they have built in Helsinki that towers over the Parliament. Books and learning above politics.

G: And the softer side of that. A liveable and lovable city for everyone. What does that look like and how do we get there?

CHAPTER 35

Aberdeen
A City in Transition

John Bone

DESPITE ITS STATUS as Scotland's third largest urban settlement, in some respects Aberdeen has, arguably, been regarded as being as culturally and economically distant as it is geographically remote from Scotland's populous central belt. Historically, the city served as the gateway and trading port for one of the nation's most extensive and productive agricultural hinterlands and the base for one of its largest fishing fleets. It also boasts one of Scotland's ancient universities, whose scholars had made a significant contribution to the Scottish Enlightenment. Industries that flourished in Aberdeen and the wider region included shipbuilding, light engineering, paper and textile manufacture and quarrying of the granite that gives the city its unique *façade*.

Aberdeen and the surrounding region also engaged in a modicum of both light and heavy engineering, albeit that this was marginal in scale in comparison to Scotland's industrial heartland. Given the region's remoteness, much of this industrial activity had been diverted to the area by active government policy aimed at enhancing development and employment in the post-war decades. Until the late 1960s and early 1970s, however, Aberdeen, and the Grampian region generally, remained economically weaker than its southern counterparts, with higher unemployment, lower average incomes and a gradually declining population (Feagin, 1990).

According to David McIntosh (1987), who served in, and as the head of, the Aberdeen planning department from 1959 to 1984, before oil the Aberdeen area was in 'a rather depressed period' and was losing population; 'something like 2,000' people were leaving annually. There were few job opportunities for young people, and wage levels were low (Lloyd and Newlands, 1987; Bentley, 1987). However, from 1970 to the OPEC-related oil price decline beginning in the early 1980s, the exploration and development of oil and gas fields brought many well-paid jobs to north-east Scotland; oil-related employment grew from 1000 in 1971 to 51,000 in 1985 (Feagin, 1990).

Aberdeen

Oil Capital

As is widely recognised, the arrival of oil fundamentally transformed Aberdeen and the surrounding region's fortunes in numerous respects, albeit that this was neither a smooth process nor one that has been unequivocally positive. Dependence on the oil industry gradually became the reality for the region, as paper, quarrying, textiles and shipbuilding precipitously declined from the 1970s onwards, while engineering activities evolved to take advantage of new opportunities, as older engineering works closed down and the engineering skills base was redirected towards the oil industry. It must be noted that this was less in terms of local businesses reinventing themselves, than the latter being taken over by larger oil industry incomers and by skilled engineering workers seeking work with incoming oil industry firms. As such, with some notable exceptions, Aberdeen was largely refashioned from without rather than from within (Hunt, 1976). Agriculture, however, remains important while fishing has carried on but with a significantly lower profile in the local economic mix.

Increasing reliance on oil and gas in Aberdeen has entailed that the performance of the local economy has become more volatile, rising and falling more in line with fluctuations in the oil price than in response to wider economic currents affecting Scotland and the UK as a whole. After an initial increase in activity that brought a large number of jobs and rising incomes to the city and region in the late 1970s, a slump in the oil price in the mid-1980s dramatically sent the local economy into recession for a time. Numerous oil jobs were lost, while house prices that had risen from significantly below to well above the national average in Scotland went into reverse gear. The city's fortunes, however, recovered in tandem with the oil price. Nonetheless, this period highlighted the precarity inherent in the area's dependence on one industry. The rise of oil and gas, however, has also affected Aberdeen and its hinterland in other ways.

Very high wages received by oil related workers during growth periods for the industry have fed the popular image of Aberdeen as a gold rush town; a not wholly unwarranted view. Expensive new cars and homes have been evident features across the city and shire, while Aberdeen saw the arrival of expensive clothing stores and other high value retailers. Nonetheless, it can be argued that in terms of cultural and leisure facilities Aberdeen has not been particularly well served, creating the impression that its economic capital had not been wholly reflected by a commensurate increase in cultural capital, or a diverse range of attractions (Bourdieu, 1984). To some extent this can be understood, at least in part, in terms of Aberdeen's relative isolation, the availability of a well-heeled 'captive audience', and the limitations for business expansion in a small city with a constrained infrastructure.

Restricted competition and high local demand may arguably have created conditions where local businesses, particularly in the leisure industry, were perhaps under less pressure to innovate to sustain profitability than those in larger conurbations, at least for a time. Until fairly recently, Aberdeen's city centre had largely failed to evolve in tandem with the area's economic and population growth, a situation also applicable to the region's transport system and road network, albeit that private housing investment has been a notable growth area. As discussed below, at the time of writing, investment in a number of these areas has increased together with optimistic plans for further development, but at a point where the city and region's economic base is in decline (Aberdeen Economic Policy Panel Report, 2018).

During the boom era, North Sea oil also had other major impacts on the area's development. As above, with the region's older industries in decline skilled workers moved into oil where technical skills, that might attract relatively modest salaries elsewhere, could be tailored towards oil sector occupations offering previously unprecedented incomes. For those beyond the oil sector, however, the picture has been less rosy. Contrary to the area's popular image, a significant proportion of the local population has come to depend on the relatively low paid service sector jobs that substantially depend on the spending power of oil related workers. As such, far from being the widely prosperous region associated with its public image, Aberdeen and the North East is an area marked by significant economic inequality. While unemployment levels remained relatively low, the spending power of oil incomes has tended to inflate the price of goods and resources, and particularly housing, stretching the more modest budgets of lower income workers.

Our dependency on the oil and gas industry has left the city vulnerable to the effects of the economic decline – job losses, falling property prices and loss of custom – the scale of harm created is having a devastating impact on the city and region. Accepting that, despite the past economic vibrancy provided by the oil and gas sector, we have had significant levels of deprivation in the city. For decades some communities have endured the poorest of outcomes with little opportunity for social and economic mobility (Aberdeen Local Outcome Improvement Plan, 2017).

As is discussed below, against this background, recent declining fortunes in the oil industry may be considered to offer opportunities for an element of socio-economic levelling out. However, the oil crisis has also been accompanied by falling employment opportunities generally, further illustrating the extent to which the region's fortunes have been tied to the industry.

Aberdeen's Changing Fortunes

Tracking Oil Prices and the Housing Market

The effects of the 2007–08 financial crisis had a muted impact on Aberdeen, as the region's oil related economy largely shrugged off the hit to consumption, house prices etc that was keenly felt elsewhere. Since the 1970s, as noted, the local economy has tended to rise and fall in tandem with the oil price. A recent indicator of this relationship is illustrated in Figures 1 and 2 below, where the fall in the oil price has coincided with an unprecedented rise in the number of properties for sale in the North East. To put this in perspective, the number of second-hand local properties for sale (based on Aberdeen Solicitors Property Centre (ASPC) 4th quarter figures each year) rose from 455 in the boom year of 2006 to 2218 in 2008, reflecting a significant increase, albeit one that subsided relatively quickly. However, the recent downturn has seen an inexorable rise in the volume of properties for sale rise to over 6000 (Aberdeen Solicitors Property Centre, n.d.) accompanied by falling prices, while this is against the wider Scottish trend.

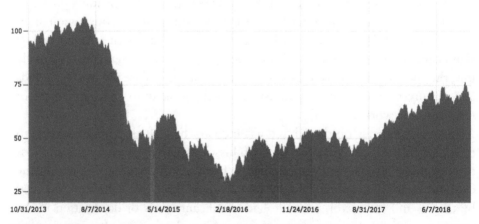

Figure 1: The Fluctuating Price of a Barrel of Oil Equivalent in US $ 2013–2018
Source: *Markets Insider.*

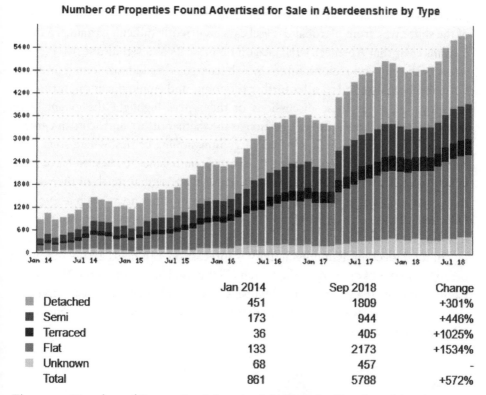

Number of Properties Found Advertised for Sale in Aberdeenshire by Type

	Jan 2014	Sep 2018	Change
▉ Detached	451	1809	+301%
▉ Semi	173	944	+446%
▉ Terraced	36	405	+1025%
▉ Flat	133	2173	+1534%
▉ Unknown	68	457	-
Total	861	5788	+572%

Figure 2: Number of Properties Advertised for Sale in Aberdeenshire (by type)
Source: home.co.uk

It is clearly the case, as noted, that Aberdeen's previous downturns have been followed by significant upturns as the price of oil has recovered. This is a view recently advanced by local property commentator, suggesting that the partial recovery in the oil price indicates that the region is again on the verge of another economic, job and, thus house price boom (BBC, 2018).

However, while some sort of recovery may occur, there are grounds for considering that the pattern of the recent past may not be relied upon in future. This view is informed by the awareness that previous downturns and subsequent booms occurred against a background of plentiful recoverable North Sea oil reserves, less global competition and a scenario where the outlook for oil as a key source of energy was much more certain.

While there are new discoveries coming on and there are new methods of recovery that are likely to make some previously uneconomic finds viable, reserves in the North Sea are in long term decline while the basin's infrastructure is aging. New finds also tend to be in smaller deposits than the giants of the past (see Figure 3). Evidently, the advent of shale has also had an impact on the global market, and particularly on mature and expensive basins like the North Sea, while the effects of the shift away from petrol and diesel cars is currently difficult to gauge. As such, it seems clear that Aberdeen's reliance on oil presents as a significant risk factor in terms of the city and region's future. Much trumpeted decommissioning prospects have also been asserted to offer further economic and employment opportunities.

However, while these discussions of themselves highlight the extent of oil industry decline, there is now a question as to whether the UK and Scottish Governments will be willing to allow partial decommissioning of rigs, where some environmental groups are now arguing that it may, on balance, be best to leave many in situ (Scottish Wildlife Trust, 2018). It is also the case that much of the work of this nature that does take place may be captured by other areas, such as Norway, Dundee and the north-east of England, who seem better prepared to capitalise on this thus far.

In total, decommissioning activity is forecast on 349 fields across the North Sea: 214 on the UKCS, 106 on the Dutch Continental Shelf, 23 on the Norwegian Continental Shelf and six on the Danish Continental Shelf. Forecast activity on the UKCS to 2025 is significantly higher than in other regions of the North Sea (Oil and Gas UK, 2017).

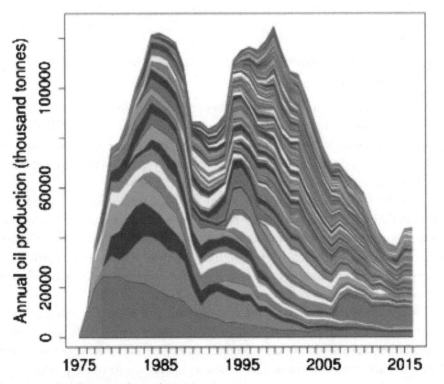

Figure 3: North Sea Oil Depletion.
Source: *The Edinburgh Geologist.*

Aberdeen Outlook

Diversification or Decline

Against this background, while some significant optimism remains regarding the pace of the decline of North Sea oil, few voices appear to challenge the notion that this is the inevitable direction of travel in the medium term. In recognition of this, as well as a push towards greater local infrastructure investment, diversifying the local economy has become an increasingly urgent priority for local authorities (Aberdeen Local Outcome Improvement Plan, 2017). Moreover, such anxieties may be understandable given the examples of other urban areas that have lost core industries. In Scotland, in areas such as Linwood and Motherwell, the closure of car and steel plants respectively devastated local economies, while the Aberdeen regional situation is potentially more profound. The fate of Flint, Michigan, for example, where the closure of the General Motors car plant saw the area collapse into widespread unemployment, poverty and crime, offers an unsettling example of the potential consequences of such a scenario (Young, 2013). That being said; however, it can be argued that Aberdeen has other assets that should allow it to avoid as dire a fate.

Aberdeen's authorities have turned their attention to the possibilities of exploiting the areas tourist potential. Beyond the relatively barren North East coastline (which has its own rugged attractions) the region provides access to some of the finest scenery in Scotland, and to a large range of castles and other historical sites. One arm of this strategy aims to develop the city's harbour area to attract cruise ships attracted by these features of the local area, and by new cultural and entertainment developments planned for the city itself (Aberdeen Local Outcome Improvement Plan, 2017).

There is a question mark, however, as to how far such developments, even if successful, might compensate for oil's decline. This plan would seem to place Aberdeen on a pathway similar to that of Inverness. However, it may be noted that, while fairly successful, the Inverness economy is currently more developed in terms of tourism, is geographically better placed, and also supports a significantly lower local population. As to the latter, a recent survey by the accountants PWC, suggested that 67 per cent of young adults intended to or were considering moving from the Aberdeen area, the majority citing the declining oil industry and consequent lack of economic prospects as the rationale for such a move. The challenge for regional and national authorities, and local businesses, then is how successful diversification might be managed to prevent a scenario where, viewed with a wider lens, Aberdeen's oil boom comes to appear as a period of hiatus in a story of long-term historical decline.

One further strategy being advanced by local politicians is in the area of new technologies. This seems sensible given some success in this area for the city's southern neighbour, Dundee. On a final note, however, new technologies of themselves – contrary to adherents of the much-promulgated (so-called) Luddite fallacy (a concept that I have argued no longer holds) are also likely to have a substantial impact on the area's labour market (Bone, 2015; Brynsolfson and MacAfee, 2011; Frey and Osborne, 2013). Automation may well have an accelerating impact on declining oil sector employment as new technologies are applied to oil extraction, as well as having effects on the local service economy, with the latter arguably being already well underway. However, these are issues that may have to be confronted well beyond Aberdeen, while the solutions, it can be argued, are likely to involve a more fundamental approach to confronting some of the issues discussed above.

References

Aberdeen City Council, 'Aberdeen Economic Policy Panel Report 2018', 2 November 2018.

Aberdeen City Council, 'Aberdeen Local Outcome Improvement Plan 2016–2026', 24 April 2017.

Aberdeen Solicitors Property Centre, available online at: www.aspc.co.uk/information/house-prices/

BBC (2018), 'Aberdeen property market "set for oil industry jobs boom"', 15 October 2018, available online at: https://www.bbc.co.uk/news/uk-scotland-north-east-orkney-shetland-45835531

Bone, J. (2015), 'False Economy: Financialisation, Crises and Socio-Economic Polarisation', *Sociology Compass*, Vol. 9 No. 10.

Brynjolfsoon, E. and McAfee, A. (2011), 'Race Against the Machine: How the Digital Revolution Is Accelerating Innovation, Driving Productivity, and Irreversibly Transforming Employment and the Economy', *Digital Frontier*.

Oil and Gas UK (2017), *Decommissioning Insight*.

Feagin, J. (1990), 'Are Planners Collective Capitalists: The Cases of Aberdeen and Houston', *International Journal of Urban and Regional Research*, Vol. 14 No. 2 pp. 249–273.

Frey, C. and Osborne, M. (2013) 'The Future of Employment: How Susceptible are Jobs to Computerisation?', available online at: www.oxfordmartin.ox.ac.uk/downloads/academic/The_Future_of_Employment.pdf

Home.co.uk (n.d.), available online at: www.home.co.uk/guides/asking_
    prices_report.htm
Hunt, D. (1976), 'Response of Industry within Aberdeen to Oil Related
    Change: some implications for urban planners', *International Journal of
    Environmental Studies*, Vol. 9: pp. 269–278.
Markets Insider (n.d.), available online at: https://markets.businessinsider.com/
    commodities/oil-price?type=wti
Scottish Wildlife Trust (2018), *Decommissioning*, available online at:
    https://scottishwildlifetrust.org.uk/our-work/our-projects/living-seas/
    decommissioning/
Young, G. (2013), *Teardown: Memoir of a Vanishing City*, CA: University of
    California Press.

CHAPTER 36

Life in the First Minister's Constituency
A Story of Govanhill

Catriona Stewart

AN AFTERNOON STROLL, should you be able to resist the temptations of half a dozen coffee shops, delis, cafes and innovative restaurants, will take you pleasantly past a queer bookshop, a record store, independent shops, an up-cycling venue and several truly bonny historic buildings.

Along this street there is a B-listed Edwardian bathhouse being redeveloped as a £6.5 million new health and well-being centre. Crumbling, yes, but worth a peek are the green and white stripes of the Egyptian-inspired Picture House. A section of tenement flats, designed by renowned architect Alexander 'Greek' Thomson, is preserved as A-listed.

In a pub filled with young professionals, community activists and hipsters with turned up jeans and no socks, *'nduja* on the menu and fancy gratins, a barman carefully slices a chunk of cucumber bought in the nearby organic supermarket and drops it into an artisan gin.

Where? A smart guess would be Finnieston, named the hippest place in Britain, and near to the chichi West End. That smart guess would, however, be wrong.

This is Govanhill. Poor Govanhill, maligned Govanhill, controversial Govanhill.

An area of terrible repute, swirling rumours and two competing realities.

One reality is that millions of pounds of targeted investment has been poured into the area in the past ten years thanks in large part to dedicated community activists who have generated enough heat and light that politicians were forced into action.

A Decade of Change

A decade ago the area, such a small square of the city's southside, was labelled a slum. Two local politicians took me for a tour, and we filmed as we went. It was, and this cannot be overstated, horrifying. Closes that had once been home to those who took great pride in their stair, stank of piss. Reeked. The refuse in backcourts was waist high.

I had worn Jimmy Choo's that day – for the filming, you see, priorities – and how I minced through the communal areas trying not to get human excrement on my heels. 'GOVANHELL' was the headline we ran across the front of the *Evening Times*. 'GROUND ZERO' we called it, across the top of two pages of the paper. There were sights that could not be unseen. Rogue landlords were up to every dodge imaginable. In one close, a flat had been subdivided to such an extent that there was only limited access to the one bathroom for 20 inhabitants.

To circumvent this issue, members of the household were doing their business in plastic bags, tying the handles tight and flinging their waste from the back windows. Unfortunately, a tall tree stood immediately outside and, well, the handles of the bags would become caught in the branches. The Jobby Tree.

We covered stories of one rogue landlord in particular who had creatively made space in one of his properties by combining the kitchen and bathroom. So, the lavatory and the oven sat flush together. Another landlord had transformed one of those long cupboards, a staple of tenement hallways, into bunk beds by inserting four shelves. We call two children sharing a bedroom overcrowding – this was four children sharing a cupboard.

These were not sights anyone would expect to see in Scotland's largest city.

One of the most notorious streets, Allison Street, is exactly that where the A-listed 'Greek' Thomson block sits. There you have your oxymoron. An A-listed slum.

Since, hundreds of flats have been taken into control of housing associations and work is currently underway to bring them to tolerable standard. In other cases, professional couples have spotted bargains at auction and are renovating former slum properties into luxury homes. Having so many properties in the ownership of housing associations is some protection from wholesale gentrification and should, hopefully, keep the area's mix of working-class community and burgeoning new middle-class.

Slum landlords are being removed from the area. Police Scotland has an enhanced strategy for Govanhill, and crime rates are falling. Cleansing services are more intensive here than anywhere else in the city. There are dozens upon dozens of community projects catering for every possible interest. There is a Big Noise orchestra working in primary and secondary schools.

The Govanhill Baths was closed by Glasgow City Council in 2001 but local people refused to accept the closure and a battle was begun. It was a neat demonstration of how passionate and motivated the community is. A trust took the Edwardian bathhouse over and it has now closed for renovation. When it opens in 2020 it will be an extraordinary boost to the area.

Inroads are being made with the Roma population – the largest in the UK – with successes at local schools and in community projects. The South City Way, a cycle route that runs through Govanhill from Queen's Park to the Merchant City, is currently under construction.

Affordable rents attract small businesses to the area, including local manufacture. The bar of our aforementioned hipster pub was made around the corner from an innovative new material based on Japanese lacquerware called Mirrl. The food scene is booming, you are spoilt for choice.

Yet, the reality for many is still harsh. The reality for many is still one of overcrowding, filthy closes and fear. If one is swatting at a cockroach as it scuttles across one's kitchen worktop, one really has no hoots to give about an organic supermarket opening up on Victoria Road, even if it does sell fresh milk by the bottle and allow you to crush your own pistachio butter.

The other reality is of those in flats where anti-social behaviour is a blight on normal life. Where infestations of mice, rats and cockroaches must be dealt with. Where multiculturalism does not make the area vibrant but makes it seem unsafe, unclean and out of control.

The Battle of Different Govanhills

During the Indyref movement a trend grew up online whereby anyone who queried whether or not the country should break away from the union was asked the question, 'Why do you hate Scotland?' This became a sort of meme, jokingly applied to anything and everything. 'I'm not so keen on haggis' – 'Why do you hate Scotland?' 'We're spending the summer on Anglesey' – 'Why do you hate Scotland?'

In Govanhill, a version of this prevails, but in reverse. Any positivity about the area is met with deep suspicion, fury even. Those who mention the positive change in the area are said to wear rose tinted glasses – a gross insult. As soon as you are accused of wearing rose tinted glasses, you're *persona non grata*.

Any positive news story I write about Govanhill inevitably leads to someone commenting that I must never have been there. When I say I live there the goalposts shift and I am told I must never have walked along the notorious Allison Street. When I reply that I walk along Allison Street daily – and at night – I am told I must be an SNP shill'.

There's another element to the issue. Nicola Sturgeon is the MSP for the area and there is a deep sense, in some quarters, that she has 'abandoned' Govanhill, though pinning people down to exactly what they mean by 'abandoned' is tricky.

Having the First Minister as elected representative has also made Govanhill a gift for the right-wing press. When I was picking my way through piss, writing about the area's ills, no-one particularly cared. When Ms Sturgeon was made First Minister in 2014, suddenly people cared and all the progress that has undoubtedly been made in the area was ignored.

Govanhill's rich history consists of the stories of its immigrant populations. Irish, Jewish, Pakistani and now the Roma. Each group has faced its challenges but there is a unique and deep distrust towards the Roma. Govanhill's astounding community spirit is also manifest in its social media presence. There are at least five prolific Facebook pages for the area, each with their own agenda and personality and with thousands of members.

Myth, Falsehood and Looking for Someone to Blame

When there were fewer ducks than usual on the pond in Queen's Park it went around on Facebook, relatively unchallenged, that the Roma had stolen and eaten them. I spoke several times to the police about this after reports from a credible source that two arrests had been made. Police Scotland categorically denied any knowledge, but it was too late – it is now lore that the Roma steal and eat ducks.

Hunting atypical wildfowl pales next to the other Roma rumour standard. Media outlets were able to print stories in 2017 that said Roma parents are selling their children on the streets for sex. Not claimed but said. A broadsheet newspaper printed, unequivocally, that Roma children are being sold by their parents on the streets for sex. I repeat that because it is a very specific charge.

The subject of the Roma came up at the place where I volunteer and a fellow volunteer told me, with a note of authority, that the children are sold from corner shops in Govanhill. 'And you know who owns the corner shops', she added.

From where does my colleague get her confidence? Her hairdresser told her. A year-long police investigation has recently concluded showing no evidence of Roma parents selling their children, but some local people still believe it to be true. The fact it was front-page news of a respected paper gives it weight.

Around Christmas 2018 a woman posted on one of the popular local Facebook pages to say she had emailed the First Minister about a disturbing incident she had witnessed the evening before on leaving Neeson's bar, a well-used local haunt. She, with a group of family and friends, saw a man 'pimping out' a young boy of around seven. She was horrified and called on Nicola Sturgeon to do something about this visible scandal taking place in her constituency.

As is standard on social media, there was a pile on. Why, asked post after post, had this woman not contacted the police? Initially she wrote back to say she felt there was no point in contacting the authorities as nothing would be done. Rather, she felt the correct route was to push Ms Sturgeon to action. This stance was rubbished and after a day or so of back-and-forth, a couple of local residents reported the Facebook post to the police. The woman was contacted and interviewed, as was another witness.

The response from the local sergeant was frank:

> In this instance we have interviewed [the witness] and the actual events she has provided us with do not reflect in any way the email she has sent to Nicola Sturgeon or the post on Facebook.

In another post, a woman was emphatic that she had reported to the police an incident where she was offered a child for sale. She had, she said, been walking along Allison Street where she was approached by two men who said, 'Ten pounds for the baby'.

The woman was absolutely adamant that the gentlemen had wanted to make an exchange – a tenner and she could take the infant away with her. Another, more plausible, take is that the chaps were begging. 'Penny for the guy' does not allow the donor to walk away with an effigy of Guy Fawkes. But the respectability these rumours – the old gypsy libel – have gained from their press attention has moved child abuse from being an unwelcome spectre to the belief that it is an everyday occurrence, publicly happening on Govanhill's streets. On one hand, it is a positive step that people are alert to the issues and care about child protection. Child sexual exploitation happens in Govanhill, of course, just as it happens everywhere, and it is a moral duty of a community to step in where it sees vulnerable children being abused.

Yet it is deeply alarming that local people now see bogeymen everywhere – and bogeymen of only one particular group. There is real social division and exclusion in the area, not helped by the proliferation of ugly rumours. Racist comments are graffitied on phone boxes. Far right groups follow the narrative closely, looking for an opportunity to use racial divisions in the area as an example that multi-culturalist doesn't work.

You have one group of people – those who have seen the area go downhill and are suffering for it – who feel patronised and belittled. You have a second group working endlessly to correct the problems but who feel frustrated and stymied.

Members of the former group say they see literally nothing being done to improve Govanhill, despite the evidence to the contrary. They want zero crime, but we live in the real world, not in a utopia. There will always be crime.

A comment on the review of Govanhill's new hipster pub claims a visitor was put off by the children begging outside. I spoke to several regular customers who say they have not once seen such a thing. Another review complains that the pub did not sell Smirnoff and so they won't be back.

It is easy to scoff at that, but what you are really scoffing at is a fear of change, a fear of people's needs being ignored. Govanhill is a microcosm of our wider political landscape. Rumour and conspiracy theory abound because of a feeling of loss of control and the threat of migration. Communities need to feel empowered and genuinely listened to otherwise they will lean towards populist politicians and public figures who make disingenuous, meaningless promises and offer simplistic solutions. This is the kind of climate where a right-wing elite could slap a solution on the side of a bus and win local votes.

The word 'vibrant' has taken on a new meaning within the borders of Govanhill. It has become a sarcastic shorthand to be used in the face of negative news' There's been a robbery? Oh, isn't Govanhill vibrant? The local primary school has a cockroach infestation? How vibrant.

But actually, Govanhill *is* vibrant. It is stimulating, full of energy, shimmering with potential. The problem with Govanhill is not the bedbugs or the overcrowding, it is that not everyone feels connected to this sense of energy. Of course, these things are of vital importance to those who are suffering from them in 21st century Scotland. However, rather than feel a sense of potential, the championing and changing of this area has added to the marginalisation and displacement felt by some.

In a country that believes it embodies fairness and social justice, the example of Govanhill throws up many acute questions. How do communities have influence in an age of truncated local government? How does positive neighbourhood change happen without gentrification or reinforcing hipster *clichés*? What is the role of the media and should not parts of it aim higher than reporting what is little more than urban folklore? And what is the relationship between the local community and its politics, and that of the national? Govanhill has had much coverage in recent years, and the vitality and dynamism of its people has many insights into how we answer these and more questions.

Section Six – The Wider World

CHAPTER 37

Defending Scotland

William Walker

SCOTLAND HAS PLAYED a part in British military history out of proportion to its size and population. Without its regiments, bases and exercise grounds, the UK would have been less able to defend itself and project power. Scotland's position in the North Atlantic and its maritime geography lent it particular importance during the Cold War, not least when providing bases for American and British nuclear submarine forces.

Since the Union's establishment, however, Scotland has not participated in military affairs as a sovereign political entity, with the rights of decision, but as an integral part of the British state. Policy has been determined in London and armed forces have been expected to show loyalty solely to the UK's Government, Parliament and crown. Scottish MPs, Ministers and defence personnel have only exercised influence when wearing their British hats. To this day, most Scots involved in military affairs, certainly in the officer class, display strong attachment to the Union.

This situation has been largely unaffected by devolution. The Scotland Act of 1998 confirmed that defence and foreign policy would remain in London's grip. Although the act gave the Scottish Parliament and Government some leeway to develop international connections, it declared unequivocally that 'the defence of the realm' and 'the naval, military or air forces of the Crown' are reserved matters. Holyrood's fealty was emphasized in an unusually lengthy and detailed concordat enjoining Scottish Ministers to

> take into account the need for the unimpeded conduct of the defence of the UK... when framing and implementing Scottish legislation or otherwise undertaking actions and functions within their competence (Concordat, December 1999).

Given the UK's reliance on nuclear bases in the Clyde, the act drew particular attention to the UK Government's exercise of 'sole control of nuclear, biological and chemical weapons of mass destruction'.

While conferring no powers of decision, the Scotland Act gave the Scottish Parliament rights to debate and vote on reserved, including military, matters. Holyrood exercised this right in January 2003 when a motion critical of the UK Government's stance on Iraq was defeated by the combined votes of Labour and Conservative MSPs. It did so again in June 2007 when an SNP motion against Trident's replacement was carried on that occasion, but without affecting the UK Government's policy that had received Westminster's consent three months previously. The unpopularity of the Iraq War and Trident's replacement, each so strongly associated with Mr Blair's Labour Government, contributed to the Labour Party's demise in Scotland, opening the way for the SNP's unexpected victory in the 2007 Scottish election. They showed that London's decisions on defence and foreign policy had repercussions in Scotland, irrespective of the Scottish Parliament's lack of sway. Indeed, the Parliament's exclusion on issues of strong Scottish interest added to independence's allure.

Defence in 'Scotland's Future'

In calling the referendum on independence, the SNP-led Scottish Government faced the difficult task, in view of its inexperience, of giving shape to the foreign and defence policy that a sovereign Scottish state would adopt if it won the referendum. It set out its stall in *Scotland's Future*, the White Paper published in November 2013. Scotland would be a small state no longer bound to a country and people that had longings to remain a great power. It would share interests and align itself with other small liberal states, especially in the Nordic region, whilst endeavouring to play a full part in international alliances and organisations. It would emphasize maritime defence given its long coastline and strategic location in the North Atlantic. Neither neutral nor pacifist, it would contribute forces to UN peacekeeping and always encourage the peaceful settlement of international disputes.

The Scottish Government proposed, amongst other things, a division of the UK's military assets in proportion to population, maintenance of the Scottish regiments, a defence force of 15,000 regular and 5,000 reserve personnel, a defence and security budget of £2.5 billion, retention of a naval shipbuilding industry, and 'refiguring the defence estate inherited at the point of independence'. The transition to a fully-fledged Scottish defence force, adapted to Scotland's foreign and security needs, was anticipated to take ten years.

The Scottish Government understood that establishing the armed forces, infrastructures and bureaucracies required in the state would be a big challenge. It was assumed, perhaps reasonably, that Edinburgh and London would be able to settle issues without enormous to-do if independence were won. The

Edinburgh Agreement of 2012 had 'committed the two governments to continue to work together constructively in the light of the outcome, whatever it is, in the best interests of the people of Scotland and of the rest of the United Kingdom' (Memorandum of Understanding, 2012).

Such constructive engagement could not, however, be expected where Trident and the future of its bases in the Clyde were concerned. Although the Scottish Government feigned confidence, this was bound to be an incendiary issue since there existed no plausible alternative locations for the submarines, missiles and their loading docks (Chalmers and Walker, 2001). The Nuclear Navy's eviction from Faslane and Coulport would therefore precipitate the nuclear deterrent's abandonment, a prospect that the rest of the UK (RUK) Government and its American, French and other allies were always likely to resist. How the eviction could be managed in practice was left vague in *Scotland's Future*, not least because the Scottish Government was reluctant to reveal the extent of its reliance on British and American expertise, finance and goodwill when carrying out the task. There was reference to a CND study suggesting that the bases' closure could be achieved within two years (Scottish CND, 2012). The study did not, however, consider the many political and logistical complications.

In the event, the red line on Trident's removal was little challenged during the referendum, mainly because the Ministry of Defence preferred to remain silent on the matter. They did so because, given Trident's toxicity north of the border, they could not trumpet the benefits that the Union's survival would bring to Scotland through the deterrent's retention. They were also reluctant to be drawn into a debate about the availability of other bases that had been little examined.

As a result, the Scottish Government was able to proclaim Trident's removal and Faslane's conversion to Scotland's military headquarters as important outcomes of independence without having to explain, beyond asserting that it would secure 'the nuclear weapons' speediest safe withdrawal', the means of achieving it. Nor did the Government acknowledge the risks that its red line would pose to agreement with London on economic and other matters. With some difficulty, it was also able to keep at bay assertions that its policy on Trident was incompatible with the intention to join NATO, a nuclear alliance.

The SNP in Westminster

The Scottish referendum defeat for Yes in 2014 left the Scottish Parliament toothless in matters relating to defence, for the time being at least. However, the 56 SNP MPs elected to the Westminster Parliament in the 2015 general election (reduced to 35 in 2017) gave the Party influence – in principle – in the

Westminster Parliament that it had never previously possessed. It also enabled the party to broaden and deepen its experience of defence affairs through participation in parliamentary debates, access to the Parliament's library and other resources in London, and representation on its Defence and Foreign Affairs Select Committees.

Any expectations that this bloc of MPs would give the SNP real sway in Westminster, and that the Scottish Government would gain influence thereby, were shown to be illusory by the decision in July 2016 to proceed with Trident's replacement by moving the project from development into manufacture. The division of votes was salutary: 322 Conservative and 140 Labour MPs in favour; one Conservative, 47 Labour, 52 SNP and seven Liberal Democrat MPs against. Including smaller Parties and independent MPs, the parliamentary majority was 355. The SNP's opposition – and Scotland's interests it would say – had been overwhelmed by the much larger bloc of Conservative and Labour MPs.

Five Years On

Looking Out on a Disordered, Insecure World

The Scottish Government noted in *Scotland's Future* that:

> The impact of world events has increasingly important implications for both domestic and foreign policy.

It assumed, nonetheless, that the states, institutions and alliances to which it would relate after independence were essentially stable and dependable. It did not anticipate the upheavals that followed (Maull, 2018). Russia's annexation of the Crimea and aggressive interventions abroad. The return to arms racing, including in nuclear weapons and cyberwarfare. The Syrian crisis and proxy wars fought across the Middle East. The US turn to isolationism and the many complications attending Donald Trump's presidency. The rise of populist movements and revival of autocracy. The general weakening of international institutions and respect for international law. The chaos and crisis of Brexit.

What this all means for Scotland is imponderable. A common opinion is that a second Scottish referendum, hastened by Brexit, might be held in the early to mid-2020s. If correct, advocates of independence would face the task of persuading voters that Scotland could prosper and fend for itself in an international environment that was much more precarious, in perception and reality, than in 2014. The section on defence and foreign policy in *Scotland's Future* – if a White Paper of similar scope were attempted – would need substantial revision. Possibly in anticipation, there has recently been announcement of an initiative to 'reboot' the SNP's defence policy, placing emphasis on the strengthening of maritime capabilities and defence of the 'High North', already being boosted by deployment of a fleet of US-supplied maritime surveillance aircraft at an upgraded Lossiemouth RAF base (Gourtsoyannis, 5 May 2018). The revision seems inconsequential so far.

Stepping into such an unstable and unpredictable international environment may encourage wariness of independence. It is unlikely, however, that defence would be any more prominent in a second Scottish referendum than in the first. So much else would press on voters' minds. It would not, however, be a secondary matter in the negotiations with RUK, the EU, NATO and the US that would follow a Yes vote, assuming that the referendum's legality were acknowledged. From their perspective, the military bases, ranges and deployments in Scotland are an important part of the Western military alliance. Scotland's future would also be intertwined with RUK's future as a military power. There would inevitably be issue-linkage as Scotland sought international recognition, entry to international organisations, agreements of various kinds with governments in London and elsewhere, and as RUK itself faced up to the Union's demise and its international consequences, including its standing in the UN Security Council.

Trident would again be vexing. By the mid-2020s, it is conceivable that the replacement programme's mounting cost, and concerns about the deterrent's vulnerability to attack or disablement, will have shifted opinion in Whitehall against keeping it, especially if the Labour Party were in office. But this cannot be assumed, so embedded is the commitment to nuclear deterrence in the UK and NATO. It remains likely that the Scottish Government would come under heavy pressure to consent to Trident's stay in Scotland or to its removal over the long term whatever that might mean. Trident would, of course, be a great bargaining chip if the Scottish Government felt able to use it without offending its supporters.

This said, Scotland would not lack international friends, nor would opposing governments avoid political risk, if it insisted on the nuclear weapons' removal. Besides serving the cause of nuclear disarmament to which so many states and NGOs are attached, Trident's continued deployment out of Faslane and Coulport would create a situation without precedent: a nuclear weapon state's basing of its *entire* nuclear force on the territory of a state seeking to become a non-nuclear weapon state under international law and member (probably) of the recently established Treaty on the Prohibition of Nuclear Weapons. Politically and legally, the problems might only be finessed if Faslane and Coulport remained sovereign base areas of RUK after independence, a proposal that would open many cans of worms. Imposition of nuclear weapons and basing rights on an unwilling Scotland, in the interest of realpolitik and to satisfy rUK's craving to remain a great power in the eyes of the world, would play badly internationally. Which is not to say that imposition would not be attempted, and that Scotland would avoid the costs of resistance.

Come what may, the challenge to Trident's future would, along with the UK's demise, turn Scotland's independence into an event of global significance and daunting political complexity, however straightforward it may appear on the surface.

'To Be Negotiated'

It is sometimes remarked that, whilst Scotland has become a distinctive polity since the Scottish Parliament's re-establishment, it is still regarded 'down south' as a territory and possession of the British state to which it remains beholden. This is certainly true in the field of defence where the military bases, weaponry and other assets in Scotland are regarded by London, and even by Washington and NATO's other member states, as the British state's necessary territories and properties – its intrinsic entitlement – in both a physical and politico-legal sense.

Scotland's nationalists have sought to end this situation just as unionists have sought to preserve it. Assertion of authority over 'defence' and its estate has been fundamental in each side's vision of the future. Defence did not, however, feature much in the 2014 referendum and would probably take a back seat next time round. It would, however, become a primary issue in relations with rUK, the EU, NATO and other states and international organizations after a Yes vote. The sign 'to be negotiated' has to be attached to the near entirety of defence issues involving Scotland. Given the experience with Brexit, it is troubling that negotiations would be entered, present trends continued, after so little preparation and with so little idea of the solutions that might be available and acceptable to governments and publics. The risk of division, indecision and delay are self-evident.

References

Chalmers, M. and Walker, W. (2001), *Uncharted Waters: The UK, Nuclear Weapons and the Scottish Question*, East Linton: Tuckwell Press.

Concordat (1999), 'Concordat between the Scottish Government and the Secretary of State for Defence'.

Gourtsoyannis, P. (2018), 'SNP defence policy to close open door to Russia', *The Scotsman*, 5 May 2018.

Maull, H. (ed.) (2018), *The Rise and Decline of the Post-Cold War International Order*. Oxford: Oxford University Press.

Memorandum of Understanding (2012), 'Memorandum of Understanding accompanying the Agreement between the United Kingdom Government and the Scottish Government on a referendum on independence in Scotland'.

Scottish CND (2012), *Disarming Trident – A Practical Guide to De-Activating and Dismantling the Scottish-Based Trident Nuclear Weapon System*, Glasgow: Scottish Campaign for Nuclear Disarmament.

Scottish Government (2013), 'Scotland's Future', Edinburgh: Scottish Government.

CHAPTER 38

Security Matters

Andrew W Neal

'NATIONAL SECURITY' WAS a matter 'reserved' to Westminster by the Scotland Act, 1998. This covered the military and intelligence services, and also 'Special powers... for dealing with terrorism' and 'The subject-matter of the Official Secrets Acts'. In the twenty years since, the scope of national security has broadened to cover a much wider range of governmental concerns and activities. As a result, while national security remains 'reserved' on paper, in practice it has become the business of the Scottish Government in several areas such as resilience planning and policing, and potentially in any part of devolved government.

The broadening of national security is a global trend. It makes sense to think of the reserved matters of defence and intelligence as the traditional 'hard' areas of national security. These have been supplemented by a wide range of other concerns in national and international security policy agendas. For example, the most recent UK National Security Strategy (NSS) from 2015 lists many non-traditional 'priority risks' such as 'cyber', 'public health', 'major natural hazards', 'decay and failure of key institutions', 'serious and organised crime', 'financial crisis', 'fuel supply', 'weather' and 'environmental events' (UK Government, 2015). Although in 1998 these would have been recognisable as potential social, economic and political problems, they would have been unfamiliar as 'national security' issues. This may still be true today, to an extent, but nevertheless they are part of UK national security policy.

This list of risks alone shows how far the national security picture has changed since Scottish devolution. If devolution was done today, it would not make sense to reserve 'national security' as a whole to the UK Government. Many 'priority risks', for example 'public health' and 'serious and organised crime', clearly overlap with devolved Scottish policy areas, such as health and policing.

It follows that national security is no longer the preserve of the military and intelligence services. The NSS envisages roles for every part of government, with continuing efforts to foster a 'whole of government' approach. The latest UK Government vision, the 'Fusion Doctrine' (nothing to do with nuclear power), goes even further to encourage input from the private and third sectors (Lawson, 2018). New agencies and institutions have been created to develop expertise, plan and co-ordinate within government, and work with stakeholders such as critical infrastructure providers. One such institution is the National Security Council (NSC), which produces the NSS. The NSC is a cabinet sub-committee created in 2010 and chaired by the Prime Minister with input from across government departments and agencies. It is supported by a National Security Secretariat of approximately 200 civil servants, which is in turn headed by the Prime Minister's National Security Advisor (UK Parliament, 2014). Related bodies include the Civil Contingencies Secretariat in the Cabinet Office, the Centre for the Protection of National Infrastructure and the Office for Security and Counter-Terrorism in the Home Office.

These developments include the Scottish Government – there are several UK-wide working groups on which the Scottish Government is represented (Scottish Government, 2011) – but are also mirrored in Scotland on a smaller scale. Scotland has created its own delivery and co-ordination bodies such as the Scottish Government Critical National Infrastructure Group, the CONTEST (counter-terrorism) Board for Scotland and Scottish Government Resilience Division. Like the 'whole of government' security strategy in Whitehall, the Scottish approach is a 'cross government effort'. The philosophy of Scottish resilience is of a piece with that of the NSS; they talk similarly of 'a different and more complex range of threats from a myriad of sources' (HM Government, 2010) and

> a complex and increasingly interdependent society…[that] leaves us, potentially, more vulnerable to a number of challenges (Scottish Government, 2012).

The risks and challenges mentioned are also similar, for example: 'terrorism, pandemic flu, volcanic ash and severe weather' (Scottish Government, 2012) or 'vulnerabilities around power supply and information technology' (Scottish Government, 2012).

The independence referendum of 2014 focused attention on the extent to which Scotland has, or could develop, independent security capabilities. As a by-product the process also produced a thorough accounting of UK security capabilities and their national distribution. For example, the Scottish Government White Paper proposed that an independent Scotland would develop its already-growing police-based intelligence capabilities (building on the 2013 integration of the Scottish police forces into the single entity Police Scotland) and create a single integrated intelligence agency (Scottish Government, 2013). At the same time, the UK Government produced a paper entitled 'Scotland Analysis: Security' – the very fact that it published separate 'Defence' and 'Security' analysis papers reveals something about the extent to which these areas have diverged; at the time of devolution, they were uttered in the same breath. While the Scottish and UK papers both contained unavoidably political and contestable statements – for example, over the extent to which the remaining UK and an independent Scotland would and could share intelligence – the UK paper in particular revealed how the Government envisages the extent of the national security architecture.

For example, it revealed the extent to which policing is now seen as central to national security in the broadest sense. While British police have had recourse to special counter-terrorism powers for many decades (at least since the 1970s) and all British police forces have had their own 'special branches' to gather intelligence and pursue cases of potential significance for national security, this is now a mainstream dimension of modern policing. Furthermore, there is a national (ie UK-wide) dimension to policing – manifested in national police databases and the National Crime Agency (NCA) – that did not exist to anywhere near the same extent twenty years ago. Scotland is very much part of this system, with the NCA sharing a Scottish base with Police Scotland at the Scottish Crime Campus at Gartcosh. The creation of the NCA was approved by both Westminster and Holyrood (Scotland Office, 2013). In the same vein, there is a European dimension to policing and security co-operation which – although European police liaison arrangements existed as far back as the 1960s – has expanded enormously since the 1990s as part of the Justice and Home Affairs policy area of the EU. Similar to internal UK police integration, this is built primarily on information sharing and databases (Monar, 2012; Bigo, 2014).

The *Scotland Analysis: Security* paper also noted that despite Whitehall providing UK-wide guidance and frameworks, resilience capabilities are mostly local. Resilience in fact has a direct link to 'civil defence', the one area of 'security' that was explicitly not 'reserved' in the Scotland Act 1998. Civil defence has origins in domestic British experiences in the World Wars, such as aerial bombardment, and was organised at a local authority level (Zebrowski, 2015). Its aim was to respond to events by putting out fires, attending to collapsing buildings, securing or shutting off water and gas supplies, maintaining bomb shelters, providing assistance to survivors, recovering and removing the dead and so on. Civil defence continued into the Cold War, with local authorities required to engage in contingency planning for a nuclear attack and the possibility that central government would cease to function. Civil defence as a term fell into disuse in the UK shortly after its appearance in the Scotland Act, but it has evolved into current civil contingencies and resilience arrangements. With direct continuity, the Civil Contingencies Act 2004 required specified bodies – including local and devolved governments, emergency services, health authorities and environmental agencies – to 'assess the risk of an emergency occurring', and make plans to prevent, reduce, mitigate or otherwise respond to them.

The reasons for the shift from civil defence to civil contingencies and resilience planning are the same as those for the broadening of national security: a perception that threats, risks and emergencies are increasingly varied and complex and no longer solely a product of military confrontation or political subversion. While the narrative of a shift from the simplicity of the Cold War to the complex risks of the 21th century is *clichéd* (but ubiquitous), the philosophical shift behind it is rather fascinating. Whereas old-fashioned threats were thought to come from external enemies or enemies within, risks may be produced endogenously through breakdowns in technological, social or economic systems, such as power supplies, transport systems, social disorder or financial crisis (Rasmussen, 2006; Hammerstad and Boas, 2014). There is no 'security' as such against the possibility of such breakdowns, only the option to manage the risks and prepare for them when they become real.

This shift in security philosophy is a key reason why the distinction between devolved and reserved matters is less clear in the security field today than it was twenty years ago. What were once the reserved area of national security and the devolved area of civil defence have merged in security doctrine. Many of the risks specified in the NSS are the same as those outlined in UK and Scottish resilience plans. It is also why institutional Scottish resilience arrangements partially mirror national security arrangements in Whitehall. Similarly, the nascent 'Fusion Doctrine' and its desire to further involve the private and third sectors borrows from the stakeholder partnerships that have long been a feature of resilience planning.

These trends of broadening national security agendas and increasing intra-governmental, multi-agency, multi-sector and multi-level co-operation are only likely to continue into the future. At the same time, the constitutional position that holds 'national security' to be a reserved area will come to look increasingly anachronistic.

References

Bigo, D. (2014), 'The (in)securitization practices of the three universities of EU border control: Military/Navy – border guards/police – database analysts', *Security Dialogue* Vol. 45 No. 3 pp. 209–225.

Hammerstad, A. and Boas, I. (2014), 'National security risks? Uncertainty, austerity and other logics of risk in the UK Government's National Security Strategy', *Cooperation and Conflict* Vol. 50 No. 4 pp. 475–491.

HM Government (2010), 'A Strong Britain in the Age of Uncertainty: The National Security Strategy'.

Lawson, E. (2018), 'The UK National Security Capability Review and the Fusion Doctrine', *RUSI*, available online at: https://rusi.org/commentary/uk-national-security-capability-review-and-fusion-doctrine, accessed 30 November 2018.

Monar, J. (2012), 'Justice and Home Affairs', in Anand, M., Erik, J. and Stephen, W. *The Oxford Handbook of the European Union*, Oxford: Oxford University Press.

Rasmussen, M. V. (2006), *The Risk Society at Wat: Terror, Technology and Strategy in the Twenty-First Century*, Cambridge: Cambridge University Press.

Scottish Government (2012), 'Preparing Scotland: resilience guidance – gov.scot', available online at: https://www.gov.scot/publications/preparing-scotland-scottish guidance-resilience/pages/1/1, accessed 30 November 2018.

Scottish Government (2013), 'Scotland's Future: Your Guide to an Independent Scotland', Edinburgh: Scottish Government.

Scottish Government (2011), 'Secure and Resilient A Strategic Framework for Critical National Infrastructure in Scotland', available online at: http://www2.gov.scot/Publications/2011/02/21095856/6, accessed 30 November 2018.

UK Government (2004), Civil Contingencies Act, 2004.

UK Government (2015), 'National Security Strategy and Strategic Defence and Security Review 2015', London: UK Government, available online at: https://www.gov.uk/government/publications/national-security-strategy-and-strategic-defence-and-security-review-2015, accessed 20 July 2018.

UK Government (1998), Scotland Act, 1998.

UK Parliament (2014), 'National Security Council: Written Questions – 215980 – UK Parliament', available online at: https://www.parliament.uk/business/publications/written-questions-answers-statements/written-question/Commons/2014-11-25/215980/, accessed 30 November 2018

Zebrowski, C. (2015), *The Value of Resilience: Securing Life in the Twenty-First Century*, Abingdon, UK: Taylor & Francis

CHAPTER 39

Who Owns the Story of Scottish Devolution and Social Democracy?

Gerry Hassan

WHO TELLS THE story of any given political moment matters, and who can place and prioritise that story so that they come to own and dominate the present perhaps matters even more? This often includes successfully presenting an interpretation of the past to justify the present: think of how Thatcherism depicted the Britain of Wilson and Callaghan in the 1970s as bitter, divided and desperate for strong leadership, or the way New Labour portrayed the Tories as out of touch and Old Labour as failing to keep up with change.

Such impulses have been just as critical to contemporary Scottish politics, chiefly ownership of the idea of the Scottish Parliament and the devolution project and, intertwined with this, the politics of the centre-left and social democracy. The former has been crucial in the contest of who can best present themselves as 'standing up' for Scottish interests and 'Scottish values', while the latter has been central to how Labour and SNP have jockeyed for political supremacy.

The Road to Devolution

In the 1980s and 1990s, the 'story' of devolution, or rather of the devolution movement, became fused with that of Scotland as a left-of-centre, social democratic nation, which was deliberately contrasted with right-of-centre, 'Tory' England. For a long time that story was controlled by the Scottish Labour Party, although the SNP sensed its political value.

Following the establishment of the Scottish Parliament in 1999, control of this narrative gradually passed to the SNP, particularly after the Nationalists formed a minority Government in 2007. Not only did the SNP portray themselves as the true guardians of devolution and social democracy (in contrast to Scottish Labour, which was caricatured as anti-devolution and quasi-Tory), but independence came to be framed in a similar way to devolution a few decades earlier, as a means of protecting Scotland's social democratic ethos and 'different' way of doing politics.

This was problematic on a number of levels. Not only had the SNP been agnostic about (and in certain quarters hostile to) devolution before the 1997 referendum, but it had also refused to sign the 'Claim of Right' and withdrawn from the Scottish Constitutional Convention in 1989, both devolutionary landmarks later claimed by the SNP (see SNP-sponsored debates in Westminster Hall, the Commons and at Holyrood in recent years). Furthermore, the rhetoric of social democracy was not matched with legislative action, a tension which had also characterised Scottish Labour in devolved government between 1999 and 2007.

Only belatedly had the SNP come around to supporting devolution. Indeed, it was Alex Salmond's major achievement gradually to persuade his sceptical party to stop worrying and learn to, if not love devolution then at least, realise its potential. Salmond played a high-profile role in the cross-party 'Scotland Forward' campaign, alongside Scottish Labour, the Scottish Liberal Democrats and celebrity backers like Sir Sean Connery, which gave him and his party a clear, visible stake in the devolution project despite the rhetoric of the last decade, ie 'Labour couldn't deliver a pizza let alone a Parliament'.

The 1999 election was important in another respect, for the SNP stated its intention to use the new Parliament's tax-varying powers to add a 'Penny for Scotland' to the basic rate. That the party then lost the election to Labour (although there were other factors), found its leadership cool on the widely-held notion that 'middle Scotland' would accept higher taxation in return for better public services. For most of the next twenty years, the party's social democratic credentials ended up resting upon non-fiscal tenets.

Scottish Labour in Office, But Not in Power

Scottish Labour's period in office from 1999 to 2007 (with Liberal Democrat support) was not a happy experience for the party. After a sustained campaign for a Scottish Parliament and coming to see it as an effective block against any future Thatcherite agenda being 'imposed' upon Scotland, it had given little thought to the policies and ideas it would actually implement. This, combined with the party's lack of autonomy, ambivalent national leadership and propensity of most of its big beasts to remain at Westminster, weakened Labour, although the consequences of this were mitigated in the early years of the Parliament by the SNP's own issues, such as coming to terms with being, for the first time, a professional political party with a sizeable parliamentary group – the only experience prior to this being the 11 MPs elected to the House of Commons in October 1974.

By default, Scottish Labour positioned itself to the left of New Labour: resisting Blairite policies such as foundation hospitals, city academies and (top-up) tuition fees, and hence able to depict its centrist managerialism as somehow 'left'. This reduced Scottish politics to a bidding war between Labour and SNP of who could be the most anti-New Labour, which became easier for the SNP after Tony Blair's decision to support the Iraq War in 2003.

The SNP *Takes Control of the Story*

Labour's troubles in office, both at Holyrood and at Westminster, allowed the SNP to present themselves as having a sense of purpose and a new 'story' for the Scottish Parliament, and eventually to claim the story of Scottish devolution as their own. In this retelling, it was SNP pressure, both electorally and via the push for independence, which had compelled Labour to support devolution, at first hesitantly in the 1970s, and then more substantially in the 1980s and 1990s.

Like many political stories, there was some truth in this, particularly regarding Labour's conversion to devolution in the 1970s. But the claim that the constitutional consensus of the 1980s and 1990s somehow hinged upon SNP pressure, when the party had absented itself from many of its critical moments prior to the 1997 referendum, was less credible. In ideological terms, the SNP's anti-New Labourism has to be put in a broader context. The working title of the SNP's 2007 manifesto was *A Culture of Independence*, and as the then deputy leader Nicola Sturgeon conceded, it was a recognition that as Labour shifted to the right, the SNP had perhaps become rather 'centralist and statist' in outlook. Governments, she added, 'should not go around getting in people's way when they don't need to'. So eradicating student debt, lightening the burden of local taxation and encouraging small businesses, argued Sturgeon, were all intended

> to give individuals a fair crack of the whip… aspirational policies about people progressing and making the most of themselves (*Sunday Times*, 8 January 2006).

It all sounded very New Labour, though paradoxically the party missed few opportunities to attack Blairism for its rightward drift.

The SNP *in Government*

If the creation of a Scottish Parliament shaped the framework for future SNP success, then the 2007 election finally realised the party's long-standing dream

of replacing Labour as Scotland's dominant centre-left party, though any prospect of doing so with a genuinely radical policy agenda had been gradually
shelved in the late 1990s. Nevertheless, there remained important points of
differentiation: tuition fees, for example, became the leitmotif of the Nationalist approach, an explicit rejection of the Blairite education agenda but also one
that flagged the difference between largely mythical Scottish traditions of 'free
education' and an increasingly marketized English approach. A long-standing commitment to unilateral nuclear disarmament also enabled the SNP to
outflank Labour on the left, albeit in a policy area over which the devolved
parliament had no control.

Alex Salmond's administration, however, was more competent than radical.
Despite plentiful rhetoric about 'social justice', the SNP allowed the Scottish Parliament's existing tax-varying powers to lapse, signalling a striking lack of interest in redistribution. Yet what resonated was the story told over the next four
years, of a Scottish Parliament which had finally found its voice, with ministers
working tirelessly to articulate Scotland's 'myths of identity', as Tom Nairn had
written in 1968, in order to 'suit everyone', casting their populist policies as
widely as possible, left, right and centre, making good on the SNP's claim to be
the 'national' party of Scotland (Nairn, 1968).

Conscious that Labour remained a barrier to achieving independence, the
SNP repeatedly depicted it as having ditched its principles and lost its soul.
Labour hit back on points of detail but ended up looking – especially as it
campaigned for a No vote alongside Conservatives in the 2014 referendum – as
if it no longer believed its own story, that Scotland was more left-wing, more
egalitarian and anti-Tory than England. Shrewdly, the SNP simply took up the
old battle cries associated with the long campaign for a Scottish Parliament and
repackaged them as arguments for independence.

There were, of course, contradictions within this Nationalist narrative: the
SNP was anti-nuclear but pro-NATO, committed to free university tuition but
content to cut grants and college places; pro-EU but opposed to the single currency and Common Fisheries Policy; economically it often talked orthodox left
but tended to act conventionally right, pledging to cut corporation tax, and
keep personal taxation low. Only in 2017, a decade into office, did the SNP
hesitantly embrace the politics of fiscal redistribution as further taxation powers were devolved, but even then, it did so while trying to keep a 'One Nation'
nationalism narrative intact.

The Scottish Government's 2013 independence White Paper, meanwhile,
was a curious mixture of 1980s left-wing rhetoric and orthodox neo-liberal

economics, which underlined the SNP's ongoing progressive dilemma (Scottish Government, 2013). So did Salmond's ecumenical welcome to

> voices to the left of the SNP's social democratic position speaking up in favour of independence,

and support 'from the entrepreneurial and more free-market perspective' (Torrance, 2015). When figures such as Tony Blair adopted such a 'big tent' approach it earned Nationalist condemnation for 'selling out', yet Salmond's similar approach attracted strikingly little criticism, even from those on the left of the independence movement.

Similarly, the SNP's economic prospectus for independence, updated by Andrew Wilson in his May 2018 Sustainable Growth Commission report, represented a significant challenge to the careful balancing act that had been the SNP's centre-left sensibilities accommodated with fiscal and global realities (Sustainable Growth Commission, 2018). The Commission acknowledged that (at least) the first decade of independence would involve major constraints on public services, an admission of reality it avoided calling 'austerity'. But faced with significant resistance from the left, inside and outside the party, the leadership seemed at first unwilling to conduct a wider debate, eventually firming up the position on an independent currency, and holding a major debate at the 2019 SNP spring conference. This saw a rare defeat for the leadership on the speed of transition to an independent currency (*Sunday Times*, 28 April 2019). Whether this alters the political dynamics within the party and the cautious centrism of the leadership remains in doubt.

Paisley and Renfrewshire South MP Mhairi Black's celebrated Westminster maiden speech in July 2015 claimed it was 'the Labour Party that left me, not the other way about'. Nationalism, she asserted, had 'nothing to do' with the SNP's advance in Scotland, rather it had triumphed on a 'wave of hope' that there was an alternative to 'the Thatcherite neo-liberal policies' propagated by Westminster (*Hansard*, 2015). This analysis was played and replayed, especially on social media platforms where Black's address became an online sensation, and by other SNP politicians elected in 2015, such as Tommy Sheppard (Edinburgh East) and Chris Law (Dundee West). It had become part of nationalist, and even national, mythology.

The election of left-winger Jeremy Corbyn as UK Labour leader in September 2015 challenged the SNP's narrative, at least regarding the British, if not Scottish, Labour Party. It required a shifting of ground and found Mhairi Black instead arguing that the 'main reason' she supported independence was the 'democratic deficit', meaning Scotland having to accept UK Governments it did not vote for. The later election of left-winger Richard Leonard as Scottish

Labour leader, in November 2017, posed another challenge to the SNP's claim to Labour's values and territory, although by this time Labour in Scotland was not in a strong position to contest them.

Interviewed by *Prospect* shortly after her election in 2015, SNP Tasmina Ahmed-Sheikh MP admitted her party's economic stance was a mix of pro-business ideas that would 'traditionally be thought of as centre or centre-right', albeit with a strong sense of social responsibility. But when challenged that she was, therefore, a Blairite, Ahmed-Sheikh sounded horrified, replying: 'Absolutely not' (Kutchinsky, 2015). She went on to suggest that the SNP's recent election victory had shifted politics away from the traditional axis of left and right, apparently unaware that this had been how the SNP had presented itself pre-1979.

The SNP also tended to co-opt figures from the Labour movement, usually after they had passed into retirement. Two of the most prominent examples of this, both courted by Alex Salmond, were former STUC General Secretary Campbell Christie and the former Communist and UCS shop steward Jimmy Reid.

In a biography of Jimmy Reid, the former SNP minister Kenny MacAskill attempted to demonstrate that the SNP and independence were the true inheritors of Labour's socialist values. MacAskill, summarising Reid's personal journey and that of Scottish politics, wrote:

> The British road to socialism had become the Scottish road to independence and we shone the light for many of the Scottish working-class (MacAskill, 2017).

MacAskill also conceded that the SNP was not the socialist party that Reid had aspired to but implied this was as good as it got in the real world. A chapter in his Reid biography entitled 'Steps on the Scottish Road' set out a conventional nationalist account of 1980s Scottish political history; latter he quotes at length a Reid essay from 2007 published in *Scottish Left Review* on the SNP and Labour in which he asserted:

> The custodianship of Scotland's national aspirations literally fell into the hands of the Nationalists. They now govern Scotland with policies that objectively can only be described as social democratic (MacAskill, 2017).

As revealing was the SNP's record in office, one of caution, competence and of folding earlier Labour-Lib Dem achievements into a story they claimed for themselves. Thus, free care for the elderly, the 'abolition' of tuition fees and free bus passes, which had all been enacted pre-2007, were combined with the abolition of prescription charges and the Council Tax freeze as proof of SNP 'delivery'. Critically, the SNP in government told a long-established story about 'progressive politics' with more aplomb than Scottish Labour.

Defining Social Democracy

Social democracy is paradoxically everywhere in Scottish politics, and yet hard to pin down – left deliberately undefined by those who claim to imbibe it. This strange state of affairs often goes unmentioned by large numbers of protagonists, whether politicians, the media or the wider policy community, almost as if no one wants to comment on the emperor's new clothes.

Thus, the early days of the Scottish Parliament featured much talk of Scotland's 'social democratic consensus', for some its virtues, and for others, those on the right such as *The Scotsman*'s Andrew Neil, its limitations. Centre-left politics in Scotland have long been heavy on rhetoric from the days of 'Red Clydeside' and the ILP, particularly as Labour and the SNP competed over who were the most authentic social democrats.

In the late 1990s, Labour easily came out on top, having legislated for a Scottish Parliament and its historic commitment to social justice. But, over time, the SNP were able to outflank Labour, not only for the aforementioned reasons of limited party autonomy and certain aspects of UK Blairite policies, but also through language and rhetoric: while Labour often appeared apologetic, the SNP told a more upbeat, positive story during Salmond's second tenure as leader (2004–14), particularly at the 2007 and 2011 Holyrood elections.

Ben Jackson has convincingly analysed the politics of Salmond, Blair and Brown as all being shaped by the need for centre-left modernisation in light of changing economic and societal realities. But where Blair and Brown had contributed to, and encouraged debate on, what social democracy was, no such debate was facilitated by Salmond – or the SNP – during its period in office (Jackson, 2012). In a subsequent analysis, Jackson also argued that, for the SNP, the role of social democracy in relation to independence has never been completely clear. Was social democracy merely an instrumental means of mobilising support for independence, or was a more powerful social democracy the ultimate vision of what an independent Scotland ought to look like? Jackson concluded that if it were the latter, the SNP in government would have pursued a very different agenda, whereas it had merely used social democracy as a framing device and mobiliser (Jackson, 2017).

All politicians of the left have a simple choice: either persuade voters to support an authentically progressive agenda or contrive a prospectus that merely identifies what they already believe packaged in the language of radical reform. In essence, both Alex Salmond and Nicola Sturgeon, in common with most of their Labour counterparts since the 1960s, opted for the latter. The danger for the party is that it will increasingly resemble what it claims to detest, ie New Labour, endlessly compromising and constantly campaigning in an attempt to reconcile free-market economics with a hazy belief in social justice. Perhaps, like other parties and movements throughout Europe, the contemporary SNP is just another example of post-ideological politics, in which the distinction between left and right has become blurred not only in the minds of political strategists, but also voters.

Scotland has seen a high degree of continuity across the devolution era, between the Labour-Lib Dem period of 1999 to 2007 and SNP one of 2007 to 2019. Both have been characterised by 'social democratic' and 'radical' rhetoric, while actually being centrist and managerialist in government. No one wants to admit it of their respective period in office but underlying both has been a soft Blairism without acknowledging the enduring influence of Tony Blair. The SNP may have successfully co-opted Labour's mantle, its 'story' of Scotland and of devolved government, but it is one that could be subject to the relentless law of diminishing returns.

A large part of the Scottish 'politics of difference' has consisted of diverging from the rest of the UK by *not* doing things, and by *not* standing up to vested interests and insider groups. One major question for the SNP as incumbents is how long a politics of the domestic status quo that avoids major redistribution can continue to present itself as centre-left and social democratic? The SNP have stolen what were once the Scottish Labour Party's accounts of social democracy and devolution, and hence, modern Scotland. Under Scottish Labour these became stories of the political establishment – of a party about power, patronage and the insider class, and hence laid the seeds of the party's long-term decline. The SNP in adopting thee perspectives has itself become the party of the political establishment, and of patronage and the interests of the insider class, in an age of anger and insurgency. All politics follows the rule that what comes up must come down, and the SNP will have to hope that they can ride this wave to the successful conclusion of a second Indyref. Otherwise the party will have to face major strategic choice about its future direction, how it does politics, and the kind of Scotland it aspires to create.

References

Hansard (2015), HC Debs, vol. 598 cc. 775–77, 14 July 2015, available online at: https://publications.parliament.uk/pa/cm201516/cmhansrd/cm150714/debtext/150714-0002.htm

Jackson, B. (2012), 'The Moderniser: Alex Salmond's Journey', *Renewal: A Journal of Social Democracy*, available online at: www.renewal.org.uk/articles/the-moderniser-alex-salmonds-journey/

Jackson, B. (2017), 'The State of Social Democracy and the Scottish National-
    ists', in Hassan, G. and Barrow, S. (eds.), *A Nation Changed? The SNP and
    Scotland Ten Years On*, Edinburgh: Luath Press.
Kutchinsky, S. (2015), 'The SNP has a right wing – and here she is', *Prospect*,
    June 2015, available at: www.prospectmagazine.co.uk/magazine/inter-
    view-tasmina-
    ahmed-sheikh-the-snp-has-a-right-wing-and-here-she-is
MacAskill, K. (2017), *Jimmy Reid: A Scottish Political Journey*, London: Bite-
    back Books.
Nairn, T. (1968), 'The Three Dreams of Scottish Nationalism', *New Left
    Review*, 49, available online at: https://newleftreview.org/I/49/tom-nairn-
    the-three-dreams-
    of-scottish-nationalism
Scottish Government (2013), 'Scotland's Future: Your Guide to an Independent
    Scotland', Edinburgh: Scottish Government.
Sustainable Growth Commission (2018), *Scotland: The New Case for Opti-
    mism: A strategy for inter-generational economic renaissance*, Edinburgh:
    SNP, available online at: www.sustainablegrowthcommission.scot/
Torrance, D. (2015), *Salmond: Against the Odds*, Edinburgh: Birlinn, 3rd
    edition.

CHAPTER 40

The Art of Leaving and Arriving
Brexit, Scotland and Britain

Fintan O'Toole

Does the Afterlife Exist?

THIS THEN IS WHAT the afterlife of dead things looks like. Many obituaries have been hastily written over the last couple of years but one of them is the mirage of Brexit itself. When did Brextinction occur? On 24 June 2016. The project was driven by decades of camped-up mendacity about the tyranny of the EU and sold in the referendum as a fantasy of national liberation. It simply could not survive contact with reality. It died the moment it became real.

Even if Theresa May were a political genius – and let us concede that she is not – Brexit was always going to come down to a choice between two evils: the heroic but catastrophic failure of crashing out, or the unheroic but less damaging failure of swapping first-class for second-class EU membership. These are the real afterlives of a departed reverie.

If the choice between shooting oneself in the head or in the foot is the answer to Britain's long-term problems, then we can sure that the wrong question is being asked. Over the past three years it has become ever clearer that Brexit is not about its ostensible subject: Britain's relationship with the EU. The very word Brexit contains a literally unspoken truth. It does not include or even allude to Europe. It is British exit that is the point, not what it is exiting from. The tautologous slogan 'Leave Means Leave' is similarly (if unintentionally) honest: the meaning is in the leaving, not in what is being left or how.

Paradoxically, this drama of departure has really served only to displace a crisis of belonging. Brexit plays out a conflict between Them and Us, but it is surely obvious that the problem is not with Them on the continent. Firstly, it is with the British Us, the unravelling of an imagined community and secondly, within that and claiming ownership rights is an English Us – with severe consequences for England, the rest of the UK and Ireland. The visible collapse of the Westminster polity played out week-in and week-out over recent years may be a result of Brexit, but Brexit itself is the result of the invisible subsidence of the political order over decades.

England and Brexit

If you think like this, it makes sense to see Brexit as a re-assertion of the true English character, a last-gasp rescuing of its distinctiveness from the incoming tides of Euro-blandness. And thus, to see self-parodying eccentrics like Boris Johnson and Jacob Rees-Mogg, not just as the saviours of this endangered Englishness but embodiments of it. Eccentricity was a revolt against the tyranny of conformity. The more it flourished, the more the English could distinguish themselves as a nation of free thinkers.

The idea of eccentricity has a long history as a signifier of English freedom. England's glorying in eccentrics (actually only those of the male and upper-class variety), so the story went, contrasted favourably with the conformism of slavish continentals and was thus a kind of personal tribute to the virtues of the English constitution and character.

This idea had more than an element of religious prejudice. Protestants thought for themselves, while Catholics (especially the French) were mindless followers of authority. Eccentricity was the proof of the value England placed on individualism: only in England could you be free to behave in a manner that most of society regarded as odd. John Stuart Mill, the great theorist of British liberalism, was quite explicit about this. In *On Liberty* he wrote that:

> Precisely because the tyranny of opinion is such as to make eccentricity a reproach, it is desirable, in order to break through that tyranny, that people should be eccentric (Mill, 1859).

Eccentricity was a revolt against the tyranny of conformity. The more it flourished, the more the English could distinguish themselves as a nation of free-thinkers and portray England (and hence Britain) as not what it actually is a normal European country.

The English Masses

Of course, this was always a myth. In the 1940s, George Orwell evoked a self-image of the English masses that was the opposite of eccentric:

> the gentle-mannered, undemonstrative, law-abiding English... the orderly behaviour of English crowds, the lack of pushing and quarrelling, the willingness to form queues (Orwell, 1947).

Perhaps the English valued their eccentrics precisely because they were actually much more obedient and orthodox than they liked to acknowledge.

In any case, upper-class male eccentricity was meant to be free of damage – the invariable modifier of 'eccentric' in the English language was 'harmless'. And so, it was: when your ruling class is running a vast empire and your practical industrialists are leading the world, you can afford a decorative eccentric or two. The eccentric Englishman was a self-conscious indulgence, a way of disguising the relentless reality of global domination. The English liked to see even their empire, not as a ruthless machine, but as an almost accidental side effect of curious gentlemen wandering off the beaten track.

Brexit has a way of reviving habits of mind that no longer conform to reality. Except this time there is a twist, the harmless eccentric has mutated into the harmful kind. The rise to prominence of an eccentric Eurosceptic Toryism can be seen as some sort of heritage industry play: a sort of geo-political farce in the style of 'Downton Abbey', but that would be to mistake style and code for substance. While the former have a familiarity and even comfort in evoking past cultural norms and the ritual humiliation of the masses, what this is being used for in the *über*-Brexiteer vision is a Britain and England of Them and Us which is both utopian and dystopian, and drawing from the past to import Britain into a turbo-charged, free-wheeling, deal-making, spivs on steroids version of the future. It is the collective responsibility of numerous different forces in Britain that it has had such traction. Step forward the British Labour Party and what went wrong long before Jeremy Corbyn, the Lib Dems, and the timidity of too many constitutional reformers through the years.

What Went Wrong with Britain?

The other afterlife that is in front of us is that of Britain itself: the state called the United Kingdom of Great Britain and Northern Ireland – a name and territory it has only held from 1922. There have been successive rebellions and mutinies in the last two generations, most obviously the Scottish and Welsh experiments in self-government, and the Northern Irish trauma of the 30-year Troubles. Post-1997, Edinburgh, Cardiff and in a more stop-start way, Belfast, have developed as alternative political centres with their own dynamics and heartbeats, and agendas increasingly ignored and found incomprehensible by the heart of the British political state. It is not a way to run a sustainable state in the long run.

It may seem strange to call this slow collapse invisible since so much of it is obvious: the deep uncertainties about the union after the Good Friday Agreement of 1998 and the establishment of the Scottish Parliament the following

year; the consequent rise of English nationalism; the profound regional inequalities within England itself; the generational divergence of values and aspirations;
the undermining of the welfare state and its promise of shared citizenship; the
contempt for the poor and vulnerable expressed through austerity; the rise of a
sensationally self-indulgent and clownish ruling class. But the collective effects
of these inter-related developments seem to have been barely visible within the
political mainstream until David Cameron accidentally took the lid off by calling the EU referendum and asked people to endorse the status quo.

What we see with the mask pulled back and the fog of fantasies at last
beginning to dissipate is the revelation that Brexit is much less about Britain's
relationship with the EU than it is about Britain's relationship with itself. It is
the projection outwards of an inner turmoil. An archaic political system carried
on even while its foundations in a collective sense of belonging were crumbling.
Brexit in one way alone has done a real service: it has forced the old system to
play out its death throes in public. The spectacle is ugly, but at least it shows
that a fissiparous four-nation state cannot be governed without radical social
and constitutional change.

In the aftermath of June 2016, the EU have continually expressed exaspera-
tion that the British have really been negotiating not with them, but with each
other. But perhaps it is time to recognise that there is a useful truth in this. Brexit
is really just the vehicle that has delivered a fraught state to a place where it can
no longer pretend to be a settled and functioning democracy. Brexit's work is
done – everyone can now see that Westminster is dead. It is time to move on
from the pretence that the problem with British democracy is the EU and to
recognise that it is with itself. After Brextinction there must be a whole new
political ecosystem. Drop the dead dodo, end the mad race for a meaningless
prize, and start talking about who you want to be, entailing the architecture that
connects and relates the peoples of the four nations of the UK and which dis-
mantles the rotten, decaying pretensions and illusions at the centre of political
power. Easier said than done when even in a floundering and collapsing edifice
ruling elites never give up their place and importance voluntarily. Even in late
crisis and the world of afterlives it is going to require effort.

The Scottish Question, Self-Determination and National Freedom

Scotland as an increasingly self-governing nation has been a leading force in
attempting to remake the idea of Britain, and increasingly, in surveying the
wreckage looking for new arrangements. The British elites have had all sorts of

last notices and warnings of the need to change their ways, the biggest of which was the 2014 independence referendum. A popular and civic engagement about what sort of country Scotland aspired to be and where it saw its collective future produced a re-energised public sphere: one beyond even the comprehension of the SNP to marshal and understand. It isn't very surprising then that this northern popular uprising proved beyond the grasp of the British Government to recognise they were in 'last saloon' territory. So, it has proven, with Cameron and the entire Westminster political tribe considering Scotland a closed discussion. Have Theresa May or Jeremy Corbyn one original insight or suggestion with regard to Scotland post-2014 and even more post-Brexit? To ask the question is to underline the paucity of their thinking.

An independent Scotland would face many of the same limits on its freedom of action as it does now. The power of oligarchies and markets and inequalities to restrict democratic choice would not disappear. Freedom does not arrive just because you declare it. And if it ever does arrive, it is complicated, constrained and contested. Scots, coming late to the business of national independence, also come to it with few illusions. Too much has happened to too many dreams of national liberation for any sensible citizen to believe in a great moment of transformation after which everything will be simpler, purer, better.

But national freedom isn't meaningless either. Room to manoeuvre can be expanded. Democratic spaces can be opened up. The terms of the struggle between public and private interests can be renegotiated. Citizens can become more confident of their power to insist on decency and dignity. A place can be defined as a society and a culture as well as an economy. And the greater the constraints, and the more naked the power of unaccountable elites, the more vital it is that whatever collective freedom remains is grasped.

Like everything else, though, even this qualified freedom has a price. Some are literal – the financial losses that have to be set against financial gains. But there's another kind of reckoning to be done, one that is more abstract but perhaps in the long-term more important. National freedom isn't another word for nothing left to lose. It is another word for no one left to blame – that is, except yourself. If you make your own choices, you become responsible for their consequences.

This is, especially for small nations which have long been part of a larger imperial whole, a severe loss. There is a deep and abiding satisfaction in imagining how wonderful you would be if only those foreign bastards would let you. Being free means having to live with the dawning realisation that you might not be so wonderful after all.

Freedom in this sense is not an illusion – it is an act of deliberate disillusion. What has to be broken free of is not just the big bad Them. It is also the warm, fuzzy Us of the nationalist imagination – the Us that is nicer, holier, more caring. Us and Them politics even has its limits in progressive Scotland. What a free country quickly discovers is that the better Us of its imagination is not already there, fully formed, just waiting to blossom in the sun of liberation. It has to be created and to do so you have to genuinely decide that you want it.

WB Yeats described this kind of freedom well in the early years of the Irish Free State in the mid-1920s. He and his artistic collaborators were under attack for daring to put on stage ugly images of an Irish reality. Yeats drew attention to a crucial distinction between national pride and national vanity:

> The moment a nation reaches intellectual maturity, it becomes exceedingly proud and ceases to be vain and when it becomes exceedingly proud it does not disguise its faults (Foster, 2003).

What Yeats meant is that before a nation becomes free, it has to wallow in national vanity, creating an idealised picture of a special place and of a people with a unique destiny. When it acquires freedom, it has to replace this vanity with a national pride that consists in having the self-confidence to tell the truth about yourself. Nationalism is a form of myth-making; independence demands a lot of myth-breaking. It has to replace the distorting mirror of fantasy with the sharp reflection of a real self.

This kind of national pride is hard work. You have to decide what are the things your nation should be proud of and how it is going to achieve them in reality. In Scotland's case, this might mean moving away from claiming a special culture of egalitarianism and towards an honest appraisal of the massive structural inequalities that call that comforting self-image into question. It might mean, as Gerry Hassan argued so cogently in his book *Caledonian Dreaming*, abandoning the notion of Scotland as a wonderfully democratic society and getting to grips with the realities of social division and exclusion (Hassan, 2014). Without this hard work though, political independence lacks its necessary foundation of psychological independence. The country remains in thrall to a mythic version of itself. It is much easier to send an external government packing than it is to cut yourself off from the cosy and comforting self-image that dependent cultures create for themselves. But when you're on your own, those self-images cease to be warm and fuzzy, and turn toxic.

This is largely what happened to Ireland. It gradually disengaged from London rule. But it has struggled to disengage from the exaggerated notions of Irish specialness that were built up through that conflict. National vanity continued to hold sway: Ireland didn't have to deal with its deeply problematic realities because it was uniquely blessed. It was holier, happier, more cultured, more Gaelic, more spiritual, than anywhere else.

In more recent times, this archaic sense of a unique destiny was replaced with another set of equally delusional exaggerations: Ireland as the richest, most successful, most globalised economy in the world, where banks would grow forever, and property bubbles inflate to infinity. These delusions can be seen as compensation for centuries of repression, but they have made it hard for Ireland to deal with its own, humdrum, non-exceptional realities in everything from poverty and mass emigration to the victimisation of children and women.

Scotland's situation at the point of potential independence is infinitely better than Ireland's was in the 1920s. It does not risk the violence that stained Ireland's sense of its better self. Whatever happens, Scotland will not suffer the consequences of partition which, in Ireland's case, meant that the ideals of a pluralist democracy were lost in the creation of two mutually exclusive sectarian states. And Scotland has, as Ireland did not have at independence, the context of an EU which, for all its faults, gives small nations a set of international institutions within which they can make themselves heard and which will provide a special welcome to Scotland after the trials of Brexit.

These advantages give Scottish independence, by historical standards, a remarkably fair wind. If it happens, it will also create its own energy of euphoria. But fair winds and moments of ecstasy do not last very long in a harsh environment of long-term global instabilities. Nationalism is a rocket fuel that can get you out of the orbit of an old order but burns quickly and leaves you dependent on much more complex and subtle systems of guidance to get you through the lonely expanses of historic space. Nationalism on its own is never enough. Look at Ireland. Look at anywhere in the world. It does not matter how 'civic' and inclusive your nationalism is, and this is the prevailing story of contemporary Scottish nationalism – it is still a nationalism – it can only take you so far.

Those guidance systems will have to be calibrated to Scotland as it is and the world as it is, not to any nostalgic belief that the conditions of an idealised older Britain can simply be recreated in 21st century circumstances. For an outsider like me, this is what is actually most interesting about the possibility of Scottish independence. It is not that Scotland might become a new state, but that it might become a new kind of state. For independence to be meaningful, Scotland would have to start with an acknowledgement that many of the things to which it appeals – the power of government, the legitimacy of democratic institutions, the equality of citizens – are in crisis. They cannot be assumed; they have to be radically reinvented.

After Brexit

New Beginnings?

How then is it possible to escape the different interpretations of Us and Them as the UK stutters and staggers to some kind of endpoint? The political mindset which has captured England as Britain did not arrive overnight, but has deep roots and traditions, and will not be easily defeated. Problematic, conservative forces are not just found in the Brexiteer outliers and Theresa May's limited leadership, but in those claiming otherwise: the self-declared radicals of the Corbynista project and new found centrist evangelicals in search of a new party and voice, both of whom seek a future Britain in different and unattainable versions of the past.

The rest of us across this archipelago have responsibilities beyond our own territorial politics: first, to map out and connect the emerging politics of self-government and self-determination while seeing the search for statehood as not an end in itself but a desire for a different politics and idea of the state; second, the Brexit debacle is fast tracking numerous issues that are a mixture of bubbling under, supposedly under control, stuck in constitutional permafrost, or provisionally decided or 'parked' by the centre. The most obvious are the Scottish and Northern Irish questions, but there will be numerous issues that emerge from the other side of any Brexit that we can only at the moment guess at.

Finally, there is the question for all of us about what future beckons for England. Some of my interventions on Brexit have met the response that I am caricaturing England to the extent that a comparison would be to attempt to understand Ireland through the eyes of the IRA (Goodhart, 2019). The point I have been trying to get over is that the English political imagination, or accurately, a noisy, influential section of it, has been captured by forces who offer a caricature of England: of un-reconstructed history, of Us and Them, and a politics which is anti-modern, intolerant, and anti-democratic.

Scotland is already halfway out of the ruined building; but how you conduct yourself in the face of provocation and England's journey into self-delusion has implications for the future you embrace and make? A quiet transformation of a country, its politics and sense of itself has gathered force over the previous twenty years. It may now require a different set of skills in the context of Brexit Britain and its fantasies, but within the chaos and tumult, Scotland can take solace in that it has friends in many places, in Ireland, the EU and across the world, and can draw from them to chart a new course. We have to aspire to more than reducing civic life to Us versus Them. Scotland has that chance. Welcome to taking charge of your own future.

References

Foster, R.F. (2003), *WB Yeats: A Life: Volume Two: The Arch-Poet 1915–1939*, Oxford: Oxford University Press.

Goodhart, D. (2019), 'Looking for the soul of England', *New Statesman*, 6 February 2019.

Hassan, G. (2014), *Caledonian Dreaming: The Quest for a Different Scotland*, Edinburgh: Luath Press.

Mill, J.S. (1859), *On Liberty*, 2016 reprint, London: CreateSpace Independent Publishing Platform.

Orwell, G. (1947), 'The English People', in *Essays*, 2002 edition, New York: Knoft.

After the First Twenty Years and the Next Scotland

Simon Barrow and Gerry Hassan

How Scotland Has Changed

THIS BOOK HAS surveyed and assessed a social landscape, politics and civic culture in Scotland that has undergone far reaching changes over the past twenty years, partly spurred by the devolution settlement and the genesis of the Scottish Parliament, and partly stretching well beyond the formal fabric of both.

Without doubt there has been a remaking of politics, power and who has voice during the past two decades. At the same time, there has been (of course) both continuity and discontinuity across the public sphere. But within all of that, it feels as if something fundamental has shifted. The idea of Scotland as 'a village' in political terms, a place where those with the contacts and influence take the decisions and others acquiesce, has been challenged and disturbed. It has been shown to be both limiting and false; a kind of corporatized, incorporated society that benefits the governing classes and civic tribes, rather than releasing energy and empowering communities to play a significant part in shaping their own destiny.

On the retreat too are many of the self-ingested caricatures and restrictions associated with Scotland being assigned (and dismissed) as belonging to a 'Celtic fringe' – a term which presupposes a range of common features and characteristics in the various peoples so labelled. It also implies an essentially dependent relationship between an assumed core and a designated periphery with another part of 'the British Isles', lowland England. The term, it should be noted, is

> essentially an English and metropolitan – and so outsider – construct. It also brings with its considerable ideological baggage arising out of England's historically fraught relations [and]... a pattern of English colonisation and cultural imperialism (Ellis, 2003).

Of course, the two decades marked by the establishment of the Scottish Parliament and a significant re-claiming of Scottish affairs within Scotland have not seen the 'cultural cringe' disappear entirely. The interpretation of the Brexit vote by many in England shows that attempts to marginalise Scotland are still alive (and that they are often not about Scotland). This peripheralization and regionalisation of Scotland has accelerated at Westminster post-Brexit vote as the British political classes and unionism has seemed to give up trying to understand and govern the divided kingdom that is the UK.

Moreover, there has been a profound shift in political gravity in the UK with two contradictory trends: the accumulation of power and status in a London-centric view of the world, and the development of alternative political centres of power in Edinburgh and Cardiff (and Belfast until the recent suspension of Stormont). Scotland's now assertive political autonomy and voice will not and cannot be reversed, but whatever our constitutional effect, we will have to continue living on a set of islands where 'the London-effect' – the interests of a political and economic elite – has huge impact on us.

Scotland's Futurescape

The key challenge at the end of this collection of essays is the task of beginning to assess, on the basis of an acknowledgment of the broad trends identified over the past twenty years, how we can more effectively embrace the Scotland of the future. This entails looking at how and where we can have more open conversations, creating spaces to develop thinking, ideas and practices which are grounded in real change and which go beyond superficialities and sound bites.

As noted in the introductory chapter, and as has become evident throughout the book, the futurescape of Scotland is being created every day in the here and now. This is an enormous positive. It is happening in thousands of ways, both small and unidentified and large and acknowledged, across the length and breadth of the country. These changes are not simply an epiphenomenon of the generation of a set of devolved institutions over twenty years, but about changes in both consciousness and agency brought about by civic and cultural engagement – a practical politics which refuses to be defined or appropriated by 'the political' as it is conceived of by parliaments and parties.

At the same time, however, the limits of 'continuity Scotland' and the technocratic mindset have been thrown into sharp relief over the past two decades. For all the rhetoric saying otherwise this has been the dominant strand of the devolution era – whether under Labour or the SNP. Its limitations have become more and more obvious. An inability to embrace the new or confront big questions, and a desire to accrue and maintain power and authority for its own sake, have not allowed the changes coming from the wider public sphere to reshape the formal political arena in ways that represent a clear break from the institutions and mindsets of top-down control.

The social democratic tradition in Scotland has many achievements to its name, but it has become, over the devolution era, increasingly a defensive outlook, aspiring to defend what we have, particularly from the post-war social compact, redressed in language and values tailored to here. It has not been hugely creative and outward looking, economically, socially and democratically. Yet, we should not be too hard on ourselves, for the last two decades have been a harsh climate for centre-left politics the world over, to which Scotland cannot be completely immune.

The Languages of Living with Many Scotlands

Too many conversations about our nation are posed as either/or. Thus, there are endless debates on whether Scotland is a conservative country or a radical nation; whether it is different from the rest of the UK, or not that different; whether it is Scottish nationalist or unionist. These debates miss that it is possible to be two things or even more at once. Scotland clearly is a conservative nation in many respects and has had a long outlook on many public issues – economic, social, ethical and moral – where it has not embraced change easily. But it is also a nation with a radical, dissenting tradition, which at times has asked serious questions of those with power: the 2014 Indyref being only the most recent. Even that most famous of binary debates – the referendum – at its best allowed for a rich interpretation of Scotland's potential futures; but it was clearly not this for everyone.

The world of binary Scotland is the articulation of the divided Scotland trope, used through the ages to pathologize difference and raise self-doubt and lack of confidence. It has said that Scotland is too divided – between Protestant and Catholic, Highland and Lowland, West and East, SNP and Labour – to be a fully functioning self-governing nation. It has always been a deception and a deflection to say just put up with the way things are and the status quo. Instead, we should not duck these challenges, but embrace them and celebrate the many Scotlands that are within our borders and multiple identities which exist and say loudly that difference and diversity makes us stronger not weaker.

Moreover, to do this we have to take on the parts of our society who want to retreat to their respective bunkers and live in a monocultural nation, emphasising only their identities and traditions, while trying to deny others their place and voice.

This means we have to talk about and confront toxic Scotland. Unreflective tribalism of any expression – left, nationalist, unionist, centre or right – harms and hinders our wider body politic. However, such deformations do not exist in a political vacuum. They occur in an environment where political leadership is wary of taking risks, facing challenges or mapping out new directions. Related to this is the complexity, diversity and ambiguity of living in an age where, on the one hand, social media has coarsened as well as enlivened discourse, and where elements of public life that previously operated through traditional gate-keepers have weakened, along with old hierarchical codes and boundaries.

This leaves Scotland with the momentous task of negotiating a fresh set of ethics and ideals for living together in a way that respects diversity while seeking justice, accountability, participation and a necessary degree of social harmony. That conversation, which also needs to take environmental sustainability as its foundation, feels like it has hardly begun. Indeed, the general noise and vituperation of political life, and the disruption or disaggregation of ideas and institutions that previously glued together the UK, have allowed little adequate space for it to happen.

This touches on another important issue effecting how we are, or can be, 'together' as a nation, and as part of a bigger set of relationships within Britain and Europe. Scotland used to be a very violent society. This is a country that systematically belted school children until 1987; and in which Glasgow was until recently the 'murder capital of Europe', a record it has now thankfully lost. But we still have too much of a culture of violence, exclusion and blighted lives hanging over large parts of our society, including, damningly, in what can be described as relatively prosperous economic times for the majority of the population.

Creating a different future involves facing our demons as well as celebrating our virtues. In the past, many assumed a common or dominant religious framework for doing that. This no longer persists. Scotland is a mixed belief society. Secularisation has eroded trust and confidence in hierarchies claiming transcendent validation, the narratives they relied upon and the power they wielded to enforce them. This is a good thing overall, we would argue. But it leaves a significant task of re-forging social and cultural bonds, creating cross-communal conversations and reaching collective agreements of the kind that can nourish a genuine sense of commonality as well as diversity. This is, simultaneously, a sociological and spiritual task.

So, what, in practical terms, will help bring the Scotland of the future into being on the basis of the immediate conditions and challenges we have outlined? We suggest below a number of possible initiatives – none of which are unrealisable or utopian, but all of which require courage and investment.

Idea Scotland

In the politico-social realm there is an urgent need to nurture new centres of policy, ideas and experimentation. One expression of this would be the creation of more think tanks: a flawed model perhaps, but one area in which Scotland suffers by their relative absence. At present there are only two independent-ly constituted think tanks in the conventional sense: Reform Scotland and the Institute of Public Policy Research (IPPR) Scotland. There is also the hybrid Common Weal, which has positioned itself as a pro-independence do-tank and produces many interesting reports. However, it has been plagued by a lack of solid funding (being supported by crowdfunding) and what some see as a lack of proper process in its work: both of which make the case for more substantive initiatives needing to occur.

More than a decade into the SNP as a party of government the absence of an independent minded and supportive (but autonomous and challenging) think tank for the current party of government is a telling omission. The SNP over the entire devolution period has been focused on first, a party strategy, and then winning and utilising the agencies of the state. What it has hitherto shown is a lack of interest or understanding in creating new institutions and autonomous capacity.

A possible model for the SNP to follow is provided by Labour, and the centre-left's involvement, in the creation of IPPR following a succession of Labour defeats in the 1980s. People sympathetic to Labour, but not bound by them, created this new body with support of the party leadership. But the whole project came not from the party or the leadership, but from those operating in proximity rather than conformity to the party. A similarly scoped initiative in Scotland is sorely needed – and indeed has more propitious terrain to start with, since the SNP have not yet suffered electoral defeat, but is surely facing a stalling of its project without fresh ideas and inspiration. The Growth Commission, technocratic and managerial in style, unimaginative and constrained in output, showed how not to do this (Sustainable Growth Commission, 2018). A different style and approach are required.

In this area, the think tank issue is but one expression of a wider malaise. Indeed, the current form of think tankery and wonkery needs challenging. Scot-land (and Britain) needs resourced thought spaces which are not simply tied to parties, corporations or the policy round, but which can re-tell the story of change and focus our imagination, as well as our practical energies, on patterns of living which re-found the political, rather than simply conform to its expecta-tions. The name and form of such bodies are yet to be arrived at and will require bold experimentation to realise them.

Invoking Popular Sovereignty

Both nationalists and unionists need to recognise that the present nature of constitutional politics and disputation is not sufficient to refit Scotland for the future. Political choices – about who governs, where and how – have to be made, of course. But the tradition of invoking popular sovereignty is needed to prevent these debates from becoming stale, unproductively fractious and log-jammed. 'A Claim of Right' is a powerful strand in the Scottish political tradition which can help here. There have been three previous claims: 1689, 1843, and 1988 (the latter in relation to the Thatcher Government and the democratic deficit). The Scottish Parliament recently re-invoked the last Claim in a 2012 vote (while Westminster accepted it as recently as 2018).

There is now an obvious relevance to the possibility of a fourth Claim which takes the tradition of popular sovereignty and gives it practical expression. This would sketch the principles of a new constitutionalism and the principles of political power, and further differentiate Scotland from the broken shipwreck of what is accurately called 'the English constitution' (a phrase used in the last Claim, referencing Bagehot).

Popular constitutionalism is evident the world over these days. It is the process whereby the making of new constitutions – once the preserve of the great and the good – has more and more become owned and created by the popular will; indeed, in many studies the participative nature of the process is deemed to be as important as any constitution's actual content. Iceland's (unfulfilled) experiment is one recent example in northern Europe. Citizens' Assemblies are a growing phenomenon, and one which Scotland can fruitfully make use of.

That said, the era of Scottish Constitutional Conventions (which while referencing a different political tradition was actually a top down talking shop) is over. The attraction of such a set of arrangements in the era of high Thatcherism made sense, but no longer. We can surely do much better. More-over, given the need to develop the Scottish Government and Scottish state in participatory ways, now is the time to further initiatives in popular sover-eignty with state support and legitimacy. For example, through the creation of a Citizens' Assembly looking to map out the country's future constitution-ally (and which could draw on the Irish example of such assemblies). This is something that the SNP and the Greens are now arguing for. The question is how and when it will be established. It needs to be set up and mandated by the Government in negotiation with civic organisations. Citizens' Assemblies (we are not restricted to just one) seeking to bring together a demonstrable cross sections of Scotland as a whole, could assist in breaking out of the log-jam on the independence and related questions, which have become fixated on process and timing, and instead get to the substance of what it is we are trying to decide and achieve.

Mapping Future Scotland

The underlying practical question about future Scotland still remains – how to think about and address the 'what comes next'. The last decade has seen an absence of national futures projects, and indeed there have not been any substantial public futures initiatives since Scotland 2020 and Glasgow 2020 (in which one of the authors was heavily involved).

Democratising the idea of the future and building 'future literacy' involves creating a national set of conversations in which people from all walks of life deliberate and decide on their preferred future Scotland, rather than it be owned and curated in a closed way by experts and institutions – which the two afore-mentioned projects showed the potential of. Framed in this way it can be a powerful mobilising tool.

However, to gain traction it requires resourcing, encouragement and engagement of people and places, in intermediate spaces where they have independence and integrity from the system, and alongside this, an interface with institutions of representation and governance nationally and locally. This latter point is not to control the project or its outcomes, but to offer a genuine line of communication – hopefully two-way – that increases the chance of change being embraced and implemented.

All of the above suggestions could help encourage and grow debate and potential in the country. They are all evolutionary rather than revolutionary, in that they go with the grain of the best of our traditions and instincts, seeking popular involvement rather than top-down manipulation. They would also take time, effort and money. The next Scotland cannot be built on the cheap and inclusive democracy is not a luxury but the condition of a negotiable, liveable future. It is also about challenging the retreat to minimal change Scotland, which can too often dominate the current system, mainstream politics and media framings. Likewise, a connective national conversation about the future, in involving the full diversity of the country (not simply the imaginings of the usual suspects in the Central belt) would by definition move away from the kind of Scottish essentialism which can infect both nationalist and unionist conceptions about how that future can be created, reducing vision to instrumentalism.

Viviculture

An Ideal for Living

The point of a civic-driven process to move the next Scotland forward is not simply that it involves people in the creation of their own future (vital though that is), but that it moves from the abstract to the concrete, from the general to the particular. That involves asking 'big questions' that need to be fleshed out with tangible narratives, examples and inspirations. Questions such as:

What kind of Scotland do we want to live in? In what ways will it be different from the here and now – and different beyond the presently framed constitutional question?

What kinds of change and change makers do we need to encourage?

How do we effect a different kind of state – this being an implicit offer in the 2014 independence argument? Such a state doesn't come about by osmosis; it needs to be willed into being (Barrow and Small, 2016).

All of this requires a political imagination, leadership and the engagement of differing philosophies and worldviews – ones that both emerge from and sustain a rich ecology of public debate and ideas. 'Ideals for living' requires emotional intelligence and humility. Critically they require the creation of an evolving political strategy to give them voice and agency, an awareness of timescales (operating in both the short and longer-term at the same time), and connectivity to the lived experience of everyday Scotland. This entails recognising that politics has to be centred on an understanding and celebration of viviculture – the love and nurturing of life and all that sustains it.

A politics of this kind would look very different from one that concentrated on the abstracts of the constitutional question – whether pro- or anti-independence. Nicola Sturgeon, to her credit, attempted this during the 2014 referendum, when she invoked a young child born in Scotland that year, named Kirsty, and imagined her potential life-chances (Sturgeon, 2012). We need more of this humanly (and humanely) scaled political conversation in Scotland. We need to be able to talk of a future that involves uncertainty and risk; that allows for doubt, unevenness, variety and contingency, rather than a false belief that we can control and predict everything. That prospect has to be more attractive and plausible for the next Scotland than more technocracy or 'better the devil you know', lowest-common-denominator thinking.

In contrast, the move towards a globally conscious, locally rooted and viviculture focused politics entails the creation of shared spaces and places where people can see themselves both reflected and included; where they can be and see themselves as active agents, and where they feel they can have a genuine say and voice. From this flows a very different manner of public debate and conversation, one which has due care for how we interact and relate to each other, gives importance to real lived experience and human testimony, and understands the importance of empathy and self-reflection. If this sounds too idealistic for some, such qualities are present in today's Scotland in many places, such as the journalist writings of Dani Garavelli and Peter Ross: the latter's *Daunderlust* collection being one of the great reads of the 2014 Indyref year capturing the human stories beyond the politics; or in the sensational success of Darren McGarvey's *Poverty Safari* (Ross, 2014; McGarvey, 2017). None of these perspectives are about abstractions or obtuse social theory but grounded in everyday Scotland and an understanding of the importance of viviculture, and what we need a lot more of.

This necessitates a politics and sensibility which goes beyond the tendency of left vanguardism and believing itself to be an enlightened elect, and the right's propensity to believe still that 'there is no alternative' and no other viable way to run the world. Too many radicals the world over have fallen into the *cul-de-sac* of miserablism and trying to tell people how wrong we are all living our lives, and that unless we change, we are away to hit economic disaster or environmental apocalypse (Duncombe, 2007). Similarly, in a far-reaching critique of left politics, the US writer Jonathan Matthew Smucker has argued that too often radicalism has too much emphasis on the self-serving practice of moralists and sainthood which leads to a *cul-de-sac* and avoids the challenge of contributing to an alternative popular morality and ethics (Smucker, 2017).

Finally, because of the age of constant change a sizeable portion of politics across the West is actually about invoking the past. We see this on the reactionary and populist right. But we also see it on the left: in the US opposition to Trump and elements of Black Lives Matter and even #MeToo movements, the Corbynista takeover of Labour on both sides of the argument, and in the Scottish independence debate. The US community organiser Michael Gecan has talked of re-enactment politics, whereby protestors act out past scripts, which once had power and potency, to increasingly diminishing returns (Gecan, 2004). In his argument, people increasingly play to a narrow cast of true believers, have a degree of self-righteousness and lack of awareness of how this comes across to people who don't share their passions. Gecan thinks much of the US left is prone to such behaviour, as have been parts of pro-independence opinion here post-2014.

Such a penetrating critique would ask demanding questions relevant to today's Scotland. Who are the main audience or target of any activities? Is it people on your own side, your opponents, media or the undecided? What is your power analysis, both of your own power in its depth, credibility, allies and potential sympathisers, and what is your power analysis of your opponents? Re-enactment politics are too often about insiders who are both actors and audience, essentially talking to themselves and giving themselves standing ovations in public. For all their radical and sometimes even revolutionary rhetoric, there is both a nostalgia for past struggles and even a restoration politics, harking back to previous and supposedly simpler times.

A politics that is not about re-enactment, that is not primarily invested in revisiting past triumphs and defeats, would be one that moved a further step towards making real the Scotland of the future. It also would be concerned with ensuring that it is informed by decent, humane and compassionate values, and that it is also, critically, reachable in the not too distant future.

Changing the Conversation

Changing Scotland requires an understanding of the ecologies, cultures and dynamics of public life, and the creation of William Mackenzie's 'community of the communicators' (see introduction) – one that recognises who has voice and who hasn't, along with the silences, omissions and gaps (Mackenzie, 1978). The environment for conversation and exchange in the public sphere has changed dramatically in recent decades. The timespan of the last twenty years covered in this book has been influenced by domestic and wider factors – from the decline of traditional media and authority to the rise of social media, all of them seen in the Indyref. This produced a 'Big Bang' of energy and engagement, followed by subsequent retrenchment, but in a context where what is 'normal' has been substantially altered.

Scotland is still – as charted here – marred by huge inequalities, poverty, powerlessness and a democracy which is simply not pluralist and diverse enough. These characteristics have not been addressed by the climate of the country post-2014, because some siren voices have taken it upon themselves to shout or abuse others in making their case. Some of the most passionate Yes and No supporters on the independence question have reduced politics to a form of trench warfare in which they see their side 'winning' through a war of attrition which shows little concern for the wider costs and causalities in public life.

There are shortcomings here on all sides. First, a politics of faith and certainty is ill-fitted to the 21st century world. Second, it creates a mindset of tribalism, 'othering' and fixed positions – ergo, all No supporters are unionists, or worse 'Yoons', and everyone on the Yes side is a 'nationalist' peddling grievance politics. We would instead like to imagine a politics where people are not fixed in each other's minds as ontological 'Yes or No voters', simply as people who voted Yes or No. This is a fundamentally different way of seeing voters and politics.

The 'true believer' Indyref mindset tends also to ignore the big questions facing us as a society: climate change; the hollowing out of democracy across the West; the powerful forces aiding inequality. They tend to assume that as long as their political perspective gains control of the organs of governmental power, then everything else will be okay. Even to state such a view is to recognise its conservatism and intellectual paucity.

The future of Scotland and its politics is not the preserve of politics alone. Instead, it is to be found in the fundamentals of how we interact and care for each other, in the relationships which bind us together, how we invest time and attention in one another and how we build trust and connections.

Pivotal in all this is how we speak, listen and engage, noting who is speaking and not speaking, the noise of public life and the silences behind and between those who we are addressing. Scotland has come far in its journey from a society in which the rules were made by tradition, deference and elites, to one where, while all these things still matter, there is a much more open, unpredictable public sphere. This means we have to pay more attention, not less, to how we behave and act in public life.

This is one of the main challenges emerging from our book, something that has to be collectively addressed, and which will have huge consequences for the future Scotland we create and live in. It is a significant positive that in recent years hundreds of thousands of citizens who weren't previously involved in public life have chosen to become engaged. But at the same time, we have to reflect on how to have conversations that extend beyond those we agree with and our own echo chambers. More than that, we have to nurture and nourish the forces and aiders of social change and address the issues that hold us back. This is vital if we are serious about creating the 'Scotland the Brave' that we claim we want to live in. It is indeed time to be bolder and be more courageous. Being respectful and understanding toward others is central to that and to making our collective future a better one.

References

Barrow, S. and Small, M. (2016), *Scotland 2021*, Edinburgh: Ekklesia Publishing and Bella Caledonia.

Duncombe, S. (2007), *Dream: Re-Imagining Progressive Politics in an Age of Fantasy*, New York: New Press.

Ellis, S.G. (2003), 'Why the History of "the Celtic Fringe" Remains Unwritten', *European Review of History*, Vol. 10 No. 2.

Gecan, M. (2004), *Going Public: An Organiser's Guide to Citizen Action*, New York: Anchor Books.

Mackenzie, W.J.M. (1978), *Political Identity*, Harmondsworth: Penguin.

McGarvey, D. (2017), *Poverty Safari: Understanding the Anger of Britain's Underclass*, Edinburgh: Luath Press.

Ross, P. (2014), *Daunderlust: Dispatches from Unreported Scotland*, Dingwall: Sandstone Press.

Smucker, J.M. (2017), *Hegemony How-To: A Roadmap for Radicals*, Chico/Edinburgh: AK Books.

Sturgeon, N. (2012), 'Bringing the powers home to build a better nation', Strathclyde University, 3 December, available online at: https://www2.gov.scot/News/Speeches/better-nation-031212

Sustainable Growth Commission (2018), 'Scotland: The New Case for Optimism: A strategy for inter-generational economic renaissance', Edinburgh: SNP, available online at: https://www.sustainablegrowthcommission.scot/

CONTRIBUTORS

NEAL ASCHERSON IS a writer and journalist who worked first at the *Manchester Guardian* and then at *The Scotsman* (1959–1960), *The Observer* (1960–1990) and the *Independent on Sunday* (1990–1998). He is the author of numerous books including *The King Incorporated: Leopold II and the Congo* (1963), *The Polish August* (1981), *The Struggles for Poland* (1987), *Games with Shadows* (1988), *Black Sea* (1995), *Stone Voices: The Search for Scotland* (2002), and *The Death of the Fronsac: A Novel* (2018).

JUDE BARBER is an Architect-Director at Collective Architecture. The 40-strong, employee-owned and controlled studio specialises in housing and civic buildings. Key projects include the award-winning Glasgow Women's Library in Bridgeton, Govan's Water Row Masterplan, Calton Hill City Observatory, Seven Lochs Wetland Park, Barmulloch Residents' Centre and Cumbernauld Community Enterprise Centre.

SIMON BARROW is Director of the beliefs, ethics and politics think tank Ekklesia. From 2000 to 2005 he was assistant general secretary of Churches Together in Britain and Ireland, the official ecumenical body. He has written and contributed to numerous books, recently editing *Scotland 2021* (with Mike Small – Bella Caledonia/Ekklesia, 2016) and *A Nation Changed? The SNP and Scotland Ten Years On* (with Gerry Hassan – Luath Press, 2017). He is also co-founder and chair of the Scottish Football Supporters Association, and lives in Leith, having relocated to Scotland from England in 2010.

JOHN BONE is Senior Lecturer in Sociology at the University of Aberdeen. His research interests are in global political economy, social change and social theory. His work involves applying a developing theoretical model – fusing sociological theory with new understandings of the individual emerging from the cognitive science revolution – to explore various ways in which the contemporary trajectory of global development and neo-liberal economic policy is affecting individuals and communities in terms of identities, working lives, well-being, social polarisation and social cohesion.

MIRIAM BRETT grew up in the Shetland islands, but now lives in London. After graduating in International Relations, she worked in policy and advocacy for the left-wing think tank Common Weal, before taking up the post of economic adviser to the SNP in Westminster. Miriam now works in critical analysis of the International Monetary Fund.

CRAIG DALZELL is the Head of Policy and Research at the think-and-do tank Common Weal. He holds a Master's degree and PhD in Laser Physics and Opto-electronics from the University of Strathclyde and previously worked in the commercial laser industry but has, via a convoluted series of events, since found himself immersed in Scottish political research. His previous work has included investigations into the economics of fracking, currencies and banking, social security, and statistics.

GILLIAN EASSON is the Director of Creative Dundee, a network organisation which connects and amplifies the city's creativity. Founded as a blog in 2008, Creative Dundee has grown as a result of, and in response to, the opportunities and challenges of the city. Creative Dundee has since been cited as influential catalyst for the increase in the profile of Dundee in an external review of Scotland's creative city networks. Gillian previously worked in the areas of education, enterprise and employability skills development – designing the connections between people and better opportunities.

BRIAN MARK EVANS is Professor of Urbanism and Landscape at the Mackintosh School of Architecture, Glasgow School of Art, director of the Glasgow Urban Laboratory and in 2019 was invited to become City Urbanist for Glasgow working in an independent capacity. He was previously Artistic Professor of Urban Design and Planning at Chalmers School of Architecture in Gothenburg and from 1990–2015 was a partner with Gillespies LLP, the international design practice where he developed the disciplines of landscape planning and urban design and pioneered ecological urbanism. From 2005 until 2010 he was Deputy Chair and Chair of Design Review with Architecture and Design Scotland and before that an Enabler with the Commission for Architecture and the Built Environment (CABE) London. He is a founding Director and Academician of the Academy of Urbanism, London. Professor Evans is author, editor and contributor to numerous books and articles and speaks widely on the contemporary and future city, urbanism, urban design and landscape planning.

ANNA FOWLIE was brought up in the Highlands, went to Inverness High School then to the University of Edinburgh. She graduated with an MA (Hons) in History of Art in 1986 and went on to get a postgraduate qualification in Personnel Management at Napier Polytechnic on day-release. She worked in HR in local government for 16 years, then at COSLA and Scottish Government on children's policy until starting as Chief Executive of the Scottish Social Services Council in November 2009. From April 2018, she has been Chief Executive of Scottish Council for Voluntary Organisations. In her personal life, she is a lawn bowler, keen baker and reader of crime fiction and married with two grown up daughters.

DOUGLAS FRASER has been a business and economy editor at BBC Scotland since 2008. He was previously based at Holyrood as a political editor of *The Herald*, and of the *Sunday Herald* and he covered education, the Highlands and the arts for *The Scotsman*.

KATIE GALLOGY-SWAN is an advocate working in women's rights for international feminist NGO ActionAid. She cares about where power lies and is interested in how it can be released and redistributed. She has formerly worked in campaigns and research roles at Govanhill Baths, Electoral Reform Society Scotland and Common Weal, and sits on the Management Committee of Compass. She holds an honours in Social Anthropology from Harvard University and began a Masters in Violence, Conflict and Development at SOAS in 2018 focusing on women and movement-building in post-conflict environments.

DAVID GOLDBLATT was born in London in 1965 and, for his sins, inherited Tottenham Hotspurs from his father. In 2006 he published *The Ball is Round: A Global History of Football* (Penguin), which has established itself as the definitive social, political and sporting history of the global game. In 2014 he published *The Game of Our Lives: The Meaning and Making of English Football* (Penguin), which was the winner of the William Sports Book of the Year Award 2015. Along the way there have been a lot of other books (on Brazilian football, on the history of the Olympic games), a lot of journalism and broadcasting (BBC Radio 4, *The Guardian* and *Observer*, the *New York Times*) and a regular visiting professorship at Pitzer College, Los Angeles. He has lived in Bristol for almost 15 years and has, for yet more sins, acquired Bristol Rovers. His next book, a sequel to *The Ball is Round*, will be published in 2019, *Football is First: The Global Game in the Twenty First Century*.

GERRY HASSAN is Research Fellow in contemporary history at Dundee University. He has previously been a Research Fellow at the University of the West of Scotland and IPPR Scotland and has written and edited over two dozen books on Scottish and British politics including *The Strange Death of Labour Scotland* (with Eric Shaw, 2012), *Caledonian Dreaming: The Quest for a Different Scotland* (2014), *Independence of the Scottish Mind: Elite Narratives, Public Spaces and the Making of a Modern Nation* (2014), *Scotland the Bold: How Our Nation Changed and Why There is No Going Back* (2016), *SNP Leaders* (edited with James Mitchell, 2016), *A Nation Changed? The SNP and Scotland*

Ten Years On (edited with Simon Barrow, 2017) and *The People's Flag and Union Jack: An Alternative History of Britain and the Labour Party* (with Eric Shaw, 2019).

RICHARD HOLLOWAY is a writer, broadcaster and cleric. He was Bishop of Edinburgh from 1986 to 2000 and Primus of the Scottish Episcopal Church from 1992 to 2000. From 1990 to 1997 he was a member of the Human Fertilisation and Embryology Authority and was chair of the BMA Steering Group on Ethics and Genetics. He was also a member of the Broadcasting Standards Commission and is a former chair of the Scottish Arts Council and current chair of Sistema Scotland.

LUCY HUNTER BLACKBURN worked for twenty years in public administration, mainly in the civil service. She is now an ESRC-funded doctoral student at the University of Edinburgh, specialising in student finance, on which she has published extensively. She blogs at adventuresinevidence.com and is a board member of Sceptical Scot.

BLAIR JENKINS has held some of the most senior roles in Scottish media, including Director of Broadcasting at Scottish Television and Head of News and Current Affairs at both STV and BBC Scotland. In 2008 he chaired the independent Scottish Broadcasting Commission set up by the Scottish Government to make recommendations on the future of the industry. From 2012–14 he was Chief Executive of Yes Scotland, the campaign for a Yes vote in the referendum on Scottish independence.

LAURA JONES is a co-founder of the award-winning independent publisher 404 Ink and a freelancer working primarily in book production and promotion for clients across the country. She is crime writing festival Bloody Scotland's Digital and Social Media Manager whilst also sitting on the board and co-ran the Saltire Society's virtual literary festival #ScotLitFest.

GEORGE KEREVAN is an economist, journalist and documentary filmmaker. He served three terms in the 1980s and 1990s as an elected Labour member of Edinburgh Council, where he chaired the economic development committee and was responsible for creating the capital's conference centre, main business park, and central banking district. He is also a former SNP MP (for East Lothian) and served on the Treasury Select Committee.

CAITLIN LOGAN is a journalist at Scottish political news website *CommonSpace*. She is particularly interested in issues around feminism, equality, and human rights, and volunteers with The Young Women's Movement. Previously, she has worked and volunteered in a varied mix of roles in the third and public sectors, including research and data analysis. At LGBT Youth Scotland, she conducted research into LGBT young people's experiences of life in Scotland and research into prejudice-based bullying in schools commissioned by the Equality and Human Rights Commission (EHRC).

KARYN MCCLUSKEY worked in the police for 22 years in Sussex, Lancashire, West Mercia, Strathclyde and Police Scotland. In September 2016 she took up the post of Chief Executive for Community Justice Scotland. She was Director of the Scottish Violence Reduction Unit for the previous decade, which proposed a different way of addressing violence in Scotland. They developed injury surveillance, gang intervention and gang exit and focused on preventing knife carrying and injury. She helps support Medics Against Violence charity in Scotland, set up in conjunction with the Violence Reduction Unit. Karyn trained as a registered nurse, has a BSc and MSc in Psychology and is a fellow by distinction of the Faculty of Public Health. She received Honorary Doctorate from University of Glasgow for work on prevention of violence and an Honorary Masters from the Open University. She is an Honorary Lecturer at the University of Glasgow. She has worked in a variety of areas within the NHS, East Africa and HM Prisons. She has published work on Armed Robbery teams, Alcohol and Violence Interventions in a clinical setting and Violence Reduction. She is a board member of Simon Community Scotland tackling homelessness and is on the Board of the Scottish Professional Football League.

GERRY MCCARTNEY completed his training at the Glasgow Centre for Population Health where he produced the first synthesis of the causes of the excess mortality in Scotland and Glasgow. Gerry continued to work part-time as a GP in Paisley throughout this training period. In 2010 he took up post as Head of the Public Health Observatory and Consultant in Public Health at NHS Health Scotland. His main interest is in the causes and solutions to the higher mortality and wider health inequalities in Scotland, on which he has published extensively. He also has research interests in the evaluation of public policy interventions and in the public health implication of (un)sustainability. He has recently been honoured with a Fellowship of the Faculty of Public Health and an Honorary Professorship at the University of the West of Scotland.

JIM MCCORMICK is Associate Director Scotland with the Joseph Rowntree Foundation (JRF), an independent organisation working to solve poverty in the UK. He is a member of the Social Security Advisory Committee (SSAC) and an advisory board member of Business in the Community (BITC) Scotland. He was appointed by the Social Security Minister to chair the independent Disability and Carers Benefits expert advisory group and was previously Director of the Scottish Council Foundation think tank. Interests include music, languages and Greenock Morton FC.

JAMES MCENANEY is a lecturer, journalist and former secondary school English teacher. His work focuses on education policy, government transparency and wider issues of policymaking. He has written extensively for publications such as *The Herald*, *The Guardian*, *The Times Educational Supplement Scotland* and *CommonSpace*. His first book is *A Scottish Journey: Personal Impressions of Modern Scotland:* a contemporary interpretation of Edwin Muir's 1935 book *Scottish Journey.*

MAIRI MCFADYEN is a creative ethnologist, freelancer and cultural activist. She has a background in academic research and teaching, completing her PhD on the aesthetics and poetics of traditional song at the University of Edinburgh's Department of Celtic and Scottish Studies (2012) and pursuing further postdoctoral research. She is currently a research associate at Heriot Watt's Intercultural Research Centre (IRC) developing a creative ethnological practice. Mairi has experience of teaching aspects of Scottish Studies, cultural politics and traditional arts in both higher education and non-formal contexts and has worked for various arts and cultural organisations, including TRACS (Traditional Arts and Culture Scotland), Local Voices and the Scottish Centre for Geopoetics. From 2013–2015 Mairi was involved as a core organiser for National Collective, the creative cultural campaign for Scottish Independence.

MALCOLM MACLEAN is a Glasgow Gael and visual artist who has transitioned into an arts producer and heritage consultant based in the Outer Hebrides. He co-founded Scotland's first Gaelic arts centre, *An Lanntair*, in Stornoway, and went on to lead the national Gaelic arts agency, *Pròiseact Nan Ealan* for 25 years. There he co-founded the national festivals association *Fèisean Nan Gàidheal* and the *Ceòlas* summer school and helped originate the Gaelic television service. Producer credits include the *St Kilda Opera*, the international touring exhibition, *An Leabhar Mòr/ The Great Book of Gaelic* and the BAFTA winning arts TV series, Tacsi. He became Chair of UNESCO Scotland in 2013 and is currently special adviser to *Ionad Hiort*, the remote-access St Kilda Centre,

NEIL MCINROY is the Chief Executive of the Centre for Local Economic Strategies (CLES). Tasked with advancing progressive economics for people and place, CLES and Neil apply practical policy which seeks an economy that advances social justice within environmental limits. Neil regularly advises national and local governments across the UK and internationally.

FERGUS MCNEILL is Professor of Criminology and Social Work at the University of Glasgow where he works in the Scottish Centre for Crime and Justice Research and in Sociology. Prior to becoming an academic in 1998, Fergus worked for a number of years in residential drug rehabilitation and as a criminal justice social worker. His many research projects and publications have examined institutions, cultures and practices of punishment and rehabilitation and their alternatives. Currently, Fergus is working on two major projects: 'Distant Voices: Coming Home' is a major, multi-partner three-year Economic and Social Research Council/Arts and Humanities Research Council project exploring re-integration after punishment through creative practices and research methods; in particular song-writing and sharing. Persuasive Punishment is a British Academy funded Mid-Career Fellowship which critically examines the emergence and contours of 'mass supervision' and how we might best respond to it.

MICHAEL MARRA works in research strategy at the University of Dundee with personal specialism in economics and development. He is a graduate of the London School of Economics and the University of Glasgow. He has worked in the UK and Scottish Parliaments and as Head of Policy for a major development NGO. Michael is an elected City Councillor in Dundee.

NASAR MEER is Professor of Race, Identity and Citizenship in the School of Social and Political Sciences at the University of Edinburgh, a Royal Society of Edinburgh Research Fellow, and Principal Investigator of the Horizon 2020 funded Governance and Local Integration of Migrants and Europe's Refugees (GLIMER). He was previously Professor of Comparative Citizenship and Social Policy at the Faculty of Humanities and Social Sciences at Strathclyde University.

ANNE MULLIN qualified in medicine at the University of Glasgow and has been a GP in Govan for 25 years. She is committed to social change and social justice and is a member of the Deep End Group of GPs.

ANDREW W NEAL is Co-Director of the Centre for Security Research (CESER) and Senior Lecturer in Politics and International Relations at the University of Edinburgh. He is the author and editor of numerous books and articles on security and its politics, including *Security in Small Nation, Scotland, Democracy, Politics* (Open Book Publishers, 2017), which came out of ESRC-funded research he led in the run up to the 2014 independence referendum. He is currently completing a monograph on the changing relationship between security and political practice at Westminster.

JEMMA NEVILLE is a writer with a background in human rights law and outreach. Her first book, *Constitution Street*, explores the experience of neighbourhood on one single street, set against the context of constitutional change in Scotland and the UK. Blending interviews, narrative non-fiction and poems, *Constitution Street* is a living constitution for a liminal land. Jemma is Director of the national development agency for community-led arts, Voluntary Arts Scotland. She was the inaugural Community Fellow at the Institute of Advanced Studies in

Humanities, University of Edinburgh, and was shortlisted for *The Guardian's* International Development Journalism Award. Originally from Dundee, Jemma is now an adopted Leither and can be found sitting by the Shore with her dog Bonnie.

ANGELA O'HAGAN is a researcher and lecturer at Glasgow Caledonian University with long experience in equalities and public policy in Scotland and Europe, with a particular interest in equality analysis and scrutiny of public policy, particularly budget processes. She is Convenor of the Scottish Women's Budget Group and Co-Convenor of the European Gender Budgeting Network.

FINTAN O'TOOLE is a columnist, writer and commentator, who has been literary editor and drama critic for the *Irish Times* for which he has written since 1988. He is the author of numerous books including his two bestselling critiques of the fall and aftermath of the Celtic Tiger: *Ship of Fools: How Stupidity and Corruption Sank The Celtic Tiger* (2009) and *Enough is Enough: How to Build a New Republic* (2010). His most recent book is *Heroic Failure: Brexit and the Politics of Pain* (2018).

LESLEY ORR is a Research Fellow at the Centre for Theology and Public Issues, University of Edinburgh. She is a historian, theologian and activist for gender and social justice. Her current research interests (all with a focus on 20th century Scotland) include war resistance and peace movements, the history of women's aid, and the historical relationship between faith and feminism. She is a co-editor of the forthcoming *Wiley Blackwell Companion to Religion and Peace*. She has extensive experience of work in NGOs and the public sector, including the Scottish Government. Lesley has had longstanding involvement in the ecumenical movement, particularly in relation to challenging gender inequality, violence and abuse in faith communities and wider society, and is a member of the Iona Community.

SUE PALMER IS a former primary headteacher in the Borders, is a literacy specialist, writer, presenter and 'childhood campaigner'. She has written over 250 books, software packages and TV programmes for schools on aspects of literacy and many hundreds of articles for the educational and national press. Over the last ten years, her books on child development in the modern world – notably *Toxic Childhood* (second edition, 2015) – have led to frequent media appearances and comments about changes in children's lifestyles. Her latest book, *Upstart: The Case for Raising the School Starting Age and Providing What the Under-Sevens Really Need*, was published in 2016. Sue chaired the Scottish Play Commission, served on the Scottish Government's Early Years Task Force and currently chairs the Upstart Scotland campaign.

DOUGLAS ROBERTSON taught housing and sociology at the University of Stirling, for 30 years, and recently retired, though he continues to undertake research and writing commissions. Recently, he has completed work on rent restriction, for Shelter, the disruptive repercussions and local policy responses to Airb&b across Europe, for the Scottish Government, an assessment of the impact of bank closures on communities in Highland Scotland, for HIE, and the challenge of initiating common repair in multi-owned property, for the RICS and BEFS. Douglas also regularly writes and is asked to comment on housing policy matters on various platforms.

KIRSTEIN RUMMERY is Professor of Social Policy at the University of Stirling, a senior fellow of the Centre on Constitutional Change and Co-Director of the Centre for Gender and Feminist Studies. She researches international social policy regarding gender, disability and ageing.

ALAN SINCLAIR is an independent policy analyst who has written on early years development and is author of *Right from the Start: Investing in Parents and Babies*. He was previously Director of Skills and Learning at Scottish Enterprise and Chief Executive of the Wise Group.

MIKE SMALL is an activist, writer and publisher, originally from Aberdeen. He is co-founder and editor of the pro-independence site *Bella Caledonia*, and author, editor and publisher of numerous books on politics, both in Scotland and internationally, and social change.

JIM SPENCE is a freelance football broadcaster and columnist, based in Dundee. He has worked for BBC Scotland both as a freelance and a staff journalist for over 25 years, and has presented various radio programmes such as *Sportsound, Ninety Minutes*, and *Beyond the SPL*. He also presented the sport on *Good Morning Scotland*, and worked for BBC Scotland flagship football show *Saturday Sportscene*, and still contributes to the programme, as well as *Sportsound* on radio, from football matches all over Scotland. He has covered both the international, and club sides in matches abroad. He was previous a law lecturer, and for many years combined that career with broadcasting, before pursuing journalism full-time.

CATRIONA STEWART is a journalist and columnist with *The Herald* and *Evening Times* who she has been writing for since 2009. She has also written extensively in the Scottish press including the *Scottish Daily Mail, The Big Issue in Scotland, The Scotsman* and *Scottish Farmer*.

ANDY SUMMERS is an architect and a photographer based in Glasgow. He is a co-founder and co-producer of the Architecture Fringe, a self-initiated grass-roots organisation and festival exploring architecture within its broader cultural and socio-political contexts. Andy is currently a design tutor at the Edinburgh School of Architecture and Landscape Architecture at the University of Edinburgh. Throughout 2013 and 2014 Andy was one of the national organisers with National Collective, the pro-independence artist-led campaign group. Working in a core team, Andy led the organisation and production logistics of the 32-day 28-date national tour of Scotland which was the Yestival. Andy also co-organised and co-hosted the one-day cities and architecture conference entitled Place at Summerhall.

LAURA WADDELL is a publisher at a large publishing house, a critic, and writer based in Glasgow. She sits on the boards of Scottish PEN and Gutter magazine, and her writing has appeared in publications including the books *Nasty Women, The Digital Critic, Know Your Place* and *the Guardian, Times Literary Supplement, The List, McSweeneys, 3:AM Magazine* and *the Scottish Review of Books*.

WILLIAM WALKER is Emeritus Professor of International Relations, University of St Andrews. His publications include, with David Albright and Frans Berkhout, *Plutonium and Highly Enriched Uranium: World Inventories, Capabilities and Policies* (1997); THORP *and the Politics of Commitment* (1999); with Malcolm Chalmers, *Uncharted Waters: The UK, Nuclear Weapons and the Scottish Question* (2001); 'The UK, threshold status and responsible nuclear sovereignty', *International Affairs*, March 2010; and *A Perpetual Menace: Nuclear Weapons and International Order* (2012).

ANDY WIGHTMAN is a Member of the Scottish Parliament and a writer and researcher on land rights, governance and democracy. He is the author of publications including *Who Owns Scotland (1996), Scotland: Land and Power* (1999), *Community Land Rights: A Citizen's Guide* (2009) and *The Poor Had No Lawyers* (2010).

RUTH WISHART is a journalist, broadcaster and commentator. She has written extensively in the press including *The Scotsman, The Herald, The Guardian* and *Daily Record*, been a broadcaster and commentator, and contributed to public life across a range of issues, and in particular, arts and culture.

TALAT YAQOOB is a feminist activist and has been working in Scotland's third sector for over ten years. She is the chair and co-founder of Women 50:50, which campaigns for at least 50 per cent representation of women in elections and is the Director of a national organisation working on women in science, engineering and technology. She has a background in equalities research, public affairs and social justice campaigning.

Luath Press Limited

committed to publishing well written books worth reading

LUATH PRESS takes its name from Robert Burns, whose little collie Luath (*Gael.*, swift or nimble) tripped up Jean Armour at a wedding and gave him the chance to speak to the woman who was to be his wife and the abiding love of his life. Burns called one of the 'Twa Dogs' Luath after Cuchullin's hunting dog in Ossian's *Fingal*. Luath Press was established in 1981 in the heart of Burns country, and is now based a few steps up the road from Burns' first lodgings on Edinburgh's Royal Mile. Luath offers you distinctive writing with a hint of unexpected pleasures.

Most bookshops in the UK, the US, Canada, Australia, New Zealand and parts of Europe, either carry our books in stock or can order them for you. To order direct from us, please send a £sterling cheque, postal order, international money order or your credit card details (number, address of cardholder and expiry date) to us at the address below. Please add post and packing as follows: UK – £1.00 per delivery address; overseas surface mail – £2.50 per delivery address; overseas airmail – £3.50 for the first book to each delivery address, plus £1.00 for each additional book by airmail to the same address. If your order is a gift, we will happily enclose your card or message at no extra charge.

Luath Press Limited
543/2 Castlehill
The Royal Mile
Edinburgh EH1 2ND
Scotland
Telephone: +44 (0)131 225 4326 (24 hours)
email: sales@luath. co.uk
Website: www. luath.co.uk